THE CONFEDERATE
NATION
1861–1865

MONTICELLO
EDITIONS

THE CONFEDERATE NATION: 1861–1865
Emory M. Thomas

EXPLORATION AND EMPIRE
The Explorer and the Scientist in the Winning of the American West
William H. Goetzmann

WORLD OF OUR FATHERS
Irving Howe

THE CONFEDERATE NATION

1861–1865

Emory M. Thomas

From The New American Nation Series
Edited by Henry Steele Commager
and Richard B. Morris

**MONTICELLO
EDITIONS**

HISTORY BOOK CLUB · NEW YORK

For Frank E. Vandiver

Contents

CONTENTS

Illustrations

These illustrations, grouped in a separate section, will be found following page 166.

1. Edmund Ruffin, Southern radical
2. Drawing of Charleston, South Carolina
3. Music cover, "Virginian Marseillaise"
4. Drawing of Montgomery, Alabama
5. The inauguration at Montgomery
6. A Unionist depiction of Jefferson Davis' inauguration
7. Jefferson Davis
8. Christopher G. Memminger, secretary of the treasury
9. Judah P. Benjamin, journeyman cabinet member
10. George W. Randolph, secretary of war
11. Josiah Gorgas, chief of Ordnance Bureau
12. R. M. T. Hunter, secretary of state and senator from Virginia
13. Alexander H. Stephens, vice-president
14. Stephen R. Mallory, secretary of the navy
15. The Great Seal of the Confederacy
16. Robert E. Lee
17. Thomas J. "Stonewall" Jackson
18. P. G. T. Beauregard

Maps

Editors' Introduction

N ATIONALISM has been a perennial theme in American historiography, but surprisingly enough historians have devoted but scant attention to the analysis of Southern nationalism. Yet the brief and tragic experiment of the Confederate States of America with nationalism provides a laboratory scarcely less interesting than that provided by the American States between 1774 and 1789. Because historians are camp followers of victorious armies, most of them take for granted the triumph of the first American bid for nationalism and the failure of the Southern. Yet, on the surface at least, the Old South of the fifties and sixties boasted more and more persuasive ingredients of national unity than had the American states in 1774. For the South—and the Confederacy—had, among whites at least, far greater ethnic homogeneity than had the United States of the 1770s, for less than one percent of the population of the Confederate States was foreign born. It acknowledged a greater degree of religious unity than could be found in the original States —for outside Maryland and Louisiana the whole of the Southern population was not only Protestant but evangelical. It displayed a substantial economic unity, with concentration on staple crop agriculture and on slaves as a work force. By modern standards it confessed pronounced class differences, but by its own standards it could boast that it was a classless society, for all whites could claim membership in an upper class: here was a principle of social philosophy which speedily took on the authority of a moral and a religious principle and provided the South with one of the most powerful of all the forces making for national unity—a common ideology. Nor, for all its inferiority in population and resources, was the Confederacy without military advantages: a territory more extensive than any which had ever been conquered in the whole of modern history; interior lines of communication; a long military tradition and superior military leaders; and a not unreasonable expectation of a foreign intervention which would rescue the South as French and Dutch intervention had rescued the new United States during the Revolutionary war. Perhaps most important of all was the elementary consideration that the South did not have to win on the field of battle in order to achieve independence, for it could afford to lose all the battles and all the campaigns and still triumph as long as it was prepared to settle simply for independence with no demands on the Union except the elementary one that it let the Sisters depart in peace.

With all these advantages, why did the South lose? That is the question to which Professor Thomas addresses himself in *The Confederate Nation: 1861–1865,* and whose answer he seeks down almost labyrithine ways. Was the failure political and constitutional; was it perhaps impossible for a government based on the principle of decentralization and state rights to fight and win a modern war? Was it military, insofar as the Confederacy never achieved unity of command, and never exploited its resources effectively? Was it economic and financial—reliance on an agrarian economy which, with the success of the Union blockade, was unable to provide essential manufactures? Was it diplomatic—the failure of King Cotton to vindicate his sovereignty? Was it, in the end, moral—the inability of a crusade for slavery to rally support from those Old World states whose recognition and support was, in the end, essential to victory?

In *The Confederate Nation* Professor Thomas has reflected the powerful and persuasive political, cultural, and racial claims of Southern nationalism against the background of the economic, the diplomatic, and the moral, which proved less responsive to importunate demands for national independence. He has traced the evolution of that section which we know as the Old South into the Confederate States, and then the fortunes and misfortunes of the embryonic Confederate nation as it embraced defeat and yielded to disintegration. In the course of this review he provides us with a picture of an alternative American nationalism—a nationalism which, with all its roots in America, had in many respects more in common with the nationalism of the Old World than with that of the New.

The Confederate Nation: 1861–1865 is a volume in the New American Nation series, a comprehensive, cooperative survey of the area now embraced in the United States. Other aspects of this era are set forth in David Potter's *Impending Crisis,* Clement Eaton's *Growth of Southern Civilization,* Russel Nye's *Society and Culture in America: 1830–1860,* and in forthcoming volumes on the Civil War, constitutional development, and the culture of the war and the postwar years.

HENRY STEELE COMMAGER
RICHARD B. MORRIS

Preface

A T some early point in our correspondence about this book, Professor Henry Steele Commager stated that a new history of the Confederacy needs "not so much new information, as new and fresh ideas." To be sure, the literature of the South as short-lived nation is extensive. Still, there is "new information" here. For the most part, though, I have emphasized "new and fresh ideas"—my own and those derived from recent research and scholarship on the Confederacy by others.

I have attempted to write a narrative interpretation. The Confederacy lived briefly; but the human drama involved all but dictates that its historian be a storyteller. The Confederate era was an extended moment during which Southerners attempted simultaneously to define themselves as a people and to act out a national identity, all the while engaged in total war for corporate survival. The momentous nature of these events and the centrality of this experience in the American and Southern past demand that its historian offer interpretations and attempt to derive the meaning of it all.

During my research, and in the organizing, writing and revising of this book, many people have given generously of their time and talents. Naturally I owe a great debt to other scholars upon whose works I have built. Many friends within the historical profession have helped with ideas and advice. I would like to thank especially Eleanor Brokenbrough of the Confederate Museum, Louis H.

Manarin of the Virginia State Library, John M. Jennings and Howson Cole of the Virginia Historical Society, Richard B. Harwell of the University of Georgia Library, and the staffs of the Library of Congress, the National Archives, the Alderman Library at the University of Virginia, the University of Georgia Library, and the Southern Historical Collection in the University of North Carolina Library at Chapel Hill. I much appreciate the indulgence and advice of series editors Richard B. Morris and Henry Steele Commager, as well as the kindness of Corona Machemer at Harper & Row. Finally I thank my family and friends who "got me through it" with understanding and love.

EMORY M. THOMAS

CHAPTER 1

The Social Economy of the Old South

O N an October Tuesday in 1859 an old man with long silver hair
poured disconsolance into his diary; Edmund Ruffin was sixty-
five years old and prepared to die. "I have lived long enough,"
Ruffin wrote, "a little more time of such unused & wearisome passage of time will make my life too long."[1]

Behind Ruffin's lament was a deep-seated sense of frustration and
failure. He had not failed at the normal activities at which people
fail and about which they then consume their later years fretting and
worrying. Ruffin had been a highly successful Virginia planter and
an esteemed agricultural scientist, he had most of the trappings of
personal and vocational success, but in the one great passion of his
mature life, he was frustrated. The old man had devoted the last
fifteen of his sixty-five years to the dream of Southern independence. He perceived the planter civilization of the South in peril; the
source of that peril was "Yankee" and union with "Yankees." Thus
he preached revolution. Ruffin was a rebel with a cause, a secular
prophet, but his cause lacked a constituency, and the prophet lacked
sufficient honor in his own beloved South.

On that same October Tuesday in 1859, less than two hundred
miles from the plantation where Ruffin brooded, events were taking

[1]William Kaufman Scarborough (ed.), *The Diary of Edmund Ruffin*, I, *Toward Independence, October, 1856–April, 1861* (Baton Rouge, La., 1972), 348. The standard biography of Ruffin is Avery O. Craven, *Edmund Ruffin, Southerner: A Study in Secession* (New
York, 1932).

1

place which promised to brighten his mood considerably. Perhaps even as Ruffin wrote, United States Marines under the command of Colonel R. E. Lee stormed a fire engine house at Harpers Ferry, suppressed an attempted slave insurrection, and captured its leader Captain John Brown. Like Ruffin, Brown was an aging zealot and a rebel, who, on the night of October 16, had attempted to seize the town of Harpers Ferry along with the United States arsenal there and establish a base for what he hoped would be a massive slave insurrection, "to purge this land with blood." On October 18, however, Brown's raid was an apparent failure just thirty-six hours after it began. Oddly, John Brown seemed unperturbed by his failure; *"Let them hang me,"* he said.[2]

If Brown was unruffled, Ruffin was jubilant when he learned of the abortive raid and its consequences. The news acted like an emotional tonic on him. "Such a practical exercise of abolition principles is needed to stir the sluggish blood of the South," he wrote. On November 21 he contemplated attending Brown's execution, scheduled for December 2 in Charlestown, but considered the difficult journey and the cold weather and resisted his "strong inclination." As the execution date drew nearer, though, Ruffin succumbed to his feelings, and at six-thirty on the morning of November 26, he set out for the " 'seat of war.' "[3]

When he arrived in Harpers Ferry, Ruffin visited the fire engine house and other shrines of the raid. He found friends and began to feel a part of the event he had come to witness; once in Charlestown his zeal to participate became almost manic. When he suffered the ignominy of arrest as a "suspicious person" and learned to his distress that only military personnel would be able to view Brown's execution, he attempted to make some military connection. Finally Colonel Francis H. Smith, superintendent of the Virginia Military Institute (VMI), offered Ruffin a place in his corps of cadets and furnished Ruffin with a rifle and uniform overcoat for the occasion.[4]

"Ludicrous" was how Ruffin described his appearance: a sixty-

[2]Brown to "Dear Brother" Jeremiah, Nov. 12, 1859, Lawrence [Kansas] *Republican,* Dec. 8, 1859, cited in Stephen B. Oates, *To Purge this Land with Blood: A Biography of John Brown* (New York, 1970), p. 335.

[3]Scarborough (ed.), *Ruffin Diary,* I, 348–367. A good narrative account of Ruffin at Harpers Ferry is Kenneth L. Smith, "Edmund Ruffin and the Raid on Harpers Ferry," *Virginia Cavalcade,* Autumn 1972, 29–37.

[4]Scarborough (ed.), *Ruffin Diary,* I, 361–368.

five-year-old man with white locks flowing over the collar of a bor-
rowed overcoat, stumping along in a formation of teen-aged boys
for two miles to the execution grounds. For Ruffin, though, the
opportunity to take part in the execution more than compensated
for the embarrassment.

To Ruffin's delight, the VMI cadets were stationed closest to the
gallows, about fifty yards away. John Brown seemed to Ruffin a
"willing assistant" in the grisly business at hand. Giving no sign of
fear or concern, he walked where he was led and stood alone and
unbending over the trap for an interminable ten minutes while the
fifteen hundred troops took their assigned positions. Ruffin carefully recorded Brown's every twitch and convulsion during the transit from life to death. In his diary Ruffin praised Brown's "animal
courage" and "complete fearlessness of & insensibility to danger &
death."

His praise was grudging, though, and later Ruffin resented public
references to Brown's courage, lest the villain appear less villain-
ous.[5] Ruffin remained in Charlestown for several days after the
execution and collected a few of the pikes Brown had brought to
Harpers Ferry to arm his followers. Ruffin labeled and shipped
some of them to Southern politicians as propaganda weapons, tangible evidence of Yankee perfidy.[6]

What inspired Ruffin to leave home in late November, journey
fourteen hours by train, go without adequate sleep, and expose
himself to ridicule in the company of boys to watch a stranger die?
Obviously part of the answer lay in Ruffin's emotional and mental
composition. His journey to Charlestown was a caricature, the extreme expression of a true believer. But to dismiss Ruffin as a
demented zealot would be to ignore those other white Southerners
who to some degree shared his zeal. The essential fact of the Confederate experience was that a sufficient number of white Southern
Americans felt more Southern than American or, perhaps more
accurately, that they were orthodox Americans and Northerners
were apostates. Southern sectionalism became Southern national-

[5]Although there are numerous eyewitness accounts of Brown's execution, Ruffin's
diary is one of the best. *Ibid.*, 368–371. Oates, *Purge this Land* provides a good
secondary narrative, pp. 337–352.

[6]Scarborough (ed.), *Ruffin Diary*, I, 371–376. Some of the pikes Ruffin had claimed
were still stored at Harpers Ferry the following spring. Alfred W. Barbour to Ruffin,
Mar. 15, 1860, Ruffin Papers, Virginia Historical Society, Richmond.

ism and underwent trial by war. The degree of Ruffin's enthusiasm was unique and extreme; his persuasion was not. The answer to the riddle of Ruffin's behavior—and by extension that of the South—was what Southerners expressed in one syllable: "cause."

Regarding another American struggle for independence, John Adams wrote to Thomas Jefferson in 1815 that their revolution of 1776 had been complete "in the minds of the people . . . before a drop of blood was shed at Lexington."[7] The same was true of the Confederate revolution. The Confederate experience began in the Old South, not as a nation or a would-be nation, but as the cause.

The Southern cause was the transcendent extension of the Southern life style; the cause was ideology. In this context "ideology" is not synonymous with "dogma" or "doctrine." Rather, Southern ideology was a belief system, a value system, a world view, or *Weltanschauung*. It was the result of a secular transsubstantiation in which the common elements in Southern life became sanctified in the Southern mind. The South's ideological cause was more than the sum of its parts, more than the material circumstances and conditions from which it sprang. In the Confederate South the cause was ultimately an affair of the viscera.

During the middle third of the nineteenth century, Southerners began to close their minds to alternatives to their "way of life"; they celebrated and sanctified the status quo and prepared to defend and extend it against threats real or imagined. In this process interests and institutions became ideals and goals. Questions about the Southern way of life became moral questions, and compromises of the Southern life style became concessions of virtue and righteousness. The Southern world view developed both positive and negative perspectives. The cause was Janus-faced: it stood *for* a distinctive Southern life style and *against* the Yankee alternative. Indeed, it is often difficult to determine for any given time whether love of things Southern or hatred of things Northern was the dominant motive force.[8]

[7]Adams to Jefferson, 1815, cited in Bernard Bailyn, *The Ideological Origins of the American Revolution* (Cambridge Mass., 1967), p. 1.

[8]Emphasis on ideology in the American experience is well expressed in Bailyn, *Ideological Origins*, pp. v–x; Eugene D. Genovese, "The Slave South: An Interpretation," in *The Political Economy of Slavery: Studies in the Economy and Society of the Slave South* (New York, 1965), pp. 13–39, and *The World the Slaveholders Made: Two Essays in Interpretation* (New York, 1969); Eric Foner, *Free Soil, Free Labor, Free Men: The Ideology*

If the raw materials of life in the ante-bellum South were the positive roots of the Confederate ideological cause, then a proper study of the cause must first examine the components of that life style. Such a study is more easily proposed than accomplished. Life in the Old South was more than a little like the house that Jack built: each element depended upon every other element in the whole. The Southern bodies social, economic, intellectual, and political were decidedly commingled. And at the center of Southern experience lay a fundamental paradox: Southerners were at the same time Southerners and Americans.

More than other Americans, Southerners developed a sectional identity outside the national mainstream. The Southern life style tended to contradict the national norm in ways that life styles of other sections did not.[9]

But if Edmund Ruffin represented an intense Southern commitment, others such as Andrew Johnson responded with similar intensity to their American identity. By turns since about 1830 or so, Southerners have been either a peculiar people who pursued a counterculture outside and opposite the American mainstream or products of the American experience no more peculiar than most other Americans.[10]

In terms of social structure, popular mythology derives much of its view of the South from the moonlight-and-magnolias legend,

---

of the Republican Party before the Civil War (New York, 1970), especially pp. 1–10; and Raimondo Luraghi, *Storia della guerra civile americana* (Turin, Italy, 1966), especially pp. 5–103, and "The Civil War and the Modernization of American Society: Social Structure and Industrial Revolution in the Old South before and during the War," *Civil War History*, XVIII (1972), 230–251. In his brilliant essay "The Historian's Use of Nationalism and Vice Versa," published first in Alexander V. Riasonovsky and Barnes Riznik (eds.), *Generalizations in Historical Writing* (Philadelphia, 1963), and later in *The South and the Sectional Conflict* (Baton Rouge, La., 1968), David Potter uses nationalism in such a way as to imply (at least) ideology.

[9]Cf. Charles G. Sellers, Jr., *The Southerner as American* (Chapel Hill, N.C., 1960); Howard Zinn, *The Southern Mystique* (New York, 1959); and F. N. Boney, "The Southern Aristocrat," *The Midwest Quarterly*, XV (1974), 215–230, which express in different ways a contrary viewpoint.

[10]Updated expositions of the Southern-American theme are Sheldon Hackney, "The South as a Counterculture," *The American Scholar* 42 (1973), 283–293; and George B. Tindall, "Beyond the Mainstream: The Ethnic Southerners," *Journal of Southern History*, XL (1974), 3–18. The most complete explanation of the problem is in C. Vann Woodward *The Burden of Southern History*, enlarged edition (Baton Rouge, La., 1968), and *American Counterpoint: Slavery and Racism in the North-South Dialogue* (Boston, 1971).

which portrays a society of two well-defined tiers. Plantation aristocrats formed the upper stratum; slaves and "po white trash" the
lower. Planters were bona fide gentle folk who set the tone and pace
of Southern life. "Trashy whites" made little impact. While they
believed themselves superior to bonded blacks, in reality—so the
legend goes—the "po whites" were of little worth and less consequence than the happy and loyal "darkies." Such was life in the
never-never South.

Aside from the romance of moonlight and magnolias, much of the
lingering appeal of the old legend stems from the fact that it portrays a society that was 'different." More precisely, it portrays a
society dominated by landed aristocrats: the South as aristocracy in
contradiction to the middle-class democracy supposedly characteristic of America.[11]

But the time is long past when thoughtful people conceived of
Southern society in such simplistic terms. In fact, there was potential tension between aristocracy and democracy in the social structure of the Old South. Genuinely "great" planters were relatively
few in number. In 1860 only about 2,300 people owned as many as
one hundred slaves and extensive acreage. Approximately 8,000
Southerners owned as many as fifty slaves and significant arable
land. Naturally these numbers usually represent heads of families
and thus the planter class was perhaps five times larger than the
number of slaveholders. Still, in 1860 there were 1.5 million heads
of families in the South, and of these only 46,000 met the rule-of-
thumb criteria for planter status: land and twenty or more slaves.
Only about one-fourth of the South's heads of families in 1860
owned any slaves at all, and of these an estimated 60 percent owned
no more than five.

From these data emerges a picture of a fairly broad-based status
pyramid in Southern society. In contrast to the moonlight-and-
magnolias model, facts indicate that the vast majority of whites
outside the planter class were neither "po" nor "trash." Census
data and tax records confirm the existence of a large class of small
planters and yeoman farmers. There was a Southern "mudsill," but
even among landless hunters and "squatters," class distinctions
were ambiguous. Mountain folk who retained a sturdy pioneer heri-

[11]The most common elaboration of the legend is Margaret Mitchell, *Gone with the
Wind* (New York, 1936).

tage and independence may have paid few taxes and resisted the efforts of census takers, but they were not poor. In short, research in hard data on the Old South has led to what one historian has termed the "discovery of the middle class."[12]

While the existence of a Southern middle class composed of small planters and yeoman farmers, together with a small group of towns-people (merchants, craftspeople, and the like), alters the traditional view of an aristocratic South, it does not necessarily overturn it. The important questions are: what was the role of those Southerners whose social position lay somewhere between planter and slave, and how much influence did they have? Scholars have offered at least three possible answers.

First, it may have been that the planters were not the "real" South after all, that the middle class, or "plain folk," were in fact the backbone of the Old South. Planters depended upon plain folk politically for votes, economically for vital skills and jobs, and so-cially for deference and companionship if nothing else.[13]

A second answer to the riddle contends that the planter aristoc-racy did not in fact exist. "Aristocrats" were merely plain folk with land and slaves, *nouveaux riches* whose behavior was conditioned by plebeian origins, not by any aristocratic code.[14]

A third explanation focuses upon evolutionary change in the ante-bellum South. Once upon a time, in the colonial South, there were wise and gentle aristocrats, but the spread of the "cotton kingdom" changed "the land of the country gentlemen." Gradually, in the early 1800s, cotton culture spread, and in time social mobility declined. By mid-century the planter class had degenerated into a group of cotton capitalists who ruthlessly exercised their traditional political hegemony and practiced a kind of thought control by domi-nating politics, press, pulpit, school, and society. The plain-folk majority were unwitting victims of the cotton kingdom, which, "like

[12]See Clement Eaton, *The Waning of the Old South Civilization, 1860–1880* (Athens, Ga., 1968), and *The Growth of Southern Civilization, 1790–1860* (New York, 1961), for a summary statement in chapters 1 and 7 respectively; and Frank L. Owsley, *Plain Folk of the Old South* (Baton Rouge, La., 1949), for the pioneer statistical analysis. William E. Dodd, *The Cotton Kingdom* (New Haven, Conn., 1917), speaks to the same point and offers statistical support.

[13]This is the implication of Owsley's research in *Plain Folk*, pp. 133–149.

[14]This view is essentially that of W. J. Cash in *Mind of the South* (New York, 1941), pp. 3–102.

the rising industrialism of the North, . . . placed material profits above human rights."[15]

Each of these accounts of the role and influence of Southern plain folk in effect Americanizes the Old South. If the real Old South was actually the mass of forgotten nonplanter whites, or an amalgam of frontier coon hunters some of whom happened to be wealthy, or a class of well-meaning farmers escorted into folly by selfish leaders, then the Old South was at heart a middle-class democracy well within the American tradition. None of these contentions, however, adequately explains why this one group of American middle-class democrats so despised another group of American middle-class democrats as to dissolve the Union and fight to perpetuate that dissolution. Moreover, if the plain folk were really the backbone of Southern society, why did they follow the planters out of the United States and into a desperate war for the sake of planter interests?

Regardless of the numbers of plain folk, the fact remains that aristocracies are by definition small groups of people. Whether or not Southern aristocrats were but one step removed from frontier farmers is not as significant as the fact that the planters believed in a landed aristocratic ideal and acted out that belief. However coarse their manners and tastes, the planter class pursued planter class interests and for the most part led the rest of the South into the same course.[16]

If the planters as a neofeudal ruling class did indeed represent the last gasp of a landed order against Northern capitalism, then the Old South represented a denial of the middle-class democracy that has characterized American society.[17] To the degree that the antebellum South was a planter-dominated, working aristocracy, the Old South was more Southern (perhaps more European) than American.

That planter interests prevailed in the South and that this denoted an un-American aristocratic tradition is a matter of observa-

[15]This analysis, very subtly expressed, is from Eaton, *Growth of Southern Civilization* and *The Freedom of Thought Struggle in the Old South,* revised and enlarged edition (New York, 1964).

[16]This point is well made in C. Vann Woodward's masterful critique of Cash's *Mind of the South,* "The Elusive Mind of the South," published first in the *New York Review of Books* (December 4, 1969) and later slightly altered in Woodward, *American Counterpoint,* pp. 261–283.

[17]See Genovese, "The Slave South," *Political Economy,* pp. 13–39.

tion, not theory; yet qualification is necessary. The planters exercised hegemony in Southern society because nonplanter whites deferred to their social "betters" and because Southern plain folk in the main accepted planter values and ideology.

Southerners as a people blended the traits of aristocracy and democracy within the same social structure. They did so in part because of the ambitions of the plain folk to become planters and because of the *noblesse oblige* of the planters toward their farmer neighbors. Kinship was important too, as was economic interdependence. Class consciousness existed among some nonplanters but was slow to develop among the masses. Resentment came hard to a farmer who yearned for a big house like his neighbor's, who appreciated the neighbor's inquiries about the health of an ailing child, who claimed kinship with his neighbor, and who sold the neighbor hogs and hay several times a year.

Beyond these factors was also the existence of a persistent folk culture in the Old South. Compared with other Americans, white Southerners were a homogeneous people ethnically and culturally. And compared with other Americans, Southerners tended to retain the more primal relationship with people and place characteristic of folk culture. Personal, as opposed to institutional, values and relationships were pervasive.[18] Southerners of all social stations were mobile people; significantly, they measured wealth in terms of moveable slaves instead of immobile acres of land. But when Southerners moved, they tended to recreate in a new location the same sort of society and folk culture they left.

In terms of social structure, consideration of the South as an expression of a unique folk culture permits the rejection of both the moonlight-and-magnolia fantasy and the conception of Southern society as middle-class democracy. However powerful the Southern planter class, it could not ignore the more numerous and often prosperous yeomen. However numerous the Southern middle class,

[18]"It was an aspect of this culture that the relation between the land and the people remained more direct and more primal in the South than in other parts of the country. . . . Even in the most exploitative economic situations, this culture retained a personalism in the relations of man to man which the industrial culture lacks. Even for those whose lives were the narrowest, it offered a relationship of man to nature in which there was a certain fulfillment of personality." David M. Potter, "The Enigma of the South," *Yale Review*, LI (1961), 142–151, republished in *South and Sectional Conflict*, pp. 3–16.

in accepting planter leadership, it hardly pursued traditional middle-class interests. United by the series of personal relationships which characterize folk culture, planters and plain folk formed an essentially solid Southern society.[19]

Southern folk culture was an adhesive factor that bound people together and offered them identity with each other and with geographical location in the Old South. The presence of 4 million black slaves within the Southern body social was another matter.

Racial slavery was the most distinctive feature of Southern life. The slave system conditioned the whole of existence for nearly 4 million black Southerners, who were its victims. And the black presence in the South incalculably affected the lives of both slaveholder and nonslaveholder whites in ways far beyond the purely economic impact of slave labor.[20] So important was slavery to the Old South's ideological cause that in 1861 Confederate Vice-President Alexander H. Stephens pronounced it the "cornerstone" of the Southern nation.[21]

The black presence in the South was at once a source of general tension and of white adhesion: slavery and the system of racial subordination were always prone to insurrection and racial upheaval within the South and under increasing attack from outside the South.[22] White Southerners believed that slavery was crucial to

[19]Although Potter's article (ibid.) remains in good repute, few historians have attempted to expand the folk culture theme and to offer examples of folk culture in action. An exception is Bertram Wyatt-Brown, "The Antimission Movement in the Jacksonian South: A Study in Regional Folk Culture," Journal of Southern History, XXXVI (1970), 501–529. An earlier treatment of Southern personalism in action is Charles S. Sydnor, "The Southerner and the Laws," Journal of Southern History, VI (1940), 1–23.

[20]As Ralph Ellison (quoted in William Styron, "This Quiet Dust," Harpers, April 1965, 136) observed a century later, "Southern whites cannot walk, talk, sing, conceive of laws or justice, think of sex, love, the family, or freedom without responding to the presence of Negroes."

[21]After stating that the "Old" Union "rested upon the assumption of the equality of races," Stephens explained, "Our new Government is founded upon exactly the opposite ideas; its foundations are laid, its cornerstone rests, upon the great truth that the negro is not equal to the white man; that slavery, subordination to the superior race, is his natural and moral condition." The full text of the speech, delivered in March 1861, is in Frank Moore (ed.), The Rebellion Record, I, (New York, 1861–1864), 44–49.

[22]See especially William W. Freehling, Prelude to Civil War: The Nullification Controversy in South Carolina, 1816–1836 (New York, 1965); and Steven A. Channing, Crisis of Fear: Secession in South Carolina (New York, 1970), for full expositions of this view. William L. Barney in The Secessionist Impulse: Alabama and Mississippi in 1860 (Princeton,

their life style and, correctly, that powerful elements in the Republican Party were committed to the extinction of the institution.[23] The slave system was the most threatened feature of ante-bellum life, and as such it was the most heavily defended. Planters believed that they would remain planters only so long as slavery persisted, and they had no interest in committing class suicide.

The South's plain folk, too, generally recognized their stake in the slaveholders' world. When in 1859 North Carolinian Hinton Rowan Helper wrote his *Impending Crisis in the South,* he tried to tell his fellow plain folk how the planters were "using" them, and he tried to show how the slave system worked to keep rich people rich and poor people poor. Helper contended that slavery was a class weapon in that the system allowed planters to work their extensive acreage and barred others from access to both land and labor. His case was convincing—in the abstract. Certainly the violent response of the planter leadership in suppressing the book indicated that it had struck an exposed nerve.[24]

In the real world of the Old South, however, plain folk and planters were bound by ties of self-interest and racial solidarity. Freeing a captive population of 4 million would injure the plain folk economically and perhaps physically as well. The slave system was hard and often brutal, and as an institution, slavery fed the basest desires of masters and degraded the humanity of slaves.[25]

Racism was a national character flaw in nineteenth-century America which differed in degree, not in kind, from section to section;[26] northern whites might have done the same as Southerners had they

N.J., 1974) speaks to the same point in a broader context.

[23]See Foner, *Free Soil, Free Labor, Free Men,* 103–148.

[24]Jack J. Carduso, "Southern Reaction to *The Impending Crisis,*" *Civil War History,* XVI (1970), 5–17.

[25]For a realistic portrayal of the physical rigors of the slave system, see Kenneth M. Stampp, *The Peculiar Institution: Slavery in the Ante-Bellum South* (New York, 1955). See John Hope Franklin, *The Militant South, 1800–1861,* (Cambridge, Mass., 1956); and Stanley M. Elkins, *Slavery: A Problem in American Institutional and Intellectual Life* (Chicago, 1959), for strong statements about the general effect of the slave system on masters and slaves respectively.

[26]On Northern racism see especially Leon F. Litwack, *North of Slavery 1790–1860* (Chicago, 1961); Foner, *Free Soil, Free Labor, Free Men;* Eugene H. Berwanger, *The Frontier Against Slavery: Western Anti-Negro Prejudice and the Slavery Extension Controversy* (Urbana, Ill., 1967); and C. Vann Woodward, "White Racism and Black 'Emancipation,'" *New York Review of Books* (Feb. 27, 1969).

been able to adapt the slave system to their enterprises. But slavery remained a Southern institution. Not only did the South's "peculiar institution" differ from the Northern system of labor; it differed from contemporary slave regimes in other parts of the Western world as well. Slavery was the South's unique answer to twin demands for labor and racial subordination.[27]

Slavery in the American South tended to be more personal than institutional. While the authoritarian features of the abstract system tended to destroy black identity and personality, investigations of the human reality reveal the presence of a strong black identity and community. At its root, racial slavery in the Old South was a basic human relationship: the relationship between master and slave predates human history. And because it was human, it existed in an infinite variety of modes. It was grounded in love, hate, and indifference. Within the framework of the peculiar institution, blacks and whites interacted in ways that were servile, oppressive, cruel, friendly, cooperative, and gentle—all human. On this basis only could Southern whites rationalize slavery and face the threats to it from outside the South. Slavery, as Stephen Vincent Benét wrote, was "the unjust thing that some tamed into mercy, being wise, but could not starve the tiger from its eyes."[28]

Agriculture lay at the base of the Old South economy, but as with social structure, a central issue was the degree of Americanness of that economy. Just as Southern society was a blend of landed aristocracy and American-style social democracy, so the Southern economy was a mixture of precapitalist seigniorialism and laissez-faire capitalism. The result was an enigma—not a never-never world of courtly agrarians or a mere mutation of American capitalism but something *sui generis.*[29]

Like most areas of the world in the nineteenth century that produced raw materials for more diversified, industrialized areas, the

[27]See David Brian Davis, *The Problem of Slavery in Western Culture* (Ithaca, N.Y., 1966); and Genovese, *The World the Slaveholders Made*, pp. 3–113.

[28]Regarding the human dimension in slavery and race relations see Genovese "The Slave South," *Political Economy*, for emphasis on the masters; John W. Blassingame, *The Slave Community: Plantation Life in the Ante Bellum South* (New York, 1972), and Eugene D. Genovese, *Roll, Jordan, Roll: The World the Slaves Made* (New York, 1974), for emphasis upon the slaves; and Robert William Fogel and Stanley L. Engerman, *Time on the Cross*, 2 vols. (Boston, 1974), for emphasis upon both slaves and masters. The Benét lines are from *John Brown's Body* (New York, 1927), p. 333.

[29]See Potter, *South and Sectional Conflict*, pp. 191–194.

South occupied a disadvantageous economic position in relation to the North and western Europe. Southern plantations produced mostly staple raw materials, and planters had to sell them on an open world market. For manufactured items, Southerners depended upon the protected industries of Europe and the North. The vicissitudes of agriculture—droughts, floods, diseases, and soil exhaustion—combined with this unfavorable market position to render the South a colonial appendage of the North and an underdeveloped nation to European capitalists.[30] Nevertheless the South produced ample wealth: sugar, rice, tobacco, hemp, and assorted grains in quantity, and in any given year after 1845 an estimated two-thirds of the world's cotton supply.[31] Most of these staples left the South raw; Southerners seemed content to produce crops without all but the most elemental processing, such as the ginning of cotton. As a result, capital flowed out of the South and into the hands of more sophisticated capitalists in the North and Europe. Southern planters, when they were able to accumulate capital or command credit, tended to invest in more land and slaves. Consequently the South expanded production of raw staples without broadening its economic base.[32]

By 1860, industrial capitalism had made few inroads in the South. Isolated centers, chiefly on the seaboard and in the upper South, took advantage of the section's industrial potential, and a few Southern industrialists were able to adapt slavery to factory conditions and thus demonstrate novel potential for the South's peculiar institution, but these were exceptions. On the whole, the Southern economy was agrarian.[33]

[30]The classic statement of this view is Thomas P. Kettell, *Southern Wealth and Northern Profits, as Exhibited in Statistical Facts and Official Figures* (New York, 1860). Harold D. Woodman, *King Cotton and His Retainers: Financing and Marketing the Cotton Crop of the South* (Lexington, Ky., 1968), offers an updated perspective but nevertheless terms the "king" a "puppet monarch."

[31]Stuart Bruchey (ed.), *Cotton and the Growth of the American Economy* (New York, 1967), p. 7.

[32]For a good brief statement on the Southern economy see Douglas C. North, *Growth and Welfare in the American Past*, 2nd edition (Englewood Cliffs, N.J., 1974), pp. 87–95. More extended analyses are in Douglas C. North, *The Economic Growth of the United States, 1790–1860* (New York, 1966); and Stuart Bruchey, *The Roots of American Economic Growth, 1607–1861* (New York, 1965).

[33]A foremost booster of industry in the Old South was J. D. B. DeBow in *DeBow's Review* (New Orleans, 1846–1864) and *The Industrial Resources of the Southern and Western States*, 3 vols. (New Orleans, 1852–1853). Robert S. Starobin's *Industrial*

One reason for the South's industrial lag was top-heavy income distribution. Manufacturers require markets, and the majority of Southerners, slaves and plain folk, were not consumers in any significant sense. Members of the planter class had money and were often conspicuous consumers, yet planter tastes were either too sophisticated or too crude for home-grown manufacturing. Infant Southern industry offered little to compete with European luxury items or Northern agricultural implements, and, for apparent reasons, slaveholders had little need of labor-saving devices. However much the South suffered from a dearth of industry, market realities offered small encouragement to those in a position to remedy the situation.[34]

This analysis seems to support the agrarian view of the Old South: that Southerners were marginal to American capitalism and simply produced for a world that exploited them. In fact, though, the supposedly prodigal planters were making a better return on their investment in land and slaves than they could have made in almost any other venture.[35] A good reason why planter class Southerners did not commit their energy and resources to industrialization was that they could make substantially more money planting. Even when all the variables were counted—factors such as the high initial cost of slave labor, maintenance of slaves too young and too old to work, losses owing to deaths and runaways—the weight of evidence, statistical and otherwise, indicates that slaveholding paid in the Old

Slavery in the Old South (New York, 1970) displays the available potential and limited success already demonstrated for the use of slave labor in manufacturing. Case studies of industrial enterprise are Charles B. Dew, *Ironmaker to the Confederacy: Joseph R. Anderson and the Tredegar Iron Works* (New Haven, Conn., 1966); and Broadus Mitchell, *William Gregg, Factory Master of the Old South* (Chapel Hill, N.C., 1928). Genovese, *Political Economy*, pp. 157–220, offers a summary explanation of why the Southern commitment to industry remained so small.

[34]Genovese, *Political Economy*, pp. 157–220.

[35]The foundation of much of this research is John R. Conrad and Alfred H. Meyer, "The Economics of Slavery in the Ante Bellum South," *Journal of Political Economy*, LXVI (1958), 95–130, and *The Economics of Slavery and Other Studies in Econometric History* (Chicago, 1964). The best summaries of the debate over the profitability of the slave system are Harold R. Woodman, "The Profitability of Slavery: A Historical Perennial," *Journal of Southern History*, XXIX (1963), 303–325; and Stanley L. Engerman, "The Effects of Slavery upon the Southern Economy: A Review of the Recent Debate," *Explorations in Entrepreneurial History*, 2nd ser. IV (1967), 71–97. See also Fogel and Engerman, *Time on the Cross*, I, 59–106; and Hugh G. J. Aiken (ed.), *Did Slavery Pay?* (Boston, 1971).

South. There is even reason to believe that slave labor on Southern plantations was more efficient than free labor on Northern farms.

Exploding the agrarian myth of profitless plantations does not necessarily establish the existence of cotton capitalism in the Old South. Southern planters, and indeed many subplanters, did employ the tools of capitalism. They depended upon credit in the money market, produced cash crops, sold those crops in a free market, made profits, and reinvested part of those profits in capital improvements—more land and slaves. Southerners were not mystical agrarians who subordinated the nineteenth-century priorities of getting and spending to romanticizing their mint juleps, but neither was the planter class in the mainstream of American capitalism.[36]

The Southern economy was basically precapitalist due to three salient features. First and most important, Southerners employed slaves instead of free labor. The use of slave labor limited flexibility in the size and skills of a work force. Planters did buy, sell, and rent slaves, but seldom in strict accord with seasonal labor demands. Both economically and emotionally, buying and selling involved more than hiring and firing. One of the striking characteristics of slavery was a sense of paternalism almost completely absent in free-labor capitalism. Paternalism did not necessarily involve kindness—a paternalistic slaveholder could be authoritarian or indulgent in the process of caring for "his" people—but merely a sense of responsibility of master for slave. This sense of responsibility extended, of course, beyond working hours and often encompassed more than physical needs. In the free-labor North, not only was the worker unbound, the employer was also free to hire and fire at will and free, except for wages, from personal obligations toward his workers. Slaveholding, then, was more than a degenerate mutation of capitalism. The South's peculiar institution was the base of an equally peculiar economic structure.[37]

A second factor that made the Southern economy unique was its overwhelming dependence upon agriculture. Although the North was still predominantly agricultural and industry was mostly domes-

[36]See Genovese, *Political Economy*, pp. 275–287; and Eugene D. Genovese, "Race and Class in Southern History: An Appraisal of the Work of Ulrich Bonnell Phillips," *Agriculture History*, ILI (1967), 345–358.

[37]Foner, *Free Soil, Free Labor, Free Men*, pp. 11–39; and Potter, *South and Sectional Conflict*, pp. 191–194; Genovese, *Roll, Jordan, Roll*, 3–112.

tic, American capitalism was becoming industrial and urban. The Old South shared neither tendency and so stood apart from the thrust of the national economy. This is not to suggest that capitalism can never exist in a rural setting, but that the Old South at this stage of economic development did not ride the dominant currents of the American economic mainstream. True, during the 1850s Southern cities and industries grew faster than before—perhaps the Southern economy was simply following national trends at a great distance—but even allowing for dynamic factors in the Southern economy, the Southern experience differed from the national norm in kind as well as degree.[38]

Finally, American capitalism in the nineteenth century, like slaveholding in the South, was not an economic system in a cultural vacuum; there was cultural baggage associated with it. However much the South employed some of the economic tools of capitalism, Southerners as a whole did not adopt its culture. In what one recent scholar has termed the "lazy South," addiction to the work ethic never became widespread. Thrift was not a virtue of the planter class, and they seem to have honored Poor Richard's sayings most in their breach.[39]

In sum, the social economy of the Old South was significantly at odds with American trends and traditions during the mid-nineteenth century. Differences alone, however, cannot explain the cause—cannot explain the intensity with which Edmund Ruffin and people like him pursued revolution. The cause was grounded in the raw materials of Southern life: slavery and race, planters and patricians, plain folk and folk culture, cotton and plantations. But to become the cause and inspire revolution, the elements of Southern social economy had to affect the Southern mind and emotions.

[38]In addition to the works cited in note 33 above see Genovese, "The Slave South," *Political Economy*, 13–28.

[39]This idea is expanded by C. Vann Woodward, "The Southern Ethic in a Puritan World," *William and Mary Quarterly*, XXV, 3rd series (1968), 343–370. The essay deals with David Bertelson's book *The Lazy South* (New York, 1967), which speaks to this point at some length.

CHAPTER 2

Cultural Nationalism
in the Pre-Confederate South

P RESTON Brooks had a sharp temper, but essentially he was a
gentle man. He was "to the manor born" in upcountry South
Carolina in 1819, and during youth and young manhood, his life
was generally comfortable. Brooks was not especially talented at any
one activity but displayed competence at law, soldiering (in the
Mexican War), planting, and politics. He was physically handsome
and under normal circumstances gracious and genial. In 1856, at
age thirty-four, Brooks was serving his second term in the Congress;
his colleagues there judged him undistinguished but affable.[1]

On May 19, Brooks visited the Senate chamber and heard part of
a speech by Charles Sumner of Massachusetts. Sumner spoke on
"The Crime Against Kansas" and said a number of highly inflamma-
tory things about slaveholders in general and about South Carolinians and South Carolina Senator Andrew P. Butler in particular. In
Sumner's phrase, Butler was a "Don Quixote" who had taken "the
harlot, Slavery" as his "mistress." Sumner pronounced Butler and
South Carolina worthless and accused Butler of "an incapacity of
accuracy," among other euphemisms for lying. Senator Butler, an
aged uncle of Brooks', was not in Washington when Sumner delivered his oration, and Brooks felt he must answer the Northerner's
harsh words.

[1]James E. Walmsley, "Preston Smith Brooks," in Allen Johnson and Dumas Malone (eds.), *Dictionary of American Biography* (New York, 1929); Alvy L. King, *Louis T.
Wigfall: Southern Fire-eater* (Baton Rouge, La., 1970), pp. 25–34.

Brooks waited until he had read the printed version of Sumner's speech and debated with himself and friends over when and how best to respond. Then, on May 21, two days after he had heard the speech, Brooks attempted to intercept Sumner outside the Capitol; he failed and grew frustrated as well as angry. The next day, shortly after a noon adjournment, Brooks stalked Sumner in the Senate chamber. He waited impatiently as the room cleared, and Sumner continued to work at his desk. At last Brooks strode to Sumner's desk, called his name, and stated that his speech had been a libel upon Butler and South Carolina. Sumner started to stand up, but Brooks broke off his prepared statement in mid-sentence and began striking Sumner with a gutta-percha cane. After several measured blows, Brooks lost control and flailed madly at Sumner's head. Stunned and blinded by his own blood, Sumner attempted first to cover himself with his arms and then to flee. He was so desperate that as he strained to stand up he wrenched his desk from the bolts that secured it to the floor. While Sumner staggered about blindly, Brooks continued his assault until his cane splintered. In less than a minute Sumner lay senseless in the arms of a bystander, and Brooks had strode from the chamber with friends to clean a small cut on his head from the recoil of his cane.[2]

Although Brooks' temper fired the intensity of the beating, there is no doubt that the caning of Sumner was premeditated. Nor was Brooks alone in his deed. His immediate confederates advised him and accompanied him to the Senate chamber, and after the fact, Southerners participated vicariously by applauding Brooks and approving his motive if not always his means. The obscure congressman became a hero in the South, and more than a hundred Southerners sent him canes to replace the one he had broken on Sumner's head. Although Brooks resigned from the House after surviving an attempt to expel him—every Southern Congressman voted no—his constituents in South Carolina returned him in triumph in the subsequent election.[3]

In several ways the caning of Sumner was a classically Southern

[2] *Alleged Assault upon Senator Sumner* (House Report, No. 182, 34 Congress, I Session); David Donald, *Charles Sumner and the Coming of the Civil War* (New York, 1960), pp. 289–296; Robert L. Meriwether (ed.), "Preston S. Brooks on the Caning of Charles Sumner," *South Carolina Historical and Genealogical Magazine*, XII (1951), 2–3.
[3] *Ibid.*

act. More than anything else Brooks' deed expressed what Robert Penn Warren has called that "instinctive fear—that the massiveness of experience, the concreteness of life will be violated: the fear of abstraction."[4] Although reflection confirms the notion that Brooks' action was symbolic, Brooks himself seemed more concerned with what was real and direct than he did with pose or gesture. He answered metaphors and innuendoes with blows. To the degree that there was a corporate Southern mind, Brooks acted out its most salient quality: the primacy of the concrete over the abstract, of action over contemplation. At the same time, Brooks gave expression to a characteristic extension of the Southern mental focus on the here and now and real—what W. J. Cash has described as "puerile individualism" and defined as "the boast, voiced or not, on the part of every Southerner that he would knock hell out of whoever dared to cross him."[5]

In the South, physical circumstances and folk culture encouraged development of rule by men instead of law and institutions. Paradoxically, while Southerners depended on legal absolutes in Congress to preserve slavery, law on slave plantations was essentially what planters said it was.[6] And among the South's plain folk, individualism expressed as a violent assertion of self was common. Of course, southern individualism was only partially negative; it also fostered a sturdy independence and a secure self-image. But however expressed, individualism hindered the development of a sense of corporate identity in Southern communities and produced a high degree of provincialism as a by-product. At best, individualistic Southerners lived out Ralph Waldo Emerson's essay "Self-Reliance"; at worst they answered insults with blows in the chamber of the United States Senate.[7]

[4]The Warren quote is cited in Albert Murray, *South to a Very Old Place* (New York, 1971), p. 22, in the context of a discussion of the concrete in the Southern mind.

[5]W. J. Cash, *Mind of the South* (New York, 1941) p. 44. Other southern "Mind" studies include William R. Taylor, *Cavalier and Yankee: The Old South and American National Character* (New York, 1961); Clement Eaton, *The Growth of Southern Civilization* (New York, 1961), chapter 13, and *The Mind of the Old South*, revised edition (Baton Rouge, La., 1967); and Rollin G. Osterweis, *Romanticism and Nationalsim in the Old South* (New Haven, Conn., 1949).

[6]Charles S. Sydnor, "The Southerner and the Laws," *Journal of Southern History*, VI (1940), 3–23.

[7]David M. Potter, "The Enigma of the South," *Yale Review*, LI (1961), 142–151, and David Bertelson, *The Lazy South* (New York, 1967) deal with the primacy of

Southerners are not the only Americans with a deserved reputation as proud, violent people, but in the Old South, violence tended to be more personal and more socially acceptable than elsewhere. Slavery, after all, depended upon physical force or the threat of force, and from childhood, slaveholders were accustomed to striking their chattels with impunity, because blacks struck whites at the risk of their lives. Planter-class Southerners codified personal violence in a *code duello* that persisted in law or practice long after its abandonment in other sections of the United States. That they also celebrated corporate violence is clear from the relatively high numbers of Southern military schools and militia units that took seriously the study and profession of arms.

The planters' penchant for violence was a model for the plain folk, if indeed they needed a model. In the rural South, often only slightly beyond the frontier stage of development, the plain folk defended and asserted themselves according to their own code of violent behavior. In addition, nonslaveholders shared responsibility with slaveholders for the internal security of slavery, and plain folk shared with planters legal sanction to "discipline" Southern blacks. Finally, the high degree of personalism which characterized Southern folk culture encouraged direct, personal confrontation. In the case of Charles Sumner's "Crime Against Kansas" speech, for example, while many critics spoke about "intemperate" language and "malignity," Preston Brooks took Sumner's insults personally, nominated himself to defend his uncle's honor, and confronted Sumner individually and violently.[8]

Brooks' action was an enormous personal overreaction, but satisfaction for a personal affront was only part of his motive. As Brooks pointed out, Sumner had insulted not only Butler but also South Carolina and the South. Brooks was simultaneously defending personal and familial honor and attacking a critic of his homeland and way of life. He was acting out the ultimate thrust of Southern culture and polity during the late ante-bellum period: to defend the Southern way of life and assert its superiority over the emerging American norm, even by force.

---

individual, as opposed to corporate, identity from opposite points of view; both scholars, however, acknowledge the central importance of personalism in the South.

[8]The classic statement on Southern violence is John Hope Franklin, *The Militant South* (Cambridge, Mass., 1956). See also Cash, *Mind of the South*, pp. 44–45.

Most people live in a state of tension between what they are and what they want to be, but this tension was especially intense in the Old South. Southerners lived with a heritage that professed the ideals of liberty, equality, and democracy, but these ideals were not easily reconciled with the reality of slavery, racism, and aristocracy.[9] In an attempt to do so, Southerners adopted elaborate defense mechanisms. Behind Brooks' caning of Charles Sumner lay a culture devoted to the celebration of Southern reality and the identification of the Southern status quo with an ideal romantic vision. Only on this basis—believing themselves to be the last best hope of Western civilization—could Southerners defend themselves against attacks from outside. The corporate Southern mind had become comfortable with the potential for guilt that pervaded a life style largely grounded in slavery. And the Southern belief in most of the rationalizations for that life style gave birth to a national ideology.

Where did the process begin? Perhaps Southern churches are the best place to look for the origins of cultural nationalism in the Old South. There the Southern mind, conditioned by reverence for the concrete and characterized by assertive individualism, blended with a unique religious tradition to mold intellectual and cultural life.

During the middle third of the nineteenth century, one of the most striking characteristics of Southern religious feeling was its homogeneity. Religious skeptics, Jews, and Roman Catholics (except in Louisiana and Maryland) were a small minority among overwhelming numbers of Protestant Christians. Of those, Quakers, Unitarians, and liberal sects were an even smaller minority. The dominant denominations were Baptist, Methodist, Presbyterian, and Episcopalian. In most communities of the seaboard South, Episcopalians and Presbyterians tended to be among the richer classes, yet even these denominations were more orthodox and evangelical than they had been in the colonial era. Hence, the mass of Southern whites acknowledged a fundamental religious emphasis upon sin and salvation. Camp meetings and interdenominational revival services, plus the ease and frequency with which Southerners attended services of various denominations (indicated in the letters and diaries of the period), attest to the religious homogeneity among evangelical Protestants in the Old South. Moreover, the religious em-

[9]See the essay of Charles G. Sellers, Jr., in "The Tragic Southerner" in his *The Southerner as American* (Chapel Hill, N.C., 1960).

phasis upon a strict moral code provided a common standard of behavior that affected church members and nonmembers as well. However much Southerners railed against the Puritan origins of their New England brethren, they themselves had incorporated much of the Puritan heritage into Southern-style evangelical Protestantism.[10]

At or near the heart of the faith was the conviction of human sinfulness. Paradoxically, this deep consciousness of sin in this world and perfection in the next served as a bulwark of the Old South status quo. Many Southern clergymen found divine sanction for racial subordination in the "truth" that blacks were cursed as "Sons of Ham," and justified bondage by citing Biblical examples.[11] More subtly, the hellfire-and-damnation emphasis of Southern Protestantism served as a kind of inverse support for the hedonistic aspects of the Southern life style. The Old South probably deserved much of the scorn heaped upon it by Northern critics as being a land of sloth and lust. Seemingly, Southerners indulged in corn liquor and camp meetings with equal zest. Perhaps the practice of their fundamentalist faith satisfied the need for confession and purgation. Hearing their sins exposed and denounced from the pulpit of a church or the stump of a camp meeting, Southern sinners were sufficiently freed from guilt to thank the preacher for a fine sermon and go sin some more. In short, if all are wrong, then none are guilty. The Southern appropriation of Puritanism seemed to offer comfort in the universality of the human condition. Thus, hedonism and fundamentalism coexisted in the Southern soul, and the same conservative faith which inspired John Brown to violence in an attempt to abolish slavery justified the South's peculiar institution to Southerners.[12]

Southern Protestantism made severe demands upon Southerners as individuals; the common conviction called upon them to live

[10]Clement Eaton, *A History of the Old South: The Emergence of a Reluctant Nation*, 3rd edition (New York, 1975), pp. 451–461; W. W. Sweet, *The Story of Religion in America* (New York, 1939), pp. 322–447; Eaton, *Mind of the Old South*, pp. 200–223; Clement Eaton, *The Freedom-of-Thought Struggle in the Old South*, revised and enlarged edition (New York, 1964), pp. 300–334.

[11]Eaton, *History of the Old South*, p. 378; Cash, *Mind of the South*, pp. 82–84. See also Ernest T. Thompson, *Presbyterians in the South, 1607–1861* (Richmond, Va., 1963); William W. Sweet (ed.), *Religion on the American Frontier: The Baptists, 1783–1830* (New York, 1931), and Donald G. Mathews, *Religion in the Old South* (Chicago, 1977).

[12]Cash, *Mind of the South*, pp. 55–60.

upright lives in response to the righteous demands of a strict father-God, and, whether they were obedient or rebellious children, they acknowledged the existence of individual moral obligations. About society, however, Southern Protestantism had much less to say. Religion in the South was essentially personal; it did not, as elsewhere, inspire reform or create in believers a zeal to perfect human society. Southerners believed in the power of Protestant Christianity to regenerate individuals, but when the church entered the arena of social justice, it had "quit preaching and begun meddling."[13]

It was no accident that Unitarianism and transcendentalism attracted so few Southerners. The Unitarian faith and the transcendental philosophy tended to exalt humanity and to call it to perfection in this world. Southerners were not so optimistic. They perceived reality as rooted in human frailty, and because they could not alter the human condition, they accepted and even celebrated their humanity. Significantly, this was as true among Episcopalians as among Baptists, even though the former expressed themselves with liturgical formality and the latter with emotional spontaneity.

Because the religious response seemed to fulfill whatever introspective and contemplative needs the Southerner had, secular culture, traditional arts and letters, in the Old South tended to reinforce what was instead of inspire dreams of what might be. It was in secular culture that Southerners made visible the romantic vision of their world, demonstrating a peculiarly Southern mutation of the romantic mood which characterized Western Europe and the United States in the nineteenth century. Romanticism in the North and West tended to inspire reform movements and the pursuit of ideals beyond present grasp; flights from reality were onward and upward. Southern romantics tended to pursue ideals which justified or sanctified things as they were in the South. Southerners prized oratory and fought duels as romantic expressions that linked them to a body of sacred tradition. Reading themselves into the novels of Sir Walter Scott, they held jousting tournaments. They recognized a direct line of aristocratic descent among a landed class from feudal lords, through English squires, to themselves. In the Southern "belle"—the lady aloof on her pedestal as ornament and object—Southerners fashioned an ideal for female behavior modeled in part

[13]For a case-study comparison of Northern and Southern religious attitudes toward reform, see Eaton, *Mind of the Old South*, pp. 205–209.

at least upon the medieval concept of courtly love. The male counterpart of the belle was the "cavalier"—the courtly horseman who defied "roundhead" vulgarity. Of course, much of this romantic self-image was myth; yet because it was believed, it was real to the Southern mind.[14]

Home-grown *belles-lettres* for the most part amounted to a romantic celebration of contemporary Southern life or of the "Southern" features of the American past. Some Southern writers expressed these things well—John Pendleton Kennedy of Maryland and William Gilmore Simms of South Carolina, for example. Kennedy, in "plantation romances" such as *Swallow Barn*, portrayed the nobler features of the slaveholders' society and paternalistic harmony in relations between masters and slaves. Simms' best works, his melodramatic tales of the American Revolution, lauded patriotic planters and made Tories of meaner folk. His most memorable characters, though, were backwoods adventurers who modeled a classless "hell-of-a-fellow" spirit.[15] Simms actively involved himself in South Carolina politics and consciously used his creative talents to project favorable images of the South, though without ever quite finding acceptance in the Charleston society he championed. So much did he give to Southern propaganda that he wrote in the epitaph he composed for himself, "Here lies one who, after a reasonably long life, distinguished chiefly by unceasing labors, has left all his better works undone."[16]

While Kennedy and Simms projected a romantic South, the Southern writer who was perhaps the epitome of Southern romanticism was Edgar Allan Poe. As Vernon L. Parrington wrote:

His ideals ran counter to every major interest of the New England renaissance: the mystical, optimistic element in transcendentalism; the social

---

[14]See Osterweis, *Romanticism and Nationalism;* Anne Firor Scott, *The Southern Lady: From Pedestal to Politics* (Chicago, 1970); Emory M. Thomas, *The American War and Peace, 1860–1877* (Englewood Cliffs, N.J., 1971), pp. 37–38; and especially Raimondo Luraghi, *The Rise and Fall of the Plantation South* (New York, 1978), pp. 15–82.

[15]On Southern writers in general, see, Jay B. Hubbell, *The South in American Literature, 1607–1900* (Durham, N.C., 1954); and Vernon Louis Parrington, *Main Currents in American Thought,* II, *The Romantic Revolution in America, 1800–1860* (New York, 1927), 1–172. On Simms see especially Jon L. Wakelyn, *The Politics of a Literary Man: William Gilmore Simms* (Westport, Conn., 1973). J. V. Ridgely, *John Pendleton Kennedy* (New York, 1966) is the standard biography of Kennedy.

[16]Cited in Parrington, *Main Currents,* II, 130.

conscience that would make the world over in accordance with French idealism, and meddled with its neighbor's affairs in applying its equalitarianism to the Negro; the pervasive moralism that would accept no other criteria by which to judge life and letters—these things could not fail to irritate a nature too easily ruffled. The Yankee parochialisms rubbed across his Virginia parochialisms.[17]

As critic, short story writer, and poet, Poe alone among ante-bellum Southerners attracted an enduring readership. He did so by indulging his taste for form and beauty and by absorbing "the indolent life of the planter gentry, shot through with a pugnacious pride of locality, with a strong dislike of alien ways, with haughtiness, dissipation, wastefulness, chivalry."[18]

Southern poets, too, generally indulged romantic tastes and reinforced their readers' appreciation of things Southern. Obvious examples include William Grayson (*The Hireling and the Slave*), Paul Hamilton Hayne, and Henry Timrod.[19] About the South, Timrod wrote in *The Cotton Boll:*

> Ye Stars, which, though unseen yet with me gaze
> Upon this loveliest fragment of the earth!
> Thou Sun, that kindlest all thy gentlest rays
> Above it, as to light a favorite hearth!
> Ye Clouds, that in your temples in the West
> See nothing brighter than its humblest flowers?
> And you, ye Winds, that on the ocean's breast
> Are kissed to coolness ere ye reach its bowers!
> Bear witness with me in my song of praise,
> And tell the world that, since the world began,
> No fairer land hath fired a poet's lays,
> Or given a home to man![20]

Although traditional intellectuals in the Old South (Poe excepted) did not produce much of lasting merit, it would be a mistake

[17]*Ibid.*, 55.

[18]*Ibid.*, 54. On Poe see also Arthur Hobson Quinn, *Edgar Allan Poe: A Critical Biography* (New York, 1941); and Edd Winfield Parks, *Edgar Allan Poe as Literary Critic* (Athens, Ga., 1964).

[19]Jay B. Hubbell, "Literary Nationalism in the Old South," in David K. Jackson (ed.), *American Studies in Honor of William Kenneth Boyd* (Durham, N.C., 1940), pp. 175–200; Edd Winfield Parks, *Henry Timrod* (New York, 1964); Rayburn S. Moore, *Paul Hamilton Hayne* (New York, 1972); and Parrington, *Main Currents*, II, 98–107.

[20]Paul H. Hayne (ed.), *The Poems of Henry Timrod* (New York, 1873), p. 128.

to dismiss the South as a cultural wasteland. Beneath the level of *belles-lettres,* Southern cultural life was rich and richly in tune with the Southern life style. The Southern people—planters, plain folk, and slaves—were accustomed to active lives in the outdoors. They rode, raced, hunted, and for the most part spared little time for systematic contemplation of life beyond their experience and their immediate physical world. Southern popular culture reflected this focus and in some of its aspects creatively enhanced the Southern life style.[21] Southerners supported indifferent theater and in the late ante-bellum period indulged in the general banality of minstrel show comedy and music, yet even minstrel companies, to the degree that they appropriated the zest of "bottom-rail" humor and generated a mood of carefree abandon in "walk-around" numbers, were a link between formal culture and authentic popular culture of Southern people.

Predictably, Southern architecture was an art form more often developed in private homes than in public buildings. The influence of Thomas Jefferson faded during the middle third of the nineteenth century, and Southerners turned to Greek Revival, adapting the columned Greek temple to functional as well as esthetic purpose. In cities like Charleston, Savannah, and New Orleans, Southerners constructed spacious homes with columns, verandas, and courtyards in relatively small spaces with a maximum sense of privacy. In the country, Southerners built homes which combined aristocratic pretense with openness to nature. At its best Southern architecture blended form and function, took advantage of natural surroundings, and gave expression to the individuality of the builder and owner.[22]

Among the plain folk, the "three P" house was a good example of the harmony which often existed between form and function. "Three P" stood for two pens and a path. The home started out as one log or board "pen" with a roof. Later the family built a second

[21]Eaton, *History of the Old South,* pp. 403–404, 451.

[22]On Southern architecture see Lewis Mumford, *The South in Architecture* (New York, 1941); T. F. Hamlin, *Greek Revival Architecture in America* (New York, 1944), and *Benjamin Henry Latrobe* (New York, 1955); J. C. Bonner, "Plantation Architecture of the Lower South on the Eve of the Civil War," *Journal of Southern History,* XI (1945), 370–388; Edward and Elizabeth Waugh, *The South Builds* (Chapel Hill, N.C., 1960); and Frank E. Everett, Jr., *Brierfield: Plantation Home of Jefferson Davis* (Hattiesburg, Miss., 1971).

pen near the first, and still later connected the two pens with a covered breezeway. The family cooked and ate in one wing of the house, slept in the other, and used the breezeway as a sort of outdoor living room in pleasant weather.[23] Eventually the owner might add a second story and columns. And at each stage Southerners reconciled the reality of outdoor life in a warm climate with their romantic vision of Greek grandeur.

Some of the people who spent leisure time on the verandas or breezeways read books. More of them, like their black neighbors in slave quarters or cabins, simply told stories. Flannery O'Connor once said about traditional Southern conversation, "I have Boston cousins and when they come South they discuss problems, they don't tell stories. We tell stories."[24] In the Old South stories were an authentic cultural form. Among illiterate Southerners, many poor whites and most blacks, folk tales were the only "literature" available. From this source came the Uncle Remus tales, the Davy Crockett legend, and more.[25]

Southern humorists such as Augustus Baldwin Longstreet (*Georgia Scenes*), William Tappan Thompson (*Major Jones's Courtship*), Johnson J. Hooper (*The Adventures of Captain Simon Suggs*), and George Washington Harris (*Sut Lovingood's Yarns*), created a popular literature of stories about crude characters and absurd situations.[26] One of the most revealing examples of the importance of stories in Southern culture is the relatively obscure work of John B. Lamar. Planter and political confidant of his brother-in-law Howell Cobb, Lamar was a man of cosmopolitan tastes. He traveled widely in North America and Europe and managed several plantations belonging to himself and his relatives. Significantly, however, this urbane man of the world who once contemplated moving to France was also the author of a collection of *Homespun Yarns* published during the 1840s. Lamar's yarns linked planter aristocrat with storytelling tradition and revealed the earthiness (polite earthiness in

[23]Everett Dick, *The Dixie Frontier* (New York, 1948).

[24]"Recent Southern Fiction: A Panel Discussion," *Bulletin of Wesleyan College*, XLI (1961), 11.

[25]See Daniel W. Patterson, "Folklore," in Louis D. Rubin, Jr. (ed.), *A Bibliographical Guide to the Study of Southern Literature* (Baton Rouge, La., 1969), pp. 102–118.

[26]Eaton, *Mind of the Old South*, pp. 130–151; Franklin G. Meine (ed.), *Tall Tales of the Southwest* (New York, 1937); Edmund Wilson, *Patriotic Gore: Studies in the Literature of the American Civil War* (New York, 1966), pp. 507–519.

Lamar's case) that lay just beneath the somewhat artificial facade of formal culture in the Old South.[27]

In music, as in literature, popular culture was more creative than sophisticated forms. Folk songs and black spirituals, which may be the most important American contributions to music, were genuinely Southern, part of a distinctive regional culture. Folk tunes were usually simple. Plaintive or sad lyrics often provided a counterpoint to happy tunes. Spirituals and worksongs, too, contained an internal paradox: they spoke of deliverence in the next world but often meant liberation in this. Through their music, black and white Southerners expressed a common emphasis upon concrete life situations.[28]

Cultural life in the Old South, then, celebrated the Southern world as it was and linked the Southern reality to romantic visions of courtly love, chivalry, Greek temples, feudal knights, cheerful peasants (slaves). Because of their religious beliefs more than anything else, Southerners did not expect too much of themselves and appreciated nobility all the more when it surfaced in flesh and blood. Hence they dreamed not of an abstract world as it might become in the future but of their real world as it resembled model civilizations of the past.

Nationalism is a compound of many interdependent elements. In the Old South a unique social economy combined with a distinctive "mind," religious spirit, life style, and culture to produce a nascent nationalism. Almost imperceptably during the nineteenth century, hopes, values, fears, preconceptions, and beliefs in that portion of the United States dominated by slaveholding planters diverged from national norms. Still, Southerners remained Americans as long as it was politically possible.

Politics concerned ante-bellum Southerners as a statement of power relationships, and was the vehicle through which they expressed their ideology and attempted to transform it into action. The nineteenth century was still fairly young when some Southern

[27]Mildred Lewis Rutherford, *The South in History and Literature* (Atlanta, Ga., 1907), pp. 306–316.
[28]Patterson, "Folklore," pp. 107–118; Sterling Stuckey, "Through the Prism of Folklore," *Massachusetts Review*, IX (1968), 417–437; John W. Blassingame, *The Slave Community: Plantation Life in the Antebellum South* (New York, 1972), pp. 41–76; Eaton, *Growth of Southern Civilization*, pp. 172–173; Georgia Writers' Project, *Drums and Shadows: Survival Studies among the Georgia Coastal Negroes* (New York, 1972).

Americans foresaw their section as a minority bloc with special interests. As a consequence, Southern politicians increasingly occupied themselves in national councils with defending and advancing sectional interests, while Southern political thinkers dealt often and deeply with the dilemma of a democratic minority.[29]

Like the ideology it asserted, Southern politics expressed the persistent tension between Southern and national emphases. Southern political leaders and thinkers were at the same time advocates of a sectional interest and of the national interest. Two factors were critical determinants of the Southern political stance. First, during the nineteenth century the South moved from the center of the American political mainstream to the backwater as an increasingly self-conscious minority bloc. Second, the Old South had never been a monolith politically or otherwise, and even as members of a minority bloc, Southern politicians often had difficulty acting in concert.

Perhaps the most dramatic demonstration of the dynamic involved in the South's political relationship with the rest of the Union was the career of John C. Calhoun. He was born in the South Carolina back country during the Revolutionary era; his father had fought in the Revolutionary War and was a planter of moderate means. As a young man, Calhoun enjoyed one of the best educations available (Moses Waddell's academy, Yale, and Judge Tapping Reeve's law office in Litchfield, Connecticut) and entered state politics as an upcountry opponent of the hegemony of low-country planters in South Carolina. He soon established himself in the state legislature and in Charleston society, and in 1810 won election to the United States House of Representatives.

Calhoun entered national politics as a nationalist. He was a War Hawk who supported James Madison's war with England. He continued a nationalist after the War of 1812, voting for the protective tariff of 1816 and introducing the bill which chartered the Second Bank of the United States. Calhoun served as secretary of war in the administration of the last of the Virginia dynasty of presidents, James Monroe. In 1824 and 1828, he won election as vice-president

[29]John Alden's *The First South* (Baton Rouge, La., 1961) suggests that Southern sectional concern predated the nineteenth century and was a factor in the Revolutionary era. See also Irving H. Bartlett, *The American Mind in the Mid-Nineteenth Century* (New York, 1967), pp. 73–93.

and at the outset of Andrew Jackson's term was heir apparent to the presidency.

By the end of Jackson's first administration, however, Calhoun had resigned the vice-presidency and abandoned his nationalist political stance. He stood with South Carolina in the Nullification Crisis and spent most of the rest of his career in the Senate defending Southern sectional interests. Calhoun changed, as did the South's political relationship with the rest of the country during those crucial two decades between 1810 and 1830. When Calhoun first went to Congress, the South was in tune with national politics. By 1830, the South was in the minority on such issues as tariffs and slavery. Southern politicians in increasing numbers were falling back upon the state rights political philosophy to defend sectional interests. By the time Calhoun died in 1850, the section of slaveholders and plantations had become a permanent minority in a nation increasingly characterized by free labor capitalism, reform enthusiasm, and social democracy.[30]

Such political circumstances led Calhoun and other Southern political thinkers to ask hard questions about the structure of American politics. In the name of slaveholding planters, Calhoun questioned the potential tyranny of a democratic majority over the rights and property of a minority and sought answers in the construction of "concurrent majorities"—that is, majorities based upon more than raw numbers of voters, majorities of classes and sections combined with that composed of ballots. George Fitzhugh carried Calhoun's analysis a step further. During the 1850s the Virginia planter wrote books (*Cannibals All* and *Sociology for the South*) in which he struck at the basic assumptions of free labor and contended that the masses might fare better under some form of benevolent despotism, which Fitzhugh believed already existed on Southern plantations. Such discussions, rendered moot by the advance of liberal democracy in the nineteenth century, were nonetheless important. By dissenting and proposing alternatives, they revealed the essen-

[30]The best biography of Calhoun is still Charles W. Wiltse, *John C. Calhoun*, 3 vols. (New York, 1944–1951). Others include Margaret L. Coit, *John C. Calhoun: American Portrait* (Boston, 1959); Gerald N. Capers, *John C. Calhoun—Opportunist: A Reappraisal* (Gainesville, Fla., 1960); and Richard N. Currant, *John C. Calhoun* (New York, 1963). On the nullification crisis see William W. Freehling, *Prelude to Civil War: The Nullification Controversy in South Carolina, 1816–1836* (New York, 1965).

tially un-American side of Southern political thought.[31]

Like Southern writers, Southern political thinkers ultimately saw a romantic vision: the reincarnation of Greek democracy in the nineteenth-century South. Again Calhoun led the way. To Americans, already conditioned by their recent struggle for independence to admire the Greeks, he offered the South as a replica of Greece in its golden age. Like ancient Athenians, Southerners held slaves; like the Greeks, Southerners lauded the equality of free people who in terms of wealth and status were anything but equal.[32] The Greek model seemed to justify slavery at the same time that it spoke to the aspirations of yeoman democrats in the words of Pericles: ". . . we enjoy, as between [free] man and [free] man complete equality of legal status. In our public life individual talent is the one thing valued. Preferment depends on merit, not on class; nor does obscurity of rank prevent any from making his contribution to the common weal."[33]

Greek democracy not only cloaked the Southern status quo with respectability; it offered the vision of a social and political system superior to the North's. Thus, as early as 1838, Calhoun could assert that:

Many in the South once believed that it [slavery] was a moral and political evil. That folly and delusion are gone. We see it now in its true light, and regard it as the most safe and stable basis for free institutions in the world. It is impossible with us that the conflict can take place between labor and capital, which makes it so difficult to establish and maintain free institutions in all wealthy and highly civilized nations where such institutions as ours do not exist. The Southern States are an aggregate, in fact, of communities, not of individuals. Every plantation is a little community, with the master at its head, who concentrates in himself the united interests of capital and labor, of which he is the common representative. These small communities aggregated make the State in all, whose action, labor, and capital is equally represented and perfectly harmonized. Hence the harmony, the union, the stability of that section which is rarely disturbed, except through the action

[31]On Fitzhugh see Eugene D. Genovese, *The World the Slaveholders Made: Two Essays in Interpretation* (New York, 1969), p. 118 ff. The best brief analysis of the Southern political mind is Bartlett, *American Mind*, pp. 73–93.

[32]See Parrington, *Main Currents*, II, 94–98.

[33]Quoted in C. E. Robinson, *Hellas: A Short History of Ancient Greece* (Boston, 1948), p. 78.

of this Government. The blessing of this state of things extends beyond the limits of the South. It makes that section the balance of the system; the great conservative power, which prevents other portions, less fortunately constituted, from rushing into conflict. . . . Such are the institutions which these deluded madmen are stirring heaven and earth to destroy, and which we are called on to defend by the highest and most solemn obligations that can be imposed on us as men and patriots.[34]

To sustain this vision of the South as heir to Greek democracy and home of balanced political economy, Calhoun more than anyone else advanced the tactic of state rights and raised it to the level of gospel. In theory, sovereign states had made the compact of union, which was the Constitution. If worse came to worst sovereign states might dissolve the compact and leave the Union. Worse need not come to worst, however, for unless a state's or the states' rights were abridged the Union was a good thing and the compact secure. Left to manage their own affairs Southern states need not fear interference with slavery, inimical trade laws, ruinous taxes, and the like, because the federal government had not the power to impose its will upon the states.

The Civil War rendered forever invalid the state rights political theory so closely associated with the Old South and so firmly connected with the secessionist origins of the Confederacy. Still, in 1860 state rights was a viable doctrine in Southern minds if only because it seemed the sole way to protect slavery. But it was more than a defense mechanism. State rights political theory was also in harmony with Southern life. The vaunted Southern emphasis upon individualism and especially the localism inherent in the South's folk culture found political expression in state rights. Thus when Southern Senators spoke of the "Sovereign State of Alabama" or wherever, they were only partially playing a game with their Northern colleagues. They were expressing their political and cultural code as well, and they were generally sincere in this expression. By 1860 Southerners had employed the rhetoric of state rights so long and so well as to transform a political theory into an article of faith.[35]

During the 1850s the South's reliance upon state rights as a

[34]Richard K. Crallé (ed.), *The Works of John C. Calhoun*, 6 vols. (New York, 1854), III, 180–181.

[35]Emory M. Thomas, *The Confederacy as a Revolutionary Experience* (Englewood Cliffs, N.J., 1971), pp. 7–8.

political weapon grew increasingly intense and more futile. The foremost national political issue of the decade following the Mexican War was slavery in the territories. Southerners believed their civilization had to expand to survive. They insisted that slaveholders had the same right to take their property (slaves) into the territories as Northern emigrants had to take theirs. Expansion was not only necessary economically; it promised political advantage as well in the form of more Southern congressmen. Also, expansion was vital to defuse what William L. Barney has termed the "Malthusian time bomb" produced by the multiplication of black Southerners. As the slave population increased within a limited land area, Southern whites feared not only falling slave prices but increased racial violence as well.[36]

State rights, however, was essentially a limiting doctrine. Under its cover, politicians were able to say "thou shalt not" to the national government and to defend against encroachments upon state and local matters. In the 1850s, though, Southerners sought to defend and extend at the same time. By embarking, however hesitantly, upon compromises over slavery in the territories—such as the Compromise of 1850 and the Kansas-Nebraska Act—Southerners opened themselves to the possibility of compromise on other issues as well. If slavery could be the subject of national debate and territorial limitation in California or Kansas, then slavery might be nowhere secure. When their minority circumstance forced Southern politicians to abandon the absolutes of their state rights position in search of expansion, they exposed the weakness of their doctrine as well as their numbers.

The South's political alienation from the nation as a whole was a progressive movement which gathered converts and intensity with the passage of time. In 1814 New Englanders at the Hartford Convention were making thinly veiled threats of secession in protest against "Mr. Madison's War." Then, Southerners struck the nationalist pose. During the Nullification Crisis in 1832, Calhoun believed he was averting the distasteful extremes of submission or disunion. Nevertheless South Carolina stood alone, and Southern leaders who favored secession were still renegades. By 1850 politicians in

[36]See William L. Barney, *The Secessionist Impulse: Alabama and Mississippi in 1860* (Princeton, N.J., 1974), pp. 3–26, and *The Road to Secession: A New Perspective on the Old South* (New York, 1972), pp. 3–21.

South Carolina and Mississippi were seriously advocating disunion but finding few allies elsewhere. In 1860, Southern politicians perceived secession as a real possibility and few opposed disunion on the basis of political principle.

Eleven Southern states and rump segments of two others eventually left the Union and formed the Confederacy, and it is tempting to think of those states as a unity. Nineteenth-century reality was neither so simple nor so tidy. Just as the South was never static in its relationship with the rest of the United States, so also were Southerners seldom really united in terms of political policy.[37]

There were many Souths. Topographically the section varied from the swamps of Louisiana to the mountains of western Virginia; culturally Southerners included such diverse peoples as Creoles, European immigrants, mountaineers, the first families of Virginia, and Texas frontiersmen. So it is no surprise that Southerners embraced a variety of political persuasions. On the crucial issue of secession, Southern voters and politicians tended to favor disunion most where the slave-plantation system and the ingredients of Southern cultural nationalism were strongest, mainly in the cotton states of the deep South. In the upper South, where slaveholding planters did not dominate the social economy quite so strongly and where the elements of Southern nationalism were not so pronounced, the stance on secession was more ambiguous. And even in the deep South there were areas populated mostly by yeoman farmers whose loyalty to the plantation-slave system was at least suspect.

Thus the secessionist leadership feared not only threats from Northerners without; it became increasingly alarmed over apostasy within. Should the border South fall away from the Southern world view and convert to Yankeeism, then the deep South would be an even smaller fraction of the American body politic.[38] In 1860 and 1861, for reasons both positive and negative, Southerners made

[37]For a reasoned statement on Southern "unity" see Barney, *Road to Secession,* pp. 85–102.

[38]The most concise statement of the "internal" (intra-Southern) apprehensions of the secessionists is William W. Freehling, "The Editorial Revolution, Virginia, and the Coming of the Civil War: A Review Essay," *Civil War History,* XVI (1970), 64–72. More extended analyses of the problem are Steven A. Channing, *Crisis of Fear: Secession in South* Carolina (New York, 1970), and Michael P. Johnson, *Toward a Patriarchal Republic: The Secession of Georgia* (Baton Rouge, La., 1977).

their break. Secessionists hoped that their nation would prosper and feared that this was their last chance to save a life style that had become sacred.

The Southerner's vision of the Yankee had become stereotypical and malignant: the North was home to a set of self-righteous money-grubbers whose personalities were a match for its cold climate; "Yankee" was synonymous with pious frauds and pasty faces; worse, Yankees sought power and pelf at Southern expense. Union with such people had never been desirable; now it was no longer possible.[39] As David F. Jamison, president *pro tem.* of South Carolina's secession convention phrased it:

I trust that the door now is forever closed from any further connection with our Northern Confederacy. What guarantees can they offer us more binding, more solemn, and with a higher sanction, than the present written compact between us? Has that sacred instrument protected us from the jealousy and aggressions of the Northern people, which commenced forty years ago, and which ended in the Missouri Compromise? Has it protected us from the cupidity and avarice of the Northern people, who for thirty-five years have imposed the burden of sustaining this Government chiefly upon the South? Has it saved us from abolition petitions, intended to annoy and insult us, on the very floors of Congress? Has not that instrument been trodden under their very feet by every Northern State, by placing on their books statutes nullifying the laws for the recovery of fugitive slaves? I trust, gentlemen, we will put no faith in paper guarantees. They are worthless, unless written in the hearts of the people. As there is no common bond between us, all attempts to continue as united will only prove futile.[40]

Southern diarist Mary Boykin Chesnut recorded an even more direct statement of Southern chauvinism. During the crisis at Fort Sumter she repeatedly heard women say, "God is on our side." When she asked, "Why?" the response came, "Of course, He hates Yankees! You'll think that well of Him."[41]

On the eve of secession, a sense of distinctiveness, apprehension over the future of slavery and racial tranquility, and the persistence of folk culture added a dynamic quality to the ideology of the plant-

[39]Taylor, *Cavalier and Yankee*, p. 24.
[40]Quoted in *The American Annual Cyclopedia . . . 1861* (New York, 1865), p. 648.
[41]Mary Boykin Chesnut, *A Diary from Dixie*, ed. by Ben Ames Williams (Boston, 1949), p. 38.

ers and transformed Southern sectionalism into Southern national-ism. This much is background, the "prehistory" of the Confederate States of America. The Confederacy's official history began in Montgomery, Alabama, where cause became nation.

CHAPTER 3

Foundations of the Southern Nation

J OHN Locke had been dead a long time in 1861. Southern secessionists, however, resurrected him and the American revolutionaries of 1776, for whom he was the essential political patriarch.
Southerners perceived their political circumstances as being parallel to those of the Founding Fathers: both sets of revolutionaries
believed that they were dissolving Lockean compacts—the British
Empire and the United States of America. For a time, the secessionists argued, these compacts had served the best interests of the
contracting parties. Then, just as George III and his Parliament
threatened the well-being of the American colonies, so Abraham
Lincoln and his Republican Congress threatened the essentials of
the Southern way of life. Similar problems called forth similar solu-
tions—secession and independence—justified by the Lockean theory of the right of revolution.[1]

In both cases catharsis came only after a prolonged period of
radical activity. It has been the fashion to speak of the Southern
secessionist leaders as "fire-eaters." Applied to Edmund Ruffin and
men like him, the term is accurate to a point. Yet Ruffin and com-

[1]For examples of this comparison between 1776 and 1861, see Jefferson Davis'
inaugural address in *Journal of the Congress of the Confederate States of America, 1861–
1865,* 7 vols. (Washington, D.C., 1904–1905), I, 64–66; and "The Address of the
People of South Carolina, Assembled in Convention, to the People of the Slaveholding States of the United States," in John Amasa May and Joan Reynolds Faunt (eds.),
South Carolina Secedes (Columbia, S. C., 1960), pp. 82–92. See also Emory M. Thomas,
The Confederacy as a Revolutionary Experience (Englewood Cliffs, N. J., 1971), pp. 1–2.

pany were more than side-show performers; they were dedicated revolutionaries as well. With no less zeal and skill than James Otis or Sam Adams, the fire-eaters pursued their radical cause. Compare, for example, Ruffin's activity at Harpers Ferry with that of Sam Adams at the Boston Tea Party. Throughout the South those who shared the intensity of Ruffin's persuasion engaged in similar activities. By 1861, major institutions of Southern society—press, pulpit, and school—were repeating the Southern line. Secession was not just a spontaneous restatement of Lockean theory; it was the culmination of years of radical tactics and revolutionary propaganda.[2]

By February 1, 1861, seven Southern states had reenacted, they believed, the revolutionary "secession" of the Founding Fathers. In the process, Southerners had been preoccupied with a political philosophy whose end was revolution and with radical agitation whose goal was dissolution of the Union. In February 1861, however, the time for rending a nation was past; the time for making a nation from independent republics had arrived. Secession was basically a negative process. Once secession was accomplished Southern leaders faced the challenge of doing something positive: creating the Confederate States of America. To do this, representatives from six seceded states—South Carolina, Mississippi, Florida, Alabama, Georgia, and Louisiana (Texas completed the secession process late and her delegates arrived later)—gathered in Montgomery, Alabama, on February 4, 1861.[3]

If delegates to the convention at Montgomery were seeking a proper setting in which to shed the euphoria of secession and to grapple with the hard realities facing the proposed Southern nation, they chose the right place. In 1861, Montgomery was a conveniently located state capital, the home of Alabama radical William Lowndes Yancey and not much else. The town spread over seven hills on the south bank of the Alabama River and afforded convenient access by rail and river to the seaboard, gulf, and Mississippi Valley regions

[2]Thomas, *Revolutionary Experience*, pp. 23–38; Avery Craven, *The Coming of the Civil War*, 2nd revised edition (Chicago, 1957), pp. 272–282; and Ulrich Bonnell Phillips, *The Course of the South to Secession*, ed. by E. Merton Coulter (New York, 1964), pp. 128–149.

[3]Because Texas seceded on February 1, 1861, and alone among the seceded states required a popular referendum to complete the process of disunion, that state's delegates arrived late at Montgomery. The Texas delegation participated only in the final debates on the permanent Constitution.

of the deep South. Yet despite its claim to being the capital of the black belt—that layer of dark, rich soil which bisects the state—Montgomery's cotton trade had been declining for a number of years. Industry had made little impact on the local economy, and Montgomery was essentially an overgrown country crossroads—overgrown because fifteen years before, in 1846, the town had become the capital of Alabama. Montgomery's primary business was politics, normally a seasonal enterprise that seldom penetrated the town's basic somnolence for long.[4]

Approximately 9,000 people, half black, half white, lived in Montgomery in 1861.[5] At first most of the white natives reacted with excitement to the gathering of secessionist delegates to the convention. In time, however, as the convention proceeded with its work and curiosity seekers and "place mongers" crowded into Montgomery, some residents of the town lost their earlier enthusiasm and became annoyed at the intrusion of so many outsiders. The outsiders returned this sentiment.[6] Montgomery's physical facilities may have been adequate for a Southern state capital, but as cradle of the Confederacy the town had marked deficiencies. Main Street, extending about a mile up from the Alabama River to the state capitol, was less than a grand boulevard; only eighteen years earlier, a team of oxen had drowned in one of the many mud holes which yawned in the street.[7] Unpaved lanes meandered off Main Street to genuinely fine homes, but visitors encountered difficulty picking their way along poorly constructed or nonexistent sidewalks and even became lost on streets which one observer complained had been "laid out before the surveyor's compass was in use." The capitol building, with its neoclassic facade, domed cupola, and hilltop site, was imposing; yet one of Montgomery's more urbane visitors judged the structure not "a peculiarly stately pile, either in size or architectural effect." Moreover, Montgomery had very few other buildings available with which to accommodate a national government. There were two moderate-sized hotels—the Exchange, which

[4]Varied descriptions of Montgomery in 1861 include H. G. McCall, *A Sketch, Historical and Statistical, of the City of Montgomery* (Montgomery, 1885), pp. 5–13; T. C. DeLeon, *Four Years in Rebel Capitals* (Mobile, Ala., 1892), pp. 23–35; and Rembert W. Patrick, *Jefferson Davis and his Cabinet* (Baton Rouge, La., 1944), pp. 319–324.

[5]Bureau of the Census, *Eighth Census, Population* (Washington, D. C., 1865), 9.

[6]DeLeon, *Four Years,* 28.

[7]Everett Dick, *The Dixie Frontier* (New York, 1948), p. 152.

catered to the better class of people and in normal times to Alabama legislators, and Montgomery Hall, which usually housed traveling salesmen and livestock traders. Both hotels impressed their guests as filthy, insect infested, and exorbitantly expensive. Significantly, the Confederate Congress debated and passed the act concerning the members' pay in secret session to discourage the proprietors of Montgomery's hotels from adjusting their bills to match the congressmen's salaries. Montgomery's mosquitoes, alive and hungry in February, made a stronger impression upon many of the town's visitors than did anything else about the place.[8]

Perhaps because most of them were used to life's finer things, delegates were sometimes loud in their complaints about the service in Montgomery's restaurants and creature comforts in the town. Three members of the Georgia delegation donned white kid gloves and like finery to attend a party given by a local judge, only to discover that the affair was no more than "ordinary 'tea drinking.'" One of these same three complained about the "great uniformity" of suppers, which "commence with oyster soup, then comes fish salad and fried oysters, then grated ham or beef and sardines with waffles and coffee or tea, then cakes and jellies, Charlotte Russe and what is considered here the greatest delicacy called 'Ambrosia' which is nothing but sliced oranges and grated cocoanut."[9] Mary Boykin Chesnut, wife of South Carolina delegate James Chesnut, Jr., recorded in her famous diary, "For a fortnight I have not gone to the dinner table. Yesterday I was forced to dine on cold asparagus and blackberries, so repulsive in aspect was the other food they sent me."[10]

Of course, not everyone found Montgomery so unpleasant. It was a provincial town, a good place for the secessionists to get down to the hard work of founding a nation, but certainly not a pretentious

[8]Patrick, *Davis and his Cabinet*, pp. 319–322; DeLeon, *Four Years*, pp. 23–24; J. B. Jones, *A Rebel War Clerk's Diary*, ed. by Howard Swiggett, 2 vols. (New York, 1955), I, 35–36; Mary Boykin Chesnut, *A Diary from Dixie*, ed. by Ben Ames Williams (Boston, 1949), p. 19.

[9]T. R. R. Cobb to wife, Montgomery, February 8, 1861, A. L. Hull (ed.), "The Correspondence of Thomas Reade Roots Cobb, 1860–1862," *Southern History Association Publications*, II (1907), 167. Cobb's letters present the best first-hand account of the Convention.

[10]Chesnut, *Diary*, p. 51.

cradle for the new Southern nationality. No doubt many of the delegates wondered why they were there.[11]

In fact the choice of Montgomery as the site of the secessionists' convention revealed a great deal about the process of disunion just completed by the states of the deep South. The seven separate secessions which took place during the forty-three days between December 20, 1860, and February 1, 1861, were not spontaneous risings of an untutored mass of people. However fundamental and unreconcilable were the issues which provoked the Southern separation, the break with the Union did not just happen; people had to make it happen. In every Southern state were radical secessionists whose agitation transformed Southern ideology into Southern nationalism. Their zeal was genuine, and in the minds of fellow Southerners their cause was authentic; otherwise, they would have become generals with no armies. Yet the task of the radicals, as they perceived it, was more than educating and agitating; it was to plan carefully the process of their revolution as well as to proclaim its substance.

For many years the radicals had debated among themselves the tactics of their hypothetical coup. Two basic problems confronted them. First, should the Southern nation originate from concerted action by all or most of the Southern states, or should the states secede separately and then act in concert? Second, should the slaveholding border states be a part of the original Southern nation; or would it be wiser to induce the upper South to act as a buffer against reprisals from the North and then allow time to tell just how Southern the border really was? As it happened, partly by design and partly by accident, the radical leadership followed a compromise course in solving both of these tactical problems.[12]

South Carolina seceded alone, but not quite as separately as it appeared. "Cooperationists," as the advocates of concerted action

[11]Narrative accounts of Montgomery's selection are A. J. Gerson, "The Inception of the Montgomery Convention," American Historical Association, *Annual Report, 1910* (Washington, D.C., 1912) 179–187; and Charles Robert Lee, Jr., *The Confederate Constitutions* (Chapel Hill, N.C., 1963), pp. 9, 16, 19–20.

[12]The tactics of separate state secession are discussed in detail in Dwight Lowell Dumond, *The Secession Movement, 1860–1861* (New York, 1931), pp. 113–145. The problem of the border South is treated in William L. Barney, *Road to Secession: A New Perspective on the Old South,* (New York, 1972), p. 118; and in Craven, *Coming,* p. 435.

called themselves, were numerous and well placed in South Carolina. Actually "cooperationist" was an ambiguous label; some adopted it literally and believed in Southern unity before all else; others were cooperationists out of the fear of rash action and wished to explore with other Southerners all avenues of obtaining Southern rights before rending the Union; still others assumed a cooperationist stance to conceal from themselves and/or others unionist sympathies in hopes that "cooperation" would slow, then stall the secession band wagon. In South Carolina cooperationists were converted to the "straight-out" position only after several attempts to initiate combined action failed. Two of these tries were crucial. Christopher G. Memminger, lawyer and cooperationist leader, visited Virginia in the aftermath of John Brown's raid in December 1859 to try to induce that state to join South Carolina in calling a convention of Southern states for the purpose of united disunion. The Virginia General Assembly listened politely to Memminger's plan and cordially told him that Virginia would wait and see a while longer. Then in October of 1860, South Carolina Governor William Henry Gist wrote confidential letters to the governors of the deep Southern states counseling simultaneous secession in the likely event of Abraham Lincoln's election in November. The replies to Gist's letters were more cautious than he had hoped. Accordingly Memminger, Gist, and most of the other South Carolina cooperationists fell into line with those who advocated separate secessions, led by Robert Barnwell Rhett, Sr.[13]

Rhett, a lawyer, planter, politician, and owner of the influential Charleston *Mercury,* had been crusading for secession and separate state action for a long time. He savored the moment when South Carolina dissolved its union with the United States and stood alone as the Palmetto Republic. However, Rhett himself saw to it that South Carolina's colors were not nailed so securely to the mast as they seemed. On the last day of 1860 South Carolina's secession convention adopted a set of resolutions, authored by Rhett, which proposed a convention of seceded states to be held in Montgomery on February 13, 1861. This convention was to form a Southern

[13]Lee, *Confederate Constitutions,* pp. 4–6. The best recent study of secession in South Carolina is Steven A. Channing, *Crisis of Fear: Secession in South Carolina* (New York, 1970). Laura A. White's *Robert Barnwell Rhett: Father of Secession* (New York, 1931) is the standard biography of Rhett.

Confederacy and to draw up a constitution based upon that of the United States. Rhett's resolutions further provided for the dispatch of South Carolina delegates to Montgomery and of commissioners to every slaveholding state.[14]

At the time that South Carolinians were planning to hold a convention in Montgomery, the state of Alabama was still in the Union. Rhett, in contact with the radical leadership in other states, had chosen Montgomery as the convention site and proposed an agenda with ground rules for the convention in order to bring the Southern nation into being as soon as possible and to offer a program for unity which would calm the cooperationists' anxieties throughout the South. The South Carolina Program promised Southern union before the inauguration of the Republican administration in Washington, and it provided for continuous communication among the Southern states through the network of commissioners. These fifty-two ambassadors of revolution, sent not only from South Carolina but from Alabama, Mississippi, Georgia, and Louisiana as well, lost few opportunities to press for immediate secession in their assigned states. They also counseled adoption of the South Carolina Program as the next step after secession.[15]

The radicals' tactic, as it emerged, was to convene as many disunited states as possible, as soon as possible. If the states of the upper South should choose to secede with the cotton South, well and good. If they should choose to wait, perhaps even better. Yancey probably stated this view best in a letter to Virginia newspaper editor Roger A. Pryor. "A well conducted Southern policy," Yancey wrote, "would seem to demand that, when such a movement [secession] takes place by any considerable number of Southern States, Virginia and the other border States should remain in the Union, where, by their position and their councils, they would prove more effective friends than by moving out of the Union, and thus giving the Southern Confederacy a long, hostile border to watch. In the event of such a movement being successful, in time Virginia and the other border States, could join."[16] The Southern radicals were not

[14]*Journal of the Convention of the People of South Carolina* (Columbia, S.C., 1862), p. 92.

[15]Dumond, *Secession Movement*, pp. 135–136; Lee, *Confederate Constitutions*, pp. 7–12.

[16]Yancey to Pryor, cited in Alan Nevins, *The Emergence of Lincoln*, 2 vols. (New York, 1950) I, 407.

clairvoyant; yet the selection of Montgomery as the convention site was an accurate prediction of the new nation's geographical center and an index of how carefully the radicals had managed their coup.

The assembly at Montgomery of fifty delegates from seven seceded states represented a great victory for Southern radicals. But much remained to be done—nothing less than the creation of a Southern nation.

To all appearances, the Montgomery Convention did its work well. There was at Montgomery, according to one delegate, a perfect "mania for unanimity." And in just five days the delegates adopted a provisional constitution, elected a provisional president and vice-president, and resolved themselves into the provisional Congress of the new nation. Appearances, however, were deceiving. Even in the midst of their triumph, the Southern radicals found themselves called upon to compromise their Southernism and to calm their ardor. The Confederacy created at Montgomery was not exactly what the super-Southerners like Rhett, Ruffin, and Yancey wanted. The convention's moderate majority was interested in preserving what it believed was the Southern status quo in the new nation; it was not willing to expand or intensify that status quo. The differences were subtle but important. The fire-eating radicals who had devoted much of their lives to Southern nationalism found themselves suddenly elevated to roles as irrelevant elder statesmen in the Southern nation. In the end few if any of them made any significant contribution to the Confederacy. Having worked and planned so long to give birth to it, more than one of the radicals became disillusioned with the infant nation; thus in response to the Confederacy's constitutional prohibition of the African slave trade, South Carolinian L. W. Spratt lamented, *"our whole movement is defeated.* It will abolitionize the Border Slave States—it will brand our institution. Slavery cannot share a government with democracy—it cannot bear a brand upon it; *thence another revolution. It may be painful, but we must make it."*[17]

[17]Cited in Barney, *Road to Secession,* p. 207. Nearly every historian of the Confederate South has remarked upon the conservative nature of the Montgomery Convention and the early disappearance of the fire-eaters from positions of power and influence in the Southern nation. For examples see Clement Eaton, *A History of the Southern Confederacy* (New York, 1954), p. 51; and Frank E. Vandiver, *Their Tattered Flags: The Epic of the Confederacy* (New York, 1970), pp. 18–21.

To understand the subtle schism between what the Confederacy was supposed to be and what it became, it is necessary to look at some of the men who assumed leadership at Montgomery and during the processes of secession which brought them to the convention. The mechanics of disunion were important because they significantly affected the actions and attitudes of the Montgomery delegates and they revealed most clearly the tension between the rival themes of radical theory and constructive action coexisting in the Southern political mind.

South Carolina's situation was especially instructive. The Palmetto State had both a long tradition of secessionist notions and a heritage of unionism and moderation. In the spring of 1860 South Carolina radicalism seemed to have reached a low ebb; the National Democrats, who proposed to save the South and the Union through the Democratic Party, gained control of Carolina polity. As a result, when the Democrats refused to adopt a platform containing strong guarantees for slavery, the state delegation to the Democratic Nominating Convention followed, rather than led, the Southern walkout in Charleston.

The subsequent sectional division of the Democratic Party and the strong probability of Lincoln's election in the fall of 1860 discredited South Carolina's National Democrats and gave radical secessionists the leverage they needed. Even so, South Carolina might not have been the first state out of the Union had it not been for its conservative constitution, which required the legislature instead of the voters to select presidential electors. When the legislature convened on November 5 to choose electors, a national Republican victory appeared certain. Accordingly, Governor Gist kept the solons in session to await the election results. Once Lincoln's victory was sure, Gist requested a secession convention, and his legislature issued a call for elections. From this point the die was cast. Unionists made poor showings when they dared to run for convention seats, and most of the cooperationists, convinced that ultimately South Carolina would not secede alone, supported separate state action. The convention met on December 17, and three days later by a unanimous vote of the delegates South Carolina seceded. Had an outbreak of smallpox not forced the body to move from

Columbia to Charleston, the process would have been even shorter.[18]

The Palmetto Republic made not one, but two declarations of independence, in which the convention attempted to explain and justify disunion. The "Declaration of the Immediate Causes of Secession," drafted by Memminger, focused on threats to slavery and slavery expansion made by the North during the recent past and likely to be made by the Republican Party in the near future. The "Address to the Slaveholding States," drafted by Rhett, was an extended dissertation which began with the Constitutional Convention of 1787 and rambled through a long catalog of sectional issues and crises, demonstrating Southern righteousness and Yankee perfidy at every point.[19]

Rhett and Memminger shared a zeal for disunion; both were sincere Southern nationalists, yet the difference in the documents they produced was revealing. Rhett had been dreaming of a separate Southern nation for more than half of his sixty-one years. An austere, reserved man, he abstained from liquor and comradeship. About the South, though, Rhett had no reservations and exercised little control over his emotions. Rhett's vision of what the South had been and should be was deep and fixed; Southern ideology had made him an ideologue. All this came through in his "Address"; it was a fundamental appeal to Southern nationalism.[20]

Memminger, on the other hand, although he had absorbed the Southern life style as deeply as Rhett, had come late to Southern nationalism. Born in Germany and orphaned in Charleston at a very young age, Memminger had acquired the education and background to go with his native abilities and had become a successful lawyer in his adopted city. His mind was flexible; he was a tactician instead of an ideologue. Once convinced that moderation was suicidal and cooperation futile, Memminger became a straight-out seces-

[18]White, *Rhett*, pp. 191–195; Channing, *Crisis of Fear*, pp. 141–285; Ralph Wooster, *The Secession Conventions of the South* (Princeton, N.J., 1962), pp. 11–22. Wooster points to the meager vote total of Benjamin F. Perry, the state's most respected unionist, in the election of convention delegates as evidence of South Carolina's throughgoing radicalism in 1860. Perry received only 255 votes, against no less than 1,300 for each of his five secessionist opponents.

[19]These documents are most available in May and Faunt, *South Carolina Secedes*, pp. 76–92.

[20]White, *Rhett*, pp. 188–190.

sionist. He shared his countrymen's hopes and, more important, he knew their fears. Thus, while Rhett's "Address" appealed to hopes for a neo-Greek democracy, Memminger's "Declaration" dwelt upon fears for the sanctity and expansion of slavery. Both Carolinians were hyper-Southern; but while Rhett espoused eternal principles, Memminger sought successful stratagems.[21] Georgian T. R. R. Cobb expressed the difference. "Rhett," Cobb wrote to his wife, "is a generous hearted and honest man with a vast quantity of cranks and a small proportion of common sense." "Memminger," he added, "is as shrewd as a Yankee, a perfect ——— metamorphosed into a legislating lawyer."[22]

Besides Rhett and Memminger, there were six other South Carolinians in the Montgomery delegation; not surprisingly the old moderates, unionists and National Democrats, were not on hand. The most influential was Rhett's cousin Robert W. Barnwell, briefly a United States senator and president of South Carolina College. T. R. R. Cobb said, "Barnwell is a very gentlemanly old man, full of politeness [and] modesty and attracts my kind feelings . . . I do not rate his talents very high." Barnwell served as elder statesman, in both his delegation and in the convention, and was important in his opposition to the fanaticism of his cousin Rhett.[23] However united the South Carolinians often appeared, they were, most of them, men of the main chance. Together they shared an allegiance to Southern nationalism; as individuals they sought to serve conspicuously. At this juncture, only time would tell whether they would serve as ideologues like Rhett or as tacticians like Memminger. Significantly, the delegation did not unite behind the candidacy of Rhett for president of the Confederacy.[24]

The Mississippi experience was similar to that of South Carolina. Radicals in both states had tried to provoke secession in 1850 and 1851. Both had seen their hopes founder when the other Southern states failed to unite on the issue and their fellow Carolinians and Mississippians shrank from seceding alone. The events of 1860 renewed secessionist hopes, and Mississippi radicals were quick to seize their opportunity. In the 1860 presidential election John C.

[21]Lee, *Confederate Constitutions*, pp. 22–25; White, *Rhett*, pp. 188–190.
[22]Cobb to wife, Montgomery, February 12, 1861, "Correspondence," 174.
[23]Lee, *Confederate Constitutions*, pp. 25–29.
[24]White, *Rhett*, pp. 194–195; Chesnut, *Diary*, p. 5.

Breckinridge, the Southern Democrat, received 59 percent of the vote in Mississippi; John Bell, the Constitutional Union moderate candidate 36.2 percent; and Northern Democrat Stephen A. Douglas only 4.8 percent.[25] Shortly after Lincoln's election, Governor J. J. Pettus called a special session of the Mississippi legislature to debate the fate of the state, and the solons called for elections to a convention.[26]

Mississippians elected a strong secessionist majority to the state convention. The radical leadership was composed of relatively young lawyers and planters, men on the make who had the most to lose if the slave-plantation system were to die or fail to expand. The cooperationists and unionists were older men and politically more conservative (Whiggish) than the secessionist-democratic majority.[27] On January 9, 1861, an ordinance of secession carried the convention, 84 to 15; eventually, ninety-eight of the convention's one hundred members signed the ordinance.[28]

The Mississippians at Montgomery faithfully reflected the radical leadership of their state. For the most part they were young planters and lawyers who held few slaves and whose greatest service and status appeared to be in the future. Although the Mississippi delegation was representative and capable, it is interesting to note who was *not* included. None of the really great cotton planters was there; the old line secessionists, Pettus, John A. Quitman, and L. Q. C. Lamar, were noticeably absent; and those who were in Montgomery proved to be less doctrinaire than expected.[29] Perhaps there was a hint of nascent moderation in Mississippians at the secession convention. In the aftermath of secession, that body passed (66 to 13) a resolution against renewing the African slave trade. Significantly, Mississippi and Mississippi Senator Jefferson Davis had been among the leaders of the movement to reopen that trade as recently as 1859. Davis, however, was now pursuing an ambiguous course; in the

[25]Wooster, *Secession Conventions*, pp. 26–28. The best studies of secession in Mississippi are Percy Lee Rainwater, *Mississippi: Storm Center of Secession 1856–1861* (Baton Rouge, La., 1938); and William L. Barney, *The Secessionist Impulse: Alabama and Mississippi in 1860* (Princeton, N.J., 1974).

[26]Barney, *Secessionist Impulse*, pp. 195–196.

[27]Wooster, *Secession Conventions*, pp. 29–35; Barney, *Secessionist Impulse*, pp. 50–60, 76–100, 285–296.

[28]Wooster, *Secession Conventions*, pp. 36–37; Rainwater, *Mississippi*, p. 212.

[29]Lee, *Confederate Constitutions*, pp. 29–32; Thomas B. Alexander and Richard E. Beringer, *The Anatomy of the Confederate Congress* (Nashville, Tenn., 1972), pp. 354–389.

aftermath of Lincoln's election he had advised against immediate secession. Having accepted the risks and dangers of secession, Mississippians seemed more concerned about tactics designed to solidify their revolution than about doctrinaire proposals designed to carry the revolution to its logical extreme.[30]

Alabama secessionists had a far more difficult task than their counterparts in Mississippi and South Carolina, much to the chagrin of the state's foremost secessionist, William Lowndes Yancey. Born in Georgia in 1814, Yancey grew up in Troy, New York, attended Williams College, then returned south to "read law" with South Carolina unionist Benjamin F. Perry. After some experience as a lawyer and newspaper editor in South Carolina, he moved to Dallas County, Alabama, where his reputation as a courtroom orator quickly led him into politics. Yancey soon forsook the unionist persuasions of his legal preceptor and during the 1840s became a strong advocate of Southern rights. To answer the Wilmot Proviso of 1846, which proposed making land gained in the Mexican War free soil, he formulated the Alabama Platform, insuring the protection of slave property in the territories, and walked out of the Democratic convention of 1848 when his platform was not adopted. During the 1850s Yancey abandoned hope of seeking the South's salvation in the Democratic party or the Union, and thereafter he devoted his skill and influence to Southern independence. The next time he walked out of a Democratic convention, in Charleston in 1860, most of the delegates from six other Southern states followed. This triggered the sectional split in the party which facilitated Lincoln's election and led to South Carolina's secession.[31] Then, in November, Breckinridge carried Alabama; but the candidates of moderation, Bell and Douglas, had a combined vote total of 41,526, which compared respectably to Breckinridge's 48,831.[32]

Governor Andrew B. Moore was a strong secessionist, more than

[30]Wooster, *Secession Conventions,* p. 48; Barney, *Secessionist Impulse,* pp. 6–7. Ronald T. Takaki, in *A Pro-Slavery Crusade* (New York, 1971), argues cogently that the movement to reopen the slave trade was more rhetorical than real—a way for Southerners to convince themselves that their peculiar institution was morally defensible while challenging the North to make painful concessions to Southern special interest.

[31]The standard biography of Yancey is still John W. DuBose, *The Life and Times of William Lowndes Yancey,* 2 vols. (Birmingham, Ala., 1892).

[32]Wooster, *Secession Conventions,* pp. 49–51; Dumond, *Secession Movement,* p. 271. The best studies of secession in Alabama are Clarence P. Denman, *The Secession Movement in Alabama* (Montgomery, Ala., 1933); and Barney's superb *Secessionist Impulse.*

willing to comply with his legislature's authorization to call a state convention in the event a "Black Republican" was elected president. Campaigns for delegate seats were brisk. Alabama cooperationists divided sharply in their response to the secession question —some favored eventual secession, others were covert unionists, and many wavered between these poles. Consequently the cooperationist cause lacked unity and direction.[33]

Geographical conditions and political heritage complicated the situation. North Alabama was traditionally the home of small farmers and Jacksonian Democrats. Holding few if any slaves and revering the political memory of Andrew Jackson as frontier nationalist, north Alabamians were almost solidly cooperationists. Alabama urbanites, the few there were, also generally voted cooperationist moderation. In Mobile and Montgomery, however, the influence of planter residents and large slave populations added to the radical count. South and central Alabama had the geographical hallmarks of secessionism: plantations, cotton, and slaves. In 1850 and 1851, however, the north Alabama Democrats had joined the central and south Alabama Whigs to squelch the radicals. In 1860 the Whigs went over to secession, and, united with the state's secessionist Democrats, they produced a working radical majority in the Alabama convention.[34]

As in Mississippi, the secessionist leaders in the state convention were young planters and lawyers with relatively few slaves—men with a stake in the continuance of the Southern status quo. Cooperationists, as a group, were older, less wealthy and held even fewer slaves than the strong secessionists.[35]

In preliminary tests the Alabama convention split by a narrow vote of 54 to 46 in favor of secession. With only an eight-vote working majority the radicals were careful. They erred once—Yancey made a fiery speech in which he labeled all who opposed secession as traitors, and secessionist leader Thomas H. Watts quickly softened Yancey's diatribe. In the end, on January 10, the secession ordinance passed 61 to 39; thereafter fifteen of the dele-

[33]Wooster, *Secession Conventions,* pp. 51–52.
[34]*Ibid.,* pp. 63–66; Barney, *Secessionist Impulse,* pp. 245–285; Durwood Long, "Unanimity and Disloyalty in Secessionist Alabama," *Civil War History,* XI (1965), 257–273.
[35]Barney, *Secessionist Impulse,* pp. 61–76, 267–285.

gates who voted against the ordinance signed it.[36]

Moderation made itself heard more clearly in the convention after Alabama seceded; the body went on record opposing the renewal of the African slave trade, and narrowly defeated a motion to exclude members of the secession convention from representing the state at Montgomery. In fact the convention chose its Montgomery delegation (with one exception) from outside its membership; that exception was David Peter Lewis, a unionist who fled the Confederacy in 1863 and did not return until after the war. Early gossip among the delegates at Montgomery was full of concern that Union men and "reconstructionists," who supposedly desired to rejoin the United States, were a majority in the Alabama delegation. Such rumors were exaggerations. Alabamians clearly chose secession, but they did so with reservations, and prudence guided the state's selection of an essentially moderate delegation.[37] Significantly, Yancey, the man who had worked as hard as anyone in the South to bring the Confederacy into existence, was not selected for his state's delegation, and Lewis, the avowed and persistent unionist, was. Nevertheless, with the exception of Lewis, the members of the Alabama delegation accepted secession and committed themselves to the new nation. As a group, they were sensible secessionists who cared most about making their revolution work.[38]

In 1860 the state of Florida was essentially an extension of Alabama and Georgia. In terms of population it was quite small; the entire population, approximately 78,000 whites and 63,000 blacks, was less than that of New Orleans.[39] On the heels of Lincoln's election, Governor Madison S. Perry charged his legislature to call a state convention and the members complied. Perry was present in Charleston when South Carolina seceded, and presumably shared with other radical leaders in Florida the object lesson in disunion he had learned. On December 22 the voters chose secession convention delegates, electing forty-two secessionists and twenty-seven cooperationists. There was no marked difference in the backgrounds of the two factions. Apparently the best index of secession

[36] *Ibid.*, pp. 301–302; Wooster, *Secession Conventions*, pp. 56–59.

[37] Wooster, *Secession Conventions*, p. 60; Lee, *Confederate Constitutions*, pp. 33–37.

[38] Lee, *Confederate Constitutions*, pp. 33–37.

[39] *The American Annual Cyclopedia . . . 1861* (New York, 1865), p. 314.

or cooperation in Florida was proximity to Georgia and Alabama. Northern counties were more likely to elect cooperationists because their voters wanted to wait and see what Georgia and Alabama did about secession. Florida cooperationists, as a group, favored united secession.[40]

When the convention met in Tallahassee the secessionist majority voted down other attempts at delay and on January 10 adopted a secession ordinance 62 to 7; when the choice became union or disunion, twenty cooperationists went along.[41] To attend the Montgomery Convention, the secession convention chose Jackson Morton, a Whig and leader of the cooperationist cause in Florida, and secessionist Democrats James Patton Anderson and James Byron Owens. All three were active in Montgomery.[42]

Georgia had the most land and the most people of any state in the deep South and was therefore crucial to the secessionist cause. Moreover, that state was the vital hinge between the seaboard and the gulf South. Back in 1850 a convention of Georgians had frustrated the radical secession scheme by agreeing to wait and test the Compromise of 1850 rather than attending a Southern convention and concerting secession. The Georgia Platform, a strong ultimatum to the North to abide by the 1850 Compromise, had dealt a death blow to the secessionists' hopes at the time.[43] By 1860 circumstances and minds had changed. On December 6, Howell Cobb, President James Buchanan's secretary of the treasury and acknowledged leader of Georgia Democrats, resigned his national office and publicly announced his support for secession. Cobb's brother T. R.

[40]Wooster, *Secession Conventions*, pp. 67–79. The standard study of secession in Florida is Dorothy Dodd, "The Secession Movement in Florida, 1850–61," *Florida Historical Quarterly*, XII (1963), 3–24, 45–66.

[41]Wooster, *Secession Conventions*, pp. 71–74; William Kaufman Scarborough (ed.), *The Diary of Edmund Ruffin*, I, *Toward Independence, October, 1856–April, 1861* (Baton Rouge, La., 1972), 525–526.

[42]Lee, *Confederate Constitutions*, pp. 32–33.

[43]The literature of Georgia's secession is extensive. A new and exciting study is Michael P. Johnson, *Toward a Patriarchal Republic: The Secession of Georgia* (Baton Rouge, La., 1977). For the state's response to the Compromise of 1850, see Richard Shryock, *Georgia and the Union in 1850* (Durham, N.C., 1926). Other important studies include Ulrich B. Phillips, "Georgia and State Rights," American Historical Association *Annual Report*, 1901 (Washington, D.C., 1902), II; T. Conn Bryan, "The Secession of Georgia," *Georgia Historical Quarterly*, XXXI (1947), 89–111; Horace Montgomery, *Cracker Parties* (Baton Rouge, La., 1950); and Ulrich B. Phillips, *The Life of Robert Toombs* (New York, 1913).

R. Cobb had long been among the radical leaders, and Robert Toombs, Whig senator and erratic genius, also joined the campaign for immediate secession. To counter this powerful secessionist triumvirate were three highly respected Georgia moderates: Alexander H. Stephens, who believed immediate secession unwise but agreed to abide by his state's decision, Herschel V. Johnson, Douglas' Democratic running mate in 1860, and Benjamin Harvey Hill, who lent strong Whig support.[44]

In November, Georgia Governor Joseph E. Brown, a staunch secessionist, requested from his legislature a million-dollar appropriation with which to arm the state and a convention to vote secession. The legislature debated two weeks before agreeing to call the convention. The delay was an accurate indication of the division in Georgia's political mind. Campaigns for 301 delegate seats at the convention were intense. The radicals used every tactic at their disposal. Howell Cobb, not himself a candidate, traveled throughout the state campaigning for straight-out secessionists. Toombs returned to Washington to see for himself whether compromise was possible, then on December 23 dispatched dramatic telegrams to Georgia's leading newspapers reaffirming his support for immediate secession. Results of the delegate elections on January 2 promised a close but clear secessionist majority in the convention. Still, Governor Brown apparently juggled the vote totals supplied to the press to make it appear that the popular vote overwhelmingly favored immediate secession. Authorized by the convention to keep the actual count a secret, Brown reported the vote as 50,243 to 37,123 for secessionists; an accurate count shows that a slim majority of Georgians in fact voted for cooperationists (42,714 to 41,717).

When the convention met in Milledgeville on January 16, advocates from South Carolina, Alabama, and Mississippi were present to make speeches and stir up secessionist enthusiasm. The Governor's final trick was to inject into the proceedings a resolution of the New York legislature promising support to the President of the United States in putting down the "insurgent" South Carolinians.[45] Though the secessionists had the necessary votes from the begin-

[44]Wooster, *Secession Conventions,* pp. 82–91.

[45]Wooster, *Secession Conventions,* pp. 82–91; Dumond, *Secession Movement,* pp. 205–207; Louise B. Hill, *Joseph E. Brown and the Confederacy* (Chapel Hill, N.C., 1939), pp. 33–45; Lee, *Confederate Constitutions,* pp. 16–18; Michael P. Johnson, "A New Look at the Popular Vote for Delegates to the Georgia Secession Convention," *Georgia Histor-*

ning, these emotional tactics no doubt aided the radicals. A motion to delay secession, the moderates' chief test, failed 133 to 164. On January 19 secession carried 208 to 89, and Georgia committed itself to the South Carolina Program.[46]

Georgians were the most numerous and probably the most talented of the delegates at Montgomery. Both Cobbs were there; Howell Cobb was elected president of the convention, and T. R. R. Cobb was an active member of the committee that drafted the permanent Constitution. Stephens, who attended although he had expressed some reservations when chosen by the Georgia convention, was a moderating force in the debates, and his election as Confederate vice-president was an index of the convention's moderate temper as well as Stephens' new-found loyalty. Toombs was a somewhat enigmatic figure at Montgomery. Originally he had hoped to become president of the Confederacy; when the hope proved illusory, he made his peace with Stephens and led a "loyal opposition" to the Cobbs.

The Georgia delegation well reflected the secession process which brought them to Montgomery. Of the ten delegates, three were Democrats and seven Whigs, four had been cooperationists, and six had been leaders of the straight-out secessionists. Most of the time this diverse group acted together—a significant commentary upon the convention's determination to present a united front.[47]

In Louisiana secessionist sentiment was slow to form until the crisis of 1860 and 1861. The radicals had made little headway in the state, whose principal city, New Orleans, was a national trading and transportation center and whose most characteristic crop, sugar, was protected by the national tariff. When the fever of disunion struck, however, it became an infectious contagion. In the 1860 presidential election, Breckinridge Democrats carried Louisiana by only a narrow plurality. Lincoln's election, though, disenchanted many of the Whiggish supporters of the Constitutional Unionist

---

the Popular Vote for Delegates to the Georgia Secession Convention," *Georgia Historical Quarterly*, LVI (1972), 259–275.

[46]Wooster, *Secession Conventions*, pp. 91–92.

[47]Lee, *Confederate Constitutions*, pp. 37–42. T. R. R. Cobb to wife, Montgomery, February 6, 1861; February 9, 1861; February 11, 1861, "Correspondence," 164, 169, 171–172. Alexander and Beringer, *Anatomy*, pp. 354–389.

moderate Bell. Thus when Governor Thomas O. Moore called for a convention to consider secession the legislature complied.[48]

On January 7, Louisianians elected eighty straight-out secessionists, forty-four cooperationists, and six undecided delegates to the state convention. As in Georgia, the radicals reported a greater popular vote margin for secessionist delegates than was actually cast. The New Orleans *Daily Delta* gave secessionist candidates 54.2 percent of the vote; the actual returns indicate secessionists received 52.3 percent. Louisiana cooperationists, however, were more inclined toward secession than their counterparts in other states, especially since the convention met after five states had already seceded. Louisiana secessionists tended to be richer and larger slaveholders than their brethren elsewhere and to come from parishes where cotton was the principal crop. The cooperationists came either from the farmer class of the northern parishes or from the sugar-planting regions in the southern part of the state.[49]

The convention voted secession on January 25 by a majority of 113 to 17. Louisiana then accepted the South Carolina Program and chose six delegates to the Montgomery Convention.[50] These delegates, like Louisiana's radical leaders, were wealthy slaveholders committed to the Confederacy. Men of means, they determined that a Southern nation could best protect those means; well satisfied and well treated by the status quo, they went to Montgomery to preserve it.[51]

Texas was exceptional. Governor Sam Houston, an unalterable foe of secession, refused to call the legislature into session or to heed radical demands for a convention. In the impasse a number of influential secessionists took it upon themselves to call an extralegal convention. Houston countered by calling a special session of the legislature, hoping it would denounce the proceedings; but it did just the opposite, approving the idea of a convention. Relying upon

[48]Roger W. Shugg, *Origins of the Class Struggle in Louisiana: A Social History of White Farmers and Laborers During Slavery and After 1849–1875* (Baton Rouge, La., 1939), p. 157; Jefferson Davis Bragg, *Louisiana in the Confederacy* (Baton Rouge, La., 1941), pp. 1–20.

[49]Charles B. Dew, "Who Won the Secession Election in Louisiana?" *Journal of Southern History*, XXXVI (1970), 18–32; Wooster, *Secession Conventions*, pp. 101–107, 115–120.

[50]Wooster, *Secession Conventions*, pp. 107–112.

[51]Lee, *Confederate Constitutions*, pp. 42–45.

the right of Texans expressed in the state constitution to alter or
abolish their government and upon this belated legislative approval
for legitimacy, the Texas secession convention met in Austin in late
January and passed 152 to 6 a resolution favoring secession. On
February 1, Texas formally voted to secede (166 to 8); included in
the ordinance was the provision that it be referred to the voters for
final approval. The popular vote confirmed the convention's actions
by more than three to one, and in time even Houston acquiesced
in the action and coexisted with the Confederacy.[52]

Because of the necessary referendum and the relative tardiness of
the state's secession, the Texas delegation arrived in Montgomery
too late to debate the provisional Constitution or to help elect the
president and vice-president. Indeed the delegation did not offi-
cially claim its seats until the permanent Constitution was in its final
stages of debate. Most colorful among the Texans was Louis Tre-
zaunt Wigfall, a South Carolina native who had moved to Texas
because he owed too much money and had fought too many duels
in South Carolina. A staunch fire-eater, Wigfall persisted in his
doctrinaire Southernism as senator in every Confederate Congress.
Among the less colorful Texans was John H. Reagan, who became
postmaster general of the Confederacy.[53]

Including the Texans, fifty men served in the Montgomery Convention. Although two-fifths of them had been cooperationists in
their home states, it is safe to say that with one or two exceptions
all of the delegates endorsed by their presence the *fait accompli* of
secession and wished their new nation well.

Secession was a radical act, and the process of disunion was the
product of radical men and tactics. The Montgomery Convention,
on the other hand, was a moderate, even conservative, body.[54] This
paradoxical sequence of radicalism followed by moderation is understandable only in the context of the delegates' background and
recent experience. Even the most radical delegates realized that
disunion had been not the unanimous choice of the Southern people, but often the tenuous choice of an emotional moment. And

[52]Wooster, *Secession Conventions*, pp. 121–135; Marguis James, *The Raven: The Story
of Sam Houston* (Indianapolis, Ind., 1929), pp. 404–417; Llerena Friend, *Sam Houston:
The Great Designer* (Austin, Tex., 1954), pp. 329–350.
[53]Lee, *Confederate Constitutions*, pp. 45–47.
[54]*Ibid.*, pp. 47–50.

most of the delegates realized that if the Confederacy were to survive, it needed the good will and support of at least its own people and if possible people in the upper South, Europe, and even the North. The Confederates made a revolution to preserve and protect the Southern status quo from encroachment. At Montgomery they attempted to frame a government which would do precisely that.

February 4, 1861, was sunny and warm. Most of the Montgomery delegates had been in town several days and, naturally, had discussed informally the work they were about to do. As the delegates took their seats in the state capitol, they knew pretty well what would happen on the first day. William P. Chilton of Alabama acted as host and called the convention to order. Then the delegates unanimously elected Barnwell of South Carolina temporary president of the convention, presented their credentials, unanimously elected Howell Cobb convention president, appointed a committee to draw up rules, and adjourned. All had gone according to the script.[55]

On the second day, February 5, the delegates began testing this harmony. Debate began on the first of the difficult questions: what was the convention empowered to do? From a series of resolutions, amendments, and substitutes and a gentleman's agreement came the delegates' ambitious answer: draft a provisional Constitution, elect a provisional president and vice-president, and then draft a permanent Constitution while sitting as the provisional Congress.[56] In normal times these would have been high-handed actions for legalistic Southerners. But these were not normal times, and the delegates felt compelled to create an instant government in order to quell fears that the Confederates were not in earnest. Many people both outside the new nation and within it believed secession to be a bluff and assumed that the Southerners had left the Union only temporarily in order to get better terms for themselves inside it. The contrary was true. The delegates at Montgomery tried to outdo each other in zeal for the permanency of their break with the North. Stephens of Georgia, for example, mindful of his cooperationist record, took pains to declare disunion irrevocable and compromise impossible. "The delegation from Georgia," President

[55]*Ibid.*, pp. 51–55; *Journal of Congress*, I, 7–16.
[56]Albert N. Fitts, "The Confederate Convention," *Alabama Review*, II (1949), 86–87; Lee, *Confederate Constitutions*, pp. 55–59; *Journal of Congress*, I, 17–22.

Cobb wrote his wife, "are acting with perfect unanimity on all questions."[57]

Having agreed upon their mission, delegates next voted to conduct much of their business in secret sessions which promised fewer public poses from the delegates, encouraged free debate, and still allowed the convention to present a united front. With these preliminaries behind them, the delegates began the substantive business of drafting a provisional Constitution.

A committee of twelve chaired by Memminger worked steadily for two days and nights and on the afternoon of February 7 presented their results. Next day the delegates debated the document and about midnight unanimously adopted it.[58]

Memminger's committee used the United States Constitution as its model. The common assumption was that the work done in Philadelphia in 1787, with a few adjustments, would serve the Southern nation well enough—as long as Southerners were free to construe it properly. There were significant differences, however. The preamble of the new Constitution spoke of "sovereign and independent states" instead of "we, the people" and invoked "the favor of Almighty God." The delegates passed over potentially divisive points about tariffs and slavery and agreed to deal with them at more leisure when they took up the permanent Constitution. The provisional Constitution provided for an item veto by the president, thus eliminating the practice of attaching unrelated riders to legislation; included a procedure to be followed in the event of presidential disability; and combined district and circuit court systems into a single district system in which each state constituted a district. Aside from these adjustments, the provisional government was little different in structure from that of the United States.[59]

After adopting the provisional Constitution, the convention adjourned late on the night of February 8 and agreed to hold elections for provisional president and vice-president the following day.[60] So far there had been amazingly little politicking on the subject.[61]

[57]Howell Cobb to wife, Montgomery, February 6, 1861, Ulrich B. Phillips (ed.), *The Correspondence of Robert Toombs, Alexander H. Stephens and Howell Cobb*, American Historical Association *Annual Report*, 1911, II (Washington, 1913), 557.

[58]Lee, *Confederate Constitutions*, pp. 58–63; *Journal of Congress*, I, 25–39.

[59]Lee, *Confederate Constitutions*, pp. 63–72. The full text is on pp. 159–169.

[60]*Journal of Congress*, I, 39.

[61]Howell Cobb to wife, Montgomery, February 6, 1861, Phillips (ed.), *Correspondence*, p. 537; J. L. M. Curry, *Civil History of the Government of the Confederate States with some Personal Reminiscences* (Richmond, Va., 1907), p. 52; T. R. R. Cobb to wife, Montgomery, February 3, 1861, "Correspondence," 160.

Rhett believed he had earned the honor. However, since honor must be bestowed rather than grasped, Rhett had not sought it openly, and his fellow South Carolinians did not put him forward.[62] Howell Cobb was a contender but had said he did not want the job; and some, including his brother T. R. R. Cobb, believed him.[63] A few delegates favored Toombs, and so did Toombs; but support for the fiery Georgian never grew, as his erratic statesmanship and hard drinking made him unacceptable to those delegates who demanded propriety and respectability. According to Stephens, Toombs was "tight every day at dinner" and "about two days before the election" Toombs was *"tighter* than I ever saw him."[64] Yancey was unacceptable for some of the same reasons. He had so long been indentified with radicalism that many were afraid of him. Stephens was the third Georgian under consideration, but although he was an energetic member of the convention, his eleventh-hour conversion to the Confederacy was a strong point against him, and in his own delegation were men whose political memories of Stephens were long and unpleasant. From the beginning the name most often mentioned was Jefferson Davis.[65]

Davis had many of the qualifications which the Montgomery delegates sought. He had been a strong Southern rights man—but not too strong, like Yancey and Rhett. His public experience had been broad; he had been congressman and senator, had graduated from West Point, fought with distinction in the Mexican War, and served the Pierce administration as secretary of war. This military background was important; for even though the Southerners repeatedly told themselves and others that the North would not fight to restore the seceded states to the Union, their words were more hopeful than confident, and just in case they might be wrong, they wanted a constitutional commander-in-chief who would command. Few delegates knew Davis well; few people ever did. In time many of them would make judgments of Davis the man; but for the moment his public record was more important than his private life. And if Davis seemed a bit aloof, so much the better—dignity was important in the

[62]R. B. Rhett, Jr., "The Confederate Government at Montgomery," in Robert Underwood Johnson and Clarence Clough Buel (eds.), *Battles and Leaders of the Civil War,* 4 vols. (New York, 1884–1887), I, 101–103.

[63]Howell Cobb to wife, Montgomery, February 3, 1861, Phillips (ed.), *Correspondence,* pp. 536–537; T. R. R. Cobb to wife, Montgomery, February 6, 1861, "Correspondence," 164.

[64]Lee, *Confederate Constitutions,* p. 78 and n.

[65]*Ibid.,* pp. 72–79; Ralph Richardson, "The Choice of Jefferson Davis as Confederate President," *Journal of Mississippi History,* XVII (1955), 161–176.

government of a revolutionary nation, and Davis looked like a president.[66]

By the time the convention could turn its full attention to the choice of a president, three state delegations (Florida, Mississippi, and Alabama) favored Davis. Louisiana and South Carolina were uncommitted; Davis and Cobb had supporters in both delegations. Georgia was the least committed, having three serious contenders in its own delegation. At this juncture Cobb repeated his disclaimer and "immediately announced his wish that Davis should be unanimously elected." Accordingly every delegation except Georgia met in caucus and agreed upon him.[67] The Georgians met at ten o'clock on February 9, an hour before the convention was to reassemble to vote. To the Cobbs' chagrin, Stephens emerged as Georgia's choice for vice-president, and the other state delegations agreed to vote for him. Thus Howell Cobb's magnanimity in refusing to contest the presidency not only cost him the opportunity of leading the Confederacy; it also advanced the career of his Georgia rival.[68]

When the convention gathered on the ninth, the election, which had been so uncertain the night before, became a *pro forma* ceremony. The convention elected Davis and Stephens unanimously, thus preserving the appearance of unity and harmony. In the process delegates effectively snubbed the old radical secessionists in favor of "safe" Southerners.[69]

On February 11, the Monday following Friday's election, Howell Cobb administered the oath of office to Vice-President Stephens. The day was Stephens' birthday, and because Davis was still en route to Montgomery from his plantation near Vicksburg, Mississippi, Stephens stood alone in the limelight. Small and slight of build, he was not physically impressive, and his stooped posture made him appear older than his forty-nine years. In the old Union he had been a national leader, and he was known to be a learned

[66]There exists no "standard" biography of Davis. William E. Dodd's *Jefferson Davis* (Philadelphia, 1907) is still good. Hudson Strode's *Jefferson Davis*, 3 vols. (New York, 1955–1964) is tedious and excessively eulogistic. Although it is a general history of the Confederacy, Frank E. Vandiver's *Their Tattered Flags* contains perhaps the best balanced portrait of Davis. The best brief treatment is in Rembert W. Patrick, *Jefferson Davis and His Cabinet* (Baton Rouge, La., 1944), pp. 27–76.

[67]Lee, *Confederate Constitutions*, p. 76; Fitts, "Confederate Convention," 91–99.

[68]T. R. R. Cobb to wife, Montgomery, February 11, 1861, "Correspondence," 171–172.

[69]*Journal of Congress*, I, 40; Horace Montgomery, *Howell Cobb's Confederate Career* (Tuscaloosa, Ala., 1959), p. 24 ff.

man. Now he was vice-president because he had been a cooperationist, because he was a Georgia Whig, and because his friends in
the Georgia delegation had worked for his election. What his public
career had not fully revealed about him thus far was the degree of
his attachment to principles and the doctrinaire bent of his mind.
He once wrote an associate that principles were the "pole star of my
existence."[70] As long as Stephens had followed his principles into
vain conflicts as a spokesman for a minority South, his leadership
had been consistent and effective. Now, however, Stephens no
longer represented a minority. He was called to help lead the cause
which he had so long proclaimed. The unanswered, indeed
unasked, question was whether his principles could survive the transition from the political outs to the political ins. His nimble shift
from union to secession indicated that his principles could bend
instead of break. He threw himself into his new task with enthusiasm
and energy and for a while was second to the President not only in
office but also in influence. But Stephens' ascendancy was brief; it
corresponded with that period of time during which the Confederacy was what he had hoped it would be, a national extension of the
ideology of the Old South. When the exigencies of the Confederacy's war prompted other Southerners to reexamine and redefine
the substance of their ideological position, Stephens resisted the
apostasy. Clinging to his principles he became an enemy of the
administration he once had served.[71]

President-elect Davis arrived in Montgomery on February 16. A
large crowd followed him from the railroad station to the Exchange
Hotel. There Yancey welcomed him and proclaimed that "the man
and the hour have met!" As Davis offered his thanks, the symbolism
of the moment was perfect. Yancey, the fire-eater, surrendered the
stage to Davis, the statesman. The radicals' hour was over; sensible
men had come to Montgomery to carry out a revolution made by
others.[72]

Two days after his arrival, Davis was inaugurated provisional

[70]Stephens to J. Henly Smith, Crawfordville, Ga., May 8, 1860, Phillips (ed.),
Correspondence, 470. The best work on Stephens is by Stephens himself, *A Constitutional
View of the Late War Between the States*, 2 vols. (Philadelphia, 1868). The standard
biography is Rudolph Von Abele, *Alexander H. Stephens: A Biography* (New York, 1946).
[71]See James Z. Rabun, "Alexander H. Stephens and Jefferson Davis," *American
Historical Review*, LVIII (1953), 290–321; Patrick, *Davis and His Cabinet*, p. 41.
[72]Lee, *Confederate Constitutions*, p. 79. See also Thomas, *Revolutionary Experience*, pp.
38–42.

president. An estimated ten thousand people, more than the town's population, watched the procession to the steps of the capitol, then thronged in front of the building to witness the ceremony. Before taking the oath of office, Davis delivered an inaugural address.[73] Davis was known as a logician; but his address strained logic. He began by drawing the common parallel between what Southerners had done and what their grandfathers had done in the American Revolution. Then after invoking "the right of the people to alter or abolish governments," he abruptly asserted, "it is by abuse of language that their act [forming the Confederacy] has been denominated a revolution."[74] Only in the context of the moment in Montgomery did Davis' revolution-no-revolution non sequitur make sense. The new President was supposed to allay fears, and he knew it; consequently most of his speech was a recital of how unchanged was the Southern status quo. "We have changed the constituent parts," he said, "but not the system of our Government."[75] Davis' message was clear: we have exercised the right of revolution, he was saying, but we did so only to preserve the Southern life style. Davis believed what he said, and none of his listeners seemed to question his logic.

Now the convention turned to its final task as a constituent assembly, the permanent Constitution. While a drafting committee worked, the convention took up its role as provisional Congress and began debating and enacting legislation.[76] Committee members worked long and hard at their assignment and sandwiched their labors on the Constitution between sessions of Congress. T. R. R. Cobb, for example, spent mornings with his congressional committee, afternoons in sessions of Congress, and nights with the constitutional committee.[77]

On the last day of February the draft was ready for debate. For ten days the delegates doubled as members of the provisional Con-

[73]Lee, *Confederate Constitutions*, pp. 79–81.

[74]*Journal of Congress*, I, 64–65.

[75]*Ibid.*, 66.

[76]*Ibid.*, 41–93. The drafting committee was composed of Walker and Smith of Alabama, Morton and Owens of Florida, Toombs and T. R. R. Cobb of Georgia, DeClouet and Sparrow of Louisiana, Clayton and Harris of Mississippi, and Rhett and Chesnut of South Carolina.

[77]T. R. R. Cobb to wife, Montgomery, February 12, 13, 14, 15, 22, 23, and 25, 1861, "Correspondence," 172–178, 236, 239–241.

gress in the morning and of the constitutional convention in the afternoon. Finally, on March 11, they unanimously adopted the Constitution. In just thirty-five days, less than half the time it took the Founding Fathers to write the United States Constitution, the delegates had laid the foundation of the Southern Confederacy.[78]

The ubiquitous Robert Barnwell Rhett, who was chairman of the drafting committee, had some definite ideas about what should and should not be included in the permanent Constitution. However, few of Rhett's ideas prevailed either in his committee's draft or in the final document. The preamble spoke of states acting in their "sovereign and independent character" but also of establishing a "permanent federal government." During the debates the delegates considered clauses about the right of secession from the Confederacy and about nullification. But the convention shrank from incorporating these revered Southern principles in the Constitution, and only the relative ease of the amendment process (initiated by convention of only three member states) spoke to the nullification issue raised by South Carolina in 1832. The delegates were satisfied to affirm state sovereignty in general terms and trust future generations to understand the meaning of the phrase. Nevertheless the assertion that they were creating a "permanent federal government" might have left future generations in a quandary had one or more states chosen to secede from the Confederacy.[79] Interestingly, no one seems to have suggested a return to the frame of the only American precedent for genuine confederation: the Articles of Confederation.

Like the provisional Constitution, the permanent document was an altered version of the United States Constitution. Some of the basic changes from the United States Constitution included in the provisional framework reappeared in the new document: the item veto, prohibition of the slave trade, strictures against tariffs, a district court structure, and a procedure to be followed in case of presidential disability. Rhett and some of the South Carolina delegates were bitterly disappointed about the prohibition of the slave trade but found themselves almost alone in this matter.

As might be expected, the Constitution expressly protected slavery in the Confederacy and its territories—"No . . . law denying or

[78] *Journal of Congress*, I, 851–896.
[79] Lee, *Confederate Constitutions*, pp. 82–83, 88–89, 101–102.

impairing the right of property in negro slaves shall be passed." The Constitution also forbade "internal improvements" and restricted the Congress from making appropriations not specifically requested by the executive branch unless the appropriations received a two-thirds majority vote in both houses. Congress was authorized to grant seat and voice to cabinet members so they might join debates over bills which concerned their departments. The Confederate Post Office was required to become self-sustaining within two years. The Confederate president was to serve six years but could not succeed himself. These provisions were adjustments in the old Constitution designed to realign its checks and balances and make the government as responsive and efficient as possible.

Significantly, the convention retained the "three-fifths clause" about the counting of slaves when determining a state's population for the purposes of taxation and congressional representation. The "necessary and proper" clause (Article I, Section 8, of the U.S. Constitution), too, remained, as did the theoretical basis of judicial review implied in the authorization of Congress to create a Supreme Court. On balance and in theory, the Confederate executive was probably stronger than his United States counterpart. Although he could not serve more than one term, that term was six instead of four years, and he had the power of item veto and strong control over appropriations.

Ironically, the most striking feature of the Confederate Constitution was not its Southern orientation. The permanent Constitution prescribed for the Confederacy much the same kind of union which the Southerners had dissolved.[80]

Although the Montgomery Convention spent only ten days debating the Constitution before adopting it unanimously, it was during these deliberations that the sacred harmony of the convention came closest to shattering. Just as the Philadelphia Convention

[80]Lee (*ibid.*, pp. 171–210) has an appendix in which the United States and Confederate Constitutions are printed side by side and in which alterations in the United States document are italicized in the Confederate frame. His exegesis of the permanent Constitution (pp. 82–140) is outstanding. Lee's conclusions about the document (pp. 141–150) are at some variance with the interpretation expressed here. He holds that the Confederate Constitutions were "the ultimate constitutional expression of the state rights philosophy and the state sovereignty concept in nineteenth-century America" (p. 150). Perhaps in the strictly literal sense this is true; no other "constitutional expression" existed in nineteenth-century America.

in 1787 had had a crucial "Great Debate" over state representation in Congress, so the Montgomery delegates had a great debate over admission of new states into the Confederacy. Led by Rhett, William P. Miles of South Carolina, and T. R. R. Cobb, convention radicals proposed to exclude nonslave states from the Confederacy. The moderates, Toombs, Stephens, and the president, who expressed his opinion privately, wished to leave the door open. The radicals feared reconstruction and even suggested that there was a move afoot to restore the old Union under the Confederate Constitution. Moreover, they feared that if nonslave states were admitted, free soil in the South would lead to "free-soilers" and doom the Confederacy to battle abolitionists all over again. The moderates argued that trade and transportation systems (the Mississippi River, for example) might in time attract free states to the Confederacy; they did not wish arbitrarily to exclude them and, with them, the hope of expansion into the west and perhaps into Mexico. The Montgomery Great Debate ended in compromise, as had the debate in Philadelphia in 1787. John G. Shorter of Alabama proposed that new states be admitted to the Confederacy by a vote of two-thirds of the House of Representatives and the Senate, with each state casting one vote in the Senate. The convention adopted Shorter's compromise, thus keeping the door open to free states, while the radicals found some comfort in the fact that free states would have to secure more than a simple majority vote to enter the slaveholders' union.[81]

The Great Debate at Montgomery was the last real obstacle in the way of the convention. When the delegates completed the Constitution, they could consider the Confederacy founded and themselves founding fathers. During the Great Debate, the radicals had made their last stand to extend and intensify the slaveholders' ideology, while the moderates resisted because they were satisfied to retain the Southern status quo and because they believed that in the real world nothing more than that was possible. The moderates won, as they had won other essential points at Montgomery, because the fundamental goal of the Southern revolution was the preservation of the Southern life style as Southerners then lived it. Southerners generally had adopted radical rhetoric and tactics to transform their ideology into nationalism; but once that transformation had oc-

[81] *Journal of Congress*, I, 876–893; Lee, *Confederate Constitutions*, pp. 112–116.

curred in secession, the radicals became superfluous. Confederates did not believe they needed to make new worlds; they were more than content with the world they already had. At Montgomery the moderate majority tried to codify the Southern status quo and to present a favorable image to the South and the rest of the world, and with the founding of the Confederacy they believed they had succeeded.

CHAPTER 4

Southern Nationality Established

A map of Charleston Harbor is perhaps as close as cartographers can come to sensual expression. The city of Charleston occupies a V shaped peninsula formed by the confluence of the Ashley and Cooper Rivers. Because the south Atlantic coastline is geologically advancing into the ocean, a torso-shaped body of water separates the city from the sea. Charleston Harbor is enclosed by low-lying mainland, marsh-covered islands, and sandy spits. At the "neck" of the harbor, Charleston's channel to the Atlantic, Sullivan Island to the north and Morris Island to the south arch toward each other like collar bones and define irregular curves in the harbor shoreline behind them. Rising from the water, between the tips of Sullivan and Morris Islands lies a manmade blemish on the harbor body. At roughly the position of a geographical sternum is Fort Sumter.

When South Carolina left the Union, Sumter was unfinished; when completed the fort would dominate the entrance of Charleston Harbor and effectively control access to the port city from the sea. Supporting Sumter were other fortifications clustered about the harbor entrance. These works, too, were in various stages of construction and occupied by a small garrison of sixty troops from the United States Army whose headquarters was at Fort Moultrie on Sullivan Island. On December 19, 1860, the presence of American troops in Charleston presented no official complications. On December 20, however, the soldiers were a "foreign army" in possession of some Palmetto Republic real estate. South Carolina could hardly defend its pretensions to being an independent republic while the United States manned its military strongpoints. On the other hand, the troops were servants of the United States government entrusted with the care of government property. They could not simply abandon their posts and their duty just because some hot-headed Carolinians asked them to leave.[1]

South Carolina's secession convention anticipated the problem, and on December 24 three commissioners from the convention set out for Washington to open diplomatic relations with the United States and to arrange for the transfer of public property from one government to another. Meanwhile South Carolina's recently inaugurated Governor Francis W. Pickens and Major Robert Anderson, commander of the garrison at Moultrie, maintained the status quo. Based upon informal communications through intermediaries, Pickens believed he had an understanding with Washington that nothing would happen in Charleston Harbor until the commissioners had dealt with President James Buchanan. Anderson had orders to do nothing hostile, to protect himself and his post, but not to make martyrs of himself and his men. The Major was a Kentuckian with some sympathy toward the South. Nevertheless he was also an army officer with a strong sense of duty, and in the crisis he consistently chose duty over sympathy.[2]

For six days the situation remained static but tense. Advisors, official and otherwise, exhorted Pickens to seize the forts and send Anderson's troops packing. Anderson all but pleaded with his government to give him precise instructions. His position at Fort Moultrie was indefensible; South Carolina militia could storm the place any time they wished, and from sand hills only a hundred yards outside the walls of the fort they could shoot down anyone attempting to serve Moultrie's guns.[3]

[1]Standard studies of the Sumter crisis include Samuel W. Crawford, *The Genesis of the Civil War: The Story of Sumter, 1860–61* (New York, 1887); Roy Meredity, *Storm Over Sumter* (New York, 1957); W. A. Swanberg, *First Blood* (New York, 1958); and Abner Doubleday, *Reminiscences of Forts Sumter and Moultrie in 1860–61* (New York, 1876).

[2]The commissioners were James Orr, Robert W. Barnwell, and James H. Adams. See Swanberg, *First Blood*, pp. 34–40, 85–93, and "Memorandum of verbal instructions to Major Anderson . . . ," in *War of the Rebellion: A Compilation of the Official Records of the Union and Confederate Armies*, 70 vols. in 127 (Washington, D. C., 1880–1901), ser. I, I, 117.

[3]Crawford, *Sumter*, p. 100.

By an odd coincidence, Edmund Ruffin was one of the first Confederates to notice any change in the delicate situation in Charleston Harbor. The old man had come to Charleston to witness the secession process, and another interested observer, Governor Madison S. Perry of Florida, invited Ruffin to Tallahassee to attend the Florida secession convention. On the evening of December 26, Ruffin was gazing out at the ocean from the upper deck of a steamboat bound for Fernandina when he heard two cannon shots from Fort Moultrie, about four miles astern. He wondered at the noise and assumed that the shots "must have been a signal for something. . . ."; when he heard no more firing, he dismissed the incident.[4]

In fact the two shots were a signal; they announced the arrival of Major Anderson's command at Fort Sumter. At dusk on the twenty-sixth the "foreigners" moved quickly and quietly across the mile or so of water, and when the main body of troops reached the island fort, a rear guard at Moultrie fired two cannon to signal two boats loaded with the garrison's dependents and provisions to pull for Sumter. Later the dozen men at Moultrie spiked its cannon, burned the gun carriages, and joined the rest of the command at Sumter. So carefully did Anderson plan and execute his move that Charlestonians did not discover it until the morning of the twenty-seventh.[5]

Reaction in the city to the concentration at Fort Sumter was immediate and ominous. Volunteer troops and local militia units filled the streets of the town while the more curious residents crowded into steeples and cupolas to view the spectacle of Yankees at Sumter. The Charleston *Mercury*, edited by Robert Barnwell Rhett, Jr., termed Anderson's action an "outrageous breach of faith" and advised patriotic women to begin rolling bandages.[6]

Governor Pickens, who in the face of considerable criticism had pursued what he believed to be a moderate and generous policy toward the United States, was more than a little embarrassed; Anderson had responded to forebearance with trickery and had committed what many of the Governor's constituents would view as an

[4]William Kaufman Scarborough (ed.), *The Diary of Edmund Ruffin*, I, *Toward Independence, October, 1856–April, 1861* (Baton Rouge, La., 1972), 514–516.
[5]Swanberg, *First Blood*, pp. 96–103; Crawford, *Sumter*, pp. 102–108.
[6]Mary Boykin Chesnut, *A Diary from Dixie*, Ben Ames Williams (ed.), (Boston, 1949), p. 4; Charleston *Mercury*, December 28 and 31, 1860.

act of war! Pickens sent his military aide, Colonel J. Johnston Pettigrew, to Fort Sumter to demand an explanation from Anderson and "courteously but peremptorily" to order the Federals to return to Moultrie. Anderson listened to the Governor's message, protested his ignorance of any agreement to maintain the status quo in Charleston's forts, and firmly refused to leave Sumter. Later in the day Pettigrew, with a rifle battalion, took partial revenge on behalf of Pickens by storming Castle Pinckney, a small, weak fortification located on a shoal at the mouth of the Cooper River. In the days that followed, Carolinians seized and manned the land fortifications which surrounded Sumter. Pickens permitted mail, wives, and officers to pass between Fort Sumter and Charleston but forbade resupply of the garrison and thus added the tactic of siege to the war of nerves between himself and Anderson.[7]

"Anderson has opened the ball," remarked one Charlestonian who was perhaps more perceptive than he knew.[8] When the dutiful Major concentrated at Fort Sumter, he created an impasse from which there was no graceful exit. The presence of United States troops at Fort Moultrie was a diplomatic incident; a besieged garrison at Sumter transformed incident into crisis. Once Anderson made his move from an untenable position on what in essence was the mainland to a defensible island, he could hardly afford to back down.

The concentration at Sumter and Sumter's location also limited the options of South Carolina. An attack on Fort Sumter promised success, but the cost of such victory might well be war between the United States and South Carolina, and secessionists realized that war, at this stage, was a bad idea.[9]

Thus the impasse remained and the crisis grew. Anderson, with four months' supply of provisions, could afford to wait, and President James Buchanan, with only three months left in his term of

[7]Charleston *Mercury*, December 28, 1860; Pickens to Anderson, December 28, 1860, *O.R.*, ser. I, I, 113; Anderson to Cooper, December 30, 1860, *O.R.*, ser. I, I, 114; Anderson to Cooper, December 31, 1860, *O.R.*, ser. I, I, 120; and Crawford, *Sumter*, pp. 109–112.

[8]Chesnut, *Diary*, p. 4.

[9]See Grady McWhiney, "The Confederacy's First Shot," *Civil War History*, XIV (1968), 5–14; Richard N. Current, "The Confederates and the First Shot," *Civil War History*, VII (1961), 357–369; and Ludwell H. Johnson, "Fort Sumter and Confederate Diplomacy," *Journal of Southern History*, XXVI (1960), 441–477.

office, was determined to wait. On January 5 the President did dispatch two hundred soldiers and additional arms and supplies to Fort Sumter aboard an unarmed merchant ship, *Star of the West.* When the ship reached Charleston Harbor, South Carolina batteries on Morris Island and at Fort Moultrie opened fire, and in accord with her orders the *Star of the West* turned about and steamed away. Buchanan's gesture was essentially symbolic; the *Star of the West* incident heated tempers without solving anything, and the lameduck President did not repeat the effort to resupply or reinforce Anderson.[10]

As the weeks passed, however, the focus of the Sumter crisis narrowed; because Anderson's provisions were dwindling, the issue became resupply. Mercifully for Anderson and Pickens, as the crisis deepened, responsibility for its resolution broadened. Anderson had the full attention of his ultimate commander-in-chief. And when the South Carolina delegates at Montgomery signed the provisional Constitution of Confederacy, Pickens became one among several state governors instead of the head of a sovereign republic, and Fort Sumter became the problem of Jefferson Davis and the Confederate government.[11]

As spring came to the new capital at Montgomery, the world looked rosy enough to inspire confidence. Relations with the United States were not yet established, but every day the Confederacy existed the Southern nation became more a fact of life in the world. True, the United States had made an issue of maintaining troops at Fort Sumter and at Fort Pickens near Pensacola, but there seemed a chance the stalemate over government property might be resolved peacefully, and if not, any armed conflict would last only long enough for the Southerners to demonstrate their determination to be a separate nation. Even if a war should drag on a bit, the Confederates were steadfast in their commitment and in the belief that they could confirm their national existence in blood. If necessary the Southern cause and Southern cotton could make their claims in Europe and secure aid or intervention on behalf of the Confederacy

[10]Anderson to Cooper, December 31, 1860, *O.R.*, ser. I, I, 120; Frank W. Klingberg, "James Buchanan and the Crisis of the Union," *Journal of Southern History,* IX (1943), 455–474; Allan Nevins, *The Emergence of Lincoln,* 2 vols. (New York, 1950), II, 340–343.

[11]Davis to Pickens, March 1, 1861, Dunbar Rowland (ed.), *Jefferson Davis, Constitutionalist: His Letters, Papers, and Speeches,* 10 vols. (Jackson, Miss., 1923), V, 58–59.

from a wider world. For the present, Jefferson Davis' first priority was the creation of a working government; then that government could act for the Southern people and negotiate the Confederacy's rites of passage into the family of nations.

After George Washington, Davis was in a position unique among American presidents, in that he had the opportunity to construct an entire executive branch of government by himself. Davis had few political debts associated with his election. Nor did he lead a political party into power—indeed, the Confederacy never developed political parties. The Confederate President was thus unencumbered as he began to fill the new nation's patronage vacuum.

Davis did not lack helpers in his task. The lure of office made a magnet of Montgomery, and the already overfilled town bulged with would-be cabinet members, clerks, generals, bureau chiefs, and colonels. The mails carried petitions to the President or to men who might have his ear from many more potential public servants, and the numbers tended to grow geometrically as Davis chose his cabinet members and as they in turn selected their staffs. However free the President should have been to select his cabinet on the basis of merit and public virtue, in fact his choices reflected the demands of politics and geography.[12]

Obviously the cabinet required a "South Carolina seat." Davis wanted Robert Barnwell to be secretary of state because he was a South Carolinian and because he had led the state's delegation to vote for Davis as president instead of Rhett. Barnwell declined the offer but proposed Memminger as secretary of the treasury, and Davis acceded to the request. Memminger had a reputation, acquired while he was chairman of the ways and means committee of the South Carolina House of Representatives, for a conservative but quick financial mind, and indeed the frugal Charleston lawyer organized his department using the structure created by Alexander Hamilton as a model.

Fortunately, Memminger did not begin his tenure with an empty treasury. On February 8, 1861, the provisional Congress began its

[12]See Harrison A. Trexler, "Jefferson Davis and Confederate Patronage," *South Atlantic Quarterly*, XXVIII (1929), 45–58; Haskell Monroe, "Early Confederate Political Patronage," *Alabama Review*, XX (1967), 45–61; and Paul P. Van Riper and Harry N. Scheiber, "The Confederate Civil Service," *Journal of Southern History*, XXV (1959), 448–470.

session with the happy duty of accepting a loan from Louisiana of $500,000 in specie seized as state property from the New Orleans mint and United States Customs Office. This action set what became an unhappy precedent; gifts, loans, and the printing press became the chief sources of support for the Confederate government. On the last day of February, Congress authorized a $150-million loan in the form of 8-percent bonds and provided for repayment by levying an export duty on Confederate cotton. While this loan drained patriotic Southern banks of much of their specie, Congress tapped a more available Southern resource, agricultural produce. The idea was to get Southern planters to lend their crops; then the government could convert the goods into other forms of wealth or barter for its needs with the pledged staples. Under the act of May 16, Memminger's department could issue $50 million worth of 8-percent bonds and immediately print $20 million worth of treasury notes to circulate in lieu of specie.[13]

As a basis of fiscal policy, loans and paper money backed by loans were not very sound. Memminger well knew that in the long run the Confederacy would have to establish a more stable source of revenue and meet its financial needs by some system of taxation. But in 1861 he believed that the government's needs were both extraordinary and temporary; there would be time enough for fiscal restraint when the Southern government was firmly established and the situation became normal. Moreover, like Hamilton, Memminger allowed himself to hope that the government's instant debt would be creative in that it would stimulate Southern patriotism by making the Confederacy's citizens its creditors. The initial success of these loans and faith accorded the treasury notes cheered Memminger and confirmed his hopes.[14]

Memminger's wishful thinking presupposed peace to be the normal Confederate condition, and he was not alone in this presupposition. The Southern leaders at Montgomery had intoned the official liturgy of "peaceful secession" so often that many of them had come

[13]Rembert W. Patrick, *Jefferson Davis and His Cabinet* (Baton Rouge, La., 1944), p. 51; Richard C. Todd, *Confederate Finance* (Athens, Ga., 1954), pp. 1–3, 25–34; *Journal of the Congress of the Confederate States of America, 1861–1865,* 7 vols. (Washington, D.C., 1904–1905), I, 31–32. The standard biography of Memminger is still H. D. Capers, *The Life and Times of Christopher G. Memminger* (Richmond, Va., 1893).

[14]Todd, *Confederate Finance,* p. 34; Patrick, *Jefferson Davis and His Cabinet,* pp. 212–216.

to believe it.[15] The President, though, could not afford to be so sanguine; and therefore the needs of the War Department had high priority. There is evidence that Davis preferred Braxton Bragg, a professional soldier, for war secretary; but he realized that governments are political constructions and thus felt obliged to choose a civilian politician to run the War Office. The cabinet required an Alabamian in a prominent place, and Leroy Pope Walker wanted the War Office. Initially the choice appeared fortuitous. Walker had been a lawyer and active Democratic politician; he was also a hard-working administrator. Davis hoped that his own talents, which he believed were more military than political, would meld well with those of Walker, and for a brief time they did.[16]

Walker's first task was to create a national army large and strong enough to deter a war or if necessary fight one with the United States. Each Southern state had militia organizations in service, and some, such as South Carolina, had been diligent about securing arms and equipment for their state troops. Early in 1861 the Confederate Congress authorized the creation of a provisional army of 100,000 men. To get these troops Walker asked state governors to raise regiments and then transfer the units to the national army. The War Office provided generals and staff officers and, in theory at least, could employ the troops and their officers in any way it pleased once they mustered into the provisional army.

As Walker began to make requisitions, he had to deal with a flood of soldiers and would-be soldiers. He had to arm, equip, and billet his nascent army and move men and equipment to the probable fronts of a war most people hoped would never occur. Before long, no doubt, Walker wondered why he had ever wanted to be secretary of war.[17] Some governors, such as Perry of Florida, were most cooperative about meeting Walker's troop requisitions; others were less helpful. Brown of Georgia all but inundated the War Office with questions, objections, and reasons for delay and noncompliance

---

[15]See for example T. C. DeLeon, *Four Years in Rebel Capitals* (Mobile, Ala., 1892), p. 27.

[16]Patrick, *Jefferson Davis and His Cabinet*, pp. 104–106.

[17]Frank E. Vandiver, *Ploughshares into Swords: Josiah Gorgas and Confederate Ordnance* (Austin, Tex., 1952), pp. 56–57; James M. Matthews (ed.), *Statutes at Large of the Provisional Congress of the Confederate States of America* (Richmond, Va., 1864), p. 104; Patrick, *Jefferson Davis and His Cabinet*, pp. 106–110.

and then complained that Walker would not answer his letters.[18]

Despite myriad difficulties, Walker was able to assemble some sort of army by the time the Sumter crisis came to a head in mid-April 1861. Excluding 5,000 South Carolina militia stationed in Charleston, the Confederacy boasted an army of approximately 62,000 men. Many of these troops existed only on paper, "in transit" to and from their places of muster or "held in readiness" in their home states. Nevertheless troops were already manning the former United States installations which the Confederate states had seized and then, in response to a request from Congress in Montgomery, ceded to the Southern government. The Confederates had troops patrolling the Rio Grande and the Indian frontier in Texas and manning the approaches to New Orleans and Mobile. Eight thousand Southerners had reported to General Braxton Bragg at Pensacola; there the United States still held Fort Pickens, an island fortress like Sumter, and thus controlled the entrance to Pensacola Harbor. General Pierre G. T. Beauregard was in command of the South Carolinians at Charleston, and Confederates were in position at Fort Pulaski guarding Savannah. On the Mississippi River, Confederates were surveying locations to protect against any advance downstream by the United States.

War had not begun, so there was no obligation to do more than deploy troops. Indeed, no one quite knew what these troops would do if war did break out, and Walker made no claims to being a grand strategist. He talked about capturing Washington but in fact arranged his troops in an essentially defensive posture and prepared most carefully to defend against water-borne invasion. The extensive inland frontier was of less immediate concern for the simple reason that no one could predict with certainty where that frontier would be. Until the upper South made up its mind about the Confederacy, there was little the War Office could do about massing troops on land frontiers which were in a state of flux.[19]

To support the growing army, the Confederacy had erected skele-

[18]J. B. Jones, *A Rebel War Clerk's Diary*, Howard Swiggett (ed.), 2 vols. (New York, 1935), I, 63–64; Patrick, *Jefferson Davis and His Cabinet*, pp. 110–111. For examples of the volume and tone of Walker's correspondence, see *O.R.*, ser. IV, I, 119–218.

[19]Walker to Davis, April 27, 1861, *O.R.*, ser. IV, I, 247–254; Patrick, *Jefferson Davis and His Cabinet*, pp. 111–112.

tal organizations of supply and service. On the same day that he signed the act creating the War Department, the President, taking advantage of the ambiguity of the Confederacy's status vis-à-vis the United States, sent Captain Raphael Semmes, late of the United States Navy, into the North to purchase weapons, ammunition, and machinery with which to make more. Later the War Office dispatched Artillery Captain Caleb Huse to Europe on a similar mission.

These agents enjoyed some success, but the hard fact was that the Confederacy had an immediate shortage of arms and ammunition.[20] Accordingly, as he divided and delivered arms contributed by the states, the new chief of ordnance, Josiah Gorgas, began planning to manufacture his supplies in the South. The Pennsylvania-born Gorgas had spent twenty years in the "old army," becoming an expert on ordnance. He resigned his United States commission and went South for several reasons: his wife was a Southerner, his Southern friends were resigning, and the Union seemed to have little appreciation of his talent and experience. While Gorgas organized, Secretary Walker had to turn down volunteers who could not furnish their own weapons, and squabble with recalcitrant governors for control of such items as knapsacks and saltpeter.

Davis placed two old friends, Lieutenant Colonels Abraham C. Myers and Lucius B. Northrup in charge of quartermaster and commissary respectively, but by mid-April these officials had done little more than prepare estimates of how much their operations would cost.[21] Aided by a honeymoon period of patriotic enthusiasm, Walker's office produced an army during its first two months of life.

For secretary of the navy, Davis at first favored Congressman John Perkins of Louisiana but nominated Stephen R. Mallory of Florida, apparently without regard for any political consideration other than that of including a Floridian in his cabinet. Mallory had not been an ardent secessionist, and he had reputedly been responsible for a deal with United States President Buchanan by which Florida promised not to attack Fort Pickens and Buchanan promised not to

[20]Davis to Semmes, February 21, 1861, O.R., ser. IV, I, 106–107; Cooper to Huse, April 15, 1861, O.R., ser. IV, I, 220; Gorgas Report, April 20, 1861, O.R., ser. IV, I, 227–228; Walker to Davis, April 27, 1861, O.R., ser. IV, I, 247–252; Huse to Ordnance Bureau, May 21, 1861, O.R., ser. IV, I, 343–346.

[21]Vandiver, Gorgas, pp. 3–65; Richard D. Goff, Confederate Supply (Durham, N.C., 1969), pp. 8–19.

reinforce the fort. Jackson Morton and James B. Owens had political memories long enough to hold up Mallory's confirmation for a week. As it happened, Mallory was the only one of Davis' cabinet appointees whose confirmation Congress delayed. Too, Mallory did not enjoy a good social reputation with the women of the Confederate inner circle. According to Mary Chesnut, the Secretary not only associated with women of questionable virtue; he was also given to relating his adventures to any and everyone whenever he had had a glass or two of wine. In spite of all this, Mallory became a good secretary of the navy. He had been chairman of the United States Senate Committee on Naval Affairs and knew about ships and the men who served them. Moreover, Mallory had an innovative mind, and the Confederate Navy required more than conventional wisdom.[22] By late April 1861, the Southern Navy could claim but two uncompleted ships in its fleet.

Secretary Mallory managed to serve at the same post throughout the life of the Confederacy; only one other cabinet member, Postmaster General John H. Reagan, did the same. Born in Tennessee, Reagan had spent much of his youth wandering from place to place and from job to job. Finally he settled in Texas, where he became a district judge and by 1861 a congressman. Traditionally in American politics, the postmaster general is a political appointee whose talent or lack of talent has nothing to do with his appointment. The Confederate President named Reagan because he liked him, because he needed a Texan, and because the Texans liked Reagan.[23] Well aware of the problems inherent in the constitutional provision which required the Post Office to become self-sufficient within two years, Reagan approached his difficult task with vigor and made the Southern mails move about as rapidly and efficiently as circumstances permitted.

During his first two months in office he did two wise things. First,

[22]*Journal of Congress*, I, 75; Patrick, *Jefferson Davis and His Cabinet*, pp. 244–247. The standard biography of Mallory is Joseph T. Durkin, *Stephen R. Mallory: Confederate Navy Chief* (Chapel Hill, N.C., 1954). Davis to Congress, April 29, 1861, *O.R.*, ser. IV, I, 266; Chesnut, *Diary*, pp. 8, 10–11; Tom H. Wells, *The Confederate Navy: A Study in Organization* (University, Ala., 1971), pp. vii–ix, 6, 11–12.

[23]The standard biography of Reagan is Ben H. Procter, *Not Without Honor: The Life of John H. Reagan* (Austin, Tex., 1962). John H. Reagan, *Memoirs, with Special Reference to Secession and the Civil War*, John H. McCaleb (ed.), (New York, 1906), pp. 109–110; Patrick, *Jefferson Davis and His Cabinet*, pp. 272–276.

he announced that his department would not assume responsibility for mail service until June 1, 1861; until that date the old service continued. Southern postmasters continued selling United States postage stamps and sending their receipts to Washington. Even though this expedient proved awkward when the Confederacy and the United States went to war with each other, the grace period allowed Reagan to organize his department and plan its operation. Second, Reagan called a convention of important Southern railroad officials and presented them with a coordinated plan for mail routes and rate schedules. The railroad men proved cooperative, not only with Reagan, but also with Secretary of War Walker, who asked low rates and high priority for rail shipments of troops and supplies. Even though Reagan's post office had yet to deliver its first piece of mail in the spring of 1861, it had made a good beginning.[24]

The Confederacy owed its existence as much to William Lowndes Yancey as to any other man. Yet the Alabama fire-eater posed the same kind of problem to Davis that Rhett did; both were root-and-branch radicals whose talents and tempers well suited the destruction of the old Union but ill became the construction of a new Confederacy. The South Carolinians at Montgomery had solved the problem of Rhett by rejecting his leadership; Yancey was another matter. Moderate Alabamians feared his doctrinaire influence but feared also his political power in the state and throughout the South. Ultimately Davis decided to offer Yancey a choice between the post of attorney general and a diplomatic mission to Europe. Both Davis and Yancey could save face, and the fiery Alabamian would be safely out of the way in a minor cabinet office or out of the country altogether. Yancey was miffed but accepted the European mission instead of the attorney generalship. The President then offered the minor job to a man who became a major figure in administration, Judah P. Benjamin of Louisiana.[25]

The President knew Benjamin as a colleague in the United States Senate, but the two were hardly friends. Once, over a presumed slur, Benjamin had gone so far as to demand an apology or "satisfaction" from Davis; the Mississippian had chosen to make a

[24]Reagan, *Memoirs*, pp. 130–134; Patrick, *Jefferson Davis and His Cabinet*, pp. 276–278; Robert C. Black III, *The Railroads of the Confederacy* (Chapel Hill, N.C., 1952), pp. 52–55. The standard work on the Confederate Post Office is August Dietz, *The Postal Service of the Confederate States of America* (Richmond, Va., 1929).

[25]Patrick, *Jefferson Davis and His Cabinet*, pp. 157–158.

courtly apology before the Senate, and the matter ended. Benjamin had been born of Jewish-English parents on the island of Saint Croix in 1811; he moved to Charleston with his parents and at age fourteen entered Yale. During his junior year, he left Yale suddenly; rumors of undefined misconduct followed him. At age eighteen he settled in New Orleans to seek his fortune and there began an eventually successful law practice. The ambitious young Jew married a Roman Catholic creole belle who shortly thereafter moved to Paris. Benjamin maintained his estranged wife and the fiction of his marriage while he turned his considerable energy to his personal advancement. He became a successful sugar planter and embraced the good life of a Southern gentleman with the zeal of a convert. Then in 1852 he entered Louisiana politics as a Whig and won election to the United States Senate. Benjamin did not become a Democrat until the late 1850s or a secessionist until even later. Short and round, with a dark, full beard, he was unimpressive until he opened his mouth; then urbanity, charm, and intellect displayed itself in full measure. Stephen Vincent Benét portrayed Benjamin as "the dapper Jew,/Seal-sleek, black-eyed, lawyer and epicure,/Able, well-hated, face alive with life,/Looked round the council-chamber with the slight/Perpetual smile he held before himself/Continually like a silk-ribbed fan./Behind the fan, his quick, shrewd, fluid mind/Weighed Gentiles in an old balance." A contemporary admirer said of him, "Hebrew in blood, English in tenacity of grasp and purpose, Mr. Benjamin was French in taste."[26]

Although Congress had created a Department of Justice—the first in the American experience—for the Attorney General to command, once that department was in operation Benjamin had little to do. He wrote opinions on legal questions asked by other government officers and in the course of this activity acquired a great deal of knowledge about the men and mechanics of the administration. He also became Davis' "greeter," charged with meeting and charming those people too important to be ignored but not important enough to intrude for long upon the President's busy schedule. During the first months, Benjamin became more valuable than his

[26]*Ibid.*, p. 158. Biographies of Benjamin include Robert D. Meade, *Judah P. Benjamin: Confederate Statesman* (New York, 1943); and Rollin C. Osterweis, *Judah P. Benjamin: Statesman of the Lost Cause* (New York, 1933). The "contemporary admirer" was T. C. DeLeon, *Belles, Beaux and Brains of the 60's* (New York, 1907), pp. 91–92.

title, and his relationship with the President began to ripen into friendship and mutual trust.[27]

Secretary of state had always been the premier cabinet post in American-style governments. When Barnwell declined the job, Davis turned to the man he had originally considered for the Treasury, Robert Toombs of Georgia.[28] The Georgian was a large man in several ways. Physically he was tall, heavy, and strong. With friends he was generous and genial in the extreme, with those he judged enemies, devastating. A personification of the hearty "hell of a fellow," Toombs scorned moderation in everything from rhetoric to wine. He had talent and brains, but he never seemed to know what he would do with them at any given moment. Beneath his braggadocio and bombast lay a profound conservatism, the most consistent trait of an inconsistent man. Toombs had begun his political life a Whig, and although he gravitated toward the Democrats in the late 1850s, he was still essentially a Southern Whig in 1861. He was an important man, and the President believed he had acknowledged that importance by asking him to be secretary of state. But Toombs had wanted to be president, and his ego was only partially salved by the gesture.[29]

The Confederacy's message to the world beyond its borders was fairly simple: the Southern nation *de facto* existed and had every right to exist. To the United States the Southerners offered a *fait accompli* and a determination to resist reunion by force as long as necessary. To Europe they added the lure of "King Cotton" as well —"white gold" in exchange for recognition and normal trade relations.

By the time Congress consented to Toomb's appointment, that body had already begun his diplomatic work for him. On February 13, 1861, it resolved to send commissioners to Washington to secure recognition for the Confederacy and settle the problems of public debts and property. On the same day Congress also resolved to assume on behalf of the general government all responsibility for "questions and difficulties" with the United States over forts, arse-

[27]Patrick, *Jefferson Davis and His Cabinet*, pp. 159–162; Hudson Strode, "Judah P. Benjamin's Loyalty to Jefferson Davis," *Georgia Review*, XX (1966), 251–260.

[28]Patrick, *Jefferson Davis and His Cabinet*, p. 78.

[29]*Ibid.*, p. 80. Biographies of Toombs include Ulrich B. Phillips, *The Life of Robert Toombs* (New York, 1913); and William Y. Thompson, *Robert Toombs of Georgia* (Baton Rouge, La., 1966).

nals, and the like. On February 25, President Davis nominated A. B. Roman, Martin J. Crawford, and John Forsyth to go to Washington as representatives of the Confederacy. The commissioners communicated with the new Republican Secretary of State William H. Seward through intermediaries, particularly Supreme Court Justice John A. Campbell of Alabama. Campbell told the Confederates that Seward had promised the evacuation of Sumter and no reinforcement for Fort Pickens. Yet Seward took no official notice of the Southerners' presence, and the United States made no move to evacuate Fort Sumter. As late as April 7, Campbell reassured the commissioners that Seward's intentions were pacific. The Lincoln government kept the commissioners in suspense as to their status and in ignorance as to the intentions of the United States regarding the forts.[30]

During this period Toombs counseled war, Davis hoped for peace, and the Sumter crisis festered. Toombs did, however, have a hand in Confederate diplomacy. On February 13, Congress resolved to send a commission of three to Great Britain, France, and elsewhere in Europe to seek formal recognition and to open trade negotiations. The President then chose Yancey, Pierre A. Rost, and A. Dudley Mann to undertake the mission, and on March 16, Toombs wrote instructions dispatching the trio first to England, then to France.[31]

Toombs' letter of instructions actually formed the basis of Confederate diplomacy throughout the nation's brief life. The Secretary of State began by restating the rationale of secession and remarking upon the tranquility with which disunion had been accomplished. The Confederacy was already, Toombs emphasized, a *de facto* nation and asked only *de jure* sanction. To enhance his point, Toombs drew an analogy between the southern sections of the United States and Italy. The British government had recognized the right of Neapolitans and Sicilians to alter their government; surely the British would do the same for the Confederates. Toombs also emphasized the permanency of the break with the North and detailed the reasons why the Confederacy would confirm with blood its claim to

[30]*Journal of Congress*, I, 46–47, 85–86; Jefferson Davis, *The Rise and Fall of the Confederate States of America*, 2 vols. (New York, 1881), I, 263–295.

[31]*Journal of Congress*, I, 49; Patrick, *Jefferson Davis and His Cabinet*, pp. 82–84; James D. Richardson (ed.), *A Compilation of the Messages and Papers of the Confederacy*, 2 vols. (Nashville, Tenn. 1906), II, 1–8.

independence if war ensued with the United States.[32]

Once the Confederate commissioners had secured official recognition from England, Toombs instructed, they were to commence negotiations leading to a treaty of "friendship, commerce, and navigation." Such a treaty, Toombs declared, would be attractive to the British because the South produced large quantities of cotton and other staples and because the Confederacy had only a small revenue tariff. If international legalities and the inherent righteousness of the cause of Southern independence were not enough to convince British statesmen to recognize the Confederacy, then British self-interest would surely do so. After all, the South might choose or be forced by a blockade to cease shipping cotton to British mills. And in such an event, Toombs estimated that the value of English manufacturing would fall by $600 million. "A delicate allusion to the probability of such an occurence might not be unkindly received by the Minister of Foreign Affairs," Toombs added. The Secretary of State closed by pointing out that the Confederacy had prohibited the foreign slave trade and only regretted that the Southern navy was not yet in a position to send patrol vessels to the West African coast to enforce the prohibition. Otherwise the Confederacy was willing and able to reaffirm all treaty obligations made while its member states were part of the United States.[33]

Naturally the Confederate message to Europe later became more expansive in scope and more refined in presentation. Yet Toombs wrote its essentials at the outset. The choice of European nations the Confederate commissioners visited and the order of these visits was significant. Britain and France possessed great navies and great appetites for Southern cotton. These circumstances and the priority given to Great Britain underscored the Southern belief that cotton was king in the real world of international relations. Having the king in captivity, the Confederates hoped to extract a heavy ransom from his industrialized subjects.[34]

It is also interesting to note in Toombs' diplomatic correspondence the not so subtle treatment of the South's peculiar institution.

[32]Richardson (ed.), *Messages and Papers*, III, 1–8.
[33]*Ibid.*
[34]The classic study of Confederate diplomacy is still Frank Lawrence Owsley, *King Cotton Diplomacy*, 2nd edition revised by Harriet Chappell Owsley (Chicago, 1957). The best recent study of wartime diplomacy on both sides is D. P. Crook, *The North, the South, and the Powers, 1861–1865* (New York, 1974).

In his instructions to Yancey, Rost, and Mann, the Secretary of State wrote euphemistically about the slavery issue as a motive for secession. After discussing political liberty and free trade, Toombs alluded to "the attempt . . . to overthrow the constitutional barriers by which our prosperity, our social system, and our right to control our own institutions were protected." Then, near the end of his instructions, Toombs carefully included mention of the prohibition of the slave trade. Thus did he anticipate and attempt to soften the objection of British abolitionists to official friendship with a republic of slaveholders.[35]

Two months after writing these instructions for the Confederacy's European mission, Toombs composed a similar letter to John T. Pickett, who had just been appointed Confederate agent in Mexico, charging him to do essentially what the commissioners in Europe were to do: secure recognition and a treaty of trade and friendship. The rationale for this approach to the Mexican government was a bit different from that offered Great Britain. To the British, Toombs suggested the attraction between economic opposites and said little about the South's peculiar institution. For the Mexicans, however, Toombs described a community of economic interest between two peoples engaged in extractive and agricultural enterprises. Toombs then added that "the institution of domestic slavery in one country and that of peonage in the other establish between them such a similarity in their system of labor as to prevent any tendency on either side to disregard the feelings and interests of the other."[36]

The attempt on the part of Toombs to project what in effect was a split image of the Confederacy to the rest of the world was a bit naïve. His instructions revealed what became a chronic problem in Confederate diplomacy. Southerners could not be all things to all people; yet they tried to be so, and as a result the Confederate diplomatic image was often unfocused. The Southern nation was by turns a guileless people attacked by a voracious neighbor, an "established" nation in some temporary difficulty, a collection of bucolic aristocrats making a romantic stand against the banalities of industrial democracy, a cabal of commercial farmers seeking to make a pawn of King Cotton, an apotheosis of nineteenth-century

[35]Richardson (ed.), *Messages and Papers,* II, 8.
[36]Toombs to Pickett, May 17, 1861, *ibid.,* II, 20–21.

nationalism and revolutionary liberalism, or the ultimate statement of social and economic reaction.

At the beginning Toombs confidently expected recognition from Europe. He was frustrated. The Confederate commissioners filled their dispatches with hope but also confessed the reality of British neutrality. Lord John Russell, British Secretary of State for Foreign Affairs, was cordial during his informal meetings with the Southerners but committed himself only to wait and see. Since English warehouses bulged with cotton from the bumper crop of 1860, England could afford to wait. When Rost spoke with the Count de Morny, a close friend of Emperor Napoleon III, the French response was similar to the English. In fact the two nations had agreed to act in concert about the "American question." Both England and France recognized the "belligerency" of the Confederacy; that is, they accorded the Southerners the rights of a warring nation and extended captured Confederates the protection of international covenants regarding prisoners. But neither government would go beyond that point at that time.[37]

Toombs was frustrated in more than his expectation of foreign recognition. He also chafed at being in an administration which he did not lead. The President was polite to him, but neither Davis nor the other cabinet members paid sufficient heed to his advice and opinions. Since no foreign nation recognized the Confederacy, the Secretary of State could not exactly lose himself in his work. On one occasion Toombs thundered to a suppliant place monger that the Department of State existed only inside his hat.[38]

The most fertile field for Confederate diplomacy in the early spring of 1861 lay much closer to home than England or France. Eight slave states of the upper South—Delaware, Maryland, Virginia, North Carolina, Tennessee, Kentucky, Missouri, and Arkansas—were still undecided about secession. It was to these states that the Confederacy looked for new members or allies; the existence of slavery was the criterion by which the Southerners identified their friends and enemies. But these eight states shared more than the institution of slavery with the seven states of the Confederacy; they also shared some degree of commitment to Southern ideological

[37]See Yancey and Mann to Toombs, May 21, 1861, *ibid.*, II, 34–48. Crook, *North, South, and the Powers,* pp. 71–97.

[38]DeLeon, *Four Years,* p. 33; Patrick, *Jefferson Davis and His Cabinet,* pp. 84–85.

values and thus an attraction to Southern nationalism. This created a serious dilemma, a crisis of identity, no less than that of deciding whether they were Southerners or Americans. The Confederates honored their heritage as Americans, but they had rejected the direction and values of the majority of their American contemporaries and had established an alternative nationality. Because the Confederacy existed as the national expression of the Southern world view, people in the border slave states, individually and corporately, faced a decision: to remain an American section or to embrace a Southern nation.

For some, such as Edmund Ruffin of Virginia, the decision was simple. On March 3, the day before Abraham Lincoln's inauguration, Ruffin left Virginia and went to Charleston to "avoid being . . . under his [Lincoln's] government even for an hour."[39] But for others in the border South the decision was agonizingly difficult. For example, Ruffin's fellow Virginian Robert E. Lee pondered his fate for quite some time before resigning his commission in the United States Army. Lee opposed secession and war; "I recognize no necessity for this state of things," he wrote. But when secession and war came, he made his decision: "With all my devotion to the Union and the feeling of loyalty and duty of an American citizen, I have not been able to make up my mind to raise my hand against my relatives, my children, my home. I have, therefore, resigned my commission in the Army, and save in defense of my native State . . . I hope I may never be called upon to draw my sword."[40] Lee's response was visceral and reasoned at the same time. Ultimately more Southerners identified with Lee than Ruffin.

On February 4, the same day that delegates from the deep Southern states met in Montgomery to create the Confederacy, Virginians went to the polls to choose delegates to a state convention. They elected forty-six secessionists and 106 moderates of varying tempers. For some time the convention's moderate majority placed its hopes upon the Washington "Peace Convention," a meeting of state delegates sponsored by Virginian ex-President John Tyler which unsuccessfully sought sectional compromise. The Virginia delegates sat during February and March, listened to speeches by

[39]Scarborough (ed.), *Ruffin Diary*, I, 557.
[40]Lee to Dear Sister [Mrs. Anne Marshall], April 20, 1861, in Captain R. E. Lee, *Recollections and Letters of General Robert E. Lee* (Garden City, N.Y., 1904), p. 26.

deep South secessionists, and voted for continued union with the North. Governor John Letcher exerted little influence upon the proceedings because he was of much the same moderate mind as the delegates. Senator Robert M. T. Hunter was a cautious secessionist, while Hunter's rival in state politics, former Governor Henry A. Wise, led the radical movement. In April, Wise, on the pretext that Virginia's convention no longer represented the wishes of its constituents, organized a "Spontaneous Southern Rights Convention" to meet in Richmond on the sixteenth. Wise hoped that the well-planned, "spontaneous" meeting would prod the regular convention into action and would become the nucleus of a "resistance party" in Virginia. The radicals took heart when on March 2 the Washington Peace Convention broke up in despair and when a delegation from the Virginia convention secured no concrete concessions from President Lincoln. But even though support for the Union in Virginia's convention eroded a bit in March and early April, Wise and the secessionist leadership were less than optimistic about immediate disunion. The radicals made more and louder speeches, but in the convention the moderates still had enough votes to keep Virginia in the Union.[41]

Because North Carolina was Southern more in terms of yeoman democracy than in terms of slaveholding aristocracy, the state shared little of the radical temper of its cousin to the south. Governor John W. Ellis led the secessionist movement, but his constituents were slow to follow. After considerable debate in the state legislature, a referendum bill summoned North Carolinians to the polls to decide on holding a convention and to elect delegates to the convention should it be held. On February 28 the voters rejected a convention by a very narrow margin and selected a strongly pro-Union slate of delegates. Among eighty-six counties, thirty voted secessionist; thirty-five voted unconditional unionist; seventeen voted conditional unionist; and four divided votes to the point of no decision. The vote was a fair index of sentiment in the state. As a

[41]Robert Gray Gunderson, *Old Gentleman's Convention: The Washington Peace Conference of 1861* (Madison, Wis., 1961); Henry T. Shanks, *The Secession Movement in Virginia, 1847–1861* (Richmond, Va., 1934); Ralph A. Wooster, *The Secession Conventions of the South* (Princeton, N.J., 1962), pp. 139–148; George H. Reese (ed.), *Proceedings of the Virginia State Convention of 1861*, 4 vols. (Richmond, Va., 1965); and William W. Freehling, "The Editorial Revolution, Virginia, and the Coming of the Civil War: A Review Essay," *Civil War History*, XVI (1970), 64–72.

rule, Democrats tended more toward secession than did Old Whigs, and secessionists were stronger in the eastern part of the state than in the Piedmont or Appalachian regions. When the Washington Peace Convention dissolved in failure, North Carolina despaired; but as long as the Union remained in a state of peaceable ambiguity, North Carolina remained in the Union.[42]

Tennessee moderate John Bell had carried his home state in the presidential election of 1860, and as a body Tennesseeans assumed essentially the same position regarding the secession crisis as did North Carolinians. As in North Carolina geography was an important factor in the population's attitude toward disunion. The yeoman-dominated mountains of east Tennessee were unionist country; the planter-oriented flatlands of west Tennessee were more receptive to secession. Middle Tennessee was divided. Although Tennessee Governor Isham G. Harris, like North Carolina's Ellis, was a secessionist, and Tennessee Democrats except for party leader Andrew Johnson tended more toward secession than did the Old Whigs for whom Bell was spokesman, on February 9 the voters soundly defeated a convention referendum and chose an overwhelmingly unionist slate of hypothetical delegates to the convention they decided not to call. As the Sumter crisis deepened in April of 1861, Tennesseeans watched and worried. But at that point not enough of them felt threatened enough by the Republican administration to leave the United States.[43]

On February 18, the same day on which Jefferson Davis took the oath as provisional president of the Confederacy, Arkansas voters went to the polls to vote on a state convention. Although they voted to hold a convention, they elected a slim but staunch majority of unionist delegates; the conservatives held an unshakable four-vote margin in the convention. After considerable wrangling and many fiery speeches, the Arkansas convention resolved to hold an August referendum on secession, and adjourned. The secessionists had tried their best and failed.[44]

[42]Wooster, *Secession Conventions*, pp. 190–194; J. Carlyle Sitterson, *The Secessionist Movement in North Carolina* (Chapel Hill, N.C., 1939).

[43]Wooster, *Secession Conventions*, pp. 173–180; J. Milton Henry, "The Revolution in Tennessee, February, 1861, to June, 1861," *Tennessee Historical Quarterly*, XVIII (1959), 99–119.

[44]Wooster, *Secession Conventions*, pp. 155–164; Jack Scruggs, "Arkansas in the Secession Crisis," *Arkansas Historical Quarterly*, XII (1953), 179–192; David Y. Thomas,

88   THE CONFEDERATE NATION

By 1861, Missouri had long been involved in North-South controversy. From the congressional debates over statehood in 1819 and 1820 and participation as some of the bloodletters in the controversy over slavery in "Bleeding Kansas" in the late 1850s, Missourians should have been accustomed to sectional crises. Yet, in spite of this experience, the secession crisis was traumatic in Missouri. Led by Governor Claiborne F. Jackson and former Senator David R. Atchison, the secessionists persuaded the legislature to call a state convention and then launched a vigorous campaign to elect pro-Confederate delegates. Unionists, however, countered with success, and on February 18, Missouri voters selected a convention slate in which not one delegate publicly favored immediate secession. When the convention assembled ten days later, the delegates made moderate member Sterling Price their presiding officer and then proceeded to examine Missouri's relations with the United States. The result was a seven-point program defining the state's position as peaceable. Missouri would remain in the Union but asked for a constitutional amendment guaranteeing the sanctity of slave property and expressed its opposition to coercion of the seceded states. Then the convention adjourned. Missouri, like other states on the border, remained in the Union but reserved the right to change its mind.[45]

With the possible exception of Virginia, no state displayed more agony of indecision about its ultimate loyalty than Kentucky. Birthplace of presidents, both of the United and Confederate States, Kentucky also claimed the compromise tradition of Henry Clay. Governor Boriah Magoffin was a Southern rights man, but Senator John J. Crittenden was the author of a major compromise proposal, an unamendable amendment to the Constitution sanctifying property in slaves south of latitude 36° 30'. Vice-President John C. Breckinridge, Kentucky's Democratic presidential candidate in 1860, backed Crittenden's scheme (presumably to rid himself of the secessionist label, which had lost him the state's electoral votes to John

---

Arkansas in War and Reconstruction (Little Rock, Ark., 1926); Thomas S. Staples, "The Arkansas Secession Convention of 1861," *Southwestern Political Science and Social Science Association, Proceedings* . . . (Fort Worth, Tex., 1925).

[45]Wooster, *Secession Conventions*, pp. 223–239; William H. Lyon, "Clairborne Fox Jackson and the Secession Crisis in Missouri," *Missouri Historical Review*, LVIII (1964), pp. 422–441.

Bell). The deep South's looming independence and the lukewarm national reception of Crittenden's compromise led Governor Magoffin in late December to call the legislature into special session to call a state convention—the first step toward secession. But even though Breckinridge endorsed the proposed convention, Kentucky's legislature turned down the Governor's request and adjourned until late March. Although the sectional crisis had deepened by the time the legislature again convened, indecision and hope for compromise still dominated that body. Kentucky continued to be divided but in the Union, committed only to the vain hope of sectional compromise.[46]

Maryland in the spring of 1861 was a border state with sharply divided loyalties. The southern and eastern shore sections of the state were extensions of eastern Virginia, while in northern and western Maryland people identified with western Virginia unionism. During the secession crisis the actions of Maryland Governor Thomas Hicks and of the Washington government were crucial. Hicks refused to call the legislature into session and thus prevented corporate action on secession; however much the Maryland secessionists fumed and threatened; they could do little without some legislative sanction. Lincoln realized that if Maryland and Virginia seceded, the Union would have to abandon Washington and lose an enormous amount of prestige and property to the Southern rebels. He played a decisive role in Maryland's fate by moving troops into the state to prevent any untoward move by disunionists. The Confederates believed, probably correctly, that large numbers of Marylanders desired to join the new nation. But the presence of an equal or greater degree of unionist sentiment, supported by the energy of Hicks and Lincoln, made Maryland a doubtful ally of the Confederacy.[47]

The last and least of the slave states was Delaware, with only 1,800 slaves. When the legislature gathered for its regular session in January, 1861, Delaware lawmakers heard speeches from Southern commissioners and received a formal invitation from Georgia to join it in secession. Never, however, did the Delaware legislature seriously

[46]Wooster, *Secession Conventions,* pp. 207–214; E. Merton Coulter, *The Civil War and Readjustment in Kentucky* (Chapel Hill, N.C., 1926), pp. 1–51.

[47]Wooster, *Secession Conventions,* pp. 242–243; George L. P. Radcliffe, *Governor Thomas H. Hicks of Maryland and the Civil War* (Baltimore, 1901).

consider disunion; indeed on two occassions it passed statements strongly condemning secession.[48]

On the eve of confrontation at Fort Sumter, then, the slave states that had remained in the Union were in great flux. It was clear, or at least should have been clear, to the Montgomery and Washington governments that nothing decisive would happen in the upper South and border states until the Confederate and United States had had some kind of showdown. As long as the two "nations" existed in undefined relation to each other, border Southerners could live suspended between them. Only when the relationship between the Union and the Confederacy crystallized as peaceful coexistence or war would a choice be necessary. Until the showdown, the slave states could watch and wait, and they did.

However much the border South wished to avoid a confrontation between the Washington and Montgomery governments, by April of 1861 both Jefferson Davis and Abraham Lincoln had good reason to seek one. Neither president wanted war, but both had to have an end to the ambiguity surrounding the secession crisis. During his first month in office Lincoln could afford to stall. He needed to form his administration, he hoped that the great mass of Southern whites would "come to their senses," and he sought support for the Union among the border states.[49] Davis, too, required time to construct his government and tc proselytize among the slave states still in the Union. By April, though, both governments had done what they could about the border South; people and governments on both sides had begun to clamor for decisive action.

In addition the crises at Fort Sumter and Fort Pickens required resolution. At Fort Pickens, Braxton Bragg's Confederates were about as numerous and as well trained as they were ever going to be, and it was apparent that the United States intended to reinforce its forces. Bragg wrote Davis that he could storm the fort but that chances of success or failure were about even, and in either event the attack would be costly. Davis hoped for better odds than that.[50]

At Sumter the situation had become critical. Major Anderson and

[48]Wooster, *Secession Conventions*, pp. 251–255.
[49]See Kenneth M. Stampp, *The Era of Reconstruction, 1865–1877* (New York, 1965), pp. 24–49, for an interpretation of Lincoln's policy in regard to the nonplanters in the South.
[50]See McWhiney, "First Shot," 5–14.

his garrison were running out of food. Women and children, dependents of the troops, left the fort in early February; but even without the extra mouths to feed, Anderson calculated that he would be starved out before mid-April. To retain Sumter the United States would have to send in supplies. To be rid of the Union presence in Charleston Harbor the Confederacy would then be compelled to open fire on the resupply ship or the fort or both. Both sides accepted the confrontation then and there.

On April 7 a federal fleet sailed for Charleston to resupply Anderson's garrison. A day later the Confederate commissioners in Washington received a letter, dated March 15 but held back by Seward, stating that the United States had no intention of abandoning Sumter. The same day, April 8, Robert Chew of the United States State Department arrived in Charleston and personally read a message from his President to Governor Pickens, which explained that Lincoln planned to send provisions to Fort Sumter but would not send more troops or arms. After Pickens had heard his tidings, Chew left in some haste.[51]

Pickens promptly relayed Lincoln's message to the Confederate military commander at Charleston, General P. G. T. Beauregard, who passed the news on to his commander-in-chief in Montgomery. Then it was Davis' turn to act. All along he had believed that war was inevitable, and although he did not wish to fire the first shot, he perceived no alternative. Accordingly, on the tenth, Secretary of War Walker sent orders by telegraph to Beauregard to demand evacuation and to reduce the fort should the demand be refused.[52]

At two o'clock on the afternoon of April 11, Beauregard sent a written demand to Anderson. Two of the General's aides, Colonel James Chesnut and Captain Stephen D. Lee, presented the note to Anderson with appropriate formality. No one involved in the Sumter confrontation missed the drama and import of what was happening. Beneath the courtesy and fastidious propriety of the proceedings, however, were the hard facts that Anderson refused to move and Beauregard meant to move him.[53]

[51]Crawford, *Sumter*, pp. 113–420.
[52]Beauregard to Walker, April 8, 1861, *O.R.*, ser. I, I, 297; Walker to Beauregard, April 10, 1861, *O.R.*, ser. I, I, 297.
[53]Beauregard to Anderson, April 11, 1861, *O.R.*, ser. I, I, 15. Anderson to Beauregard, April 11, 1861, *O.R.*, ser. I, I, 15.

After informing Chesnut and Lee of his determination to remain at his post, Anderson said, almost as an afterthought, that he would be starved out within a few days whether the Confederates fired on him or not. Chesnut reported these words to Beauregard, and the General decided to make one last effort to avoid a fight. Consequently Chesnut and Lee again rowed out to Sumter, around one o'clock on the morning of the twelfth. This time Beauregard's note requested the day and hour when Anderson could consider himself starved out and would evacuate. The Union Major conferred with his officers for almost two hours and then agreed to leave Sumter at noon on April 15, providing the circumstances regarding resupply did not change. Chesnut, the senior Confederate officer present, took only a few minutes to read Anderson's proposal and reject it. Lincoln's resupply fleet was overdue already; the Confederacy must have Sumter by the time it arrived. At 3:20 A.M., Chesnut informed Anderson that the shore batteries would open fire on Fort Sumter in one hour. The Southerners then bade somewhat emotional farewells and left Anderson to his fate.[54]

During these last few hours of peace, Edmund Ruffin was on Morris Island sleeping in his clothes among the sand fleas. The old man was determined to have a part in the fight for Fort Sumter, and so he had joined the Palmetto Guard, South Carolina Infantry. At four o'clock in the morning the Palmetto Guard rolled out of their makeshift beds and hurried to their guns. Ruffin stood by Columbiad number one, the first of the heaviest class of seacoast weapons, in the Iron Battery.

At four-thirty a thin, red arc appeared in the sky over Sumter. It was the burning fuse of a ten-inch mortar shell from Fort Johnson on the southern shore of Charleston Harbor. The shell burst about a hundred feet above the center of the fort. This was the signal, ordered by Chesnut after he left Anderson, to begin the bombardment. Mortar batteries opened soon after, and at dawn Ruffin jerked the lanyard of his Columbiad. Afterward the zealous old man claimed that his was the first shot of the war. Perhaps because of Ruffin's age and fame, no one then seriously disputed his claim. As time passed and the war became a disaster, few but Ruffin would have admitted starting it.[55]

[54]Crawford, *Sumter*, pp. 422–426.
[55]Scarborough, (ed.), *Ruffin Diary*, I, 588–589.

Fort Sumter and Anderson's garrison did not resist long. The Federals answered the Confederate fire, but they were short not only of food but also of gunpowder. At 2:30 P.M. on April 13, Anderson sent word that he was prepared to surrender, and on the afternoon of the fourteenth the stars and stripes came down from the makeshift flagstaff over Sumter. Ironically, the only casualties of the first battle in the new war occurred during the flag-striking ceremony. Some gunpowder exploded, killing one Union soldier outright and wounding five others, one mortally. When the Palmetto Guard occupied the fort later that day, the first man ashore was "Private" Edmund Ruffin. He immediately set to work gathering souvenirs to send to his "slowpoke," sometime-Southern friends in Virginia.[56]

In Washington, Lincoln responded to the attack on Sumter by calling for 75,000 volunteer troops to suppress "combinations too powerful to be suppressed by the ordinary course of judicial proceedings, or by the powers vested in the marshals by law." By so doing he accepted the challenge of armed conflict without accepting the legality of secession or the reality of the Confederacy. The flood of volunteers in the North and the enthusiastic cooperation of state governments there supported Lincoln's determination and his logic. In the border South, however, the President's call for volunteers pushed the slave states off the fence. When United States Secretary of War Simon Cameron presented the appropriate troop requisitions to state governors, middle ground between North and South disappeared. At that point the states of upper South had to answer their President's call to arms or find a new president.

Now things moved quickly. On April 17 the Virginia state convention became a secession convention by adopting 88 to 55 an ordinance dissolving the state's bonds with the Union. Delegates from the far western counties, however, strongly dissented from the majority stance, and on the evening of the seventeenth, as secessionists were celebrating in the streets, the western unionists met in a Richmond hotel to take the first step toward their own secession—from Virginia.[57]

In the wake of Lincoln's call to arms, North Carolina's Governor Ellis called a special session of his legislature and urged that body

56 *Ibid.,* 593–601.
57 Wooster, *Secession Conventions,* pp. 148–154.

to call a secession convention. Circumstances and minds had changed since the last time North Carolinians had considered secession. This time the legislature was nearly unanimous in passing the convention bill, and when the body assembled on May 20, the principal debate concerned whether to base North Carolina's secession on the right of revolution or on the traditional state-sovereignty compact theory. By the end of the day's session the convention had removed North Carolina from the Union.[58]

Governor Isham Harris of Tennessee also called his legislature back into session after receiving requests for troops from Washington. Harris, however, believed that the secession convention process would be too slow. Therefore he urged the legislature to declare Tennessee's independence and refer the *fait accompli* to the voters. The solons complied and on May 7 approved a military alliance with the Confederacy. When the voters finally made their voice heard, they endorsed secession from the United States and union with the Confederacy by more than a two-to-one majority, although eastern Tennesseans, even after the fact of secession, voted against the proceeding by 32,923 to 14,780.[59]

In Arkansas the slim majority of unionist votes in the convention before Sumter melted away. The state convention which reassembled on May 6 took only one day to pass an ordinance of secession, 65 to 5.[60]

In response to the larger conflict between North and South, Missouri conducted its own intrastate civil war. After Lincoln's call for volunteers, bands of unionists and secessionist radicals armed themselves, and when United States troops attacked a pro-Southern state militia camp near St. Louis, fighting reminiscent of "Bleeding Kansas" began in the state. The Union army held Missouri in the Union, but violence continued. The state convention reassembled in late July and took a pro-Union position; however, many secessionists, including Governor Claibourne Jackson, were not in attendence. Jackson remained with his militia and in October 1861 called the legislature to meet at Neosho in the southwest corner of the state. The assembly rump promptly declared Missouri out of the Union, and on November 29, the Confederacy admitted Missouri

[58] *Ibid.*, pp. 194–203.
[59] *Ibid.*, pp. 180–189.
[60] *Ibid.*, pp. 164–172.

and pronounced legitimate what was in essence a state government in exile. Missouri had stars in both American flags and representatives in two governments. For all practical purposes, however, the state remained in Union hands.[61]

Kentucky sought neutrality. Governor Boriah Magoffin refused the request for troops from Washington and called a special session of the legislature to address the sectional crisis. He hoped for secession, but when the legislature rejected any radical course, he settled for a proclamation of neutrality. The neutral posture, however, lasted only a few months. Confederate troops entered the state in September 1861; in response to this violation of neutrality, the legislature reconfirmed the state's allegiance to the United States. As in Missouri, a pro-Southern rump government proclaimed Kentucky's secession and gained admission to the Confederacy, and like Missouri, Kentucky actually remained in the Union. About twice as many Kentuckians joined Union armies as fought in Confederate units.[62]

One week after the firing on Sumter a Baltimore mob attacked Massachusetts troops on their way to Washington. Fearing for his capital, Lincoln sent more soldiers into Maryland, and Governor Hicks called the state legislature into special session. Members of that body were loud in their condemnation of Hicks and Lincoln, yet they never took the long step of secession. Even though Southern sympathizers sang in "Maryland, My Maryland" of "the despot's heel" and called upon listeners to "Avenge the patriotic gore/that flecked the streets of Baltimore," Maryland, like Missouri and Kentucky, was very much in the Union.[63]

Mobilization and war added six stars to the Confederate flag, but two of those states, Kentucky and Missouri, remained occupied by the enemy throughout. Thus the Confederacy gained four of the eight border states: Virginia, North Carolina, Tennessee, and Arkansas. Even if the Southern nation failed to gain all the territory it had sought, the Sumter crisis had forced genuine self-determination of peoples.

[61]*Ibid.*, pp. 238–241.
[62]*Ibid.*, pp. 214–222.
[63]*Ibid.*, pp. 243–251.

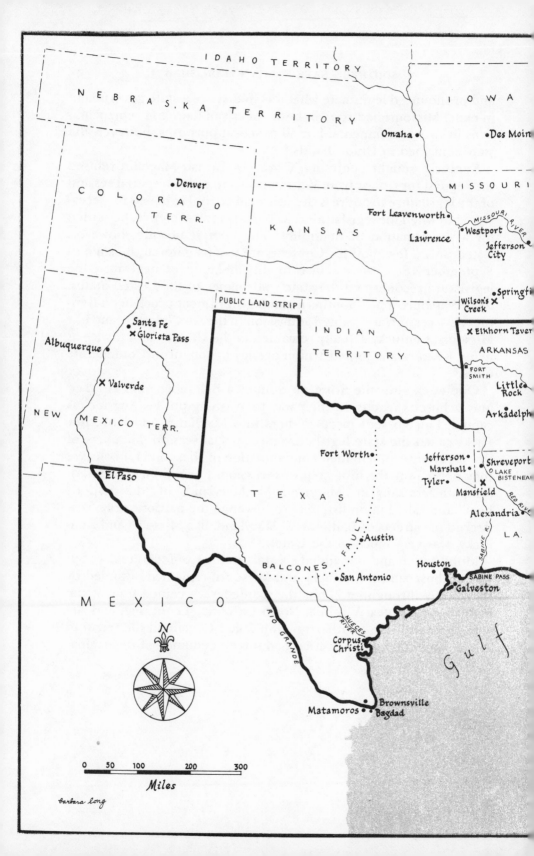

IDAHO TERRITORY

NEBRASKA TERRITORY

IOWA

• Omaha   • Des Moin

COLORADO
TERR.
• Denver

MISSOURI

Fort Leavenworth •
KANSAS
Lawrence •   • Westport
                   • Jefferson
                     City

PUBLIC LAND STRIP

INDIAN

TERRITORY

Santa Fe •
× Glorieta Pass
Albuquerque •
× Valverde

NEW MEXICO TERR.

• El Paso

Wilson's ×   × Springfi
Creek

× Elkhorn Taver

ARKANSAS

FORT
SMITH
Little •
Rock

Arkadelph

T E X A S

Fort Worth •

Jefferson •
Marshall •   • Shreveport
Tyler •   ○ LAKE
             BISTINEA
× Mansfield

Alexandria •

L. A.

FAULT

• Austin

BALCONES

• San Antonio

MEXICO

RIO GRANDE

NUECES RIVER

Houston •   SABINE PASS
          • Galveston

Corpus
Christi •

Gulf

Brownsville •
Matamoros • • Bagdad

N

0   50 100   200   300
Miles

barbara long

WISCONSIN
Lake Michigan
Detroit
Rockford
Chicago
MICHIGAN
Lake Erie
NEW YORK
CONN.
Cleveland
PENNSYLVANIA
New York
ILLINOIS
INDIANA
OHIO
Pittsburgh
Trenton
Philadelphia
Gettysburg
Springfield
Indianapolis
Columbus
WEST
VIRGINIA
(1863)
Baltimore
MD.
Washington
Annapolis
St. Louis
OHIO RIVER
Charleston
Fredericksburg
Louisville
Frankfort
Lexington
White
Sulphur
Springs
VA.
Lynchburg
Richmond
Petersburg
Norfolk
Paducah
Elizabethtown
Bacon Creek
KY.
Mill
Springs
Perryville
Saltville
Danville
NORTH CAROLINA
Albemarle Sd.
Roanoke
Island
Cairo
Columbus
FORT
DONELSON
Bowling
Green
CUMBERLAND R.
Durham Station
Raleigh
Goldsboro
FORT
HENRY
TENN.
Nashville
Murfreesboro
Tullahoma
Knoxville
Asheville
Salisbury
Charlotte
Bentonville
Fayetteville
New Bern
Jackson
Shiloh
Pittsburg Ldg.
Chattanooga
Memphis
Corinth
TENNESSEE RIVER
WESTERN
SOUTH
CAROLINA
Wilmington
FORT FISHER
Holly
Springs
Tupelo
Okolona
Columbia
MISS.
Fayetteville
Atlanta
AND
Augusta
Charleston
FORT SUMTER
CHICKASAW BLUFFS
Vicksburg
Edward's Depot
Jackson
Champion's Hill
Brierfield
chez
Five Points
Opelika
Selma
Meridian
Montgomery
Columbus
Macon
ATLANTIC R.R.
Savannah
Port Royal harbor
Hilton Head Island
Atlantic
Ocean
ALABAMA
GEORGIA
Irwinsville
OKEFENOKEE
SWAMP
on
ouge
ort
Hudson
Mobile
Pensacola
FORT
PICKENS
Lake
City
Ocean
Pond
Fernandina
Jacksonville
St. Augustine
New Orleans
FORT ST. PHILIP
FORT JACKSON
of
Mexico
FLORIDA
Bahama Islands
New Providence
Nassau

The Confederate
States
of America
1861 ~ 1865

Havana
Bahama Channel
CUBA

CHAPTER 5

Southern Nationality Confirmed

R OBERT Mercer Taliaferro Hunter, Virginian, went to Montgomery to take the Confederate government back with him to Virginia. And when Hunter set his mind to a thing, he usually succeeded.

During his youth Hunter's classmates at the University of Virginia had dubbed him "Run Mad Tom," after his initials, but since that time his name had inspired little or no frivolity. A native of the tidewater, Hunter had been congressman and senator from Virginia, and by the time of the secession crisis, he was one of the most influential men in American politics. Hunter followed John C. Calhoun politically from Whig to Democratic Party and intellectually even after the South Carolinian's death. In 1843, Hunter was chief among those who sought Calhoun's election to the presidency; in 1860 Hunter himself was a candidate. Although he had no outstanding mental or physical gifts, Hunter was "sound," and he was an expert political mechanic.

Hunter resigned his seat in the United States Senate in March of 1861 and accepted the secession convention's appointment to represent Virginia in the Confederate Congress. From the beginning his ruling passion was moving the capital from Montgomery to Richmond. The idea was not original with him, but he was the man most likely to carry it through.[1]

[1]The standard biography of Hunter is Henry H. Simms, *Life of Robert M. T. Hunter: A Study in Sectionalism and Secession* (Richmond, Va., 1935). The Calhoun connection

On May 1, in the Confederate Congress, Walter Brooks of Mississippi introduced a bill to move the capital, and a few days earlier Vice-President Stephens, in Richmond to contract an alliance with Virginia, had broached the same topic. The Virginia state secession convention had already voted to leave the Union but had made secession contingent upon voter ratification in a referendum to be held May 17. Davis had no intention of winning Virginia and then watching helplessly as Federal troops overran his prize; the Confederacy wanted Virginia before May 17. Thus Davis dispatched Stephens on April 19 and three days later sent thirteen regiments to Virginia from among those mustering in the deep South. Stephens proposed to the secession convention a "temporary military alliance" between Virginia and the Confederacy. Of course such an arrangement would make the referendum meaningless, but on this occasion Stephens was willing to rise above legalism. As he concluded his appeal to the convention for early action, the Vice-President pointed out the advantage of centralized military command at Montgomery or, he added, "it [the command] may be at Richmond. For, while I have no authority to speak on that subject, I feel at perfect liberty to say that it is quite within the range of probability that, if such an alliance is made, the seat of our government will within a few weeks, be moved to this place." Stephens and commissioners from the Virginia convention drew up an alliance the next day, and on April 27 the convention issued a formal invitation to the Confederate government to move to Richmond.[2]

On the strength of the alliance agreement that Stephens made with the Virginia convention, Congress admitted Virginia to the Confederacy on May 7. Three days later Hunter took his seat at the

---

is established in James L. Anderson and W. Edwin Hemphill, "The 1843 Biography of John C. Calhoun: Was R. M. T. Hunter Its Author," *Journal of Southern History*, XXXVIII (1972) 469–474.

[2]*Journal of the Congress of the Confederate States of America, 1861–1865*, 7 vols. (Washington, D.C., 1904–1905), I, 173–174. Fears for Virginia's safety are reflected in J. B. Jones, *A Rebel War Clerk's Diary*, ed. by Howard Swiggett, 2 vols. (New York, 1935), I, 26–27. On the Stephens mission see Davis to Letcher April 19, 1861, and Davis to Letcher (telegram) in Dunbar Rowland (ed.), *Jefferson Davis Constitutionalist: His Letters, Papers and Speeches*, 10 vols. (Jackson, Miss., 1923), V, 64–65; Stephens' speech in Henry Cleveland, *Alexander H. Stephens, in Public and Private* (Philadelphia, 1866), 729–744; and Virginia's response in *Ordinances Adopted by the Convention of Virginia, in Secret and Adjourned Sessions in April, May, June and July 1861*, pp. 3–5, and Richmond *Enquirer*, May 3, 1861.

head of the Virginia congressional delegation and immediately began his campaign to move from Montgomery. It was successful. On May 11, Congress resolved by vote of 5 to 3 (Alabama, Florida, and South Carolina) to hold its next session in Richmond. Then the wrangling began. President Davis returned the resolution with the observation that not only Congress but the entire government ought to move—or at least be in the same place. Accordingly Congress voted to move the seat of government *in toto*. Meanwhile each time Hunter walked past the marble works in Montgomery on his way to the capitol he was reportedly "in agony." The sight of tombstones triggered fear that he would sicken and die in Alabama, never to see Virginia again.[3]

Many factors motivated the decision to move the capital. For some congressmen the poor quality of accommodations at the Exchange Hotel and the voracious appetites of Montgomery's mosquitoes were decisive considerations; for others the dearth of office space for governmental activities was a prime concern. The political consequences of Virginia's secession were also involved. In 1861, Virginia was too large, rich, and powerful to ignore, and what better way of celebrating the Old Dominion's adherence to the new nation than to move the national capital to its state capital. No less important were Richmond's Tredegar Iron Works, the only facility in the Confederacy capable of manufacturing large machinery and heavy weapons. Richmond was, for a time at least, absolutely essential regardless of where the capital was. Perhaps the most often heard reason for transferring the seat of government was the proximity of Virginia to Washington and thus to Union armies. If Davis' administration was to be a war government, then why not move it near the front so that the Commander-in-Chief might better command?[4]

Hindsight has inspired serious second thoughts about the wisdom of this move. Locating the government near the front lines might indeed have helped the Davis administration direct the war, at least in the East. But Richmond's proximity to Washington worked the other way round as well. Once the Confederacy commit-

[3]*Journal of Congress*, I, 192–193, 205, 212–213, 242–243, 254–255. The Hunter story is in Jones, *War Clerk's Diary*, I, 41.

[4]Rembert W. Patrick, *Jefferson Davis and His Cabinet* (Baton Rouge, La., 1944), 321–324; Emory M. Thomas, *The Confederate State of Richmond: A Biography of the Capital* (Austin, Tex., 1971), pp. 33–34; Frank E. Vandiver, *Ploughshares into Swords: Josiah Gorgas and Confederate Ordinance* (Austin, Tex. 1952), p. 59.

ted itself to an essentially defensive war, the capital, because of its location, was vulnerable to enemy attack. And from a strategic standpoint, locating the government in Virginia limited the interest and enthusiasm of that government for operations west of the Appalachians. Finally, given the endemic limitations of transportation and communications, situating the capital on the geographical fringe of the new nation diluted the government's power and influence in the vast Southern hinterland.[5]

Still, on the balance the move from Montgomery to Richmond was no blunder. Because of its industrial importance to the Confederacy, Richmond needed protecting, especially in 1861 and 1862. If the Davis government sometimes seemed to wear blinders that restricted its vision to the war's eastern theater (a debatable point), that was a sin of administration, not location. Moreover, from the vantage of hindsight, it would appear that the North's preoccupation with "on to Richmond" hindered the Union war effort more than it threatened the Confederacy. Because Richmond was so close and because they equated Richmond's capture with the collapse of the Confederacy, the Federals devoted massive amounts of time, manpower, and materiel to the project. The taking of Richmond promised quick victory; indeed when the city finally fell, the Confederacy followed. But the illusion of quick victory at Richmond cost the United States resources that might have been better spent elsewhere. For three years Richmond was a magnet that lured Federal armies onto killing grounds and sidetracked the Union war effort into frustration. Only during the war's final ten months did Richmond become a military millstone around the Confederacy's neck, and by that time the attrition of war had nearly exhausted resistance everywhere.[6]

When Congress adjourned on May 21, the Confederates were still thinking first thoughts about Richmond. In 1861 Richmond was an old town and a young city rolled into one. Located at the falls of the James River, Richmond had long been a typical ante-bellum Southern city: a center of transportation and trade between the countryside and the larger world. Like other Southern cities, Richmond was

[5]See Jerrell Shofner and William W. Rogers, "Montgomery to Richmond," *Civil War History* X (1964), 155–166.

[6]Thomas, *Confederate Richmond*, pp. 33–34. See also Douglas S. Freeman, "The Confederate Tradition of Richmond," *Civil War History*, III (1957), 360–373.

a political center, too, and the Virginia state capitol, designed by Thomas Jefferson, dominated the city's panorama.

Unlike other Southern cities, however, Richmond had become by 1861 a center of manufacturing and industry. Its flour mills and tobacco factories processed local agricultural products, and its thriving iron industry was the largest in the South, with more than 1,500 workers (900 at the Tredegar Works) fashioning products worth $2 million in 1860. Railroads and port facilities, too, had changed Richmond's trading-post economy into major commercial enterprise.

Still, Richmond was Southern. Men of industry and capital might dominate the city's marketplaces, but planters and their wives still ruled Richmond's drawing rooms.

Whiggish politics had long characterized the city, and Richmond's voters gave the Constitutional Union ticket a two-to-one majority in 1860. Yet the city also had one of the most influential Democratic dailies in the United States, the Richmond *Enquirer,* justly called the "Democratic Bible." Industrial slaves and an un-Southern percentage of German and Irish immigrants were among Richmond's 37,910 inhabitants, but they posed no real problem for the urban aristocrats who ruled the city. The city's "Negro Ordinance" placed the municipal authorities in the role of surrogate masters to keep black people, both free and bonded, in place. And immigrant labor was important to Richmond's industrial growth. In 1861, at least, magnolias and mills coexisted in Richmond.[7]

The Confederacy came suddenly to Richmond. First the city became an armed camp—the rendezvous point, training camp, and supply base of Southern volunteer soldiers. Then, on May 29, Jefferson Davis led the governmental immigration. Davis' journey by train from Montgomery to Richmond was triumphal; at every stop along the route Southerners came to the station to cheer the new President and his traveling companions, Louis T. Wigfall of Texas and Secretary of State Robert Toombs, in "one continuous ovation." Richmond was the crescendo; cannon roared in salute as

[7]Thomas, *Confederate Richmond,* pp. 15–31. See also Samuel Mordecai, *Richmond in By-Gone Days* (Richmond, Va., 1946); W. Ashbury Christian, *Richmond, Her Past and Present* (Richmond, Va., 1912); Mary Newton Stanard, *Richmond, Its People and Its Story* (Philadelphia, 1923); and Louis H. Manarin (ed.), *Richmond at War: The Minutes of the City Council, 1861–1865* (Chapel Hill, N.C., 1966).

Davis rode through large crowds to his temporary quarters in the Spotswood Hotel. The President arrived in his capital in the morning; by late afternoon he was in the saddle inspecting troops.[8]

Approximately 1,000 government employees, from president and cabinet members to clerks, made the trip from Montgomery to Richmond. Eventually some 70,000 civil servants worked for the Confederate government. Because the Southern nation was new, opportunities for the loaves and fishes of patronage were unprecedented. So the would-be great joined the great and near great in Richmond, and the new capital became more crowded and frenzied than Montgomery had been.[9]

To command the armies which trained in Richmond and elsewhere, Davis could rely upon former United States officers who felt sufficiently Southern to resign their commissions and offer their swords to the Confederacy as Lee had done. The Confederate high command was overwhelmingly composed of Southerners and men who possessed training and experience in the "old army."

The rank-and-file Southern soldiers who flocked to Richmond lent a carnival atmosphere to the capital that partially obscured political machinations. The dress rehearsal for war that lasted for more than three months after the Sumter confrontation was a mixture of preparation and picnic for Confederate volunteers. Perhaps no military unit caught the spirit of the time as well as the New Orleans Zouaves. Recruited from the jails of New Orleans, the men of this regiment wore Turkish-style uniforms with red caps, bright blue jackets, baggy red trousers, white leggings, and black boots. They arrived in Richmond on June 7. From the hour of their coming the city's chicken population declined, and for the Zouaves, even better than robbing hen houses was eating sumptuously in a Richmond restaurant and charging the meal to the Confederate government. War was a game for some of the new soldiers, and although few played it as conspicuously as the Zouaves, most of the Southern volunteers made the best of it. Though some Richmond burgers resented the presence of their defenders, most Richmonders, in-

[8]Richmond *Enquirer*, May 30, 1861, cited in Rowland, *Jefferson Davis*, V, 102–104.
[9]Thomas, *Confederate Richmond*, pp. 44–47; Paul P. Van Riper and Harry N. Schreiber, "The Confederate Civil Service," *Journal of Southern History*, XXV (1959), 450–451; Harrison A. Trexler, "Jefferson Davis and the Confederate Patronage," *South Atlantic Quarterly*, XXVIII (1929), 45–58; Mary Boykin Chesnut, *A Diary from Dixie*, ed. by Ben Ames Williams (Boston, 1949), p. 68.

deed most Southerners, looked upon the impending war as a romantic adventure. The concentration and drilling of troops culminated, not yet in battles, but in parades and parties instead.[10]

Jefferson Davis, of course, realized that his administration would have to preside over more than politics and dress parades. Probably sooner than later the Southern nation would have to fight for its life. Many people in Montgomery had said that there would be no war; now many in Richmond proclaimed that one pitched battle would convince the United States that the Southerners were serious and thus insure Confederate independence. Davis and most of those around him were not so sanguine, and even if they were, the government had to confront at least the possibility of a full-scale war.[11]

Neither Davis as commander-in-chief nor the Confederate War Office nor the Southern corps of general officers ever wrote down a specific war plan. The best statement of Confederate strategy was Davis' plea during his post-Sumter address to Congress on April 20: "All we want is to be let alone." The Confederacy was a people acting out natiorhood; as long as the Southern nation existed the Confederates were winning the war. Like the rebels of 1776, Southerners could win by not losing. Accordingly the Davis administration looked to George Washington for strategic inspiration. By eighteenth-century standards, Washington had had an inferior army and had lost on most of those occasions when he risked battle. But Washington had won the war. He had done so by keeping his army intact and trading space and time for opportunities to strike decisive blows. Washington, like Davis, had hoped for a foreign alliance, and French troops and ships had been decisive in 1781. Yet, like Washington, Davis was determined to fight alone, if necessary, as long as it took to discourage his enemies and compel them to sue for peace.[12]

However much Davis and his generals revered Washington's ex-

[10]Thomas, *Confederate Richmond*, pp. 36–39; Bell I. Wiley, *The Life of Johnny Reb: The Common Soldier of the Confederacy* (New York, 1943), pp. 15–27; Chesnut, *Diary*, p. 75.

[11]See Walker to Letcher, June 29, 1861, *War of the Rebellion: A Compilation of the Official Records of the Union and Confederate Armies*, 70 vols. in 127 (Washington, D.C., 1880–1901), series IV, 411–412 for Davis' policy of accepting no more troops for periods of less than three years or "for the war."

[12]See Emory M. Thomas, *The Confederacy as a Revolutionary Experience* (Englewood Cliffs, N.J., 1971), pp. 43–57; Frank E. Vandiver, *Their Tattered Flags: The Epic of the Confederacy* (New York, 1970), pp. 120–121; and Russel F. Weigley, *The American Way of War: A History of United States Military Strategy and Policy* (New York, 1973), pp. 96–97.

ample, they were not so blind to the reality of nineteenth-century warfare as to believe that their struggle would duplicate precisely that of their grandfathers nearly a century earlier. Between Washington and the Confederates stood Napoleon and his object lessons in mass armies, strategic terrain, and battles of annihilation. And between the Napoleonic era and 1861 there had been considerable advances in military technology. The challenge that confronted Davis was no less than that of reconciling the heritage of Washington, Napoleon's maxims, and the industrial revolution. Davis and his generals perceived this challenge subconsciously, but they did perceive it, because the South responded logically and consistently, if not victoriously. Above all, Confederate military strategy and performance bore out Prussian military philosopher Karl von Clausewitz's dictum that a nation's warfare is an extension of its national character.[13]

Both the image and reality of Southern nationhood prescribed a defensive strategy. The Confederacy posed to the North, to Europe, and to itself as a legitimate national state, in anticipation of the doctrine of "self-determination of peoples." Given the legitimacy of their revolution, the Southern rebels were thus victims of a war of aggression waged by the North. Such a stance was important to attract European allies, capitalize upon sympathy for their cause in the North, and allow national feeling to congeal in the South. Thus a defensive posture militarily reinforced national policy, both foreign and domestic.[14]

Resources, both human and material, seemed to dictate a defensive strategy, too. The Confederacy had all too few of the prerequisites for nineteenth-century war: men, manufactures, and money. Offensive wars required more than aggressive enthusiasm; they demanded large armies and the logistical support necessary to sustain those armies during prolonged campaigns in the enemy's country. The South in 1861 had less than half as many people as the North, less than half the railroad mileage, less than one-third the bank capital, and less than one-tenth the manufacturing output. Add to those figures the fact that the United States had an existing navy with the facilities to expand it and the Confederate States had nei-

[13]See Frank E. Vandiver, *Rebel Brass: The Confederate Command System* (Baton Rouge, La., 1956), pp. 3–8.
[14]*Ibid.*, pp. 16–17.

ther, and it becomes clear that the South stood at the short end of almost every index of military might. The Confederacy would have to husband resources and spend its limited substance dearly, and the logical way to do that was to stand on the defense.[15]

However realistic and philosophically consistent a defensive strategy might be, though, it flew in the face of conventional military wisdom in 1861. Napoleonic strategy as codified by Henri Jomini in his *Summary of the Art of War* insisted that offensive action alone was decisive. Then, too, it was obvious that the Confederates could not conduct a static defense of every inch of Southern soil; there would always be too few Confederates and too much soil. Jomini and other authoritative military writers conceded that an energetic defense might take advantage of interior lines of communication and transportation to frustrate attacking armies. On paper at least, the defender might move troops and supplies from one front to another and thus gain local superiority against a much larger offensive aggregate forced to operate on a convex perimeter. But geography would work against the South in such a strategy. The Confederacy's northern frontier was in fact concave; the Appalachian mountains bisected its land mass; and its river systems, both coastal and inland, were potential highways of invasion. If the thrust of Confederate strategy was to be defensive, as circumstances seemed to dictate, then the Southerners would have to accommodate both contemporary military thought and their geographical dilemma. The accommodation they made most successfully involved the use of railroads to move troops rapidly and gain superiority in numbers at crucial points and times. As long as Southern railroads were available and dependable, Confederate strategists possessed the opportunity of massing and dispersing their forces much faster than the Northern invaders.[16]

[15]T. Harry Williams, *Americans at War: The Development of the American Military System* (Baton Rouge, La., 1960), pp. 54–55, catalogs the reasons for defense, but wonders, as have others, whether an early offensive would not have been successful and decisive.

[16]For assessments of Jomini's influence see T. Harry Williams "The Military Leadership of North and South," in David Donald (ed.), *Why the North Won the Civil War* (Baton Rouge, La., 1960); Archer Jones, "Jomini and the Strategy of the American Civil War, a Reinterpretation," *Military Affairs*, XXXIV (1970), 127–131; and Thomas Lawrence Connelly and Archer Jones, *The Politics of Command: Factions and Ideas in Confederate Strategy* (Baton Rouge, La., 1973), pp. 3–30. On the importance of railroads see Robert C. Black, *The Railroads of the Confederacy* (Chapel Hill, N.C., 1952).

As it happened (and that is perhaps the best way to express the process), the Confederacy did act out a reasoned strategy. Variously described as "offensive-defense" and a "strategy of annihilation," Southern military policy was an eclectic appropriation of the legacy of Washington, Napoleon, and Jomini, modified by geography and nineteenth-century military technology.[17]

The Confederates believed that they, like Washington, could trade space and time for opportunity. Within limits Southern armies could stand on the defense and permit penetration by their enemies. Then at a place and time of their choosing the Confederates hoped to attack and destroy the invader.

The limits were important. Washington could surrender major cities and large land areas to the British and still fight on. The much larger armies of the nineteenth century depended for logistical support upon centers of transportation and war industry. Larger armies too, made land more critical; the Confederates required a large land base for subsistence, and invading armies could despoil an area simply by marching through it. Confederates were conditioned to look upon land as the basis of wealth and social status. The culture of the Southern folk required a stable community of landholders. No one had to tell the Confederate high command that the defense of the Southern cause was intimately bound up in a defense of the soil from which that cause sprang.[18]

To prosecute the war, Union armies would have to invade the South and attempt to subdue the rebellion. Sooner or later, they hoped sooner, the Confederate forces would find their opportunity and strike. At that point defense would become offense. However, emphasizing the supposedly decisive nature of offensive action, both protagonists overlooked the significance of the rifle and Minié ball. The muskets of Napoleon's time were accurate only within one hundred yards; in the 1860s rifles increased that effective range five times. Small-arms fire rendered Napoleonic artillery tactics obsolete by forcing the bigger guns to remain at longer ranges, reducing their effectiveness in softening a point of attack. Cavalrymen, too,

[17]Davis used the term "offensive-defensive"; see Hudson Strode, *Jefferson Davis,* 3 vols. (New York, 1955–1964) I, 134. Perhaps the more correct term is "annihilation" (Weigley, *American Way of War,* p. 127).

[18]Vandiver is only slightly hyperbolic when he remarks about Confederate "geographical determinism" that "wedded irrevocably to the ground, they buried themselves in it." (*Rebel Brass,* p. 17); see also Vandiver, *Flags,* pp. 58–61.

learned the folly of charging massed infantry whose weapons' range and accuracy more than compensated for the speed and shock effect of a mounted attack. Consequently the defense had a much greater advantage than conventional military wisdom held, and ironically the Confederates were often more successful when they were unable to assume the offense.

The goal of the offensive-defensive strategy continued to be the destruction of the invading force; the Confederates hoped they could at least stop and at most destroy the armies sent against them. When the North had had enough killing, peace and independence would follow. Thus, in a way, the Confederates hoped to employ a strategy of annihilation to work a passive sort of exhaustion upon their enemy.[19]

This strategy made sense—so much sense that the Southerners adopted it naturally without thinking it out or writing it down. What Jefferson Davis did write down was the command system with which he proposed to implement his strategy. The Confederate War Office adopted a departmental command structure. This meant that Davis divided his nation into semiautonomous military departments. The Southern assumption was that each departmental commander would be able to meet the enemy threat in his department. If necessary departmental commanders could borrow troops from adjacent departments or lend battle-ready units to meet the enemy in a neighboring locale. Yet the heart of the scheme was the hope that a system of logistically self-sufficient commands arranged in a geographical cordon could fend off or destroy enemy armies. At first, when the anticipated front was limited to northern Virginia, departments were small. General P. G. T. Beauregard's geographical command at the first Battle of Manassas (Bull Run) encompassed only three counties. As the war widened, so did the size of the departments. By the winter of 1862 and 1863, Beauregard commanded a department composed of three states.

[19]Weigley, *American Way of War*, pp. 92–127; William L. Barney, *Flawed Victory: A New Perspective on the Civil War* (New York, 1975), pp. 7–9; Albert Manucy, *Artillery Through the Ages* (Washington, D.C., 1949), pp. 17–20.

COMMAND	COMMANDER	HEADQUARTERS
Dept. No. 2 (The Northwest)	Albert Sydney Johnston	Memphis, Tenn.
Northwest Virginia Army	Robert E. Lee	Valley Mountain, Va.
Army of Potomac	Joseph E. Johnston	Manassas, Va.
Dept. No. 1	David E. Twiggs	New Orleans, La.
Dept. of W. Florida	Braxton Bragg	Pensacola, Fla.
Dept. of Georgia	A. R. Lawton	Savannah, Ga.
Dept. of Fredericksburg	T. H. Holmes	Fredericksburg, Va.
Dept. of Norfolk	Benjamin Huger	Norfolk, Va.
Army of the Peninsula	John B. Magruder	Williamsburg, Va.
Mobile	J. M. Withers	Mobile, Ala.
Dept of N. Carolina	Richard C. Gatlin	Goldsborough. N.C.
Dept. of S. Carolina	Romwell S. Ripley	Charleston, S.C.
Dept. of E. Florida	John B. Grayson	Tallahassee, Fla.
Dept. of Texas	P. O. Hébert	San Antonio, Tex.

V. C. Groner to J. Cooper, September 30, 1861, *O.R.*, series IV, 631–633.

But always the home-based cordon philosophy persisted.

Davis counted on himself and his War Office to unify and direct the departmental command system. The Commander-in-Chief, however, was often less than a unifying influence, and too late did Confederates appreciate the need for unified command. Although the command structure they adopted was in some ways logical, given the Confederacy's offensive-defensive posture and the administration's political imperative to serve a land-oriented, localized populace, military logic did not always coincide with military necessity.[20]

The Confederacy's first trial by battle occurred in July of 1861. At that time the Southern nation was as ready as it could be to test its new government, army, strategy, and command system in defense of its new capital.

During May and June of 1861 the Confederacy's war had devel-

[20]For explanations and critiques of the departmental system see especially Williams, *American at War*, pp. 62–64; and Connelly and Jones, *Politics of Command*, pp. 87–136. The following list of departments and geographically designated field armies (having essentially the same function as departments) from September 1861, is indicative of the Confederate command structure during the first two years of the war.

oped a front. By mid-July Richmond had became a rendezvous and staging point from which Southern regiments fanned out toward Virginia's borders. Relatively small numbers of troops went west into the mountains of what is now West Virginia and east into the Virginia tidewater at Yorktown and Norfolk. The majority of the new army concentrated at three points to the north, between Richmond and Washington. About 3,000 men were just north of Fredericksburg at Aquia Landing on the Potomac River. Their commander was Brigadier General Theophilus H. Holmes, an "old army" man. At Winchester, guarding the entrance to the Shenandoah Valley, were 12,000 troops led by Brigadier General Joseph E. Johnston. Johnston was old army, too; in fact he was the highest-ranking officer among those who resigned from the United States Army and went south. Between Aquia Landing and Winchester and squarely astride the most direct invasion route from Washington to Richmond was the village of Manassas Junction. There, about 20,000 Confederates prepared to receive the first expected attack from the United States. In command of the troops and of this critical position was Brigadier General P. G. T. Beauregard, the "Hero of Sumter."[21]

Beauregard was a thoughtful soldier, well versed in the military thinking of his time. He was also a charismatic personality with a flair for the dramatic; his biographer has described him as "Napoleon in Gray," an assessment with which Beauregard himself would have agreed. In mid-July 1861, the General responded to Southern military circumstances in keeping with his personality and training and with the essentials of Confederate strategy.

Opposing the Southern departmental cordon in Virginia were two major Union armies. In front of Johnston's force in the valley were about 18,000 Federals under the command of Robert A. Patterson, a veteran whose career had begun in the War of 1812. At Washington, Irwin McDowell had approximately 35,000 men in

---

[21]One of the clearest and best summaries of military operations is Vincent J. Esposito (ed.), *The West Point Atlas of American Wars,* 2 vols. (New York, 1959); for the Bull Run (Manassas) campaign see I, maps 18–24. The standard camapaign study, R. M. Johnston, *Bull Run: Its Strategy and Tactics* (Boston, 1913), has been supplanted by William C. Davis, *Battle at Bull Run: A History of the First Major Campaign of the Civil War* (Garden City, N.Y., 1977). Also helpful are T. Harry Williams, *P. G. T. Beauregard: Napoleon in Gray* (Baton Rouge, La., 1955), pp. 66–80; and Douglas S. Freeman, *Lee's Lieutenants: A Study in Command,* 3 vols. (New York, 1942–1944), I, 38–80.

various stages of preparation for the march on Richmond. In an effort to complete the training of his troops, McDowell delayed as long as his government would allow him. Then on July 17 he moved, marching west from Washington to the town of Centreville. At this point McDowell's army was situated due north of Richmond and Beauregard's army at Manassas.[22]

Roughly halfway between Centreville and Manassas, flowing generally east-west, was Bull Run. The stream was the greatest natural obstacle between the two armies, and accordingly Beauregard had positioned his troops in battle order on the southern bank. Beauregard, however, had no intention of defending his Bull Run line, and plotted much grander things; a good apostle of Jomini and Napoleon, he thought in terms of concentration and decision. He proposed to Davis that Johnston leave a covering force in the valley and move by forced march and rail to Manassas. Holmes' force would also join the concentration. Then Beauregard could destroy McDowell and return the favor for Johnston. Reinforced by some of Beauregard's troops, Johnston would march rapidly back into the valley, crush Patterson's army, and sweep through Maryland to attack Washington from the north. Meanwhile Beauregard with his remnant force would move on the Union capital from the South, and at the juncture of the two armies the war would end victoriously. The entire operation, Beauregard calculated, would take less than a month.

In Richmond, President Davis, Commander of Virginia troops Robert E. Lee, and Confederate Adjutant and Inspector General Samuel Cooper heard and rejected Beauregard's plan. Beauregard's strategic thinking may have been sound and bold, but his estimates of troop strength and logistical planning were at best visionary. He had overestimated the size of Johnston's army, underestimated the strength of the Federals, and made little allowance for the state of roads and railroads in northern Virginia.[23]

From his headquarters at Manassas, Beauregard took the rejection of his grand scheme as a personal affront and grumbled about the way Richmond was managing the war. Before he could fret too

[22]Johnston, *Bull Run,* pp. 17–89.
[23]Freeman, *Lee's Lieutenants,* I, 38–43; Johnston, *Bull Run,* pp. 85–88; Williams, *Beauregard,* pp. 74–75.

long, however, McDowell began his march, and Beauregard realized that his army was outnumbered and in peril. Frantically the General called for reinforcements. Davis responded by doing on a modest scale what Beauregard had originally proposed. The President ordered Johnston and Holmes to join Beauregard at Manassas. With 9,000 of Johnston's troops and 3,000 of Holmes', Confederate numbers would roughly equal the Federals'. As a consequence Beauregard threw off his gloom and again began thinking about a battle of annihilation.[24]

On July 18 the Confederates repulsed a "reconnaissance in force" at Bull Run, and Beauregard's confidence increased. McDowell's march was cautious and his concentration at Centreville slow. On July 20, with the enemy still at Centreville and Holmes' and Johnston's troops pouring into his position, Beauregard determined to attack.[25]

Southern troop units were spread over an eight-mile front along Bull Run. Oddly, the largest numbers occupied the most defensible terrain, steeply wooded slopes that lay across the most direct route between Centreville and Manassas. Beauregard's headquarters were nearby at the home of Wilbur McLean, a local farmer. West of McLean's farm the banks of Bull Run leveled out and the countryside was open and rolling. Bull Run was fordable in several places along the Southern line, but the only bridge in the vicinity was at the extreme left of the Confederate position. Over the entire western, or left, half of his position, Beauregard had stationed only a brigade and a half of troops, comprising six regiments, or roughly 5,000 men. This imbalanced troop distribution, especially as related to terrain, did not trouble Beauregard on July 20, however; he was preparing his attack orders and cared little for considerations relating primarily to defense.[26]

When Johnston arrived with the van of his army on the Manassas Gap Railroad, he solved two of Beauregard's problems. Johnston assured Beauregard that the reinforcements from the valley would be present and ready for action on July 21. He also agreed with Beauregard that the Confederates must attack as soon as possible. And even though he outranked Beauregard, Johnston agreed to let

[24]Williams, *Beauregard,* pp. 75–77.
[25]Johnston, *Bull Run,* pp. 130–142.
[26]Freeman, *Lee's Lieutenants,* I, 48–50; Esposito (ed.), *West Point Atlas,* I, map 20.

Beauregard plan and execute the battle. This seemed logical since Beauregard was more familiar with the local situation.[27]

Accordingly, the Hero of Sumter retired to his room on the evening of July 20 to construct his attack order. The document he produced is a model of military obfuscation. The over-all concept was fine: the Southern army was supposed to converge upon Centreville from three directions and crush the enemy. But when Beauregard tried to fill in the details, his mind miscarried. His instructions were confusing at best; he wrote of "divisions and corps," which did not exist in his army, an amalgam of brigades. Beauregard's staff completed the necessary copies of the order at 4:30 A.M. on July 21 and awakened Johnston to sign them. The General was not so sleepy that he overlooked Beauregard's errors; but he signed the document anyway in hopes that the attack would take place at dawn and that Beauregard had a firmer grasp of the situation than his orders indicated.[28]

Fortunately for the Confederates, they never had to execute Beauregard's order. A Federal artillery shell crashed into the McLean kitchen while messengers were still trying to distribute the order. The shell interrupted Beauregard's breakfast and his attack. McDowell's army was on the march. The Federals first feinted at the stone bridge on the far left of the Southern line, then appeared in strength on the near side of Bull Run beyond the Confederate left flank. McDowell had struck the Southerners where they were weakest and by late morning was threatening to overrun the Confederate position.

Beauregard and Johnston did the only thing they could do. As rapidly as possible they dispatched brigades "to the sound of the firing." By 11:30 Johnston could stand the suspense no longer. "The battle is there!" he said gesturing toward the noise. "I am going!" Beauregard followed, and the two generals arrived at the scene of the action at about 12:30, just in time to have their worst fears confirmed.[29]

Remnants of two broken brigades were milling around behind a pitifully thin rank of Confederate troops on a low plateau just south

[27]Johnston, *Bull Run,* pp. 157–159.
[28]*Ibid.,* pp. 159–163; Williams, *Beauregard,* pp. 79–80; Freeman, *Lee's Lieutenants,* I, 50–52.
[29]Esposito (ed.), *West Point Atlas,* I, maps 21, 22; Williams, *Beauregard,* 81–84.

of Bull Run. Beyond the Southern line were large numbers of the enemy. In command of those Confederates engaged in the fight was Thomas J. Jackson, late of the faculty at Virginia Military Institute. Although no one knew it at the time, Jackson had just earned the sobriquet "Stonewall" when Bernard E. Bee, commander of one of the shattered brigades, attempting to rally his men by pointing to Jackson, coined his famous simile, "There is Jackson standing like a stone wall." Bee was mortally wounded soon after, and the first task undertaken by Johnston and Beauregard was to restore order to his confused troops. The commanding generals waded into the mob, found officers to lead the men, and in time stabilized the situation on the plateau.[30]

During the momentary lull, Beauregard asked Johnston to leave him in charge of the Confederate left wing and retire to a safer command post. Johnston, who was apparently a bit confused about whether he was responsible for the Confederate effort or, more precisely, whether he wanted to be, complied with his subordinate's request after some discussion. As he rode back down the Confederate line, Johnston issued more orders moving troops from the right to the threatened left.

For Beauregard the day seemed to go from bad to worse. Each time he was able to send in troops to bolster his left, more Federals appeared on that flank. As the afternoon lengthened, the Confederate battle line bent, and by two o'clock the Southerners were about a mile behind the position in which Beauregard had found them. The battle raged over the slope of Henry House Hill. Judith Henry had refused to evacuate her home, and the old lady lay dead in her bed while the fighting went on in her front yard.

Between two and four o'clock the Southerners pretty well held their own on Henry House Hill. The day had been unbearably hot and humid. The adrenaline of battle sustained the men for a time, but as the afternoon wore on and the heat intensified, more soldiers showed the effects of their hot work. Beauregard dashed along the line trying to save his battle; in the process he had a horse killed under him.

Then, beyond the dust and smoke that circled the hill, Beauregard saw new clouds of dust to the rear of his left flank. Johnston

[30]Freeman, *Lee's Lieutenants*, I, 62–65; Frank E. Vandiver, *Mighty Stonewall* (New York, 1957), pp. 160–161; Johnston, *Bull Run*, pp. 195–209.

saw them too from his headquarters. The dust indicated the approach of marching men, but neither general was quite sure whose men they were. If McDowell had been able to send a part of his army on a wide flanking march or if Patterson had followed Johnston's army from the valley, the Confederates were in deep trouble. As men materialized out of the dust Beauregard anxiously turned his field glasses on the approaching column. A flag hung limply from its standard; it was red, white, and blue. The colors were common to both the stars and stripes and the stars and bars, however. Beauregard feared the worst and wrote out a request for Johnston to prepare intermediate defenses to cover the impending retreat. The courier was ready to gallop away with the message when a soft breeze unfurled the flag enough to reveal bars instead of stripes. Two fresh brigades, commanded by Jubal A. Early and Edmund Kirby Smith, were arriving on the Confederate left; debacle turned to victory.[31]

What happened next was both natural and incredible. As the arriving soldiers ran onto the battlefield, their weary comrades mustered the strength for one last effort. They charged. And as they charged they let go a piercing scream which afterward became the "rebel yell." It was too much for the Federals. The Union battle line wavered, then broke. Here and there were significant pockets of resistance, but McDowell's army generally melted into a fleeing mob of tired, scared men.[32]

For the most part the Southerners watched their enemies run. They were as tired and scared as their adversaries; had the fresh troops on the flank been Union, the Confederates would likely have run as their enemies were doing. Johnston ordered two fresh brigades from his right flank to pursue, but heat and confusion slowed the effort. Finally, darkness and thunderstorms halted the pursuit. The battle wound down, and the soldiers straggled back to the field to find their regiments, celebrate the victory, and bury their comrades.[33]

Meanwhile the Commander-in-Chief had arrived. President Davis had remained in Richmond on July 20 to open the reassembled

[31]Freeman, *Lee's Lieutenants*, I, 65–72; Williams, *Beauregard*, pp. 85–88; Johnston, *Bull Run*, pp. 224–230.
[32]Freeman, *Lee's Lieutenants*, I, 73–79.
[33]Johnston, *Bull Run*, pp. 243–252.

2

116   THE CONFEDERATE NATION

Confederate Congress. On the day of the battle at Manassas, he boarded a train and went to find the action. Near Manassas Junction the engineer encountered the backwash of what looked like a defeated army and proceded farther only after pleas from his president. At last Davis reached headquarters, secured horses for himself and his aide, and set out to find his generals. Wounded men cheered him as he rode, and he in turn delivered romantic phrases about doing or dying. Only as he approached Johnston's field headquarters did the President learn of the Federal rout.[34]

Eventually Beauregard made his way back to Davis and Johnston, and at about midnight the three discussed their options for pressing the Confederate advantage on July 22. The Southern army was a winner, but in terms of organization, supply, and armament, the Confederates were in no condition to march on Washington. The possibilities of marching on Baltimore or into the valley to defeat Patterson's Federals existed but seemed remote. Ultimately the council of war agreed to shore up victory rather than risk defeat through recklessness; the torrential rain falling outside in the darkness reinforced the decision.[35]

Back in Richmond it had been an anxious day for a lot of people. The capital was empty of soldiers, and the fact that July 21 was a Sunday accentuated the ominous quiet. All day in the sultry heat little knots of people gathered and dispersed; every horseman entering the city from the north attracted requests for war news.

Across the street from the capitol in Mechanics Hall were the makeshift offices of the War Department. There Confederate officialdom assembled to wait out the suspense. The telegraph yielded nothing reliable. Secretary of War Walker damned his job and longed for action. The entire cabinet came and went, pacing and nervous. Howell Cobb, after sifting the fragmentary dispatches, announced that the battle at Manassas was a draw. Hot words followed, as men debated in complete ignorance. Night closed, and still the watch went on.

Then Judah Benjamin burst into the hall with real news. He had

[34]Varina Howell Davis, *Jefferson Davis: A Memoir*, 2 vols. (New York, 1890), I, 94–99.
[35]*Ibid.*, I, 102–113; Johnston, *Bull Run*, pp. 251–252. Hindsight, of course, revealed that the Confederates had lost a marvelous opportunity. Yet most historians of the event agree that the Beauregard-Johnston-Davis council of war made the only decision possible. See also Joseph E. Johnston, *Narrative of Military Operations*, ed. by Frank E. Vandiver (Bloomington, Ind., 1959), pp. 59–65.

come from the Spotswood Hotel and a call upon Varina Davis. A telegram from the President had arrived, and Benjamin had memorized the text: "We have won a glorious but dear-bought victory; the night closed with the enemy in full flight, pursued by our troops." Joy broke out. R. M. T. Hunter's tense face relaxed into smiles, John Reagan's eyes ceased to pop so far out from their sockets, and Benjamin simply glowed. The Confederacy had committed its fate to battle and won. The Southern nation was at last a reality; the cause was triumphant.[36]

On the night of July 21, 1861, the Confederate States of America was just about everything its founders had envisioned the Southern nation to be. In the minds of its citizens at least the Confederacy was the confirmed expression of Southern nationalism.

Radical means had yielded the conservative end. Secessions had led to confederation, and confederation to Constitution. That Constitution, if correctly construed, would preserve the Southern world and world view. The government of Jefferson Davis was the political expression of sensible Southerners; the old fire-eating radicals were by now mainly ornaments in the Confederate body politic. The administration had organized itself and conducted the confrontation in Charleston Harbor. Fort Sumter was a Confederate victory; not only was Charleston Harbor undefiled, but in the aftermath of the crisis the nation had reached its "natural frontiers."

The victory at Sumter had committed the South to war, but perhaps the revolution had always required blood. The government had been equal to the challenge, and Southern soil and soul were intact. Indeed the most striking thing about the conduct of Confederate statecraft and warfare thus far was its quintessential Southernness.

Mobilization for war had been a sort of gathering of the clans, and Davis as warrior chieftain was present to lead them. He had moved his capital to the front and mapped his strategy. Then Davis had been on hand to preside over his victory at Manassas. Success in battle had covered over personal animosities and sins of military administration and supply. Beauregard was once again a hero, although he shared his mantle with lesser heroes such as Jackson and martyrs to the cause such as Bee.

[36]Thomas, *Confederate Richmond*, p. 49; Jones, *War Clerk's Diary*, I, 65–66.

Hindsight, of course, reveals that the Southern celebration following Manassas was premature. Even at the time the Southern soldiers involved in the victory knew better, having learned the hard way that war was no parade and that Yankees were not pasty-faced cowards. Confederate generals, too, had reservations about the victory; they had no illusions about the logistical weaknesses the campaign had revealed. More important, the battle had more or less "happened," with precious little direction or control. The most significant order given all day had been the near-desperate command, "Go to the sound of the firing!" The battlefield had been broad beyond either Johnston's or Beauregard's comprehension, and the numbers of men involved had been too great for either general to control. If their enemies renewed the invasion—and Davis and his generals believed they would—the Confederate army would have to be more than a random collection of autonomous brigades. And commanders would have to do better than guess at the contents of each approaching cloud of dust. Naturally the success at Manassas softened the sting of the critique, but nagging doubts persisted even in the revel of victory.[37]

The vivid memories of pain and death that Confederate troops were suppressing and the awareness of failures that the Southern high command was rationalizing loomed small in the nation as a whole. The Richmond *Examiner* caught the spirit of the hour.

This blow will shake the Northern Union in every bone; the echo will reverberate round the globe. It secures the independence of the Southern Confederacy. The churches of this city should be open to-day and its inhabitants should render God their thanks for a special providence in their behalf; for yesterday morning the fate of Richmond, with many other fates, trembled in the balance.[38]

By the work of Sunday we have broken the backbone of invasion and utterly broken the spirit of the North. Henceforward we shall have hectoring, bluster and threat; but we shall never yet get such another chance at them again in the field.[39]

God was Southern, and the Confederacy would live. It was almost perfect. Even Edmund Ruffin had had a part in the triumph. The old

[37]For a critique of the military operations at Manassas see Johnston, *Bull Run,* pp. 273–276.
[38]Richmond *Examiner*, July 22, 1861.
[39]*Ibid.,* July 25, 1861.

man still belonged to the Palmetto Guards (Second South Carolina Infantry Regiment), and he had rejoined his regiment during the first week of July. With a cheese and a barrel of crackers, he appeared in their camp at Fairfax Court House one day and took up the rigors of soldiering. The troops were glad to see him, and he rejoiced that he was again serving the cause.[40]

Then on July 17 the war interrupted Ruffin's pleasure. His regiment retreated at double-quick time to join the concentration at Bull Run. Ruffin held the pace for two miles and then fell back. Fortunately the Alexandria Light Artillery was passing, and the old man rode to the new position on one of its caissons, losing his cheese, crackers, and baggage in the process.

On the morning of the battle, Ruffin was back in the ranks, but the Palmetto Guards were on the Confederate right, and the action was on the left. After waiting almost all day while the battle went on without him, the aged "private" deserted his post and set out to find the war.

Again he rode an artillery caisson to the scene of action. And again young men allowed him to fire their first shot. This time Ruffin's shot exploded near a suspension bridge over Cub Run on the Federal line of retreat and showered fragments into a body of fleeing troops. Ruffin watched with pride the distant blue figures recoil in panic as the guns of "his" battery completed the work he had begun.

Next day Ruffin visited the bridge and the site of his most recent "first shot." He was disappointed to find only three dead bodies. Later he learned that "about seven dead bodies" lay near where his shell exploded, and finally he convinced himself that at least fifteen Yankees had fallen, dead or wounded.[41]

[40]Avery O. Craven, *Edmund Ruffin: Southerner* (New York, 1932), pp. 226–227.
[41]*Ibid.*, 227–233.

CHAPTER 6

Confederate Nationality Confounded

R OANOKE Island, North Carolina, had been important in
American history before. Some time between 1587 and 1590
a colony of Englishmen sponsored by Sir Walter Raleigh had vanished without a trace from the island, beginning the intriguing un-
solved mystery of the "lost colony." Early in 1862, Roanoke Island
again commanded the attention of Americans. This time the "lost
colony" was a band of Confederate soldiers and sailors who attempted to defend the place. But this time there was no mystery;
most of the defenders were killed, wounded, or captured by Union
soldiers.[1]

Situated behind North Carolina's outer banks, Roanoke Island
was critical terrain. Control of the island promised influence in
North Carolina's extensive inland waterways and command of the
Dismal Swamp Canal, the "back door" to Norfolk.[2]

In August of 1861 the Federal navy succeeded in capturing Fort
Hatteras, which guarded the entrance to Pamlico Sound from the
sea. At that point Benjamin J. Huger, who commanded the Depart-

---

[1]The best general accounts of the battle of Roanoke Island are Rush C. Hawkins,
"Early Coast Operations in North Carolina," and Ambrose E. Burnside, "The Burn-
side Expedition," in Robert Underwood Johnson and Clarence Clough Buel (eds.),
Battles and Leaders of the Civil War, 5 vols. (New York, 1883–1887), I, 632–670.

[2]A good map of the region is in the report of Flag-Officer L. M. Goldsborough,
February 18, 1862, *Official Records of the Union and Confederate Navies in the War of the
Rebellion,* 31 vols. (Washington, D.C., 1894–1927), ser. I, VI, 554, reprinted in Haw-
kins, "Early Coast Operations," 641.

ment of Norfolk, sent a regiment of troops to garrison and fortify
Roanoke Island with the aid of some state militia from North Carolina. Then Huger inaugurated an extensive dialogue with the Confederate War Department over the boundaries of his department,
to attempt to avoid responsibility for defending Roanoke Island.
While the War Office gerrymandered military departments, work on
the island's defenses proceeded indifferently. Finally in late December 1861, Judah P. Benjamin, who had succeeded Leroy Pope
Walker as Secretary of War, assigned Henry A. Wise to Roanoke
Island and to Huger's department.[3]

Governor Wise, the former Virginia fire-eater, was a general by
virtue of political influence and his ability to recruit a "legion"
(brigade) for the Confederate army. He assumed command at Roanoke Island on January 7, 1862, while his legion was still in transit
from Virginia. However limited his military experience and talent,
Wise could easily perceive that Roanoke Island was all but defenseless.[4]

On the island were about 1,500 soldiers who were, Wise later
reported, "undrilled, unpaid, not sufficiently clothed and quartered, and . . . miserably armed with old flint muskets in bad order."
The artillery was misplaced, antiquated, and undersupplied. Wise's
naval complement consisted of a squadron of small gunboats commanded by Captain William F. Lynch. The *Sea-Bird,* Lynch's flag-
ship, carried two guns; the rest of the vessels in the squadron had
one gun each, and two were in reality tugboats with guns aboard.
Wise pronounced them "perfectly imbecile."[5]

Having acquainted himself with the sad state of his new command, Wise hastened to Norfolk to confront Huger with his needs
and then to Richmond to expedite transit of his legion. Meanwhile,
during the first week of January a Union armada of warships and
troop transports, eighty ships and 15,000 men, under the command
of Ambrose E. Burnside set sail for North Carolina. On January 20,
Captain Lynch discovered Burnside's expedition pouring through

[3]Huger to Davis, March 5, 1862, *War of the Rebellion: A Compilation of the Official
Records of the Union and Confederate Armies,* 70 vols. in 127 (Washington, D.C., 1880–
1901), ser. I, IX, 113–114; Reports of Wise, February 21, 1862, *O.R.* ser. I, IV,
123–124.
[4]Wise Reports, *O.R.*, ser. I, IX, 126–129.
[5]*Ibid.*, 129; Burnside, "Expedition," 670. The standard biography of Wise is still
Barton H. Wise, *The Life of Henry A. Wise of Virginia, 1806–1876* (New York, 1899).

Hatteras Inlet and responded by steaming back to Roanoke Island and writing a letter to the Navy Department blaming Wise for the impending disaster.[6]

Wise did not return to his command until the last day of January. The next day he established his headquarters at Nags Head on the outer banks and became violently ill with pleurisy. The General's legion was arriving slowly, and as it did, Wise dictated orders from his sickbed dispatching the troops to Roanoke Island. Eventually the Confederates on the island numbered just over 2,500. Neither army nor navy contingents had adequate ammunition for more than a skirmish.[7]

The Federals came steaming into Croatan Sound in strength on the morning of February 7. Lynch's squadron gave battle intermittently, and the army's shore batteries opened on the Union ships. Never, however, was there hope of doing more than delaying the advance of the enemy. Federal troop transports began landing operations on an all but unprotected beach in the middle of the island, and by midnight 10,000 Union troops and considerable artillery were on Roanoke Island.

Early on the morning of the eighth about 1,500 Southerners arrayed themselves around a three-gun battery on a low hill and discovered that no one knew how to serve the artillery pieces. A captain sent from Wise's headquarters was still giving lessons when the enemy's infantry appeared. The fight was more than uneven; by noon the Southerners had exhausted their artillery ammunition and had fallen back in confusion. There was nowhere to retreat. In addition to other shortages, the Confederates had virtually no small boats in which to escape from the island, and most of the Southern troops surrendered in place.[8]

One of those mortally wounded was Captain O. Jennings Wise, son of the Commanding General and until recently editor of the

[6]Wise Reports, *O.R.*, ser. I, IX, 132–142; Burnside, "Expedition," 660–662; Lynch to Mallory, January 22, 1862, in Wise Reports, *O.R.*, ser. I, IX, 147–148.

[7]Wise Reports, *O.R.*, ser. I, IX, 147; Report of Colonel H. M. Shaw, February 24, 1862, *O.R.*, ser. IV, I, 170–173.

[8]Report of Flag-Officer Lynch, February 18, 1862, *O.R.N.*, ser. I, VI, 594–597; Report of Flag-Officer Goldsborough, February 18, 1862, *O.R.N.*, ser. I, VI, 550–555; Report of Colonel H. M. Shaw, February 24, 1862, *O.R.* ser. I, IX, 170–173; Wise to Huger, Feb. 10, 1862 in Wise Reports, *O.R.*, ser. I, IX, 155–157; Burnside, "Expedition," pp. 666–668, 670; Hawkins, "Early Coast Operations," 640–645.

Richmond *Enquirer*. When General Wise recovered from his pleurisy and his grief, he sought vengeance for the debacle on Roanoke Island at the expense of Huger, Benjamin, and the Confederate War Office. Eventually a committee of Congress investigated; Wise had the time and the inclination to supply the committee with most of the evidence it considered, and not surprisingly the committee laid the blame for the defeat upon Huger and Benjamin.[9]

The battle of Roanoke Island was a classic Confederate disaster. From the beginning, the new nation was unprepared to defend the isolated island. Huger demonstrated the weakness of the departmental command structure by spending considerable time and energy trying to avoid responsibility for Roanoke Island. Nor was the War Department able to make an appropriate response even with ample warning of the Union threat. Wise was an amateur general; he spent most of his time while in command of Roanoke in Norfolk and Richmond complaining instead of doing anything effective about his problems. As a result the Confederate plan to defend the island was a farce. The navy showed itself weak and small, and the army's deficiencies in men and war materiel were all too obvious. Even before the debacle occurred, the Southerners—Lynch, Wise, Huger, and Benjamin—bent their energies exchanging blame. And eventually the unseemly sniping involved a congressional committee that took few pains to spare the feelings of the administration.

Roanoke Island was not the only disaster to befall the Confederacy during the eight months following the victory at Manassas. In fact nearly a year passed before Southerners could again celebrate a major victory, and during the period between the battle of Manassas and the opening of the 1862 campaigns, Confederate losses seemed irredeemable. In sharp contrast to the euphoria of July 1861 was the growing disillusion and gloom of the succeeding months.[10]

In early August of 1861 a party of "buffalo hunters" led by John R. Baylor invaded the territory of New Mexico and claimed it for the Confederacy. But when the adventure became a campaign, the

[9]*Richmond Enquirer*, February 25, 1862; Wise Reports, *O.R.*, ser. I, IX, 122–65; Report of the Investigating Committee, Confederate House of Representatives, *O.R.*, ser. IV, I, 183–191.

[10]Few historians of the Confederacy have sufficiently emphasized the period between July 1861 and the spring of 1862. Bell I. Wiley in *Road to Appomattox*, Atheneum edition (New York, 1968), does point out the depressing effect on public morale (pp. 49–59).

Southern troops of Brigadier General H. H. Sibley lost the battle of Glorieta Pass on March 28, 1862, and abandoned New Mexico.[11]

On August 10, Southern volunteers commanded by Sterling Price and ex-Texas Ranger Ben McCulloch defeated a Union army at Wilson's Creek in Missouri,[12] but skirmishing between small units continued during the late summer and fall with no further Confederate advances. The Confederate Congress admitted Missouri to the Confederacy formally on November 28 in the presence of Governor Claiborne Jackson, but by then Jackson's government was in exile and Missouri was *de facto* in the Union.[13] The Southerners made what turned out to be their last campaign for Missouri in March of 1862, and that campaign advanced no farther than northern Arkansas. On March 6 and 7, Confederate General Earl Van Dorn and about 20,000 soldiers attacked an equal number of Federals at Pea Ridge. The battle was essentially a draw, but the Southerners abandoned the field and their threat to southern Missouri.[14]

The Confederate attempt to hold Kentucky fared no better. On September 3, 1861, General Leonidas Polk, until recently the Episcopal bishop of Louisiana, violated Kentucky neutrality and drew a strong protest from the state legislature. Popular sentiment in the state was running against the Confederacy even as the Confederate Congress admitted Kentucky to the Southern nation on December 10, 1861. Then, on January 17, 1862, Richmond's military positions in Kentucky collapsed at the Battle of Mills Springs. Within a month the Confederacy had all but abandoned Kentucky and was fighting to hang on to some of Tennessee.[15]

[11]See Martin H. Hall, *Sibley's New Mexico Campaign* (Austin, Tex., 1960); David Westphall, "The Battle of Glorieta Pass: Its Importance in the Civil War," *New Mexico Historical Review*, XLIV (1969), 137–154; and Jerry Don Thompson, *Colonel John Robert Baylor: Texas Indian Fighter and Confederate Soldier* (Hillsboro, Tex., 1971).

[12]Albert Castel, *General Sterling Price and the Civil War in the West* (Baton Rouge, La., 1968), pp. 39–47.

[13]See two articles by Arthur R. Kirkpatrick, "Missouri's Secessionist Government, 1861–1865," *Missouri Historical Review* XLV (1951), 124–137, and "The Admission of Missouri to the Confederacy," *Missouri Historical Review*, LV (1961), 366–386.

[14]See Albert Castel, "A New View of the Battle of Pea Ridge," *Missouri Historical Review*, LVII (1968), 136–151; and Homer L. Kerr, "Battle of Elkhorn: The Gettysburg of the Trans-Mississippi West," in William F. Holmes and Harold W. Hollingsworth (eds.), *Essays on the American Civil War* (Austin, Tex., 1971).

[15]Thomas L. Connelly, *Army of the Heartland: The Army of Tennessee, 1861–1862* (Baton Rouge, La., 1967), pp. 46–99; Wilson P. Shortridge, "Kentucky Neutrality in 1861," *Mississippi Valley Historical Review*, IX (1923), 283–301.

In the mountains of western Virginia the Confederacy suffered secession and defeat during the fall of 1861. Delegates from the western counties met in Wheeling in late August. They were in effect a secession convention which framed the constitution for a new state carved from Virginia. On October 24 a popular referendum in the Virginia west endorsed the work of the convention.[16] Military efforts to hold the area for the Confederacy were uniformly unsuccessful. The major campaign led by Robert E. Lee failed at the Battle of Cheat Mountain in mid-September. By early spring the Confederate frontier in Virginia seemed about to contract still more. Stonewall Jackson and a small force of infantry suffered defeat at Kernstown in the lower, or northern, Shenandoah Valley.[17]

In November 1861, a Federal amphibious force landed at Port Royal, South Carolina, and rapidly secured a foothold on the coast between Charleston and Savannah. Lee, the Confederate departmental commander, was powerless to do more than harass his enemies, and by December planters along the Georgia–South Carolina coast were burning cotton to prevent its capture by the Union army.[18]

On the Mississippi the Confederates lost a key point at each end of the river. Early in December 1861 the United States reoccupied Ship Island near the mouth of the Mississippi. That move provided the North with a base from which to launch assaults on New Orleans and/or Mobile, although the Confederacy was able to open the Mississippi briefly in October 1862, when the ironclad ram *Manassas* damaged some Union ships. To the north the Southerners held New Madrid, Missouri, through the winter but lost the river port on March 14, 1862. It was obvious that Southern use of the river would be perilous at best.[19]

Then the South, having lost both possession and allegiance in Kentucky, began losing Tennessee, in the Confederate heartland, as

[16]See Richard O. Curry, *A House Divided: A Study of Statehood Politics and the Copperhead Movement in West Virginia* (Pittsburgh, 1964).

[17]Douglas S. Freeman, *R. E. Lee*, 4 vols. (New York, 1934–35), I, 541–587; Frank E. Vandiver, *Mighty Stonewall* (New York, 1957), pp. 204–207.

[18]Daniel Ammen, "DuPont and the Port Royal Expedition," in Johnson and Buel (eds.), *Battles and Leaders*, I, 671–691.

[19]See James M. Merrill, *Battle Flags South: The Story of the Civil War Navies on Western Waters* (Rutherford, N.J., 1960), pp. 15–110; H. Allen Gosnell, *Guns on the Western Waters* (Baton Rouge, La., 1949), pp. 1–69; John D. Milligan *Gunboats Down the Mississippi* (Annapolis, Md., 1965), pp. 3–51.

well. Albert Sydney Johnston commanded Department Number Two, which extended from the Cumberland Gap to the Mississippi River, including most of the state. On the other side were two Union military departments and the potential, for the Union, of confused command. Johnston convinced himself that his most immediate threat was Don Carlos Buell's army. Buell, who commanded the Department of the Ohio, had a sizable force at Munfordville, Kentucky, and seemed to Johnston about to advance on Nashville. Accordingly Johnston made his largest concentration at Bowling Green, between Buell and Nashville. Meanwhile from the adjacent Union Department of Missouri came an amphibious assault up the Tennessee and Cumberland Rivers.

The Federal army commander of this expedition was Ulysses S. Grant, who at this point boasted an essentially undistinguished record in the "old army" and a command seemingly beyond his training and experience. Grant and his naval counterpart, Commodore Andrew H. Foote, were aggressive, however, and on February 2, 1862, an invasion force of 15,000 began moving up the Tennessee. Barring the invasion route were two Confederate forts, Henry and Heiman, and a small army commanded by Lloyd Tilghman.[20]

The Confederates were woefully unprepared to defend the forts. Most of Tilghman's 2,500 troops were armed with muskets left over from the War of 1812. Fort Heiman, situated on high ground on the west bank of the Tennessee, was an uncompleted work designed to protect Fort Henry, which was on level ground on the east bank. Fort Henry was all but defenseless against Foote's gunboats; winter rains had flooded many of the gun emplacements, and the parade ground was under two feet of water at the time of the Federal advance. Tilghman had repeatedly warned Johnston of his potential peril, but because Johnston was preoccupied with Buell's threat, the warnings went unheeded. Now in the face of the Union advance, Tilghman realized his position was hopeless. He evacuated Fort Heiman, dispatching all but a token garrison to Fort Donelson (eleven miles away on the Cumberland River) and at Fort Henry awaited the inevitable. The Southerners defended Fort Henry for two hours on February 6 and surrendered.[21]

[20]Connelly, *Army of the Heartland*, pp. 78–85, 102–106; Vincent J. Esposito (ed.), *The West Point Atlas of American Wars*, 2 vols. (New York, 1959), I, map 25.
[21]Connelly, *Army of the Heartland*, pp. 106–108; Esposito (ed.), *West Point Atlas*, I, map 26.

Finally, Johnston understood the dimensions of the threat posed by Grant. He countered by falling back from Bowling Green to Nashville and reinforcing Fort Donelson. By February 12, when Grant was ready to move against the fort, former Virginia Governor John B. Floyd was at Donelson in command of 15,000 Confederates, the divisions of Simon B. Buckner and Gideon J. Pillow. Floyd, Buckner, and Pillow, however, were convinced that Foote's gunboats represented the greatest danger to the fort, and the Confederates ignored their opportunity to attack Grant's infantry as it approached. Instead the Southern troops manned a line of breastworks outside Fort Donelson and waited.

On February 14 the gunboats closed on the fort and dueled with the Southern shore batteries. Donelson's guns repulsed the attack, but Floyd did not realize the extent of the damage inflicted upon the Federal fleet. That evening the Southern commander held a council of war with Pillow and Buckner, and they determined to abandon the fort and withdraw to Nashville.

Meanwhile Grant was receiving reinforcements; by morning 25,-000 Union troops enclosed the Southern lines. Both sides were suffering from the extremely cold weather, a dearth of blankets, and a shortage of rations. Near dawn on February 15, Pillow's Confederates surged forward to open an escape route and after brisk fighting during the morning achieved their objective. Floyd, however, could not believe his success. He conferred with Pillow and Buckner, delayed the breakout, and eventually recalled his army to their works. In the afternoon the Confederates repulsed a Union counterattack, and by nightfall the two armies occupied essentially the same lines as they had the night before.

Again Floyd called a council of war. This time the three commanders decided to surrender, or at least they decided to surrender their armies; Floyd and Pillow fled in the night on February 15 with about 1,500 members of the garrison. Cavalry commander Nathan Bedford Forrest, who would have no part of the surrender talk, managed to lead his troopers through a frozen swamp and onto the road to Nashville that same night.

Buckner, because he had less rank than his fellow generals, was left to surrender Donelson, 11,500 troops, and forty guns. He asked for terms on February 16. Grant demanded unconditional surrender, and Buckner had no choice but to accept. Grant thus enhanced his reputation as an aggressive commander, earned a famous nickname, and compounded the Southern ignominy. Four days after the surrender at Fort Donelson, Johnston abandoned Nashville. Then Grant's army pressed its advantage into the Tennessee Valley; by the end of March the invasion column was at Pittsburg Landing, only a few miles from Mississippi.[22]

There were bright spots in the record of Confederate arms after Manassas, but they were pitifully few and mostly of short duration. As late as March of 1862 the Confederates still had to celebrate Manassas as their last major military victory. They had had to abandon New Mexico, Missouri, Kentucky, western Virginia, and a large portion of Tennessee. The enemy threatened at Port Royal, at both ends of the Mississippi, and in eastern North Carolina. And worst of all were the humiliating ways in which the Confederates lost— especially at Fort Donelson and Roanoke Island.

To make matters even more frightening, Union General George B. McClellan, victor in the western Virginia campaigns, was raising and training a mammoth army around Washington for an assault on Richmond. Rumors put McClellan's numbers at more than 100,000, and the rumors were true. In the wake of so much failure the Confederacy appeared ready for the *coup de grâce* as the campaigning season of 1862 began in earnest.[23]

Amid the gathering gloom that pervaded the Confederate war, the Southern navy offered little hope. Secretary Mallory had gathered about him some first-rate thinkers, and he and his staff had thought some wise thoughts. Yet in the realm of deeds the navy had little of lasting consequence to show in the spring of 1862. Mallory was still hoping to buy a navy in Europe rather than construct one in the South. To this end Captain James D. Bulloch, Georgia-born veteran of the United States Navy, had already made a good beginning in England. He had, for example, contracted with the Laird shipbuilders at Birkenhead for the construction of two seagoing ironclad rams which promised to wreak havoc with the Union blockade. Yet Laird could not complete the rams for another eighteen

[22]Connelly, *Army of the Heartland*, pp. 108–125; Esposito (ed.), *West Point Atlas*, I, maps 27–30; Lew Wallace, "The Capture of Fort Donelson," in Johnston and Buel (eds.), *Battles and Leaders*, I, 401–429; James J. Hamilton, *The Battle of Fort Donelson* (New York, 1968); and Merrill, *Battle Flags South*, pp. 82–107.

[23]See Archer Jones, *Confederate Strategy from Shiloh to Vicksburg* (Baton Rouge, La., 1961), pp. 33–36.

months, and in the interim the Federals were tightening the blockade.[24]

In July of 1861 the United States, which possessed about a hundred ships, was attempting to seal the 189 openings along the 3,549 miles of Confederate coastline with fewer than thirty-three vessels. Not surprisingly, during 1861 the blockaders stopped only about one Southern ship in nine. By January 1862, though, the Federal navy had grown to three hundred ships, and during 1862 blockading squadrons were able to catch one ship in seven. The blockade was not yet ruinous to Southern trade, but Union performance was improving. And during the period when the blockade was most porous, the Confederates had been unable to ship their unfilled arms orders from Europe. Now, in 1862, the South faced a tightening blockade with little more than purchase orders in the way of a blue-water navy. The entire Confederate naval force on February 27, 1862, numbered only thirty-three ships.[25]

While waiting for the efforts of Bulloch and other purchasing agents to bear fruit, Mallory and his staff realized the necessity for immediate action to defend Southern rivers and coastal waters. The Secretary had for some time been intrigued with the feasibility of ironclad ships and the possibility that a few armored vessels might offset the North's growing superiority in numbers of conventional ships. Even though the *Manassas* had had to withdraw to New Orleans for repairs after its brief success on the Mississippi, the pioneer ironclad had demonstrated potential. Nevertheless, in October 1861, the Confederate Congress committed $2 million to the construction of small wooden gunboats.

All the while, however, work was progressing at the Gosport Navy Yard near Portsmouth on the partially burned hull of the old Union frigate *Merrimack*.[26] Back in June, Mallory's Chief of Ordnance and Hydrography John M. Brooke had drawn a design for transforming

[24]See Frank J. Merli, *Great Britain and the Confederate Navy* (Bloomington, Ind., 1971); Wilbur D. Jones, *The Confederate Rams at Birkenhead* (Tuscaloosa, Ala., 1961); and Richard I. Lester, *Confederate Finance and Purchasing in Great Britain* (Charlottesville, N.C., 1975); William N. Still, Jr., *Confederate Shipbuilding* (Athens, Ga., 1969), pp. 3–20. Bulloch recounted his and others' adventures in his *The Secret Service of the Confederate States in Europe*, 2 vols. (London, 1883).

[25]Virgil Carrington Jones, *The Civil War at Sea*, 3 vols. (New York, 1960), I, 165–166, 332; II, 247. Mallory to Davis, February 27, 1862; *O.R.N.*, series II, II, 149–53.

[26]William H. Still, Jr., *Iron Afloat: The Story of the Confederate Armorclads* (Nashville, Tenn., 1971), pp. 11–17, 47–51, 79.

the *Merrimack's* hull into the iron-plated C.S.S. *Virginia.* Mallory authorized the work and anticipated completion by November. The conversion proceeded glacially, however, and although the *Virginia's* executive officer, Lieutenant Catesby ap R. Jones, pressed the workmen to labor overtime, seven days a week, the ironclad was not in the water until mid-February 1862. It was a strange sight. The rebuilt hull, covered by a flat deck and fitted with a cast-iron ram, floated just below the waterline. An oval superstructure housing ten guns was centered on the submerged deck that protruded fore and aft. The *Virginia* was 263 feet long (the superstructure was 170 feet) and drew twenty-two feet of water. It looked somewhat like a floating roof.[27]

Finally, at 11:00 A.M. on March 8, the great ironclad steamed out of Portsmouth and down the Elizabeth River toward Hampton Roads. Despite his strenuous efforts to get the ship into action, Jones was not its captain. Franklin Buchanan, recently made commander of the James River defenses, was the senior officer on board, and Jones remained the executive officer; the *Virginia* had no real captain. In keeping with his aggressive instincts the veteran Buchanan took the ironclad immediately into action without a trial run. From several Union ships on Hampton Roads, the sizable body of water which links the James River with the Chesapeake Bay, Buchanan selected the *Congress* and the *Cumberland* as his foes. The two wooden ships lay at anchor off Newport News, and Buchanan headed for them at full speed. On the *Virginia,* full speed was little better than four knots, so the Federals had more than an hour to prepare for the encounter.[28]

Just after 2:00 P.M. the *Virginia* drew within 1,500 yards of the *Congress,* and the two ships exchanged broadsides with little effect. Buchanan then continued his course to engage the more heavily armed *Cumberland.* He intended to ram the Union ship, and as he closed, both ships blazed away at each other. Shells poured into the *Cumberland,* but answering shots merely bounced off the *Virginia.* Then the Southern craft rammed its adversary and tore a gaping hole in the starboard side. The *Cumberland* began to sink immedi-

[27] *Ibid.,* pp. 13–25; John M. Brooke, "The *Virginia* or *Merrimac:* Her Real Projector," *Southern Historical Society Papers,* XIX (1891), 3–34.

[28] J. Thomas Scharf, *History of the Confederates States Navy,* 2nd edition (Albany, N.Y., 1894), pp. 154–155 and n.; Still, *Iron Afloat,* pp. 23–29.

ately and might have dragged the *Virginia* down too had the iron-clad's ram not broken off. The *Cumberland*'s crew continued to serve their guns even as their ship sank lower in the water. At about 3:30 the *Cumberland* went down—colors still flying.

When Buchanan then turned to engage the *Congress,* the Federal commander made sail and ran his ship aground to prevent the heavy-draught ironclad from ramming him. No matter—Buchanan maneuvered the *Virginia* to within a hundred yards of the *Congress* and pounded it into submission. Near the end of the battle Buchanan sustained a leg wound, and Jones at last assumed command of the *Virginia.* [29]

The crew of the *Virginia* watched the *Congress* burn that night while news of their triumph spread abroad. Meanwhile Jones directed repair work and prepared to resume the destruction the following morning. He knew that by the next day the *Virginia* would no longer have a monopoly on iron armor. In the light cast by the burning *Congress,* a southern pilot had seen the Union ironclad *Monitor* approaching. [30]

The Federal ironclad was in Hampton Roads that morning by sheer coincidence; like the *Virginia,* it had been built as something of an experiment and towed south to support Union efforts in Virginia waters. The Federal "cheese box on a raft" was smaller (172 feet) than the *Virginia* but faster. Moreover, because its squat cylindrical turret revolved and it drew only 10.5 feet of water, it was more maneuverable and capable of delivering a more sustained rate of fire from its two eleven-inch guns. [31]

Early on March 9, Jones got the *Virginia* under way and headed for the Union frigate *Minnesota,* which had run aground the previous evening. As the *Virginia* closed on its prey, the *Monitor* intervened. For most of that morning the two ironclads battered each other at ranges seldom exceeding a hundred yards. Neither was able to inflict significant damage. Finally a shot from the *Virginia* exploded near one of the *Monitor*'s observation holes and the powder fragments temporarily blinded the Federal commander. His executive

[29]Still, *Iron Afloat,* pp. 29–32; T. Catesby Jones, "The Iron-Clad *Virginia,*" *Virginia Magazine of History and Biography,* XLIX (1941), 297–303.
[30]Catesby R. Jones, "Services of the *Virginia,*" *Southern Historical Society Papers,* XI (1183), 70–71; Still; *Iron Afloat,* pp. 32–33.
[31]On the *Monitor,* see William C. White and Ruth White, *Tin Can on a Shingle* (New York, 1957).

officer broke off the engagement, and Jones did not attempt to follow. The duel of ironclads was over, and naval warfare would never be the same again.[32]

During the two months that followed, both sides expected a renewal of the combat between ironclads. But none occurred. Neither navy was willing to chance combat under any but the most favorable conditions. The heavy-draught *Virginia* could not leave Hampton Roads without risking the danger of running aground, and the Federals feared that the *Monitor* might be rammed and sunk if it offered battle on wide waters.

Early in May the Confederate army evacuated Norfolk in the face of McClellan's threat, and the *Virginia* became a ship without a port. After frantic but futile efforts to lighten the vessel enough for it to steam up the James, the *Virginia*'s crew, on May 10, scuttled and burned it.[33]

The *Virginia*'s brief cruise convinced the Confederates that their salvation lay in ironclads, and Mallory recommitted the energies of his department to the construction of armored ships. During the spring of 1862, however, the South lost the ports of New Orleans, Memphis, and Norfolk, and with them all but five of the nascent fleet of ironclads. Moreover, the Confederates themselves had the unhappy task of destroying the ships to prevent capture. On one occasion, as Secretary Mallory was concluding a women's tour of an armored vessel, one of the women asked to see a final feature of the ship: "the place where they blow it up." Clearly, the Navy Department would have to begin again, at a time when the end seemed imminent. To his credit, Mallory persevered. But the hard fact was that the Confederate navy was much less a match for its foe in 1862 than it had been the year before. A year of stop-gap operations and attempted foreign purchases had produced few tangible results.[34]

[32]For accounts of the famous battle and its significance, see John Taylor Wood, "The First Fight of Iron Clads," Johnson and Buel (eds.), *Battles and Leaders*, I, 692–711; Jones, "Services of the *Virginia*," 65–75; Robert W. Daly, *How the Merrimac Won* (New York, 1957); and E. B. Potter and Chester W. Nimitz (eds.), *Sea Power: A Naval History* (Englewood Cliffs, N.J., 1960), pp. 262–272.

[33]Still, *Iron Afloat*, pp. 34–40. Tom Henderson Wells, in *The Confederate Navy: A Study in Organization* (University, Ala., 1971), pp. 97–98, points out the problems involved in trying to move the *Virginia* up the James and blames constructor John L. Porter for supplying inaccurate information regarding the ship's least possible draught.

[34]Still, *Iron Afloat*, pp. 79–88; T. C. DeLeon, *Belles, Beaux and Brains of the 60's* (New York, 1909), pp. 415–416.

The military failure of the Confederacy during the months after Manassas was both cause and effect of other flaws in the fabric of Southern nationhood. A "chicken-and-egg" relationship existed between the fortunes of Confederate arms and the state of Southern manpower, materiel, money, politics, and national morale. In each of these areas Southerners had tried to act like a nation and had failed.

When the first session of the first permanent Congress convened in Richmond on February 18, 1862, its members were concerned about the capacity of the Confederate military establishment to defend the nation. As the sad details of the Roanoke Island and Fort Donelson debacles became known, senators and representatives became genuinely alarmed. On March 3, in open session, the House requested the President to "communicate what additional means in money, men, arms, or other munitions of war, are, in his judgement, necessary." Presented with an opportunity to make specific requests to an ostensibly responsive Congress, Davis lost no time asking his secretaries of war and navy for estimates of their needs.[35]

Davis' response to the Congress, based upon the reports of his cabinet secretaries, was curious. He began by filling in the figures of the "blank check" to prosecute the war properly during 1862. The Confederacy required 300,000 more men, 750,-000 more small arms, 5,000 more artillery pieces, 5,000 additional tons of powder, fifty more ironclads, and an additional fleet of at least ten "of the most formidable war vessels" for service on the high seas. Then, having asked for these items, the President informed his Congress that no amount of money or legislation would suffice to procure them.[36] The requisite tools of war were not to be had at any price either within the South or abroad. The Confederacy had raised an army of 340,000 men, at least on paper, but in the multifront war in which the Confederacy found itself, it appeared that at least twice that number would be required. And before the South enlisted more men in the ranks, it had to solve the problem of properly arming those already in the field. Thus when Congress asked the President what he needed,

[35] *Journal of the Congress of the Confederate States of America, 1861–1865,* 7 vols. (Washington, D.C., 1904–1905), V, 47.

[36] Jefferson Davis to Speaker of the House of Representatives, March 4, 1862, *O.R.,* ser. IV, I, 969–970.

Davis responded by outlining his needs and then admitted that no one knew how to meet them.

In the beginning, the War Department had hoped to purchase large quantities of arms and ammunition abroad, and Caleb Huse, the Confederacy's chief purchasing agent, enjoyed considerable success. Using the South's limited amount of specie as long as possible, then offering cotton in exchange for his purchases, he contracted for military supplies of all kinds. Contracts, however, would not kill enemy soldiers; by February 1862 only 15,000 small arms had actually arrived from Europe. The Union blockade hampered Huse's efforts, as did the Confederacy's somewhat bizarre system of international barter.[37]

Josiah Gorgas, chief of the Ordnance Bureau, had the foresight not to rely totally upon foreign purchases for the tools of war. He let contracts for as much materiel as civilian manufacturers could produce and then faced the fact that the South had little or no manufacturing base to convert to war industries. In the early spring of 1862, Gorgas was in the process of reorganizing the Ordnance Bureau so that the government could create its own war industries. His plans were sound. He realized that government enterprise was necessary if the Confederacy were to be self-sufficient and hoped to involve his bureau in everything from mining operations to the production of arms and ammunition. But although the Ordnance shops, arsenals, works, and laboratories were soon producing, they were not producing fast enough. Gorgas' plans, like Huse's contracts, had not borne sufficient fruit. To make matters worse, the Confederates had lost the Nashville Ordnance Depot to fire in December and the powder works there to the Federals in February.[38] In early 1862, otherwise rational men proposed arming Southern soldiers with pikes, and General Daniel H. Hill complained about the weapons issued to his troops: "I have long believed that there was treachery in the Ordnance Dept."[39]

Other operations relating to war materiel were equally unsuccessful. In 1861 Quartermaster-General Abraham C. Myers inherited troops most of whom were clothed and shod by the states which

[37]Frank E. Vandiver, *Ploughshares into Swords: Josiah Gorgas and Confederate Ordnance* (Austin, Tex., 1952), pp. 84–104.
[38]*Ibid.*, pp. 105–109.
[39]*Ibid.*, pp. 82, 105–111.

furnished them. He also had the good fortune to secure quantities of tents, blankets, and shoes by foreign purchase. Yet Myers made few if any long-range plans, and in the spring of 1862 the troops were ill-equipped and Myers' reserves dangerously low. Commissary-General for Subsistence Lucius B. Northrup had displayed little more foresight than had Myers.[40] As early in the war as July 1861, Mary Chesnut recorded in her famous "insiders'" diary, "Now, if I were to pick out the best abused one, where all catch it so bountifully, I should say Mr. Commissary-General Northrup is the most cursed and vilified."[41]

The Southern Confederacy did not have the material resources to fight a mass industrial war. Nor did the Confederates have much success purchasing the tools of war in Europe; the tightening of the blockade, lack of specie, and the neutral posture of the European powers frustrated Confederate efforts. To fight its war for survival the South needed to organize and husband every resource it had. Some Confederate leaders realized these facts of life early in the conflict; others learned the lesson from bitter experience. But in the spring of 1862, the efforts of men like Gorgas had not yet been rewarded, and the short-sightedness of men like Myers had been only partially revealed. The hope of a short war had faded, and Southern preparations for a long war were woefully inadequate.

The short war mentality was equally evident in the Confederacy's army organization. Secretary of War Benjamin's figures were by his own admission inexact; but in his report of February 1862, more than two-thirds of the Confederate army were listed as twelve-month volunteers. The enlistment terms of these soldiers were due to expire during the campaigning season of 1862, and if the men chose not to reenlist, the Confederacy confronted disaster.[42]

After Southern soldiers found that war involved more than picnics and parades, volunteering had lagged considerably. Many Southern soldiers discouraged friends and relatives at home from duplicating their mistakes. "Jord[an] you spoke as if you had some notion of volunteering. I advise you to stay at home," a Louisianian

[40]Richard D. Goff, *Confederate Supply* (Durham, N.C., 1969), pp. 34–39.

[41]Mary Boykin Chesnut, *A Diary from Dixie*, ed. by Ben Ames Williams (Boston, 1949), p. 99.

[42]Benjamin to Davis, February—, 1862, *O.R.*, series IV, I, 955–964.

counseled his brother-in-law in October 1861.[43] Similar advice came from many homesick men during the first winter of war. Congress attempted to stimulate reenlistment by legislation that offered bounty money, furloughs, and elected officers to those who extended their service, but had little success. Between the lines of President Davis' message to Congress on February 25, 1862, was the uncertainty of a commander-in-chief who did not know how many soldiers he commanded or would command in the coming months. Davis had always opposed short enlistments, and he spoke candidly about the chaos attending reenlistment: "the process of furloughs and re-enlistment in progress for the last month has so far disorganized and weakened our forces as to impair our ability for successful defense."[44] The Confederacy, then, faced renewed Union assaults in 1862 uncertain of its manpower and all but devoid of the martial enthusiasm of the previous spring and summer.

Waning confidence in Southern military performance, foreign aid, war materiel, and manpower also infected Confederate economic and fiscal policy. The economic impact and dislocation of the war were not too widespread during the first year. Nor was the strangling effect of the Union blockade yet evident. But economic ills did exist locally, and long-range prospects were less than sanguine in early 1862.

In Richmond, for example, proximity to the battle front, the influx of the national government, and the disruption of established trading patterns with the North had produced ferment in the business community. The report of the city council's finance committee for January 1862 was especially revealing. Part of the report urged the city fathers to extend the time limit for business license applications, owing to the large numbers of new enterprises opening in the city. Another portion of the report, however, dealt with the high rate of failures among the city's established businesses. An auction company had requested the council to refund its license fee because the company had dissolved. The finance committee rejected the plea: "if this should be considered sufficient reason for remitting a tax, the Council may expect to be flooded with petitions for the remission of taxes; as it has, unhappily, been the case during the past year

[43]Cited in Frank E. Vandiver, *Basic History of the Confederacy* (Princeton, N.J., 1962), p. 121. See also Albert Burton Moore, *Conscription and Conflict in the Confederacy* (New York, 1924), pp. 6–11.
[44]*Journal of Congress*, V, 25–26.

that many persons in the city have found their business unprofitable and have stopped it; and to remit the taxes in all such cases will materially and injuriously affect the finances of the city."

Economic instability also affected the capital's food markets as rising prices plagued the city's consumers. The price of flour rose $1 Confederate per barrel between September 1861 and January 1862. During the same period the price of coffee doubled; common whiskey rose from $.65 to $1.50 per gallon; and butter increased from $.26 to $.40 per pound. To be sure, Richmond was exceptional—many localities in the Southern interior remained undisturbed by rising prices and business instability in 1861 and 1862—but Richmond was also a bellwether. Sooner or later, to some degree, the same economic problems that beset the capital affected the Confederate hinterland.[45]

The government's financial policies were little help. To his credit, Secretary of the Treasury Christopher G. Memminger advocated taxation as the proper method for financing the war. Congress, however, balked, and Memminger settled for a system involving a series of loans and treasury note issues to pay the government's expenses. By the early spring of 1862 Memminger's department was in serious trouble. The Treasury had made no concerted effort to collect staple commodities pledged to the produce loans, and planters began selling those items on which the government's credit depended. By February 1862, treasury notes—fiat money—comprised 76 percent of the government's income; at the same time, a gold dollar in Richmond was worth $1.40 in Confederate money. Only the good will and faith of the Southern people held the inflation rate that low, when in New York a dollar in gold brought only $1.01 in United States currency. In August 1861, Congress had imposed a war tax of $.50 per $100 assessed value on various kinds of property. However, Memminger had not yet constructed the administrative organization to collect the tax, and when he did, state governments undertook to pay the levies for their citizens—largely in unsupported state currency.[46]

Had the war lasted only one year, Memminger might have re-

[45]Louis H. Manarin, *Richmond at War: The Minutes of the City Council, 1861–1865* (Chapel Hill, N.C., 1965), pp. 104–107; Emory M. Thomas, *The Confederate State of Richmond: A Biography of the Capital* (Austin, Tex., 1971), pp. 70–74.

[46]Richard Cecil Todd, *Confederate Finance* (Athens, Ga., 1954), pp. 39–41, 105, 130–135, 198.

stored fiscal confidence and funded the Confederate debt with tariff revenues, but as the war continued, the flow of government paper money increased. Memminger realized the folly of unsupported paper money but could do little about it. A great deal of Southern specie—gleaned from banks under the government's first loan the previous spring—had gone to Europe for the purchase of war supplies. Cotton was white gold only when Confederates could ship it to markets. Beyond the limited amount of specie, estimated at $27 million, and the uncertain potential of cotton, the Confederacy had little in the way of economic resources, hence its reliance on fiat money and popular faith in its domestic economy. Popular faith, in turn, depended upon the capability of the government to defend the country and to stabilize the war economy. As the second year of the war began, the nation appeared to be living not only on borrowed money but also on borrowed time.

Politics and public morale both reflected and contributed to the Confederate failures during the eight months following Manassas. The provincialism which characterized the ante-bellum period, the naïvete which attended secession, and the faith in a short, easy victory seemingly confirmed at Manassas combined to convince Confederate Southerners that they were invincible. Frustration and failure came hard to a people so assured of the righteousness of their cause and so buoyed by the initial success of their revolution. Reasons for the new nation's failures were complex and fundamental, but most Confederates, even if they grasped the sources of their national frustration, had neither the time nor the inclination to attack the roots of their dilemma. Instead, they focused their concern upon men and issues nearer at hand, an exercise in corporate psychological transference. Such behavior was natural. If their cause was just and their armies were valiant, Confederates could only look to their leadership as the source of failure. Thus, in the fall and winter of 1861–62, dissent, charges of bungling, and hints of treachery further weakened public confidence and threatened to rend the fabric of Southern nationhood.[47]

The discord began at the top, among the leaders of the would-be nation. Already the administration had warred with state governors over troop and arms requisitions. Tension between state and na-

[47]See Wiley, *Road to Appomattox*, pp. 43–59.

tional governments was a constant fact of Confederate life. But in the adversity which mounted as the Confederacy approached the first anniversary of its founding, the veneer of unanimity and personal harmony among the national leaders vanished. The President and Vice-President fell out. During the early months of his tenure, Alexander Stephens had seemed to be one of Davis' trusted advisors. He made speeches supporting administration policies, and in securing Virginia's early alliance with the Confederacy, he rendered important service. Then, as military affairs assumed first call upon the government's attention, the President consulted Stephens less and less, and Stephens agreed with the administration policy of nationalism less and less. During 1862 the Vice-President found little to do in Richmond, and after that year he seldom even visited the capital. Eventually he abandoned his disgruntled silence and began publicly criticizing as "tyrannical" the administration he supposedly served.[48]

Other political leaders were similarly dissatisfied with the Davis administration and with each other. T. R. R. Cobb confided to his wife in March 1862 that the President "*would be deposed* if the Congress had any more confidence in Stephens than in him."[49] Congress did pass a bill which created the post of commanding general of all Confederate armies. Davis recognized the bill for what it was, an oblique expression of no confidence in the constitutional commander-in-chief, and accordingly he vetoed the measure. In the House, Representative Henry S. Foote of Tennessee introduced a formal motion of no confidence in the secretaries of war and navy, Benjamin and Mallory. Although the motion failed, both Benjamin and Mallory had become political liabilities to the administration.[50]

Even though no "court" and "country" political parties ever developed in the Confederate Congress, a "floating" antiadministration faction was emerging. Louis T. Wigfall of Texas, for example, had generally supported Davis' military legislation; but from early 1862 the Texan opposed Davis' strategy, domestic policy, and person in ever increasing degree. If Wigfall and men like him did not

[48]See James Z. Rabun, "Alexander H. Stephens and Jefferson Davis," *American Historical Review*, LVIII (1953), 290–321.

[49]Cited in Wiley, *Road to Appomattox*, p. 83.

[50]*Journal of Congress*, V, 15, 45–46, 48–49, 57, 66, 107–108; *Proceedings of the Confederate Congress Southern Historical Society Papers*, XLIV–LII, 1923–1959; XLIV, 23–28, 69–71, 80, 84–85.

display the cohesion of a consistent antiadministration faction, they harmed the Davis government on selected issues.

It was unfortunate for the Confederacy that no loyal opposition party ever formed. A rival party would have had the obligation to pose responsible alternatives to the administration program and might have had the discipline to forestall political vendettas against Davis by men such as Wigfall and Foote. As it happened, factors more personal than party allegiance—pre-Confederate party affiliation, stance on secession, and proximity of enemy armies to a congressman's home district or state—lay at the base of the structure of Confederate politics. Southern congressmen and senators assumed individual stances on issues which defied consistency.[51]

Perhaps the South's heritage of individualism, conditioned by rural isolation and mastery of plantation empires, fed self-assertion among Confederate leaders. Maybe Southern politicians had been naysayers so long in the United States Congress that they were unable to shuck the habit when the South became a nation. For whatever reason, even before the succession of failures following Manassas, quarrels and carping were frequent among rebel leaders. South Carolinian James H. Hammond recognized the condition even while the illusion of harmony prevailed at the Montgomery Convention. In February 1861, he wrote, "*Big-man-me-ism* reigns supreme & every one thinks every other a jealous fool or an aspiring knave."[52]

Predictably, Hammond succumbed to the general despair of March 1862. He advised his friend, Congressman W. W. Boyce, "Impeach Jeff Davis for incompetency & call a convention of the States. Ad interim make Floyd [John B.] or Price [Sterling] or Toombs [Robert] Dictator. West Point is death to us & sick Presidents & Generals are equally fatal."[53] Boyce responded to such desperate sentiments on at least two occasions that spring by telling Hammond, "I think you are even too hopeful," and "I assure you

[51]See Thomas B. Alexander and Richard E. Beringer, *The Anatomy of the Confederate Congress* (Nashville, Tenn., 1972), pp. 35–73, 335–339; David W. Potter, "Jefferson Davis and the Political Factors in Confederate Defeat," in David Donald (ed.), *Why the North Won the Civil War* (Baton Rouge, La., 1960), pp. 94–112; Alvy L. King, *Louis T. Wigfall: Southern Fire-eater* (Baton Rouge, La., 1960), pp. 127–140.
[52]Cited in Wiley, *Road to Appomattox*, pp. 100–101.
[53]Hammond to Boyce, March 17, 1862, in Rosser H. Taylor (ed.), "Boyce-Hammond Correspondence," *Journal of Southern History*, III (1937), 349.

that things are in a more critical condition than you imagine."[54]

Abrasive ambition surfaced in the military high command days after the victory at Manassas, and subsequent defeats only served to increase the discord. P. G. T. Beauregard, on July 29, 1861, wrote a letter to his friend and congressman William Porcher Miles complaining about the decision not to advance on Washington after the battle and blaming the lost opportunity on the administration. Miles read the letter on the floor of the House, and the second-guessing began in public. Davis sent Beauregard a mild rebuke, Beauregard apologized, and the rift appeared at an end. In October, however, Beauregard issued a detailed report of the battle to the War Department and the newspapers. The report overlooked few opportunities to congratulate its author, and Davis charged the General with trying "to exalt yourself at my expense." This time Beauregard did not apologize and the feud raged in the press for some time.

Tempers also flared between Davis and his other commander at Manassas, Joseph E. Johnston. On the last day of August the President asked the Senate to confirm a list of five men as full generals in the Confederate army. Johnston ranked fourth in seniority on the list behind Samuel Cooper, Albert Sidney Johnston, and Robert E. Lee, and ahead of Beauregard. Adjutant and Inspector General Cooper, the army's chief administrator, and A. S. Johnston were old friends of Davis; Lee was a new friend who had won the President's confidence. J. E. Johnston had outranked all three in the United States army, and he interpreted Davis' action as a severe affront. He wrote the President a long and bitter letter, and Davis sent a curt reply in which he told Johnston that his insinuations were unbecoming. Perhaps even more unbecoming were the semipublic quarrels between the Confederate Commander-in-Chief and two of his key subordinates.[55]

Southern men had no monopoly on highly placed dissension. Varina Davis had a difficult period as first lady of Richmond's official society. Some Virginians resented the intrusion of any "official society" into a long-established social set, and within government circles Mrs. Davis had tiffs with Mesdames Wigfall, Johnston (Mrs. Joseph E.), and Myers. The Quartermaster-General's wife called the

[54]Boyce to Hammond, March 17, 1862, and April 12, 1862, Taylor (ed.), "Boyce-Hammond," 349–352.
[55]See Wiley, *Road to Appomattox*, pp. 87–92.

first lady from Mississippi a "western woman" and as the feud progressed changed "woman" to "squaw."[56]

Southern newspapers had been enthusiastic in their support of the new nation. Even those editors who had opposed secession for the most part accepted the *fait accompli* and offered support to the Confederate government. Even in the face of the military reverses of late 1861 and early 1862, the press remained generally sanguine. There were, however, significant exceptions, and eventually the press began to reverberate with criticism and carping over the conduct of Confederate statecraft and military affairs.[57]

In Charleston, the *Mercury*, edited by Robert Barnwell Rhett, Jr., began earnest editorial opposition to the Davis government in February 1862. One of the *Mercury's* correspondents, George William Bagby, editor of the *Southern Literary Messenger*, who signed his material "Hermes," recorded his private sentiments in his journal: "We have reached a very dark hour in the history of this struggle. I do not say the cause will fail, but the chances are all against us. . . . Cold, haughty, peevish, narrow-minded, pig-headed, *malignant*, he [President Davis] is the cause. . . . While he lives, there is no hope for us. God alone can save us. Will He?"[58] And in Richmond, John M. Daniel's *Examiner* was only slightly more restrained on February 24, when the paper began its open opposition to the administration. "The Confederacy," the editor stated, "has had everything that was required for success but one; and that one thing it was and it is supposed to possess more than anything else, namely *talent.*" Then Daniel continued his attack upon the War and Navy Offices and explained his change of policy: "In common with all conscientious Southern men, we have long kept silence. . . . But there is no longer room to doubt the propriety of saying and doing all that can be said and done to surround the President with the first men in the land. We must get more talent in that Confederate government or be ruined."[59] It was a short step from criticizing the President's bad advisors to criticizing the President himself—a step the *Examiner* soon took.[60]

[56]Chesnut, *Diary*, pp. 99–109.
[57]See J. Cutler Andrews, *The South Reports the Civil War* (Princeton, N.J., 1970), pp. 448–449.
[58]George W. Bagby Journal, Virginia Historical Society Library.
[59]Richmond *Examiner*, February 24, 1862.
[60]See *ibid.*, March 30, 1862.

Naturally, semiprivate quarrels and public dissent coupled with military failures affected the morale of the Southern people. Undoubtedly Jefferson Davis had the flagging spirits of his countrymen on his mind when he wrote his inaugural address. On February 22, birthday of that other revolutionary leader, Davis took the oath of office as permanent president of the Confederacy. He wrote a good speech. He was candid with his fellow citizens, he admitted that "the tide for the moment is against us," and he confessed that it was "at the darkest hour of our struggle [that] the Provisional gives place to the Permanent Government." Then he offered hope for the future, faith in the devotion of the people, and commitment of his own energies. If he promised little in the way of specific policy changes, Davis' resolve to do better had a sincere ring.[61]

Of course, speeches would not reverse the tide of Confederate failure or lighten the nation's "darkest hour" for long. Even as Davis invoked the blessing of Providence upon his undertaking, Providence seemed to spurn the invitation by baptising the new government in a continuous downpour of cold rain. The Vice-President, when asked for a few words, said nothing, and the Richmond *Examiner* found the inaugural address so insignificant that "it might, in fact, have been omitted from the ceremony had not custom required that the President should say something on such an occasion."[62] Deeds, not words, were required if the Southern nation were to live. Nor was time on the Southern side. The 1862 spring campaigns were at hand, and in Washington, Abraham Lincoln had issued President's General War Order Number One ordering a "general forward movement" to begin on February 22, the same day on which Davis inaugurated his government.

The Confederacy to this point had been an incarnation of the Old South, and as such the Old South had been tried and found wanting. Southerners found that Confederate national survival and rigid adherence to ante-bellum Southern ideology were mutually exclusive. The ante-bellum South could not metamorphose into the "bellum" South without some fundamental alterations in its cherished way of life. Haltingly and to a large degree unconsciously, the Confederate South emerged a significant mutation of the South the nation had

[61]Dunbar Rowland (ed.), *Jefferson Davis, Constitutionalist: His Letters, Papers, and Speeches*, 10 vols. (Jackson, Miss., 1923), V, 198–203.
[62]Richmond *Examiner*, February 24, 1862.

been called into being to preserve. To fulfill Southern nationalism, Confederate Southerners had to slaughter some of the sacred cows and overturn some of the shibboleths that had previously defined them as a people.

CHAPTER 7

Origins of the Revolutionary South

I N March of 1862 Union General George B. McClellan began the campaign by which he hoped to crush the Southern rebellion once and for all. His prospects appeared bright. After elaborate preparations he transported an army of more than 100,000 men from Washington down the Potomac and the Chesapeake Bay to Fort Monroe on the tip of the peninsula between the James and York Rivers in Virginia. From there he planned to march up the peninsula to Richmond and there destroy the Confederacy's main field arm, its capital, and its government in one blow. McClellan arrived in Virginia on April 2 to join the Army of the Potomac, and the next day Secretary of War Edwin Stanton closed his recruiting offices—the ultimate statement of his confidence in the Confederacy's early doom.[1]

Standing between McClellan's host and Richmond were John Bankhead Magruder and about 10,000 Southern troops. Magruder, a West Pointer known as "Prince John" for his fastidious dress and for his skill at official entertaining, was a professional soldier who had commanded artillery with some skill in the Mexican War. But in April of 1862 many of Magruder's weapons were "Quaker guns," logs painted black to resemble cannon, and "Prince John" was all

[1] Union optimism as the campaigns of 1862 began is well described in Alan Nevins, *The War for the Union*, II, *War Becomes Revolution*, 4 vols. (New York, 1959–1971), 88–108; and Bruce Catton, *Terrible Swift Sword* (New York, 1963), pp. 250–251.

too aware that his command could not provide a proper reception for McClellan's party.[2]

Magruder held a fortified line across the tip of the peninsula from Yorktown to the Warwick River. He reasoned without much confidence that if his batteries at Yorktown and Gloucester Point could keep enemy ships out of the York, if the ironclad *Virginia* could keep the enemy out of the James, and if he were reinforced massively and immediately, then perhaps he could slow down McClellan a bit. "I have made my arrangements to fight with my small force," Magruder reported to Richmond on April 5, "but without the slightest hope of success." The next day he commented, "Reinforcements come very slowly, and will probably be too late."[3]

Magruder's mood was justified, but for the rest of April, McClellan settled down to siege operations before Yorktown, granting the Confederates what appeared to be an uneasy stay of execution. Elsewhere, however, the tide continued to run against the Confederacy.

On April 6 a Confederate army commanded by General Albert Sydney Johnston attacked Ulysses S. Grant's invasion force at Shiloh, Tennessee. In his drive up the Tennessee River, Grant had paused at Pittsburg Landing to await reinforcements commanded by Don Carlos Buell. Johnston concentrated at Corinth, Mississippi, and sought to overwhelm Grant's army by a surprise attack. "Tonight," he reportedly said, "we'll water our horses in the Tennessee River." Though the Confederates' approach was less than stealthy, the Southerners achieved surprise and ran pell-mell through Federal camps during the initial stage of the battle. Then their momentum sagged as Union resistance stiffened. Johnston suffered a mortal wound while attempting to rally his men, and command of the Southern army passed to P. G. T. Beauregard, who directed the disorganized troops as best he could and halted the Confederate attacks at dusk. The Confederates had almost fulfilled their dead

[2]Douglas S. Freeman, *Lee's Lieutenants: A Study in Command*, 3 vols. (New York, 1942–1944), I, 15–19.

[3]Magruder to Lee, April 15, 1862, *War of the Rebellion: A Compilation of the Official Records of the Union and Confederate Armies*, 70 vols. in 127 (Washington, D.C., 1880–1901), ser. I, XI, 3, 442; and Magruder to Lee, April 5, 1862 *O.R.*, ser. I, XI, 3, 425. For assessments of the "Yorktown line," see Freeman, *Lee's Lieutenants*, I, 148–153; and Joseph E. Johnston, *Narrative of Military Operations*, ed. by Frank E. Vandiver (Bloomington, Ind., 1959), pp. 112–114.

general's prophecy; they had driven the Union force back to the last defensible position before the Tennessee. But almost was not enough. Next day Grant's army, reinforced by Buell's troops, counterattacked and in fierce fighting won back lost ground. Beauregard then broke off the engagement and took his army back to Corinth. Tactically the Battle of Shiloh was a bloody draw; but from the Confederate perspective it was much less. The enemy threat in the West was still intact, and it was the Southerners who had retreated, losing ground, men, and materiel.[4]

April continued to be a bad month for the Confederacy. On April 11 the North captured Fort Pulaski near Savannah, sealing the Savannah River and further tightening the Federal blockade.[5] Two weeks later came a crushing blow. On April 25 the Confederates abandoned New Orleans to Admiral David Farragut's fleet. Confederate General Mansfield Lovell had had to gamble the city's safety upon the guns of Forts Jackson and St. Phillip down river from New Orleans. When Farragut's ships ran past the river forts, Lovell had to evacuate his small army and give up New Orleans.[6]

Thus, with the campaigning season of 1862 barely begun, the Confederate situation was well-nigh desperate. As the national expression of the Old South, the Confederacy was a failure.

At this crucial juncture in their fate, the Confederates themselves began a transformation in the Southern world as they had known it before 1861. What emerged was a Confederate South, distinct from the Souths that came before and after. Revolutions have a way of getting out of hand—of affecting institutions and lives they were never intended to affect. Though the change was often subtle and unintended, the Confederates' revolution, in the name of survival, altered many, if not most, of those traditional Southern characteristics it was designed to preserve. The war experience challenged the

[4]On Shiloh see Thomas L. Connelly, *Army of the Heartland: The Army of Tennessee, 1861–1862* (Baton Rouge, La., 1967), pp. 145–175; T. Harry Williams, *P. G. T. Beauregard: Napoleon in Gray* (Baton Rouge, La., 1955), pp. 133–140; Charles P. Roland, "Albert Sidney Johnston and the Shiloh Campaign," *Civil War History,* IV (1958) 355–382; and two recent monographs: James Lee McDonough, *Shiloh—Hell Before Night* (Knoxville, Ky., 1976); and Wiley Sword, *Shiloh: Bloody April* (New York, 1974).

[5]See Allen P. Julian, "Fort Pulaski," *Civil War Times Illustrated,* XI (1970), 8–21.

[6]See Gerald M. Capers, *Occupied City: New Orleans under the Federals, 1862–1865* (Lexington, Ky., 1965), pp. 25–53; and Charles Lee Lewis, *David Glasgow Farragut: Our First Admiral,* 2 vols. (Annapolis, Md., 1943), II, 33–77.

chief tenets of the old Southern ideology and life style, and by the spring of 1862 it had become apparent that if the Confederacy were to survive, Southerners would have to fundamentally alter their world and their world view.[7]

Perhaps no one perceived this reality more clearly than Jefferson Davis, who was, after all, in the best position to gauge the depth of Confederate failure and to assume responsibility for Southern independence and nationality. In his inaugural address on February 22, Davis had shared his vision of the nation's "darkest hour" and pledged to do better. Within the limits of legislative and administrative inertia and of his own political personality, Davis did do better.[8]

He began with his cabinet. Secretary of State R. M. T. Hunter had already submitted his resignation to accept a seat in the Senate, where he would serve as president *pro tem.* Secretary of War Benjamin was the target of much criticism from the press, politicians, and public because of the Southern war record in general and the disasters at Roanoke Island and Fort Donelson in particular. Benjamin had also made enemies among the Southern officer corps, most notably Stonewall Jackson and Joseph E. Johnston. Secretary of the Navy Stephen R. Mallory had proven the administration's second most criticized cabinet officer. Attorney General Thomas Bragg had asked to retire to his native North Carolina. His motives were unclear; perhaps the Democrat Bragg believed he could best serve the Davis government by making room for the appointment of a former Whig to his post. The remaining two members of Davis' cabinet, Secretary of the Treasury Memminger and Postmaster General Reagan, who worked well in harness with Davis, were secure.[9]

Clearly, reconstitution of the cabinet was necessary. Davis needed to find replacements for Hunter and Bragg and to decide the fates of Benjamin and Mallory. The President temporized; he made William M. Browne, an English-born newspaper editor from Georgia, *ad interim* secretary of state while he pondered the politics of reorganization.[10] Finally on March 18 he submitted to the Senate his nominations for the permanent government's cabinet.

[7]See Emory M. Thomas, *The Confederacy as a Revolutionary Experience* (Englewood Cliffs, N.J., 1971.)
[8]See Frank E. Vandiver, *Jefferson Davis and the Confederate State* (Oxford, Miss., 1964).
[9]Rembert W. Patrick, *Jefferson Davis and his Cabinet* (Baton Rouge, La., 1944), pp. 199–101, 167–182, 302.
[10]*Ibid.*, pp. 101–102.

Mallory, Memminger, and Reagan were to stay; Benjamin was shifted from War to State in order to retain his counsel and relieve his embarrassment. Thomas H. Watts, an Alabama Whig, became the new attorney general, and to the War Office, Davis called George Wythe Randolph of Virginia. Predictably the Senate divided over Mallory and Benjamin, but confirmed Davis' entire slate on March 19.[11]

Because the Confederate Congress never established a Supreme Court, Davis used his Attorneys General as *de facto* final arbiters of legal questions involving the government. So Attorney General Watts spent much of his time writing opinions on questions of law for the President and for other department heads. During his eighteen-month tenure Watts wrote one hundred informal opinions, watched over judicial patronage, and heard claims against the government. He served in the cabinet until October of 1863, when he resigned to run for Governor of Alabama.[12]

Randolph's greatest claim to fame when he took over the War Office was his grandfather, Thomas Jefferson. The Richmond lawyer had been an active secessionist, an undistinguished officer, and an unsuccessful candidate for the Confederate House of Representatives. Davis probably made Randolph Secretary of War to replace Hunter as the cabinet's resident Virginian. Consciously or unconsciously he wanted Randolph as an ornament, for he had in fact long believed that he should be his own War Secretary. Convinced that his chief talents were more military than political, Davis doubtless hoped that Randolph would oversee the internal administration of the War Office and implement the policies and strategy of the Commander-in-Chief. For a time Randolph fulfilled these hopes. But when he learned his job, Randolph displayed talent and independence beyond Davis' expectations and ultimately beyond Davis' tolerance.[13]

The cabinet reorganization, designed to improve the administration's political position and to increase its internal harmony and efficiency, had mixed results. At first the changes looked good to

[11]*Journal of the Congress of the Confederate States of America, 1861–1865,* 7 vols. (Washington, D.C., 1904–1905), II, 72–74.
[12]Patrick, *Davis and his Cabinet,* pp. 303–310; Rembert W. Patrick (ed.), *The Opinions of the Confederate Attorneys General, 1861–1865* (Buffalo, N.Y., 1950), pp. 71–167, 179–315, 329–343.
[13]Patrick, *Davis and his Cabinet,* pp. 120–131.

most Southerners, though predictably the Richmond *Examiner* disapproved violently:

Mr. Davis has sacrificed to popular clamor without yielding to public opinion. He has made so small a change. . . . All of the old members were retained, except those who wanted to get out of it. Benjamin is transferred, and Mallory left in *statu quo*. The representation of the Synagogue is not diminished; it remains full. The administration has now an opportunity of making some reputation; for, nothing being expected of it, of course every success will be a clear gain.[14]

Certainly the Davis government had to improve more than its political posture. The peril confronting the would-be nation that spring demanded not only new people but new policies. By the time Davis announced his revised cabinet, he had already inaugurated new measures.

On February 27 Congress authorized the President to suspend the writ of habeas corpus and to declare martial law in "such cities, towns, and military districts as shall, in his judgement, be in . . . danger of attack by the enemy." The act contained internal ambiguity implying that suspension of habeas corpus and martial law were the same thing. Quite aside from this, though, the act challenged the Old South's fundamental attachment to individualism and its jealous regard for civil liberties. Moreover, it clearly said that the central Confederate government did not trust state and local legal machinery to exercise the necessary discipline over a people at war.[15]

Subsequent acts of Congress in this area progressively limited the blanket authority granted the President in the law of February 1862. Nevertheless Davis' power to suspend habeas corpus endured and contributed to the government's growing centralization.[16] In his first suspension order, written to General Benjamin Huger at Norfolk on the day the act passed, the President stated what he had in mind. After telling Huger to place Norfolk and Portsmouth under martial law, Davis added, "preparation should be made for the removal of that part of the population who could only embarrass the

[14]Richmond, *Examiner*, March 20, 1862.
[15]James W. Matthews (ed.), *The Status at Large of the Confederate States of America,* . . . *First Session* . . . *First Congress* (Richmond, Va., 1862), p. 1.
[16]See John B. Robbins, "The Confederacy and the Writ of Habeas Corpus," *Georgia Historical Quarterly*, LV (1971), 83–101.

defense."[17] Davis wished to be able to arrest and detain "disloyal" Confederates without going through the time-consuming and sometimes unpredictable machinations of civil procedure. This was Davis' answer to the ever-present conflict between liberty and military necessity in wartime. That spring he resorted to martial law a number of times in a number of places to allow local commanders maximum latitude in their search for security.[18]

An extreme example occurred in the Confederate capital itself. Davis put Richmond under martial law on March 1 and delegated responsibility for its security to Brigadier General John H. Winder. The aging Marylander took his charge seriously. He banned the sale of liquor in the city, ordered all privately owned firearms surrendered to the Confederate Ordnance Bureau, required hotels and railroad companies to provide lists of their guests and passengers, initiated a passport system to control the movement of people in and out of the city, and stationed soldiers at the outskirts to enforce his regime. Winder even attempted to enforce the Hack Ordinance, a municipal regulation governing fares for hired carriages; but Richmond police had never been able to prevent overcharging, and though Winder tried, he was no more successful than the civil authorities.[19]

By March 15, 1862, Winder had confined thirty suspected traitors, spies, and Union sympathizers in the Castle Goodwin military prison. Among these unfortunates were John Minor Botts, former United States congressman from Virginia, who had declared himself a neutral, and the Reverend Alden Bosserman, pastor of Richmond's Universalist Church, who had prayed openly for the defeat of "this unholy rebellion."[20]

The General employed soldiers from his command and also hired civilian agents to do his work. So zealous were Winder's men that they confiscated patent medicine of a suspect alcoholic content and

[17]Davis to Huger, February 27, 1862, Dunbar Rowland (ed.), *Jefferson Davis, Constitutionalist: His Letters, Papers, and Speeches*, 10 vols. (Jackson, Miss., 1923), V, 207.

[18]See for example James D. Richardson, *A Compilation of the Messages and Papers of the Confederacy*, 2 vols. (Nashville, Tenn., 1906), I, 219–227.

[19]*Ibid.*, I, 220–221; Department of Henrico, General Order 4 and Special Order 43, printed in Richmond *Whig*, March 14, 1862; Emory M. Thomas, *Confederate State of Richmond: A Biography of the Capital* (Austin, Tex., 1971), pp. 81–83.

[20]Richmond *Dispatch*, April 13, 1862; Richmond *Examiner*, March 6 and April 19, 1862.

arrested druggists who filled forged prescriptions for medicinal spirits. Late in March, Winder tried to fix prices of foodstuffs in Richmond's marketplaces. The experiment lasted only a few weeks because farmers stopped bringing their produce into the city in the face of passport delays and fixed prices. Rather than confront empty marketplaces, Winder revoked his order and abandoned his price-fixing scheme.[21]

General Winder's actions were perhaps atypical. They went further than the President had orignially intended, but they were an index of how far the government would go to win independence. In April the Congress limited suspension of habeas corpus to cases involving violation of Confederate law.[22] And on April 25, Attorney General Watts wrote in answer to a query from Davis: "Let the *general* rule be that the civil jurisdiction of the courts shall be exercised as usual; and the exception prevail only when a necessity for the departure is manifest."[23] In Richmond and elsewhere civilian courts remained open and traditional law enforcement activities continued during the Confederacy's attempt to enforce internal security by arbitrary arrest.

External security, however, seemed the most pressing issue before the Davis government in the spring of 1862. On March 28 the President took a significant step toward improving Confederate military strength and away from the traditions of state rights and individualism characteristic of the ante-bellum South. At the urging of War Secretary Randolph, the President requested from Congress the first military draft on the North American continent. Davis proposed that "all persons residing within the Confederate States, between the ages of 18 and 35 years, and rightfully subject to military duty, shall be held to be in the military service of the Confederate States, and that some plain and simple method be adopted for their prompt enrollment and organization."[24] By April 16 the Congress had complied, and the Confederacy had a conscription act.

[21]Richmond *Whig*, March 17, 25, and 27, and April 30, 1862; Department of Henrico, General Order 20, printed in Richmond *Whig*, April 2, 1862; Sallie Brock Putnam, *Richmond During the War: Four Years of Personal Observation* (New York, 1867), pp. 113–114.

[22]*Journal of Congress*, II, 220.

[23]Watts to Davis, April 25, 1862, Patrick (ed.), *Opinions of Attorneys General*, pp. 73–75.

[24]*Journal of Congress*, II, 106.

The act "to Further Provide for the Public Defense" obligated all white males between eighteen and thirty-five to three-years' service or less, should the war end sooner; a second law, passed in September, raised the age limit to forty-five. Men eligible for the draft who could secure an acceptable substitute, someone otherwise ineligible, did not have to serve. Those already in service would remain, and twelve-month volunteers, the majority of the army, received a sixty-day furlough and the privilege of electing officers at the company level.[25]

A few days later, on April 21 Congress dealt with the most basic question regarding the draft: exemption. Obviously the government could not simply herd almost an entire generation into the field and leave no producers at home to support the Southern army. Too, certain groups of men possessing special skills or holding important positions in civil society were of more use to the cause at home than in the military. Accordingly Congress decided upon a "class-exemption" system in which all those in specific occupations were relieved of responsibility for military service. The classes of exemption included national and state officers, railroad employees, druggists, professors, schoolteachers, miners, ministers, pilots, nurses, and iron-furnace and foundry laborers. The War Department had discretionary power to grant other class exemptions in crucial industries or special circumstances.[26]

To enforce the conscription act the War Office first depended upon the Adjutant and Inspector General's Office and later (December 1862) upon a separate Conscript Bureau. The law removed from the states the responsibility for recruiting and organizing units for the national army, placing this responsibility with the central government, and expanding the authority of the Davis government far beyond the power merely to raise armies. The War Department used its discretionary power to subsidize the South's war industries. Those manufacturing establishments engaged in the production of essential materials had little difficulty securing draft-exempt labor; nonessential industries suffered from labor shortages and received little sympathy in Richmond. Exemption thus became a means to

[25]Matthews (ed.), *Statutes at Large . . . First Session . . . First Congress*, p. 29, and *Statutes at Large . . . Second Session . . . First Congress*, (Richmond, Va., 1863), pp. 77–79.
[26]See Albert B. Moore, *Conscription and Conflict in the Confederacy* (New York, 1924), pp. 52–53.

husband, channel, and organize the South's resources not only of manpower but of material.[27]

Naturally the draft law and its enforcement were less than perfect, and naturally many Southerners resented on principle the departure from state rights and individual liberty that conscription represented. Some of this resentment worked to the advantage of the cause. Southern men began volunteering again, if only to avoid the stigma of conscript. Yet, for motives high-minded and mean, many Southerners resisted the draft or assisted evasion by others. The substitute and exemption systems were abused. Professional substitutes took payment from their sponsors, enlisted, deserted, and sought more sponsors. State governors frustrated the exemption process by claiming more state officers than they needed and by obstructing the conscription process. The classic example was Georgia's Governor Joe Brown, who exempted more men than any other governor and fought conscription in the courts. President Davis wrote Brown extended letters—actually legal briefs—and in November of 1862 sent former interim Secretary of State William M. Browne on a diplomatic mission to seek the compliance of the Georgia Governor. The state Supreme Court in Georgia upheld the draft unanimously; still Brown persisted and withheld troops whenever possible.

On the other side, Conscription Bureau officers too often resembled kidnapers or at least "press gangs" in their efforts to enforce the draft. And Congress did not make the draft more palatable when in October 1862, in the name of exemption reform, it exempted owners or overseers of twenty or more slaves. This species of class exemption stimulated class conflict; Southern yeomen resented so blatant a symbol of the "rich man's war" as "poor man's fight."[28]

In sum, conscription as practiced by the Confederacy was never what Davis asked—"some plain and simple method . . . for . . . prompt enrollment and organization." Conscription produced only about 82,000 soldiers and more than any other issue exposed latent conflict between state and national government in the South. Fur-

[27]*Ibid.*, pp. 15–16, 161; Charles W. Ramsdell, "The Control of Manufacturing by the Confederate Government," *Mississippi Valley Historical Review*, VIII (1921), 231–249.

[28]Moore, *Conscription*, 27–82, 230–231, 255–296; 70–73; Davis to Brown, May 29, 1862, Rowland (ed.), *Jefferson Davis*, V, 254–262. Davis to Browne, November 28, 1862, Rowland (ed.), *Jefferson Davis*, V, 378–379. See also Louise B. Hill, *Joseph E. Brown and the Confederacy* (Chapel Hill, N.C., 1939).

ther, the exemption system stirred class conflict that the would-be Southern nation did not need. Yet, without conscription, the Confederacy could never have endured the campaigning season of 1862, much less the remaining years of the war; and with conscription, the Confederacy did manage to mobilize, however imperfectly, just about the entire Southern military population. There were approximately 1,000,000 white men between eighteen and forty-five in the Confederacy. At one time or another about 750,000 of these men were Confederate soldiers. If the number of men exempted from service or detailed from service to perform some vital civilian task is added to that, the total involved in the war would very nearly approximate the South's military population. Even so, figures on the comparative size of Confederate and Union armies reveal the numerical odds faced by the South. The following are "present-for-duty" totals.

DATE	CONFEDERATE	UNION
January 1, 1862	209,852	527,204
January 1, 1863	253,208	698,802
January 1, 1864	233,586	611,250
January 1, 1865	154,910	620,924

Conscription was an extreme measure, but it was doubtless necessary to keep the odds from running even more heavily against the Confederacy.[29]

While Davis was shuffling his administration and Congress was passing the habeas corpus and conscription acts, McClellan's army on the Peninsula was looming larger and more ominous. Obviously, laws and cabinet changes could have no direct effect on the immediate military threat. Accordingly, the Confederate Congress made legal provision for moving the Southern capital if necessary, authorized the Treasury Department to buy cotton, sell more bonds, and print more paper money, and on April 21 adjourned.[30] Some Southerners viewed the congressmen's hasty departure from Richmond

[29]Moore, *Conscription*, pp. 355–358; population and soldier statistics are from E. B. Long's *The Civil War Day by Day: An Almanac, 1861–1865* (Garden City, N.Y., 1971), pp. 704–706. (The Confederate army totals were from December 31 of the previous year.)

[30]Matthews (ed.), *Statutes at Large . . . First Session . . . First Congress*, pp. 28, 34.

as unseemly: "To leave Richmond at the very moment of the hazard," the *Examiner* scolded, "is not the way to encourage the army or help a cause in peril."[31] Yet there was truth in the statement of Representative Lucius Dupre of Louisiana that, "People look somewhere else than to this Congress for aid."[32] In April 1862, the salvation of the Southern nation depended on immediate military action.

Already the Confederate military mind had begun to change. The Union successes following the Battle of Manassas clearly demonstrated that the South faced a long, multifront war. The elastic strategy of offensive defense might work, but Southern military expectations needed scaling down, and success required a more modest definition. This was evident enough in Richmond, but even on the geographical fringe of the Confederacy, in Houston, Texas, newspaper editor E. H. Cushing cited the battle of Shiloh and concluded, "There will be no decisive battle. . . . Let us not deceive ourselves. . . . It [winning independence] must be done by hard knocks, long continued against an inveterate foe. And when we have gained our freedom, there will be time enough to determine when and where the 'decisive' battle was fought."[33]

Within the Confederate high command, strategic expectations were becoming more realistic and the offensive defense more elastic. Evidence of military realism appeared, for example, along the coasts of South Carolina, Georgia, and Florida. To meet the threat to the Atlantic coastline in the deep South, President Davis sent Robert E. Lee to command a newly created department. Lee, the son of Revolutionary hero "Lighthorse Harry" Lee, had been prominent in the old army of the Union. He agonized over the secession of his native Virginia but ultimately determined that he was more Virginian than American and offered his services to Governor John Letcher. Lee commanded Virginia state troops until they and he transferred to the Confederate Service, then accepted an ambiguous command in western Virginia and spent three months trying in vain to coordinate the defense of the Kanawha Valley.[34] In early

[31]Richmond, *Examiner,* April 21, 1862.
[32]Proceedings of the . . . Confederate Congresses, *Southern Historical Society Papers,* XLIV (1923), 178–183.
[33]Houston *Tri-Weekly Telegraph,* June 13, 1862.
[34]The standard biography of Lee is still Douglas S. Freeman, *R. E. Lee: A Biography,* 4 vols. (New York, 1934–1935.)

November he journeyed to South Carolina just in time to witness the Federal success at Port Royal, then spent the remainder of his time as departmental commander attempting to prevent the enemy from expanding the breach made there. Lee's actions were unpopular but successful. He essentially abandoned the coast and withdrew into the interior to concentrate his resources and draw the Federals away from their ships and floating batteries. Planters in the South Carolina and Georgia coastal lowlands reacted with understandable dismay, but Lee persisted. He constructed a viable defense line to protect the cities of Charleston and Savannah and to maintain the Charleston and Savannah Railroad. By withdrawing up the rivers, Lee was able to obstruct the passage of amphibious forces and to neutralize the superior firepower of the Union navy.[35]

In mid-March the President himself displayed a significant change of mind. In a letter to a circuit judge in Marion, Alabama, responding to criticism of his conduct of the war, Davis acknowledged "the error of my attempt to defend all the frontier." He then protested that his policy was not "purely defensive" and, referring to Shiloh, explained, "The advantage of selecting the time and place of attack was too apparent to have been overlooked, but the means might have been wanting."[36] Shiloh was an example of the offensive defense—concentrate and attack—in action; but Shiloh was less than a victory, and Beauregard still lacked "means" in the west.

Perhaps Lee of all men best understood and expressed the offensive-defense concept. In a letter written in January 1863, he summarized the strategy in three sentences. "It is [as] impossible for him [the enemy] to have a large operating army at every assailable point in our territory as it is for us to keep one to defend it. We must move

[35]Lee to Governor Joseph E. Brown, February 10, 1862, Clifford Dowdey and Louis H. Manarin (eds.), *Wartime Papers of R. E. Lee* (New York, 1961), p. 113; Lee to General Samuel Cooper, January 8, 1862, *ibid.*, p. 101; Lee to Cooper, November 21, 1861, *ibid.*, p. 87; and Lee to Judah Benjamin, February 10, 1862, *ibid.*, p. 112.

[36]Davis to W. M. Brooks, March 13, 1862, Rowland (ed.), *Jefferson Davis*, V, 216–217. For contrary views of Davis as strategist see Thomas L. Connelly and Archer Jones, *The Politics of Command: Factions and Ideas in Confederate Strategy* (Baton Rouge, La., 1973), pp. 87–136; and Grady McWhiney, "Jefferson Davis and the Art of War," *Civil War History*, XXI (1975), 101–112. On Davis' side is Frank E. Vandiver in *Their Tattered Flags* (New York, 1970), pp. 88, 94, and in "Jefferson Davis and Confederate Strategy," *The American Tragedy*, Bernard Mayo (ed.), (Hamden-Sydney, Va., 1959), pp. 19–32.

our troops from point to point as required, and by close observation and accurate information the true point of attack can generally be ascertained. . . . Partial encroachments of the enemy we must expect, but they can always be recovered, and any defeat of their large army will reinstate everything."[37]

With the proper means Davis hoped for victory, but by mid-April time was short. McClellan was cautious, but he would not respect Magruder's phantom Yorktown-Warwick line forever. Davis realized that for better or worse, he had to make some commitment before McClellan marched on Richmond.

On April 14 the President held a council of war. He had previously recalled Lee to Virginia to serve as his military advisor, so Lee and War Secretary Randolph represented the administration. Joseph E. Johnston, just returned from an inspection of Magruder's works, came with two of his subordinates, Gustavus W. Smith and James Longstreet. Johnston's army had retreated from Manassas to the Rappahannock River, where it could move to meet an attack from Washington or march to the peninsula with equal ease. Johnston, however, had neglected to tell the War Department his plans and had destroyed a massive amount of accumulated supplies at Manassas. Davis clearly desired no more such surprises from his main field army, and he wanted some plan agreed upon for dealing with McClellan.

The six Confederates met from eleven o'clock on the morning of the fourteenth until one o'clock on the morning of the fifteenth. Longstreet and the President said little, for Davis adopted the position of judge, and Longstreet was both hard of hearing and new to councils of grand strategy. Johnston and Smith advocated a stand at Richmond; Lee and Randolph favored a battle on the peninsula. In the end Davis announced in favor of meeting McClellan on the peninsula. Sooner or later, he reasoned, the Confederates would have to do battle with the blue host, and a siege of Richmond could have only one result: the destruction of the army and capital at once.[38]

---

[37]Lee to Gustavus W. Smith, January 4, 1863, Dowdey and Manarin (eds.), *Wartime Papers*, pp. 383–384. On Lee as strategist see especially Connelly and Jones, *Politics of Command*, pp. 31–48; Russell F. Weigley, *The American Way of War: A History of United States Military Strategy and Policy* (New York, 1973), pp. 92–127; and J. F. C. Fuller, *Grant and Lee: A Study in Personality and Generalship* (Bloomington, Ind., 1957).

[38]Freeman, *Lee's Lieutenants*, I, 149–151.

Johnston was less than sanguine about his prospects. He recalled later, "The belief that events on the Peninsula would soon compel the Confederate government to adopt my method of opposing the Federal army reconciled me somewhat to the necessity of obeying the President's order."[39] What Johnston did during the next month was march his men into Magruder's works and then back out again, back up the peninsula to the vicinity of Richmond. Having complied with the letter, if not the spirit, of his instructions, he prepared in mid-May to fight McClellan's army near Richmond, as he had originally intended.

The President was irked and desperate. Lee tried to mediate between the Commander and the Commander-in-Chief. Randolph packed up the War Office and prepared to supervise the evacuation of the capital. In Richmond there was wild panic for a time; Varina Davis led a sizable number of refugees who sought safety elsewhere. Among those who remained, a stoic mood surfaced; Governor Letcher and Richmond Mayor Joseph Mayo made pugnacious speeches to mass meetings, and the city's newspapers published bold editorials.[40]

Davis remained unimpressed. On May 16 he explained his ideas in a letter to his wife:

The panic here has subsided and with increasing confidence there has arisen a desire to see the city destroyed rather than surrender. . . . these talkers have little idea of what scenes would follow the battering of rows of brick houses. I have told them that the enemy might be beaten before Richmond or on either flank, and we would try to do it, but that I could not allow the Army to be penned up in a city. The boats, we ought to be, and I hope are, able to stop. Their army, when reduced to small arms and field pieces I think we can defeat and then a vigorous pursuit will bring the results long wished for.[41]

Already, Davis had expressed his determination to abandon his capital rather than submit to a siege.[42] And as McClellan's vast army of 100,000 advanced slowly on Richmond, Davis still held hope, not only of defeating the Federals, but also, with a "vigorous pursuit,"

[39]Johnston, *Narrative*, p. 119.
[40]Thomas, *Confederate State of Richmond*, pp. 92–96.
[41]Davis to Varina Davis, May 16, 1862, Rowland (ed.), *Jefferson Davis*, V, 246.
[42]Davis to speaker of the House of Representatives, March 20, 1862, Richardson (ed.), *Messages and Papers*, I, 201–202.

of destroying the invaders. When the President wrote, Richmond indeed seemed secure from naval shelling. At Drewry's Bluff, just seven miles below the capital, on May 15, the Confederates had turned back a Union flotilla. The crew of the scuttled ironclad *Virginia* manned some of the shore batteries and were once again able to fire on the Union ironclad *Monitor* when it encountered the prepared channel obstructions and torpedo mines.[43]

Still, Davis fretted over Johnston's apparent unwillingness to give battle. On May 28 the President wrote Varina Davis describing a battle aborted by swollen creeks: "Thus ended the offensive-defensive programme from which Lee expected much and of which I was hopeful."[44] Finally, on May 31, Johnston attacked. McClellan had sent two corps of his army south of the Chickahominy River, a usually sluggish stream which bisects the upper peninsula. Heavy rains, however, made a torrent of the Chickahominy and washed away bridges and fords between elements of the blue army. Johnston launched an attack upon the two isolated corps at the village of Seven Pines, but poor staff preparation and a failure in coordination among the three columns that Johnston sent to Seven Pines dulled the Confederate attack. The Southerners drove the Federals back but did not destroy them; McClellan's threat to Richmond was still very real.[45]

Johnston suffered a serious wound at Seven Pines, and at this juncture Davis made Lee commander of his army. Davis issued an address to the troops calling Seven Pines a victory and then wrote to his wife, "The opportunity being lost, we must try to find another."[46]

Lee made the Army of Northern Virginia his own and put it to work preparing field fortifications. Meanwhile Stonewall Jackson was conducting his brilliant campaign in the Shenandoah Valley. Jackson's few baffled, evaded, and battled the Federal many, drawing potential reinforcements for McClellan into the Shenandoah and defeating them. And James Ewell Brown (J. E. B.) Stuart and

[43]Freeman, *Lee's Lieutenants*, I, 209–211.
[44]Davis to Varina Davis, May 28, 1862, Rowland (ed.), *Jefferson Davis*, V, 252–254.
[45]On Seven Pines see Freeman *Lee's Lieutenants*, I, 225–243.
[46]Davis to Varina Davis, June 2, 1862, Rowland (ed.), *Jefferson Davis*, V, 264–265.

his cavalry rode completely around McClellan's army, disrupting communication and supply lines. At twenty-nine, young "Beauty" Stuart was something of a paradox—a pious *bon vivant* and a hard-fighting exhibitionist. His ride around McClellan gave expression to his flamboyant nature even as it struck a telling blow at the Federal cause.

The activities of Jackson and Stuart, besides shoring up Southern morale, convinced Lincoln in Washington and McClellan in Virginia that the Confederates were more numerous and more threatening than they actually were. Thus Lincoln withheld some of the troops intended for McClellan, and McClellan began to think more about not losing his campaign than about winning it.

Lee in the meantime planned a battle of annihilation; he determined to attack McClellan's host before it invested Richmond and his army. Federal front lines were already nearing the suburbs of the capital when Lee set his plan in motion. Between McClellan's 100,-000 and Richmond, Lee stationed 25,000 Confederates; he massed 47,000 men, the bulk of his army, near the village of Mechanicsville on the Union right flank. And while Lee shifted his forces, Jackson left the valley and drove his "foot cavalry" of 18,500 men toward Richmond and the Federal rear.

On June 25 the Seven Days campaign began; in the face of advancing Union forces, "Prince John" Magruder conducted a "demonstration" in front of Richmond designed to convince the Federals that there were many more than 25,000 Confederates between them and the city. The next day Lee unleashed what was supposed to be the crushing blow to McClellan's flank. Amid bitter fighting around Mechanicsville, however, the Southern design miscarried. Jackson was uncharacteristically late and slow, and the Confederate assault uncoordinated. But even though the Union flank survived, McClellan became convinced that his army was in grave danger. The next day, June 27, the Confederates again attacked at Gaines' Mill and temporarily broke the stubborn Federal line. In the aftermath, McClellan ordered his forces to withdraw to Harrison's Landing on the James River. Lee, when he realized the Federal intent, attempted a vigorous pursuit, hoping to crush "those people," as he termed his enemies, while they marched and before they reached the relative security of the landing. For the next three days the Confederates maintained contact but failed to apply the *coup de grâce*. Finally, after six days of heavy action, McClellan's troops occupied Malvern Hill in strength. Lee knew that this would be his last chance to smash the Federals as they withdrew, but on July 1, after his artillery dueled with Union guns on Malvern Hill and lost, he canceled his order to attack. Then in the late afternoon troop movements on the slope convinced him that the Federals were resuming their retreat, and he sent his infantry straight up the hill in hopes of overrunning a rear guard. But the Confederates found Union artillery and infantry still in strength on Malvern Hill, and piecemeal assaults failed at a bloody cost. Next morning while the Southerners buried their dead, McClellan's forces reached Harrison's Landing and sanctuary. Lee withdrew to Richmond and left McClellan undisturbed. Confederate citizens in Richmond and elsewhere hailed Lee as deliverer; the Seven Days battles had humbled the invaders and driven them away from their goal. Lee of course had had more ambitious plans and felt the disappointment of having merely defeated "those people" instead of destroying them.[47]

Meanwhile, in the war in the west the Confederacy held its own. When on May 30 Beauregard evacuated Corinth, Mississippi, Davis promptly replaced him. The Federals did not press their advantage, and Beauregard's successor, Braxton Bragg, was able to move into middle Tennessee and block further Union penetration.[48] On the Mississippi River, Memphis fell on June 6, and two months later, after a brief but brilliant life, the Southern ironclad *Arkansas* went to the bottom. With it went the South's final threat to the Union's "brown water" navy, but the Confederates still held Vicksburg and, after two full campaigning sea-

[47]On Jackson's valley campaign see Robert G. Tanner, *Stonewall in the Valley* (Garden City, N.Y., 1976); Frank E. Vandiver, *Mighty Stonewall* (New York, 1957), pp. 197–283. The standard biography of Stuart is still John W. Thomason, Jr., *Jeb Stuart* (New York, 1930). Major works on the Seven Days Battles include Freeman, *Lee's Lieutenants*, II, 489–604; and Clifford Dowdey, *The Seven Days: The Emergence of Lee* (Boston, 1964).

[48]See Connelly, *Army of the Heartland,* pp. 158–183; and Grady McWhiney, *Braxton Bragg and Confederate Defeat: Field Command* (New York, 1969), pp. 257–266.

sons, still denied the lower Mississippi to the Federals.[49]

Then in August Confederate armies in the east and west took the offensive and carried the war into the enemy's country. The Union was in the midst of moving troops from the peninsula to northern Virginia and the command of John Pope. Late in August, Jackson engaged Pope's army near the familiar field of the Battle of Manassas. Lee waited until Pope committed himself against Jackson's troops, and then, on August 30, ordered Longstreet to apply the crushing blow to the Federal flank. Although Pope's army made good its retreat across Bull Run, the second Battle of Manassas was nearly as great a Southern victory as the first.

Lee headed North, crossed the Potomac, and invaded western Maryland. At the same time, Bragg's army invaded Kentucky. One purpose of these twin invasions was liberation: the Confederates hoped to encourage Kentuckians and Marylanders to join the South. In addition, the Confederates hoped a major victory or victories on Northern soil might persuade European governments to recognize Southern independence and influence Northern voters in the upcoming congressional elections. Finally, the Southerners preferred that the war disrupt Northern harvests in 1862 instead of Southern ones. The Kentucky and Maryland invasions were limited offensives designed to achieve the same results as the offensive defense in the South: a battle or battles of annihilation.[50]

The late spring and summer of 1862 saw a minor military miracle for the Confederacy. The Southern revolution, which appeared abortive in May, had found new life. By September the Confederates had not only proven themselves capable of defense, they had shown offensive potential as well. As Lee's and Bragg's columns swung into Maryland and Kentucky respec-

[49]See James M. Merrill, *Battle Flags South: The Story of the Civil War Navies on Western Waters* (Rutherford, Vt., 1970), pp. 189–219; H. Allen Gosnell, *Guns on the Western Waters* (Baton Rouge, La., 1949), pp. 92–135; John D. Milligan, *Gunboats Down the Mississippi*, (Annapolis, Md., 1965), pp. 63–90.

[50]For these campaigns (Second Manassas and the invasions of Kentucky and Maryland) see especially Freeman, *Lee's Lieutenants*, II, 81–152; Connelly, *Army of the Heartland*, 221, 224–225; Edward J. Stackpole, *From Cedar Mountain to Antietam* (Harrisburg, Pa., 1959); and Archer Jones, *Confederate Strategy from Shiloh to Vicksburg* (Baton Rouge, La., 1961), pp. 70–78.

tively, Southern hopes soared. Nor did the spectacular reversal of military fortune escape the attention of European powers. Although the Confederates could not know it, England and France were about as close as they would ever come to intervening in the American war.

Then the fates frowned upon rising Southern hopes. As Lee's columns separated to march into Maryland and take the offensive, a Union patrol happened upon a copy of Lee's complete invasion plan wrapped around three cigars lying in a road. McClellan, again in command of Federal forces in the east, studied the document for a time, realized his good fortune, and set his army in motion to smash the dispersed invaders. Lee had to forget about his offensive and concentrate quickly to save his army from destruction. Confederate units delayed McClellan's advance through the mountains of western Maryland as best they could, and Lee drew his battle line along Antietam Creek near the town of Sharpsburg, Maryland. On September 17, as Southern troops were still arriving on the field, McClellan's Federals attempted to overrun the Southern position and drive Lee's army into the Potomac River. The resultant combat produced the bloodiest single day of the war and a tactical draw, as the Confederates allowed their lines to bend but not break. The Army of Northern Virginia survived, yet the invasion of Maryland was over, and Lee led his battered troops back across the Potomac into Virginia.[51]

In Kentucky, Bragg's army began its invasion with a series of clever maneuvers which allowed the Southerners free rein for a time, evading Don Carlos Buell's Federals. On October 4 at Frankfort, Bragg even presided over the inauguration of Richard Hawes as Confederate governor of the state. But four days later Buell overtook the Confederates; the armies collided at Perryville, and although the fight was inconclusive, the Southerners abandoned the field and the idea of liberating Kentucky. Bragg marched his army back into Tennessee. The second half of the Confederacy's twin offensive had also failed.[52]

During late autumn 1862 the Confederacy managed to pre-

[51]On Antietam (Sharpsburg) see Freeman, *Lee's Lieutenants,* II, 166–225; Shelby Foote, *The Civil War, A Narrative,* 3 vols. (New York, 1958–1974), I, 681–702.

[52]McWhiney, *Braxton Bragg,* pp. 272–336; Connelly, *Army of the Heartland,* pp. 228–245.

serve the military stalemate established by the frustration of its offensives in Maryland and Kentucky. The army of John C. Pemberton beat off an assault on Vicksburg on December 29 and retained for another six months that last Southern bastion on the river. In middle Tennessee, on December 21, Bragg's army fought a tactical draw with William S. Rosecrans' Federals (formerly commanded by Buell) at Murfreesboro (Stones River) and retired to lick its wounds in winter quarters at Tullahoma, Tennessee. In Virginia, Lee's army entrenched at Fredericksburg and repulsed the frontal assaults of the Army of the Potomac commanded by Ambrose E. Burnside.

Burnside had replaced McClellan and proved as overbold as McClellan was overcautious. Time after time on December 13, Union forces surged forward across open ground in front of Marye's Heights, and each time the Confederates stopped them cold. When the fighting ended the Army of the Potomac had suffered 12,653 casualties, the Army of Northern Virginia 5,309.

During 1862 the Confederate South began to achieve an identity apart from the Old South, and the creative efforts of Davis' government bore fruit. Talented leadership, tenacious soldiers, and the fortunes of war played their parts; but the statecraft of the Richmond government and the zeal of the Southern people for the cause combined to produce a nascent nation. By autumn the tottering experiment seemed on the brink of victory in enemy country and fulfillment at home. But the moment of near triumph was brief. By the year's end Southern armies were again on the defensive, and the South's survival as a nation still lay in the balance.

The inconclusiveness of the Confederacy's war was, on one hand, a favorable circumstance. Every day the war lasted was one more day of Southern independence, and Southerners believed they could win independence by enduring, by outlasting their enemy's will to conquer them. But wars, beyond an undefined point, seem to demand a victor. An inner dynamic takes hold and drives the combatants to a conclusion, if only to justify the death and sacrifice. The Confederate war had passed that point of no return, and hindsight confirms that the United States persisted. The Confederacy, having sacrificed blood and treasure and compromised principles on which the nation was founded, was still in a state of becoming. The inconclusiveness of the war would require more sacrifice and more compromise, and the South would become more Confederate and less Southern in the fateful year of 1863.

1. Edmund Ruffin, Southern radical.
(Museum of the Confederacy.)

2. Drawing of Charleston, South Carolina. *(Harpers Illustrated Weekly.)*

3. Music cover, "Virginian Marseillaise."   (University of Georgia Library.)

4. Drawing of Montgomery, Alabama.   *(Harpers Illustrated Weekly.)*

5. The inauguration at Montgomery.   (Library of Congress.)

6. A Unionist depiction of Jefferson Davis' inauguration.   *(Harpers Illustrated Weekly.)*

7. Jefferson Davis.
(Library of Congress.)

9. Judah P. Benjamin, journeyman cabinet member.

(Library of Congress.)

8. Christopher G. Memminger, secretary of the treasury.

(Library of Congress.)

10. George W. Randolph, secretary of war.

(Library of Congress.)

11. Josiah Gorgas, chief of Ordnance Bureau.
(Virginia State Library.)

12. R. M. T. Hunter, secretary of state and senator from Virginia.
(Library of Congress.)

13. Alexander H. Stephens, vice-president.

(Library of Congress.)

14. Stephen R. Mallory, secretary of the navy.

(Library of Congress.)

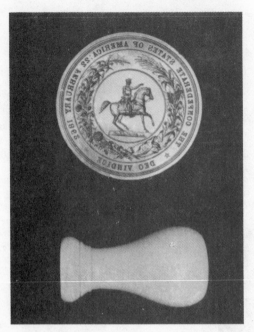

15. The Great Seal of the Confederacy.
(Museum of the Confederacy.)

16. Robert E. Lee.
(Museum of the Confederacy.)

17. Thomas J. "Stonewall" Jackson.
(Library of Congress.)

19. Joseph E. Johnston.
(Library of Congress.)

18. P. G. T. Beauregard.
(Museum of the Confederacy.)

20. Braxton Bragg.
(Library of Congress.)

21. The C.S.S. *Virginia* (née *Merrimack*) running down the frigate *Cumberland* off Newport News.

(Harpers Illustrated Weekly.)

22. The Tredeger Iron Works at Richmond. (Virginia State Library.)

23. Confederate torpedoes (mines), successful rebel ingenuity.

(Library of Congress.)

24. Double-barreled cannon, unsuccessful rebel ingenuity.

(Photo by Kenneth Kay, Athens, Georgia.)

25. "Recipe to Get Rid of Extortioners—Chain them to a stake, as above; pile their ill-gotten gains around them, and any passer-by will fire the mass. This will have the happy effect, both of ridding the community of their presence, and at the same time reducing the circulating medium."

(Museum of the Confederacy.)

26. "Master Abraham Lincoln gets a new Toy."

(Library of Congress.)

27. "Butler, the Beast, at Work."   (Library of Congress.)

TENDER.

THE LOVELY LIZZIE

Transports all the MALES in the Confederacy free of charge and with astonishing celerity!

28. Valentine card from the wartime South.   (Museum of the Confederacy.)

29. Farragut's victory on Mobile Bay.   *(Harpers Illustrated Weekly.)*

30. Drawing of Richmond, ca. 1850.

(Virginia State Library.)

31.   Richmond from the south side of the James, 1865.   (Virginia State Library.)

32.   Broadside revealing desperate days.

(University of Georgia Library.)

33. In the trenches around Petersburg, 1865.

(Photo by Mathew Brady. Library of Congress.)

34. Music cover "No Surrender."

(University of Georgia Library.)

CHAPTER 8

Foreign Relations of a Nascent Nation

S OUTHERNERS in the mid-nineteenth century maintained a cu-
riously ambivalent relationship with the wider world.[1] Drawing
upon the heritage of the eighteenth century, many planter-aristo-
crats considered themselves cosmopolites and citizens of the world;
some had given their education "a finishing polish by making a tour
of Europe."[2] They copied European fashions, listened to European
music, read English and French books, and adorned their homes
with foreign furniture and art. Yet as the nineteenth century progressed Southerners became less at ease with a Europe torn by
revolution and driven by the currents of liberal nationalism. Although Southerners shared some of the nationalist feelings of Europeans, the logical conclusion of Southern nationalism was reactionary separation, in contrast to the European trend toward liberal
unification. When reflecting upon European revolutions, Southerners quite often identified with the old order instead of the new.
Consequently they tended to become as culturally isolated from the
Old World as they were politically alienated in the New World. Like
John B. Lamar of Georgia, some Southerners might talk about
spending their later years living near Paris but in fact never trouble

[1]This observation and the interpretation expressed in this paragraph relies much
upon the analysis contained in chapter 1 of William R. Taylor in *Cavalier and Yankee:
the Old South and American National Character* (Garden City, N.Y., 1961).
[2]Daniel R. Hundley, *Social Relations in Our Southern States* (New York, 1860), p. 49.

to learn French. Lamar's love of things European was anachronistic; he identified with the European past and all but ignored its alien present.[3]

Travelers like Lamar could visit Europe, see the art and the relics of the past, and remain more or less insulated from contemporary Europeans. Diplomats could not. During the ante-bellum period the actions of Southerners in the United States diplomatic service often bore witness to the general ambivalence which characterized the South's attitude toward Europe. One of the best examples of this worldly provincialism at work was John M. Daniel, who served in Turin as United States chargé d'affaires and later as minister resident to the court of Sardinia. Daniel was a journalist and an intellectual who read Latin classics and whose favorite authors were Voltaire and Swift. In 1853 he left his newspaper, the Richmond *Examiner,* and accepted the diplomatic post at Turin.[4] His initial reactions to life in a European capital were not at all those of a cosmopolite; homesick and disillusioned, he confided to a friend back in Virginia:

The real comforts of Europe don't compare with those of the United States. The people are no where as good as ours. The women are uglier; the men have fewer ideas. . . . I am busily learning to speak French and studying what is popularly, but most falsely, termed the 'great world' and 'polite society.' I have dined with dukes, jabbered bad grammar to countesses, and am sponged on for seats in my opera-box by counts who stink of garlick, as does the whole country. I receive visits from diplomats with titles as long as a flagstaff, and heads as empty as their hearts, and find the whole concern more trashy than I have ever imagined.[5]

Daniel remained in Turin until 1860 and witnessed but misunderstood the early machinations of Count Cavour which led eventually to Italian unification. He then returned home in the midst of the secession crisis, resumed editorship of the *Examiner,* and champi-

[3]Lamar's response to Europe is recorded in his letters to his sister contained in the Cobb-Erwin collection University of Georgia Library, Athens, Ga.

[4]Material about Daniel may be found in Frederick Daniel, *The Richmond Examiner During the War* (New York, 1868); J. Cutler Andrews, *The South Reports the Civil War,* (Princeton, N.J., 1970), pp. 29–31; Allen Johnson and Dumas Malone (eds.), *Dictionary of American Biography,* 22 Vols., index (New York: 1928–1965), V, 67–68; George W. Bagby, "John M. Daniel's Latchkey," in *The Old Virginia Gentleman and Other Sketches* (Richmond, Va., 1938), pp. 110–143.

[5]The letter is cited in Daniel, *Examiner During the War,* p. 225.

oned the cause of Southern disunification.[6] He may not have been a typical Southern diplomat; he did however betray the naïveté which often lay beneath the facade of Southern worldliness. When the South became the Confederacy, the personal prejudices of men like Daniel too often became national presumptions. Confederate hopes for recognition and intervention from Europe rested upon simple faith in the righteousness of the cause and in the commercial prerogatives of King Cotton. Hindsight reveals Southern optimism to have been founded upon unreal and antique assumptions much at odds with the century of *realpolitik*. Still Southerners persisted in hoping, and as a consequence Confederate diplomacy seemed to be a series of dashed hopes—great expectations followed by greater frustrations.[7]

Perhaps it was fortunate that Robert Toombs did not last long as secretary of state. Toombs was not a diplomatic person. Moreover, he was a spokesman for the older South, a true believer in the cause, and he was convinced that Southern virtue combined with Southern cotton would win sentiment and support for the Confederacy in Europe. Because he resigned his post in July of 1861, Toombs was spared the full frustration of his hopes.

Toomb's successor in the State Department was R. M. T. Hunter, who remained in the office no longer than Toombs. Jefferson Davis chose Hunter because he was an astute politician and because he was a Virginian; Hunter took the job because it seemed important and perhaps because he aspired to be president. He performed capably enough but soon learned that the Confederate State Department was no steppingstone to power or prestige and that secur-

[6]Daniel's diplomatic dispatches are printed in H. R. Marravo (ed.), *L' Unificazione Italiana Vista dai Diplomatici Statunitensi,* III, (Rome, 1975). See also Emory M. Thomas, "A Virginian Ambassador in Torino: John Moncure Daniel," to be published in the First International Conference of American History, Italy and the United States (1776/1976), *Proceedings.*

[7]The standard study of Confederate diplomacy is still Frank L. Owsley, *King Cotton Diplomacy: Foreign Relations of the Confederate States of America,* revised edition (Chicago, 1959); and the standard work on England and the American war is still Ephraim D. Adams, *Great Britain and the American Civil War,* 2 vols. (New York, 1924). The best study of French reaction is Lynn M. Case and Warren F. Spencer, *The United States and France: Civil War Diplomacy* (Philadelphia, 1970). See also Max Beloff, "Great Britain and the American Civil War," *History,* XXXVII (1952), 40–48; Norman A. Graebner, "Northern Diplomacy and European Neutrality" in David Donald (ed.), *Why the North Won the Civil War* (Baton Rouge, La., 1960), pp. 55–78; and D. P. Crook, *The North, the South, and the Powers, 1861–1865* (New York, 1974).

ing recognition and assistance from Europe was no child's game. A policy founded on righteousness and cotton did not sufficiently impress Britain and France, and the Confederacy had little more to offer.[8]

The Confederacy's first commissioners to Europe, William L. Yancey, Pierre A. Rost, and A. Dudley Mann, were still hopeful in the summer of 1861. After all, Britain and France had recognized the belligerency of the Southern rebels. This recognition was, however, insufficient by itself. The Confederacy needed more than neutrality; it needed formal recognition and material assistance, and these tangible things the British and French were ill-prepared to offer.

Both European powers needed cotton, though not necessarily Confederate cotton, and both could imagine benefits accruing from a permanently disunited States. Yet Britain and France also realized the cost of Confederate recognition: confrontation and war with at least the United States and, if the balance of power were threatened, perhaps one or more European states as well. The "American question" involved more than the pretensions of some planter nationalists; if Europe intervened, the distribution of world power would be at stake. Accordingly France determined to act in concert with England. The Confederates not only had to persuade both powers to act; they had to persuade them at the same moment.[9]

Statesmen in London and Paris did not have to search for reasons to answer the American question cautiously. In France, Napoleon III maintained his authoritarian regime by means of a series of rather delicate domestic compromises with republican ideologues, the business community, the Church, and the army. At the same time, he attempted to emulate his famous uncle and fire French national pride through a series of international adventures on behalf of liberal nationalism. Confederates naturally hoped that Napoleon would exercise his supposedly autocratic will and intervene on the side of Southern national aspirations, as he had in Italy. But though the record of Napoleon's Italian policy was indeed instructive, its lessons should not have been comforting to Confederates. Napoleon had allied himself with Sardinia (Piedmont) against

[8]The best assessment of Toombs and Hunter as secretaries of state is in Rembert W. Patrick, *Jefferson Davis and His Cabinet* (Baton Rouge, La., 1944), pp. 78–101.
[9]Crook, *North, South, and the Powers*, pp. 71–83.

Austria in 1859, and subsequently the allied armies had beaten the Hapsburgs thoroughly at the battles of Magenta and Solferino. Then, having opened the way for a united Italy, Napoleon drew back and made a separate peace (Treaty of Villafranca) with Austria. Not only did Austria retain Venetia; Napoleon now held Nice and Savoy (his price for the Sardinian alliance), and he also sent troops to Rome to protect the Pope and the Papal States. Clearly, Napoleon III was something of an international trimmer: he had assisted Italian nationalism but then recoiled when national unification, or *Risorgimento,* seemed to threaten the Church and the established order of power relationships in Europe. However much the Emperor might thrust himself and France into the center of world politics, his audacity had limits. In truth, by 1861 France was overextended; during the previous decade French armies had fought on three continents. No wonder French public opinion displayed increasing disenchantment with the mercurial foreign policy of the Third Empire. Accordingly Napoleon III cherished his agreement to act in concert with Great Britain on the American war and clung to the safety of his Anglo alliance.[10]

Queen Victoria's government, presided over by Lord Palmerston and Foreign Secretary Lord John Russell, accepted the leadership role in the French concert and doubtless regarded British primacy as natural. Palmerston, though, was never certain of his leadership in British politics. His government survived for six years, a period which encompassed the life span of the Confederacy, but the ministry rested upon a tenuous base of compromise at home and conservative policy abroad. Since the Peace of Ghent in 1814, British statesmen had realized the greater wisdom of commercial domination rather than political subjugation in the "colonies." Palmerston and Russell thus looked with concern upon the American war. While they needed a climate of peace in North America for the sake of British capital, they also feared potential shocks to the system of power relationships among the European powers that the American war might generate.[11]

[10]*Ibid.,* pp. 14–18, 371–372; Case and Spencer, *The United States and France,* pp. 38–52; and Henry Blumenthal, *A Reappraisal of Franco-American Relations, 1830–1871* (Chapel Hill, N.C., 1959).

[11]Crook, *North, South, and the Powers,* pp. 9–14, 371–375; and Beloff, "Great Britain and the American Civil War."

The Confederacy based its initial overtures to Europe on ideals and cotton, but both England and France had active antislavery societies and large segments of the populace committed to the ideals of liberal democracy as exhibited in the North. And although both nations needed raw cotton, in 1861 both had large stockpiles from the bumper crops of 1859 and 1860. Most significantly the British were heavily invested in the American industrial revolution, and England traditionally bought Northern grain as well as Southern cotton. Indeed during the war years the United States supplied an average of 33.3 percent of England's wheat, flour, and corn imports, almost 50 percent of the nation's supply.

Aid to the slaveholding aristocracy would thus cost the British and French governments in the marketplace of public opinion. Of course in nineteenth-century Europe public opinion did not make diplomatic decisions; but in England especially the diplomatic establishment gave consideration to the impact of its actions upon the popular will. The steady performance of United States ambassadors Charles Francis Adams in London and William L. Dayton in Paris also contributed to diplomatic inertia in Europe. The Confederates had reason to hope for the future; the Southern nation might demonstrate its legitimacy on the battlefield, and the "cotton famine" would strike sooner or later. But initially Europe's answer to the "American question" was a firm "maybe."[12]

In early August of 1861, Yancey, Rost, and Mann gathered in London to present exciting news to the British secretary for foreign affairs. From Hunter they had just learned of the victory at Manassas, and accordingly they requested another informal interview with Russell. To the Confederates' surprise and chagrin, Russell refused to meet them, requesting instead that they make their communication in writing. The commissioners wrote a brief; Russell promised to consider the matter further; and Yancey, Rost, and Mann still clung to some hope of success. Yet the three men could not always agree upon their best course of action. Yancey especially was so disgruntled with his assignment

[12]Joseph M. Hernon, "British Sympathies in the American Civil War: a Reconsideration," *Journal of Southern History*, XXXIII (1967), 356–367; and Crook, *North, South, and the Powers*, pp. 1–18, 37–39, 269.

and his colleagues that he requested to be relieved.[13]

In Richmond, Davis and Hunter were impatient. By September they concluded that Yancey, Rost, and Mann had failed and that it was time to replace all three. Late in the month, Hunter recalled Yancey and dispatched Rost and Mann to Spain and Belgium respectively. For the important tasks in London and Paris, Davis and Hunter selected James M. Mason and John Slidell. Mason was a crudely charming Virginian and a former United States senator. Davis and Hunter correctly predicted that Mason's affability would win him and the Confederacy many friends among the British gentry. Slidell, an adopted Louisianian, was more subtle and ambitious; Davis and Hunter hoped that his guile as well as his charm would be effective with Napoleon III.[14]

The two commissioners left Charleston on October 12, 1861, slipped through the blockade to Nassau, and then proceeded to Cuba. On November 7 they sailed with their secretaries from Havana aboard the British mail packet *Trent*. They planned to go to St. Thomas and there board a British steamer for Southhampton. One day out of Havana, on November 8, their plans miscarried and there occurred the first and most significant crisis in Anglo-American relations during the war.[15]

As the *Trent* made its way through the Bahama Channel, the United States sloop of war *San Jacinto*, Captain Charles Wilkes commanding, approached, fired a shot across the *Trent*'s bow, and signaled it to heave to. Captain Wilkes then dispatched a boarding party, which searched the *Trent* and seized the two Confederates. Wilkes proceeded with his captives to Fort Monroe, Virginia. There he gave out the news that he had captured the Southerners and then took them to Boston, where they remained under house arrest.

Wilkes became an instant hero in the United States, but Confederates, too, were grateful to the aggressive Union captain. Search

[13]Owsley, *King Cotton Diplomacy*, pp. 64–78; W. Stanley Hoole (ed.), "William L. Yancey's European Diary, March-June, 1861," *Alabama Review*, XXV (1972), 134–142; Adams, *Great Britain*, pp. 172–180.

[14]Owsley, *King Cotton Diplomacy*, pp. 77–78, 224–225.

[15]Case suggests that the Confederacy deliberately courted capture of Mason and Slidell and cites circumstantial evidence to support the theory (Case and Spencer, *The United States and France*, pp. 190–194). The notion is intriguing but the case too weak.

and seizure in international waters had often been a thorny issue between England and the United States; indeed the Americans had gone to war in 1812 over British actions similar to those of Wilkes. The British would hardly take this affront lying down. Indeed they did not. Russell sent a firm note to the United States demanding an apology and the return of Mason and Slidell, and the London *Times* among other British newspapers, called for war with the United States over the incident. The French, too, sent a note to Washington supporting the British demands, underscoring the concert between the two European powers. Southerners greeted these events with glee. Surely the *Trent* affair offered Britain the excuse to intervene on behalf of the Confederacy.

Lincoln and his secretary of state, William H. Seward, waited as long as they dared to respond to the British note. Then, on Christmas Day, 1861, Lincoln and his cabinet settled upon a reply. The United States did not apologize; instead the government explained that Wilkes had acted "without orders" in the matter. As for Mason and Slidell, they would be "cheerfully surrendered." That the explanation and surrender were accepted bore witness to the British determination to remain neutral. The *Trent* affair provided an excuse for England to go to war with the United States, but excuse meant little without the inclination to do so. The incident was all but forgotten by the time Mason reached London on January 29, 1862.[16]

Still, there was reason for the new commissioners to be optimistic. The English and French mills seemed at last to have reached the bottom of their stockpiles of cotton; the great famine was at hand. During the first year of the war, Southerners had practiced a kind of informal embargo on cotton. President Davis was reluctant to make the embargo a matter of public policy or law, because he did not wish to give the impression that the new nation was blackmailing Europe or that the Confederacy had departed from its basic free trade posture. Nevertheless with an amazing degree of unanimity,

[16]See Charles F. Adams, "The *Trent* Affair," *American Historical Review*, XVII (1912), 540–562; Case and Spencer, *The United States and France*, pp. 190–249; Adams, *Great Britain*, pp. 203–243; and F. C. Drake, "The Cuban Background of the *Trent* Affair," *Civil War History*, XIX (1973), 29–49. Case convincingly argues the significance of the French note and provides perhaps the best overview as well. Drake contends that the United States consul at Havana shared Wilkes' hope for the capture.

Southerners withheld shipments of cotton in 1861, and in accord with laws of several states the planters reduced their cotton acreage in 1862. These actions, combined with the Federal blockade, severely reduced cotton supplies in Britain and France.[17]

Throughout 1862 the European mills were able to buy only a fraction of their normal supply of cotton, and they paid premium prices for it. When the mills ran short of raw cotton, they reduced their operating time, and when they exhausted their supplies, they shut down entirely. The working classes in England and France suffered; among mill workers an estimated 330,000 in England were unemployed during November of 1862, and in France about 220,-000 were unemployed during the winter of 1862–1863. The cotton famine destroyed many of the smaller milling operations and depressed any segment of the economy that depended on the purchasing power of cotton mill workers.[18]

As the cotton famine worsened during the early months of 1862, the Confederate position in Europe was paradoxical. On the one hand the Southerners hoped, as they had hoped all along, that the shortage of cotton would compel Britain and France to confront the United States over its blockade of the Confederacy. Such a confrontation would, the Confederates believed, result in recognition and assistance from the European powers, and to this end they blamed the cotton famine upon the Union blockade. On the other hand the Confederacy claimed that the Union blockade was in violation of international law because it was a "paper blockade," that is, Union ships did not patrol every mile of the Southern coast. Obviously, the blockade was either effective or it was not effective, and King Cotton would resolve the paradox. To secure cotton, the British and French would have to support the Confederacy, either by breaking an effective blockade or by challenging one that was ineffective.[19]

In fact the British and French fretted a great deal about the Northern blockade. Both nations were alarmed when the United

[17] Owsley, *King Cotton Diplomacy*, pp. 25–51.
[18] *Ibid.*, pp. 146–65; Case and Spencer, *The United States and France*, pp. 158–189.
[19] The effectiveness of the Union blockade is still an open question. Frank L. Owsley in *King Cotton Diplomacy* (pp. 250–291) argues the ineffectiveness of the blockade, especially in the early years of the war. Case in Case and Spencer, *The United States and France* (pp. 139–148) contends that the blockade was effective because the individuals involved believed it so. See also Robert Erwin Johnson, "Investment by Sea: The Civil War Blockade," *American Neptune*, XXXII (1972), 45–57.

States Congress enacted legislation closing Southern ports to international commerce and when the Union navy tried to seal Charleston Harbor by sinking a number of old whaling ships loaded with rocks—the "great stone fleet"—at the harbor mouth. In terms of the number of ships it seized, the Federal blockade may have been quite porous, but as a factor in Atlantic diplomacy, it was very real to the European mind.[20]

Nevertheless, for reasons which defied the Confederates' understanding, England and France clung to their lofty neutrality in the spring of 1862. Despite the presumed justice of the Southern cause, the *"Trent* affair," the blockade, and the "cotton famine," Mason and Slidell still represented a non-nation in London and Paris.

Actually the British and French had good reasons to wait and see. The "cotton famine" may have severely injured some portions of the working class; but the mill managers and owners were not nearly so disturbed. They had warehouses full of cotton cloth, the product of the cotton glut in 1860 and 1861. Faced with the prospect of rising prices for raw cotton and falling prices for their finished products, the owners and managers were content to stop production for a time. Britain and France were able to import cotton from India, Egypt, and Brazil, and in fact the British even resold increasing amounts of raw cotton to France. Moreover the price of Northern grain was declining, and British traders were able to substitute wheat for cotton without challenging the Federal blockade. There is reason to believe that the crisis in the British cotton districts was one of overproduction instead of scarcity, and that the republican press of Paris exaggerated the crisis. In both countries the American war was a convenient scapegoat upon which to blame economic ills. To Southerners' chagrin, "King Cotton" proved to be a puppet monarch whose strings the Confederacy did not control.[21]

The European powers were most anxious about the military an-

[20]Case and Spencer, *The United States and France*, pp. 126–157, 250–258; Arthur Gordon, "The Great Stone Fleet: Calculated Catastrophe," U.S. Naval Institute *Proceedings*, XCIV, (1968), 72–82.

[21]Case and Spencer, *The United States and France*, pp. 258–285; Owsley, *King Cotton Diplomacy*, pp. 224–249; Amos Khasigian, "Economic Factors and British Neutrality, 1861–1865," *Historian*, XXX (1963), 241–265; Robert H. Jones, "Long Live the King?," *Agricultural History*, XXXVII (1963), 166–169; Crook, *North, South, and the Powers*, pp. 199–206, 270; and Eugene A. Brady, "A Reconsideration of the Lancashire 'Cotton Famine,' " *Agricultural History*, XXXVII (1963), 156–162.

swer to the American question. Neither England nor France wanted to support a loser. If the Southerners proved themselves capable of perpetuating their independence, then Europe would be foolish to ignore the *fait accompli*. However, as long as the military issue remained in serious doubt, Europeans could afford to stand aside. And stand aside they did.

The Southern diplomats by 1862 had watched the Palmerston government accept the United States' explanation of the *Trent* affair and had witnessed the "mistress of the seas" submit to the Union "paper blockade." Slidell believed, correctly, that Napoleon III was sympathetic to the South but that the French foreign ministry—and for the most part the French people—favored the North. The two unofficial ambassadors had seen the cotton famine worsen without apparent effect upon the governments in London and Paris. They knew that the French minister to the United States, Henri Mercier, had visited Richmond in April of 1862 to meet President Davis, but as far as Mason and Slidell could see, the impressive string of Southern victories during the summer was having no tangible impact. Such a set of favorable circumstances surely should bear fruit, yet thus far the powers had remained aloof.[22]

Although nothing that Mason and Slidell did much influenced the British and French governments, Confederate diplomacy underwent a subtle change during 1862. While the Southern commissioners were doing their unofficial best to plead their case to European governments, Southern propagandists began the more basic task of selling the cause to broader segments of the foreign populace. The Confederate public relations effort, designed to counter the influence of "official" (United States) sources of American news, began in the mind of Secretary of State Benjamin and of a Swiss-born Mobile journalist named Henry Hotze. Hotze traveled to London in 1861 as a commercial agent and became a free-lance propagandist; then in May of 1862 he launched *The Index*, a weekly paper offering a Southern slant on scrupulously accurate news of the war. Hotze also "educated" British journalists to the Confederate cause and so expanded his influence. Secretary Benjamin, when he realized the depth and quality of

[22]A good summary of this activity in Crook, *North, South, and the Powers*, pp. 171–219.

Hotze's contribution, hastened to subsidize his efforts from Richmond.[23]

Even as Hotze prepared his first issue, in April, 1862, Benjamin appointed Edwin DeLeon, a well-connected South Carolinian who had been living in France when the war began, to coordinate Confederate public relations activities in Europe. DeLeon returned to France in July 1862, where he used government funds to subsidize the Paris *Patrie,* advanced money to Hotze, and in the summer of 1862 produced a pamphlet, *la vérité sur les États-Confédérés d'Amérique,* for the instruction of the French press and public. In September, DeLeon was able to insert a favorable article on President Davis in *Blackwood's* magazine, and the following month he wrote a piece on the ineffectiveness of the blockade for *Cornhill* magazine.[24]

The activities of Hotze and DeLeon bore witness to an increased degree of maturity in Confederate foreign relations. The Yancey-Rost-Mann mission in the summer of 1861 foundered in part at least because at the time Southerners had too naïve a faith in the righteousness of their cause and too simple a dependence on the potency of King Cotton. The *Trent* affair, the Union blockade, and the cotton famine demonstrated too well that obtaining recognition and/or intervention from the European powers was going to be no simple matter. The Confederate State Department altered its tactics accordingly. Mason and Slidell remained at their posts, but they no longer expected a grand coup in London or Paris to sweep away British or French neutrality. Instead they applied themselves to the more fundamental tasks of initiating and cultivating Southern friendships in government circles. Mason, ever frustrated by the aloof neutrality of Palmerston and Russell, sought to guide and expand sympathy for the South in Parliament. Slidell, aware of Napoleon's friendly inclinations toward the Confederacy, tried to wean the French emperor from his ministry, his people, and his dependence upon concert with England. But although they were based upon clear-eyed analysis and probably held the most promise of success, the machinations of Mason and Slidell, like those of

[23]See Stephan B. Oates, "Henry Hotze: Confederate Agent Abroad," *The Historian,* XXVII (1965), 131–154; and Charles P. Cullop, *Confederate Propaganda in Europe, 1861–1865* (Coral Gables, Fla., 1969), pp. 18–66.

[24]Cullop, *Confederate Propaganda,* pp. 67–84.

Hotze and DeLeon, came to naught. Certainly by the fall of 1862 the quality of Southern diplomacy had advanced several paces beyond the simplicity displayed by Yancey, Rost, and Mann.[25]

Ultimately the South's hopes for independence marched with its armies, and indeed when the Army of Northern Virginia invaded Maryland in the fall of 1862, Palmerston and Russell became convinced of the depth and potential of Southern separation. On September 14, Palmerston wrote to Russell about Anglo-French mediation and "an arrangement upon the basis of separation."[26] Russell responded, "I agree with you that the time is come for offering mediation to the United States Government, with a view of the recognition of the Independence of the Confederates—I agree further that in case of failure, we ought ourselves to recognize the Southern States, as an Independent State."[27]

In accord with these convictions, Russell informally approached his counterpart in Paris, Antoine Edouard Trouvenel, and discussed with Palmerston a date for a meeting of the cabinet to approve the mediation scheme.[28] Russell was still firm in this policy on October 4, when he wrote Palmerston, "I think unless some miracle takes place this will be the very time for offering Mediation."[29] And on October 7, Chancellor of the Exchequer William Gladstone let the cat out of the bag. Speaking at Newcastle, Gladstone affirmed, that, "Jefferson Davis and other leaders of the South have made an army; they are making, it appears, a navy; and they have made what is more than either, they have made a nation."[30]

Then, just as quickly as the mediation enthusiasm had developed in England, it evaporated. On October 24, Russell wrote to Palmerston, "As no good would come of a Cabinet [to consider mediation], I put it off."[31] Actually, in Palmerston's absence, a

[25]Crook, North, South, and the Powers, pp. 171–219; Case and Spencer, The United States and France, pp. 286–346; Owsley, King Cotton Diplomacy, pp. 294–336.

[26]Palmerston to Russell, September 14, 1862, quoted in Crook, North, South, and the Powers, p. 222.

[27]Russell to Palmerston, September 17, 1862, quoted in Adams, Great Britain, II, 39.

[28]Case and Spencer, United States and France, p. 337.

[29]Russell to Palmerston, October 4, 1862, quoted in Adams, Great Britain, II, 46.

[30]Quoted in Crook, North, South, and the Powers, pp. 227–228.

[31]Russell to Palmerston, October 24, 1862, quoted in Frank E. Vandiver, Basic History of the Confederacy (Princeton, N.J., 1962), p. 149.

number of cabinet members did meet informally with Russell on October 23 and decided to forget mediation for the time being.[32]

During the brief period between the rise and fall of the British mediation mania, English statesmen received and digested two significant pieces of news from North America: Antietam and the Emancipation Proclamation. On September 17, Lee's invasion of Maryland suffered its bloody repulse on the banks of Antietam Creek near Sharpsburg. In the aftermath of that battle, on September 22, Lincoln issued his preliminary Emancipation Proclamation. These events gave the British cabinet pause and weakened the French resolve to act jointly with the British. Lee's retreat into Virginia meant that Washington and Baltimore were again safe and the South was again on the defensive. Emancipation, even though it applied only to those slaves in rebel hands, introduced a moral dimension heretofore lacking in the American war. Now the war for Union was a crusade against slavery.

Important as Antietam and emancipation were, other considerations contributed to England's return to nonintervention. Mediation was attractive to free-traders who resented the Federal blockade, to liberals who supported self-determination, to conservatives who felt a kinship with landed aristocrats in the South, and to some varieties of nationalists who looked with favor upon the dissolution of the United States. But these attractions were essentially abstract. In the end British statesmen had to face the hard reality of what might follow an unsuccessful offer of mediation and subsequent recognition of the Confederacy: they had to ponder the consequences of a North American war. And if the British should be drawn into an American war, they wanted to support the winning side. In this regard, Antietam and emancipation were indecisive; neither event broke the American impasse to reveal a victor.[33]

On September 29, Lord President of the Queen's Council, George Gower, the Second Earl of Granville, a Liberal-Whig elder statesman in foreign affairs, best summarized the case against mediation and recognition. In a rambling, stream-of-consciousness-style letter to Russell, Granville observed, "We might selfishly argue that it was not politically disadvantageous to us that both parties should

[32]Crook, *North, South, and the Powers*, p. 242.
[33]See Kinley J. Brauer, "British Mediation and the American Civil War," *Journal of Southern History*, XXXVIII (1972), 49–64.

exhaust themselves a little more before they make Peace. . . . I doubt whether in offering to mediate, we should do so with any bona-fide expectation of its being accepted. . . . It would not be a good moment to recognize the South just before a great Federal Success —If on the other hand, the Confederates continue Victorious as is to be hoped, we should stand better then than now in recognizing them. In any case I doubt, if the War continues long after our recognition of the South, whether it will be possible for us to avoid drifting into it."[34]

The logic of Granville's musing was compelling, and the date of his letter especially significant. Granville wrote from the continent on September 29; first reports of the Battle of Antietam did not reach England until September 30, and news of the Emancipation Proclamation came later still. Granville's letter was only one of many in which members of Palmerston's government expressed their views on the American question. The British government considered the question still unanswered, and recoiled from answering it at the cost of becoming embroiled in a potentially debilitating foreign war.[35]

Soon after the British backed away from intervention, the French took their turn at proposing concerted mediation. The author of the French mediation note, sent simultaneously to England and Russia, was Drouyn de Lhuys, who had succeeded Trouvenel as French minister of foreign affairs in October of 1862 and who was ironically more pro-North than his predecessor. Drouyn formulated the French mediation proposal at the behest of Napoleon III. In all probability the Emperor chose this moment to offer mediation because of the effects of the cotton famine and the pressure of public opinion to reopen normal trade relations with America. Dispatched in early November, the French note met rejection in both London and St. Petersburg. Palmerston and Russell had been through the process before and turned down the French invitation for the same reasons they had resisted intervention themselves. The Russians were too committed to the United States to risk disturbing the status quo. Thus the French mediation scheme died a speedy and quiet death. Napoleon, however, had the satisfaction of doing something

[34]Granville to Russell, September 29, 1862, quoted in Vandiver, *Confederacy*, pp. 146–148.
[35]Crook, *North, South, and the Powers*, pp. 224–226.

to break the American deadlock and accepted praise from organs of French public opinion for his gesture. The only losers in the affair were the Confederates.[36]

The mediation enthusiasm in Great Britain during the autumn of 1862 was the nearest thing to intervention undertaken by the European powers during the Confederate war, although in reality diplomatic circumstances were a bit more volatile afterwards than historians have often assumed. The Powers had not declared irrevocable neutrality; they had determined to watch and wait. If there should be a significant alteration in the American situation, both Britain and France were prepared to reassess. During the first half of 1863 the Confederates had reason to believe that there were significant alterations in the South's position, especially vis-à-vis the British.

By turns that spring the Confederates and then their Northern enemies injected new elements into the international situation on the seas. At long last it seemed that the success of Southern cruisers in what Navy Secretary Mallory termed "commercial warfare" would make the Confederate navy a factor in Atlantic diplomacy. In effect the Confederates established an open-sea blockade; using foreign-built ships, they roamed the seas in search of Union commercial vessels, whose cargoes they captured or destroyed.[37]

The architect of the Confederate commercial war was James Dunwoody Bulloch, a Georgian who had served in the "old navy." Bulloch spent the war period, and the rest of his life, in England serving as purchasing agent for the Navy Department. Not only did he contract for ships and oversee their construction, he undertook the more difficult task of running the diplomatic blockade of European neutrality. Often by ruse and subterfuge, Bulloch managed to launch the most important of the South's nineteen commerce raiders. His greatest success was the *Alabama*. Built at the Laird shipyards, the ship was disguised as merchant vessel *Enrica* until its maiden voyage in July 1862. After a stroke of good fortune prevented its seizure while still at Liverpool, it sailed to the Azores for armament. Then, under the command of Captain Raphael Semmes, a

[36]Case and Spencer, *United States and France*, pp. 347–366.
[37]Frank J. Merli, *Great Britain and the Confederate Navy, 1861–1865*, (Bloomington, Ind., 1970), pp. 48–99, 117–133.

Marylander who had already served the Confederacy as purchasing agent and commander of the C.S.S. *Sumter,* the *Alabama* began preying upon United States commerce. Although the *Alabama* never entered a Southern port during its extended cruise of twenty-two months, it destroyed or captured more than sixty Northern ships.[38] It and the other Confederate raiders were primarily responsible for the doubling of marine insurance rates in the North.

In one sense, though, the *Alabama* and its fellow cruisers were too successful. News of each new capture increased pressure from the United States on the British government to broaden its interpretation of neutrality. Both England and France accepted a standard whereby neutral nations might build merchant vessels for belligerants. Under pressure from the United States, however, the powers began to take more responsibility for the transformation of their products into warships. In April 1863, the British seized the newly built *Alexandria* and held it pending a determination of its intentions at sea. The inquiry resulted in the *Alexandria*'s eventual release but served notice of a British change of heart regarding the construction of Southern ships. In the fall of 1863, Bulloch suffered his worst setback when the British government seized two "rams," ocean-going ironclads rigged with ramming spars, from the Laird yards at Birkenhead. Thereafter Bulloch's attempts to purchase and fit cruisers became fewer and less successful. The *Alexandria* case and subsequent actions seemed to indicate that the Palmerston government had decided to appease the United States; certainly the Confederate successes did not bring British support for the cause. The Confederates could not understand the apparent impotence of the "mistress of the seas."[39]

Even less could the South understand British action in the case

[38]*Ibid.,* pp. 86–98. See also Raphael Semmes, *Service Afloat, or The Remarkable Career of the Confederate Cruisers, Sumter and Alabama, during the War Between the States* (Baltimore, 1887); Douglas Maynard, "Plotting the Escape of the *Alabama,*" *Journal of Southern History,* XX (1954), 197–209; and William P. Roberts, "James Dunwoody Bulloch and the Confederate Navy," *North Carolina Historical Review,* XXIV (1947), 315–366.

[39]Frank J. Merli, "Crown versus Cruiser: The Curious Case of the *Alexandria,*" *Civil War History,* IX (1963) 167–177; Crook, *North, the South, and the Powers,* pp. 258–262, 291–309; Wilbur D. Jones, *The Confederate Rams at Birkenhead: A Chapter in Anglo-American Relations* (Tuscaloosa, Ala., 1961); Case and Spencer, *The United States and France,* pp. 427–480; and Richard I. Lester, *Confederate Finance and Purchasing in Great Britain* (Charlottesville, Va., 1975), pp. 61–132.

of the *Peterhof,* a British merchant ship captured by the Union navy in the Caribbean on February 25, 1863. The *Peterhof* carried supplies defined by the United States as contraband bound for the neutral port of Matamoros in Mexico. The Union rationale for seizing the *Peterhof* involved a very broad interpretation of international law and hinged upon the contention that its cargo would eventually reach Texas: the "continuous voyage" of a neutral ship to a neutral port included overland transportation to the belligerent Confederacy. British pride and popular resentment produced a reaction which resembled the indignation displayed over the *Trent* affair. The United States and Great Britain were once again at each others' throats over neutral rights on the high seas, and the positions were much the same as they had been on the eve of the War of 1812— only the roles were reversed. Yet the Palmerston government ultimately submitted to the United States' action in the case of the *Peterhof* and resisted the jingoism of the British press. Britain was supreme on the seas, and thus Russell embraced an interpretation of international law which in the long run would benefit his nation.[40]

Many Confederates were baffled at their enemy's seeming ability to "twist the British lion's tail" with impunity. Yet British motives in the *Peterhof* affair, as in the *Alexandria* case, were not obscure. At issue was national survival. However much British statesmen would have liked to salve national pride and put the upstart Yankees in their place, British interests demanded restraint. The European balance of power seemed once again in flux; Italian *Risorgimento,* rumblings from Prussia over German unification, and a new rising of the Poles against Russia—all pointed to the wisdom of a policy that preserved British freedom of maneuver. War with the United States would not only destroy the flexibility of British diplomacy, it would also sap British military and naval strength and drain British energy and resources. The North was stronger than the South in every available index of national power. The only way the Confederacy could secure recognition in such circumstances was to demonstrate superiority on the battlefield. Then, in a diplomatic climate dominated by power, the South would become an attractive and inexpensive ally. Until the Confederacy demonstrated decisive mili-

[40]See Stuart L. Bernath, *Squall Across the Atlantic; American Civil War Prize Cases and Diplomacy* (Berkeley, Calif., 1970).

tary strength, however, Great Britain would remain neutral.[41]

Confederates were frustrated in foreign affairs on their side of the Atlantic Ocean almost as much as they were in Europe. The Richmond government had some hope of securing an alliance with Mexico against the avaricious, land-grabbing Yankees. Friendly relations with Mexico also promised overland trade and easy access to the outside world through Mexican ports. Unfortunately for the South, Mexicans had longer memories than the Confederate Department of State. The avaricious, land grabbers in Mexican memory had too often been Southerners—as proponents of the Mexican War, Texas revolutionaries, and filibusterers.

Consequently the Confederate commissioner to Mexico, John T. Pickett, former consul at Vera Cruz, former Cuban filibusterer (he participated in a private attempt to seize the island), and ever a consummate conniver, received a cool reception in Mexico City. He realized that the liberal Juarez government in Mexico City was pro-Union and even then involved in negotiations for an $11-million loan from the United States. Therefore Pickett decided to court Juarez's conservative rival, the Church Party. He determined to endear himself to Mexican conservatives by offending the liberal government. After all, Juarez controlled only part of Mexico, and in the volatile state of Mexican politics, Pickett had reason to hope the tide would turn in favor of the Church Party. Accordingly in late 1861 Pickett, after numerous "incidents," deliberately engaged in a brawl with a United States citizen and spent thirty days in jail. After bribing a judge to secure his release, he fancied himself *persona non grata* among Juarez Mexicans and proceeded to Richmond in early 1862 to await a Church Party victory and his triumphant return to favor in Mexico. Neither dream materialized, and Pickett suffered the ultimate embarrassment of entrusting the dispatches explaining his actions to a New Orleans postmaster who turned out to be a Union spy.[42]

Confederate agent Juan A. Quintero did better in the more or less independent northern Mexican states that shared a border with the South. Quintero was only one of several agents sent by Richmond,

[41]See Crook, *North, South, and the Powers*, pp. 257–282; and John Kutolowski, "The Effect of the Polish Insurrection of 1863 on the American Civil War," *Historian*, XXVII (1965), 560–577.
[42]Owsley, *King Cotton Diplomacy*, pp. 88–119.

but his was a permanent mission, and he was the most successful. Although he claimed Confederate citizenship, Quintero had long lived in Mexico. His first assignment was to visit Governor Santiago Vidaurri in Monterrey, the capital of Nuevo León. Quintero returned to Richmond during Hunter's tenure in the State Department and brought with him assurances of Vidaurri's friendship. Quintero expressed the hope that the Confederacy might form a permanent alliance against Juarez with the states of eastern Mexico that were in Vidaurri's camp. Hunter and Davis were reluctant to embroil the Confederacy in Mexican politics but eager to have Quintero follow up his success. Thus Quintero returned to Monterrey to oversee commercial relations between the Mexican North and the American South. Cotton crossed the Rio Grande in exchange for arms, ammunition, powder, metals, coffee, sugar, and more from the outside world. Through Matamoros, the South had an outlet to Europe, albeit a risky one after the *Peterhof* seizure. The Mexicans had the satisfaction of profitable trade, tariff revenue, and presumed safety from Confederate invasion. In 1862 this trade, which gave Confederates some consolation for their failures in Mexico City, began to flourish and became a major factor in the Southern war west of the Mississippi River.[43]

Rebuffed in their attempts to deal with the Juarez Mexicans, the Confederates in 1863 had hopes that soon Juarez would no longer speak for Mexico. For some time a joint expeditionary force of British, French, and Russian troops had been in Mexico to press the demands of international creditors against Mexicans. In 1863 France assumed leadership of the coalition and gave evidence of more than monetary interest. In January a French army invaded Puebla, and although the conquest seemed leisurely, by June the French had captured Mexico City. If Napoleon III was attempting to establish a New World Empire, he certainly would require the good will of the Confederacy. The United States and its Secretary of State William H. Seward were making vague threats and invoking the principles of the Monroe Doctrine. The Confederacy could,

[43] *Ibid.*, pp. 119–120; Ronnie C. Tyler, *Santiago Vidaurri and the Southern Confederacy*, (Austin, Tex., 1973); Marilyn McAdams Sibley, "Charles Stillman: A Case Study of Entrepeneurship on the Rio Grande, 1861–1865," *Southwestern Historical Quarterly*, LXXXVII (1973), 227–240; and LeRoy P. Graf, "The Economic History of the Lower Rio Grande Valley, 1820–1875," unpublished Ph.D. dissertation (Harvard University, 1972).

under the right circumstances, be persuaded to ignore Monroe's dictum and ally with the French.[44]

Already France had renewed its mediation offer (in January, 1863), and logic seemed to indicate that Napoleon would welcome a buffer state between the North and the new French empire in Mexico. In addition, as a portent of closer relations with France, the Confederacy in 1863 secured a substantial loan—£3 million, or about $14.5 million—through the French banking house of Emile Erlanger and Company. The Confederates received high-risk terms, of course, but given the circumstances there was ample reason for financial optimism in Richmond when Congress approved the transaction on January 29, 1863.[45] Although Emile Erlanger himself was not exactly representative of hard-eyed international financiers (he was extremely sympathetic to the Southern cause, and in 1864 married the daughter of Confederate commissioner to France John Slidell), the Erlanger loan encouraged the Confederates to believe that European money was a stronger endorsement of the Southern nation than diplomatic recognition, and that financial interests might rekindle political interest.[46]

The most immediate benefit of the Erlanger loan was a restoration of faith in Confederate credit. Southern purchasing agents were able to settle old accounts and contract for more war materials on the strength of the loan. For a time, the Confederates in Europe seemed bent upon outdoing each other in spending their government's new-found wealth. In May of 1863, Collin J. McRae arrived in London with the government's mandate to consolidate purchasing activities and manage Confederate finances abroad. Because the Erlanger loan was based upon cotton and because Southern military fortunes appeared bright until mid-summer, the Confederates in Europe were able to procure and contract for increased amounts of war supplies in the first half of 1863.[47] Ultimately the Confederacy realized £1,759,894 (about $8,535,486) from the sale of loan subscriptions during 1863 and 1864. Profit, discount, and commissions

[44]Case and Spencer, *The United States and France,* pp. 386–403.

[45]Judith Fenner Gentry thoroughly discusses the loan and its historiography in her splendid article, "A Confederate Success in Europe: The Erlanger Loan," *Journal of Southern History,* XXXVI (1970), 157–188.

[46]Lester, *Confederate Finance and Purchasing in Great Britain,* p. 237.

[47]*Ibid.,* p. 48; Gentry, "Erlanger Loan," 169–173. See also Charles S. Davis, *Colin J. McRae: Confederate Financial Agent* (Tuscaloosa, Ala., 1961).

for Emile Erlanger and Company, plus market manipulations by the Confederates themselves accounted for the difference between the money figure for which the Southerners contracted ($14,550,000) and the amount they actually received ($8,535,486). Considering the circumstances under which the rebel nation entered the European money market, the Confederacy had made about the best deal possible.[48]

Thus as the military campaigning season of 1863 opened, the Confederacy had reason for renewed faith in French friendship and hope for intervention. As it happened, though, Napoleon remained a step or two ahead of the Southerners. His mediation gesture of January 1863 was precisely that—a gesture, more rhetorical than real, designed to placate French politicians. As for the Mexican venture, it was primarily a pawn in the Emperor's Austrian diplomacy; he schemed to trade Mexico to Austrian Prince Maxmilian in exchange for territorial concessions in Italy and thus reemerge as savior and guarantor of *Risorgimento.* But Napoleon was nothing if not flexible. The French, like the British, were prepared to respond to Southern victory; and like the British, Napoleon kept his options open in 1863 while surveying the rival armies.[49]

Perhaps the ultimate reality of the Southern diplomatic circumstance displayed itself, not in Europe or Mexico, but closer to home, among nations much less sophisticated than Britain and France. On August 12, 1861, Confederate commissioner Albert Pike concluded one of several treaties between his government and elements of the "Five Civilized Tribes" living in Indian territory (Oklahoma). Among quaint-sounding articles that forbade stealing horses and going "upon the warpath" was a pledge on the part of the Confederate government that the Indians would not "henceforward . . . be in any wise troubled or molested by any power or people, State or person whatever."[50] Pike, a resourceful and knowledgeable emissary, made sound suggestions to President Davis on Indian policy. The Indians sought protection against the United States, Pike pointed out, and as long as the Confederates could provide that protection, the tribes would be loyal allies. In fact Indian forces

[48]Gentry, "Erlanger Loan," 185–188.

[49]Crook, *North, South, and the Powers,* pp. 331–343.

[50]*War of the Rebellion: A Compilation of the Official Records of the Union and Confederate Armies,* 70 vols. in 127 (Washington, D.C., 1880–1901), ser. IV, I, 542–546.

fought for the South at Pea Ridge in March of 1862, and elsewhere. But after the Confederate defeat at Pea Ridge, the South was never again in a position to prevent Northern invasion of Indian territory. The United States pressed its advantage, and the Indians lost enthusiasm for the Southern cause.[51]

The Confederate-Indian situation was bluntly instructive. As in other foreign relations, the Confederacy's hopes ultimately marched with its armies, and so it was involved in a vicious diplomatic circle. To secure recognition and aid both in Europe and North America, the Confederacy had to win on the battlefield, and the surest way to win on the battlefield was to win foreign recognition and aid. The South's sometime allies in Indian territory paid no homage to King Cotton, nor did they respond to incidents touching national pride and face. They, like others among the world's peoples, did respond to power or the lack of power. Consequently they recognized and assisted the Confederacy in rough accord with the South's capacity to return the favor.

[51]See two articles by Kenny A. Franks, "The Implementation of the Confederate Treaties with Five Civilized Tribes," *Chronicles of Oklahoma* (1973), 21–33, and "The Confederate States and the Five Civilized Tribes: A Breakdown of Relations," *Journal of the West* (1973), 439–454.

CHAPTER 9

The Development of the Confederate South

D URING the early months of 1863 as the Confederacy marked
the second anniversary of its founding and the first year of its
permanent government, the new nation appeared to be normal.
The Southern nation had endured, indeed prevailed, for two campaigning seasons without the loss of truly critical land or battles.
And even though the war went on, Confederate prospects in 1863
looked far more hopeful than they had in 1862. At Richmond a
distinguished foreign visitor, Arthur James Lyon Fremantle, found
an orderly government and "at least as much difficulty in gaining
access to the great men as there would be in European countries."
On the surface at least the South seemed to have achieved wartime
stability.[1]

Yet beneath this superficial stasis the Confederacy was far from
normal. The continued strain of wartime exposed new flaws in the
fabric of Confederate nationality. On January 6, 1863, for example,
Dodson Ramseur's division of Lee's army marched through Richmond with many of its members barefoot. No wonder that in 1863
the Confederate Patent Office issued four separate patents for

[1]Walter Lord (ed.), *The Fremantle Diary: Being the Journal of Lieutenant Colonel Arthur
James Lyon Fremantle, Coldstream Guards, on his Three Months in the Southern States* (New
York, 1954), p. 164. Jefferson Davis went so far as to state in his first message to
Congress in 1863, "we have every reason to expect that this will be the closing year
of the War." Davis to Congress, January 12, 1863, James D. Richardson (ed.), *Mes-
sages and Papers of the Confederacy*, 2 vols. (Nashville, Tenn. 1906), I, 277.

wooden shoe soles; shoes were a small matter until men had to march without them.[2]

The new challenges which beset the Confederacy in 1863 were, more accurately, new versions of old challenges. They called for novel responses which transformed the Confederate South still more from its ante-bellum origins. Jefferson Davis faced a new political crisis with a Congress whose members faced their own political crises in upcoming fall elections. Southern soldiers and civilians encountered increasing shortages of supplies and provisions, and the Confederate government confronted a shortage of specie and a declining faith in inflated treasury notes. And Southern armies again faced Northern invasions during another campaigning season. These circumstances, whether interpreted as chronic problems or crises, clamored for resolution as the year 1863 began.

President Davis' new political difficulties had begun back in the fall of 1862 with his cabinet. George W. Randolph had been a capable secretary of war. By October 1862, Randolph had impressed upon Davis and Richmond officialdom the significance of the west as a theater of military operations and had argued successfully for some relaxation in the departmental command structure.[3] Beyond the Appalachians, Randolph perceived, the war demanded a fluidity too often unappreciated in Richmond. But when he attempted to act on his enthusiasm by shifting some troops in the western command without consulting the President, Davis responded by reminding Randolph of the relative powers of commander-in-chief and secretary of war. Randolph resigned in haste on November 15, and Davis accepted the resignation in greater haste. When Randolph described the war secretary's job as that of a "chief clerk," the quarrel became public and the antiadministration press elaborated upon the theme.[4]

[2]Kate Mason Rowland, Ms. Diary, Confederate Museum, Richmond, Va., *Report of the Commissioner of Patents* (Richmond, Va., 1864).

[3]For Randolph's accomplishments see Archer Jones, "Some Aspects of George W. Randolph's Service as Confederate Secretary of War," *Journal of Southern History*, XXVI (1960), 299–314.

[4]The Randolph-Davis correspondence is in Dunbar Rowland (ed.), *Jefferson Davis, Constitutionalist: His Letters, Papers and Speeches*, 10 vols. (Jackson, Miss., 1923), V, 371–372, 374–375. On the status of cabinet secretaries and clerks, the Richmond *Examiner* (November 17, 1862) commented, "Indeed, if cabinet ministers are to continue mere automations, it matters little by what names those machines are

To cope with the situation, Davis installed General Gustavus W. Smith in the War Office ad interim and cast about for Randolph's replacement. On November 22 he gave the war portfolio to James A. Seddon and thus forestalled political crisis. Seddon was a Virginian, a disciple of Calhoun, and a staunch secessionist. He was, however, more scholar than warrior, and his sickly appearance raised questions about his capacity to sustain the work load of the War Office. But he proved to be a practical and clear-eyed administrator, bowing to the President's expertise in military matters but contributing a large measure of common sense and efficiency in the day-to-day conduct of the war. Press and public reaction to Seddon's appointment was generally favorable. The Richmond *Examiner* and Charleston *Mercury,* two of the administration's most consistent critics, endorsed the new secretary, and Virginians were satisfied that one of their own was again in the cabinet.[5]

Although Seddon was the President's first choice to replace Randolph, Davis had seriously considered Joseph E. Johnston. The Virginian general had spent most of the campaigning season of 1862 recovering from wounds sustained at Seven Pines, and just about the time that the Randolph-Davis squabble came to crisis, he reported himself fit for duty. What Johnston wanted most was command of the Army of Northern Virginia, which he still considered his own. That army was now Lee's, but Johnston did merit an important command, and even though the General and the President had had their differences, Davis held Johnston's generalship in high esteem. Seddon had much to do with the solution to the problem of finding a use for Johnston, and in so doing built upon Randolph's legacy of concern for coordination of the western command. In late November, Seddon and Davis decided to make a superdepartment, a theater actually, of the Confederate heartland between the Appalachian Mountains and the Mississippi River, and command of this new military structure went to Johnston. The command included three field armies: Edmund Kirby Smith's in east Tennessee,

called." Among historians, Jones ("Randolph's Service") blames Davis for the incident; Rembert W. Patrick (*Jefferson Davis and His Cabinet* [Baton Rouge, La., 1944], pp. 127–131) blames Randolph.

[5]Patrick, *Davis and His Cabinet,* pp. 131–149; Roy W. Curry, "James A. Seddon, a Southern Prototype," *Virginia Magazine of History and Biography,* LXIII (1955), 123–150.

Braxton Bragg's in middle Tennessee, and John C. Pemberton's covering Vicksburg. Johnston's mission was coordination. Beyond this fact, however, his duties and authority were somewhat ambiguous.[6]

Aware at last of problems in the western theater, Davis resolved to view the situation at first hand. He wished to confer with Bragg, inspect the armies, visit political leaders, and show himself to the people—all in the hope, as he wrote to Lee, that "something may be done to bring out men not heretofore in service, and to arouse all classes to united and desperate resistance."[7]

Traveling first to Murfreesboro, where Bragg stood between two Federal armies at Nashville and Chattanooga, Davis made a speech to the troops, then, with commanding General Johnston in tow, hurried on to visit Pemberton at Vicksburg. On December 26 he addressed the Mississippi legislature and a few days later returned to Richmond, stopping on his way to consult with local leaders and test the climate of public opinion.[8]

Returning to the capital on the night of January 5, Davis found to his surprise a band and a modest crowd at the station. The occasion demanded a speech, and Davis rose to the occasion with accounts of Southern heroism, tales of Yankee atrocities, and exhortations to greater patriotism which stirred his audience. Yet through the speech ran a current of estrangement between President and people; Davis spoke as a visitor to the city in which he had lived for nearly two years. He protested that "constant labor in the duties of office, borne down by care, and with an anxiety which has left me scarcely a moment for repose, I have had but little opportunity for social intercourse among you," and concluded with the hope "that at some future time we shall be better acquainted."[9] As President, Jefferson Davis led the Southern revolution as capably, perhaps, as any man could have led it, but his

[6]Patrick, *Davis and His Cabinet*, pp. 132–135; For assessments of Davis, Johnston and theater command, see Frank E. Vandiver, *Rebel Brass: The Confederate Command System* (Baton Rouge, La., 1956), pp. 34–37; Archer Jones, *Confederate Strategy from Shiloh to Vicksburg* (Baton Rouge, La., 1961), pp. 96–110; and Thomas L. Connelly, *Autumn of Glory: The Army of Tennessee, 1862–1868 (Baton Rouge, La., 1971), pp. 30–38.*

[7]Davis to Lee, December 8, 1862, Rowland (ed.), *Jefferson Davis*, IV, 384.

[8]For Davis' travels see Hudson Strode, *Jefferson Davis*, 3 vols. (New York, 1955–1959, 1964), II, 343–356; and Jones, *Confederate Strategy*, 111–122.

[9]Richmond *Enquirer*, January 7, 1863, cited in Rowland (ed.), *Jefferson Davis*, V, 390–395.

political personality had severe limitations, and Confederate Southerners had to look beyond him to find inspiration for the cause.[10]

While the President was traveling to Richmond, Bragg's army fought a major battle at Murfreesboro on December 31, 1863.[11] Bragg described the battle as a victory, and Davis accepted the word but not the fact. How was he to explain Bragg's subsequent retreat to Tullahoma? Acting decisively Davis ordered Johnston to investigate the matter, then to take command of Bragg's army and send the "victorious" general to Richmond to make a personal accounting. A series of circumstances having little relation to the military situation frustrated these plans, however, and Johnston's role in the structure of command remained unclear in all but outline. Davis and Seddon probably thought of Johnston as a sort of trouble-shooter; Johnston himself believed and wrote to his friends in Congress that he had been exiled and elevated to a position of inconsequence.[12]

Having dealt with the politics of administration in the Randolph crisis, the politics of command in Johnson's theater assignment, and the politics of personality in his western tour, President Davis girded himself to face the politics of politicians when Congress came back into session on January 12, 1863.

The session lasted until May, and for the first two months the Southern solons distinguished themselves more by what they did not do than by what they did. Congress debated but did not enact bills to establish a Supreme Court, seat cabinet members in Congress, create a general staff for the army, and renew the President's

[10]On Davis and public morale see Bell I. Wiley *Road to Appomattox,* (New York, 1968), pp. 28–31, 105–108.

[11]Connelly, *Autumn of Glory,* 44–68; Grady McWhiney *Braxton Bragg and Confederate Defeat: Field Command* (New York, 1969), pp. 349–373.

[12]Davis, on the night he returned to Richmond, referred to the "victory" at Murfreesboro (Rowland [ed.], *Jefferson Davis,* V, 392). The President's instructions to Johnston are contained in letters of January 22 and February 19 (Rowland [ed.], *Jefferson Davis,* V, 420–421, 433–435). Johnston's account is in his *Narrative of Military Operations,* ed. by Frank E. Vandiver (Bloomington, Ind., 1959), pp. 161–162. To Texas Senator Louis T. Wigfall, Johnston wrote on March 8, 1863: "I am told that the President and Secretary of War think that they have given me the highest military position in the Confederacy, that I have full military power in all this western country. . . . If they so regard it, ought not our highest military officer to occupy it? It seems so to me that principle would bring Lee here. I might then, with great propriety be replaced in my old Command." (Louis T. Wigfall Papers, University of Texas Archives, Austin) See also Gilbert E. Govan and James W. Livingood, *A Different Valor: The Story of General Joseph E. Johnston, C.S.A.* (New York, 1956), pp. 166–174.

authority to suspend habeas corpus. The Supreme Court and habeas corpus bills had the support of Davis and the administration, which in part explained their failure; for in an election year, congressmen were reluctant to expand the power of the central government and were sensitive to the abuses of martial law by some commanders. Even though the Confederate Constitution made provision for a Supreme Court, Congress never passed the requisite enabling legislation. Consequently ultimate judicial authority remained in the state courts instead of the central government. Still, to an amazing degree state courts in the Confederacy upheld the prerogative of the Davis government. Hence the Confederate judicial system remained fragmented in structure but centralized in substance.[13]

Author of the general staff and the cabinet member seating bills was Senator Louis T. Wigfall of Texas. The idea of permitting commanders to appoint their own staffs had considerable merit, but the merits of the bill got lost in what became a conflict of prerogative and personality between president and senator. The President had already vetoed Wigfall's general staff proposal once, on the ground that it infringed upon presidential power, and from that moment Wigfall became an open political enemy of Davis. Wigfall reintroduced his general staff bill and offered the cabinet member seating bill as opposition measures, and as such the Senate rejected them. Thus, although the Confederate Constitution made provision for the seating of cabinet members in Congress, no member of Davis' cabinet ever got the opportunity to explain his program to Congress in person. That was not all to the bad; cabinet members were able to escape the invective of antiadministration men like Wigfall in the Senate or Henry S. Foote in the House. But it was unfortunate that Wigfall's general staff scheme, which could only have improved the normally poor quality of staff work in Southern armies, lost to personal rancor and Davis' inflexibility.[14]

The fate of these four pieces of legislation dramatized the erosion of administration influence, erosion which increased during the

[13]Wilfred Buck Yearns, *The Confederate Congress* (Athens, Ga., 1960), pp. 155, 37–38, 228; "Proceedings of the Confederate Congress," 1 Congress, II Session, *Southern Historical Society Papers*, XLVI, 9, 110; William M. Robinson, Jr., *Justice in Grey: A History of the Judicial System of the Confederate States of America* (Cambridge, Mass., 1941).

[14]See Alvy L. King, *Louis T. Wigfall: Southern Fire-Eater* (Baton Rouge, La., 1970), pp. 157–160, 166–168.

remaining two years of the Confederacy's life. That the opposition never coalesced into a party structure gave some index of its fragmentation. Ultimately antiadministration sentiment in Congress, like the attempted obstruction of national policies in some of the states, was a measure of the political metamorphosis within the Confederate South. With some allowance for individual quirks and for the limitations of Jefferson Davis' political personality, the fundamental issue which divided the Davis government from its foes was state rights versus nationalism. In the name of wartime emergency, the Davis administration had all but destroyed the political philosophy which underlay the founding of the Southern republic. Interestingly, the Confederate Congress sometimes led the way.[15]

During the final month and a half of the session, Congress debated and enacted three crucial bills which expanded still further the authority of the Richmond government. In March, Congress authorized quartermaster and commissary officers to seize private property for the use of field armies.[16] In reality the law merely legitimized the existing practice by which armies lived off the land when necessary. The army paid for the impressed items in accord with a War Department schedule of standard prices. Unfortunately for producers, the schedule consistently fixed prices below the open market value, and the government paid in depreciated currency. Unfortunately for civilian consumers, army agents often seized supplies en route to local markets and thus produced a scarcity of food and forage in Southern cities and towns. The impressment process, with its ills and inequities, was doubtless necessary as a supplement to the efforts of the Commissary and Quartermaster Bureaus, and though Southern civilians complained, they generally submitted to this infringement of property rights for the sake of the cause. Ironically that cause had originally included concern for the sanctity of private property in slaves, yet the act of March 26 gave sanction to the impressment of slaves as military laborers.[17]

[15]See Emory M. Thomas, *The Confederacy as a Revolutionary Experience* (Englewood Cliffs, N.J., 1971), pp. 73–78. The Congress too often led in the degree of rancor as well. The Supreme Court bill sparked a brawl in which Georgia Senator Benjamin H. Hill hurled an inkwell at Alabama Senator William Lounndes Yancey (King, *Wigfall*, p. 150).

[16]James M. Matthews (ed.), *The Statutes at Large of the Confederate States of America . . . Third Session . . . First Congress* (Richmond, Va., 1863), pp. 102–104, 127–128.

[17]Thomas B. Alexander and Richard E. Beringer, *The Anatomy of the Confederate Congress: A Study of the Influences of Member Chracteristics on Legislative Voting Behavior, 1861–1865* (Nashville, Tenn., 1972), pp. 139–144; Yearns, *Confederate Congress*, pp.

Congress began debating ways and means of financing the Southern nation and its war early in the 1863 session. Secretary of the Treasury Memminger reported on January 10 what Congressmen already knew too well: the policy of financing the war by issuing treasury notes had produced rampant inflation.[18] In January 1863, a gold dollar in Richmond brought three dollars in treasury notes.[19] And the trend worsened every day. Yet clearly the government needed enormous amounts of money to sustain its existence. Memminger's solution was simple and logical—for a peacetime economy. He proposed to remove as much as two-thirds of the paper money from circulation by offering to exchange non-interest-bearing notes for interest-bearing bonds.[20] On March 23, Congress enacted the policy and authorized Memminger to issue each month up to $50 million in treasury notes which could be exchanged for thirty-year bonds bearing 6 percent interest.[21] Under the provisions of this act the government printed more than $500 million worth of notes, the largest issue of notes ever made in the Confederacy, but the inflation rate discouraged investment in bonds, and only $21-million worth of notes were withdrawn from circulation. By January 1, 1864, a gold dollar in Richmond was worth eighteen to twenty dollars in Confederate notes, reflecting an inflation rate of over 600 percent. The wonder was that the government survived for another fifteen months thereafter.[22]

In January 1863, Memminger renewed his consistent plea for taxation as a necessary method of producing revenue and of restraining inflation. The treasury note authorization of March 23 was

---

116–120. See also Harrison A. Trexler, "The Opposition of Planters to the Employment of Slaves as Laborers by the Confederacy," *Mississippi Valley Historical Review* XXVII (1940), 211–224.

[18]Memminger to Thomas S. Bocock, January 10, 1863, in Raphael P. Thian (comp.), *Reports of the Secretary of the Treasury of the Confederate States of America, 1861–1865*, Appendix III (Washington, D.C., 1878), 99–115.

[19]Richard Cecil Todd, *Confederate Finance* (Athens, Ga., 1954), p. 198.

[20]See *ibid.*, pp. 110–111

[21]Matthews (ed.), *Statutes at Large . . . Third Session . . . First Congress*, pp. 97–98, 99–102.

[22]Todd, *Confederate Finance*, pp. 111, 119–120, 198. From hindsight Charles W. Ramsdell once stated, "If I were asked what was the greatest single weakness of the Confederacy, I should say, without much hesitation, that it was in this matter of finances. The resort to irredeemable paper money and to excessive issues of such currency was fatal, for it weakened not only the purchasing power of the government but also destroyed economic security among the people." (*Behind the Lines in the Southern Confederacy* [Baton Rouge, La., 1944], p. 85).

only half of the government's financial policy in 1863. The other half was a collection of measures designed to generate revenue to support government paper. On April 24 Congress passed a tax law which was stern to the point of being confiscatory. The act levied an 8-percent ad valorem tax on agricultural products grown in 1862 and taxed bank deposits and commercial paper at the same rate. The act levied a 10-percent tax on profits from buying and selling foodstuffs, clothing, and iron, thus requiring speculators in these commodites to share their profits with the government. It levied a license tax on just about every form of occupation or business, a graduated income tax whose scale varied from 1 percent of incomes less than $500 to 15 percent of incomes over $10,000, and a tax-in-kind tithe on agricultural produce and livestock: 10 percent of everything grown or slaughtered in 1863.[23]

The tax law was bitter medicine. The unchallenged income tax, for example, anticipated the United States federal income tax by fifty years. Nevertheless at first Congress received praise for its courage and wisdom. Before long, however, the difficulties of equitable enforcement became apparent. The tax in kind, especially, proved onerous, and the "TIK men," agents appointed to collect the tithe, too often acted like licensed thieves. Some dissenters declared the tax unconstitutional, and it probably was, but the President countered with the plain truth that the nation's survival depended upon collection of the tax.[24] The tax bill and other significant legislation of 1863 dealt with the problem of distributing wealth, food, and supplies among armies and people. The year before, the main thrust of government activity had been the organization of manpower when Confederates faced the challenge of reconciling state rights and individual liberties with the demands of a multifront war fought by the largest bodies of armed men ever

[23]Matthews (ed.), *Statutes at Large . . . Third Session . . . First Congress*, pp. 115–126. Todd, *Confederate Finance*, pp. 136–141.

[24]Todd, *Confederate Finance*, pp. 141–148. Todd estimates the value of taxes in kind collected from 1863 to 1865 at $62 million (p. 148). See also James L. Nichols, "The Tax-in-Kind in the Department of the Trans-Mississippi," *Civil War History*, V (1959), 382–389. On the larger issues of Confederate fiscal policy see three articles by Eugene M. Lerner, "Monetary and Fiscal Programs of the Confederate Government," *Journal of Political Economy*, LXII (1954), 506–522; "Money, Prices, and Wages in the Confederacy," *Journal of Political Economy*, LXIII (1955), 20–40; and "Inflation in the Confederacy, 1861–1865," in Milton Friedman (ed.), *Studies in the Quantity Theory of Money* (Chicago, 1956), pp. 163–178.

assembled in North America. Actually these two efforts, material distribution and manpower organization, were opposite sides of the same coin. The Confederates were learning the hard lessons of modern warfare: to survive, a combatant nation must be able to mobilize its military population, its economy, and its social institutions in support of the war. The Confederates had submitted to conscription and martial law; now they faced impressment, confiscatory taxation, and fiat currency.

For the military campaigns of 1863 the South placed more troops in the field than it ever had before or would after.[25] To sustain so large a body of consumers, the Southern economy had to do two things: produce or purchase food, equipment, and arms to supply its armies; and produce or purchase the necessities to support its civilian producers. In the spring of 1863 the nation reached critical points in each of these efforts. Southerners achieved their greatest degree of self-sufficiency in war industry and supply, but at the same time the Confederate civilian economy displayed its most alarming and dramatic symptoms of disease. Contrary to the sacred truism, a nation of farmers could indeed go hungry.[26]

The winter of 1862–1863 had been hard for Confederates. Those who lived on farms or plantations away from the war zones missed the farmers and planters who were away in the army, but as long as gardens grew and livestock survived, they could eat. Life was more difficult in areas where armies of friend or foe had marched, camped, or fought, and in areas under Union control. Those who remained on the land had to contend with broken fences, plundered chicken coops and smokehouses, and trampled crops. Many left their homes and migrated as refugees to cities and towns to find safety at the cost of privation.[27] During the winter of 1862–1863 Southerners discovered to their alarm that their economy was far more fragile and interdependent than they had previously realized.

A fundamental fact of economic life in the Confederacy was that

[25]The strength totals for December 31, 1862, and December 31, 1863, are in *War of the Rebellion: A Compilation of the Official Records of the Union and Confederate Armies,* 70 vols. in 127 (Washington, D.C., 1880–1901), ser. IV, II, 278, 380.

[26]Among the numerous specific accounts of wartime privation in the Confederacy, two general works are basic: Ramsdell, *Behind the Lines;* and Mary Elizabeth Massey, *Ersatz in the Confederacy* (Columbia, S.C., 1952).

[27]See Mary Elizabeth Massey, *Refugee Life in the Confederacy* (Baton Rouge, La., 1964)

wherever Southerners congregated in cities, towns, or armies, there was the threat of hunger. There were several reasons for this. First, Southern agriculture in ante-bellum times had thrived on the production of staple crops—cotton, tobacco, rice, sugar, and the like—but tobacco provided little nourishment, cotton even less, and Federal armies occupied or threatened the South's rice- and sugar-producing lowlands. Obviously Southern agriculture needed to convert to food production, and to that end Congress adopted resolutions and state legislatures passed laws which limited the number of acres to be planted in inedible staples. But the transition required more time and self-sacrifice than the new nation could afford. Ante-bellum agrarian inertia proved a formidable obstacle.[28]

A second reason for food shortages in the Confederacy was military. By the end of 1862 Federal troops occupied extensive croplands in regions adjacent to population centers, most significantly Southern grain- and livestock-producing areas in central Virginia and middle Tennessee. Farms and plantations which lay in the path of the war produced little or no food for the armies sent to defend them. And as the sphere of Union control increased, Confederate cropland contracted; fewer acres had to feed almost as many people.[29]

The ratio of defenders to producers in the Confederate economy was a third source of Southern supply problems. Farms and plantations were less efficient when farmers and planters were away in the army. When a Southern farmer left his fields to take the field, the farmer's wife, parents, or children were simply not able in many cases to take the place of the producer turned consumer (as soldier). Slaves on plantations and farms remained, and overseers were exempt, but masterless plantations, like masterless farms, were less productive, and plantations which continued to grow cotton or to-

[28]In his message to Congress on January 12, 1863, President Davis resorted to hyperbolic statement to express a desperate hope: "Our fields, no longer whitened by cotton that cannot be exported, are devoted to the production of cereals and the growth of stock formerly purchased with the proceeds of cotton." Davis to Congress, January 12, 1863, Rowland (ed.), *Jefferson Davis*, V, 415. For the economic legislation of state legislatures see May Spencer Ringold, *The Role of State Legislatures in the Confederacy* (Athens, Ga., 1966), pp. 40–45.

[29]This factor, so obvious as to be often overlooked, is pointed out in Frank E. Vandiver, *Their Tattered Flags: The Epic of the Confederacy* (New York, 1970), pp. 238–239. The standard work on agriculture is Paul W. Gates, *Agriculture and the Civil War* (New York, 1956).

bacco provided no sustenance for armies or urbanites.[30]

Finally, the Southern transportation system severly hindered distribution of food supplies. Railroads in the Old South had been largely farm-to-market facilities, a fact which limited their military usefulness but seems likely to have aided the Confederacy's supply effort. However, Confederate tracks and rolling stock quickly became worn as immediate military requirements commanded priority attention. The Confederates spent their limited resources maintaining the lines which linked military theaters and connected Southern subregions. The Western and Atlantic road, which connected Chattanooga and Atlanta, continued to function; the Richmond and York River line, which "merely" ran from the Confederate capital into tidewater farmlands, suffered neglect and cannibalization.

The same set of priorities which usually dictated the distribution of the Confederates' railroad energies and resources applied to other kinds of roads as well, and military necessity established first claim to the South's wagons and draft animals. Hence, for what seemed at the time the most rational of reasons, people went hungry in the midst of full cribs, barns, and smokehouses. A bountiful harvest counted for little if local railroad tracks were destroyed by foes or cannibalized by friends, if the road to town were a quagmire, or if wagons and mules were impressed to serve the army.[31]

The best case study of the results of Southern food supply problems occurred under the nose of the Confederate government in its capital. As in other cities and towns in the wartime South, Richmond's population had swollen enormously and rapidly during the two years since 1861. The increased number of government employees and wage laborers were, like salaried people everywhere, especially hard hit by currency inflation. Because the summer campaign of 1862 had despoiled the adjacent countryside, local farmers reaped an especially meager harvest in the fall, and Richmond residents had to share that harvest with a major field army. The situation was most critical in the early spring, before the new planting yielded and as supplies stored the previous autumn ran lowest. In

[30]See Ramsdell, *Behind the Lines*, pp. 1–41.

[31]On the conditions of Southern railroads the classic work is Robert C. Black III, *The Railroads of the Confederacy* (Chapel Hill, N.C., 1952). For government regulation see Richard D. Goff, *Confederate Supply* (Durham, N.C., 1969), pp. 104–111.

the spring of 1863 a set of natural and artificial circumstances rendered Richmond's food situation critical.[32]

Always before, residents of the capital, like other town dwellers, had blamed high prices and short supply upon "extortioners," an omnipresent but seldom identifiable group of Yankeelike war profiteers in foodstuffs. When in March 1863 Congress passed the impressment law, however, the city's economic enemies became more visible. In their zeal to feed the troops and restock government storehouses, commissary agents took immediate advantage of the new law by impressing food in Richmond marketplaces and along the roads leading to the city. Such indiscriminate impressment not only cut more deeply into the limited supply of food, it also discouraged farmers and gardeners from bringing produce to Richmond and thereby risking impressment at less than market value. The ardor of impressment agents soon cooled, and in time a series of court injunctions, laws, and informal understandings ameliorated the worst abuses of urban impressment, but moderation of impressment practices did not come in time to avert a crisis in the spring of 1863.[33]

Even before the advent of systematic impressment, the business of transporting produce and staple food to Richmond was tedious at best. In the absence of enabling legislation from Congress, some features of martial law persisted in the capital. Specifically, the passport system remained, which meant that to satisfy the needs of internal security, local farmers had to stand in lines and undergo delays coming and going to their market stalls. Then, on March 19 and 20, 1863, nature compounded the conspiracy to keep producers at home. Nine inches of snow fell and rendered travel difficult; then nine inches of snow quickly thawed, and travel was next to impossible on the sodden roads.

On the morning of April 2, a group of Richmond women gathered in a Baptist church near their homes. Most of them were wives of iron workers from the nearby Tredegar Works, and all of them believed that the price and supply of food in Richmond had reached intolerable levels. They determined to seek redress from Virginia

[32]The Richmond *Dispatch* (January 29, 1863) estimated that a family food bill had increased during two years of war from $6.65 to $68.25.

[33]Emory M. Thomas, *The Confederate State of Richmond: A Biography of the Capital* (Austin, Tex., 1971), pp. 111–114, 117–119.

Governor John Letcher. The group left the church and began walk-
ing toward the governor's mansion on Capitol Square, and as they
walked their number grew. By the time they assembled to present
their plight to Letcher, there were several hundred, and men and
boys had joined the female petitioners.[34]

While Letcher listened to the complaints, a Richmond gentle-
woman out for a stroll noticed the growing throng and asked a
young girl on its fringes what was happening. "Is there some celebration?" she inquired.

"There is," said the girl solemnly; "We celebrate our right to live. We are
starving. As soon as enough of us get together we are going to the bakeries
and each of us will take a loaf of bread. This is little enough for the
government to give us after it has taken all our men."[35]

Letcher offered his personal concern, but no tangible answers.
When the Governor went inside his mansion, the crowd in the front
yard turned angry and began to move toward Richmond's commercial district. Knives, hatchets, and a few pistols emerged from pock-
etbooks and skirts. Within a short time a small group of distraught
housewives had become a crowd and then a mob; petition became
riot.

Throughout a ten-square-block area the women and their male
allies broke into shops and stores and took what they wanted. Most
took only bread and other food items, but some helped themselves
to jewelry, clothing, and hats. One merchant claimed a loss of more
than $13,000 worth of goods, and the rioters took more than three
hundred pounds of beef belonging to the City Hospital as the crowd
broke into bands of leaderless looters.

Governor Letcher, when he heard the news, hurried to the scene
and tried to reason with the mob. Richmond Mayor Joseph Mayo
read the riot act to those within the sound of his voice. Letcher's and
Mayo's words, however, had no effect upon the rioters, if indeed
many heard them. The riot had been in progress for some time
when the vanguard neared one of the city's two marketplaces. There
the looters met a company of reserve soldiers drawn from workers

[34]Emory M. Thomas, "The Richmond Bread Riot of 1863," *Virginia Cavalcade*
(Summer 1968), 41–42; and *Confederate Richmond*, p. 119.

[35]Mrs. Roger A. Pryor, *Reminiscences of Peace and War* (New York, 1904), pp. 251–
259; F. N. Boney, *John Letcher of Virginia: The Story of Virginia's Civil War Governor*
(University, Ala., 1966), pp. 189–190.

in the Confederate armory. In haste some of the rioters pushed a horseless wagon across the street as a makeshift barricade. On opposite sides of the wagon, citizens confronted citizen soldiers.[36]

Then into the midst of the impasse strode the President of the Confederacy. Jefferson Davis climbed into the wagon and shouted above the confusion. First he emptied his pockets and threw what money he had with him into the mob. The gesture served to get the attention of crowd. Then Davis took out his pocket watch, glanced at the troops behind him and stated, "We do not desire to injure anyone, but this lawlessness must stop. I will give you five minutes to disperse, otherwise you will be fired upon."[37]

For long minutes no one moved. Davis had no way of knowing whether the troops at his back would actually carry out his threat. Indeed it was likely that some of the reserve soldiers recognized friends or relatives among the mob. The captain in command of the troops, however, gave his men no opportunity to ponder moral alternatives. "Load!" he commanded, and the men obeyed. Then the crowd broke and moved off. The Richmond bread riot was over.[38]

The government took no chances with its hungry citizens. The next day cannon guarded the riot scene. The War Department kept two battalions of infantry on the alert to quell any further domestic disturbance, and the military ordered newspapers and telegraph operators to reveal nothing about the "unfortunate disturbance." Accordingly on April 3 the lead editorial in the Richmond *Dispatch* concerned "Sufferings in the North,"[39] But in time, of course, news of the riot spread to the Confederate hinterland.

Significantly, the bread riot in Richmond was no isolated occurrence. During the spring a wave of riots broke out in Atlanta, Macon, Columbus, and Augusta, Georgia, and Salisbury and High Point, North Carolina. Later, on September 4, despite assurances from the Mobile *Register and Advertiser* that "there is enough food to

[36]Thomas, "Bread Riot," 44; Thomas, *Confederate Richmond,* pp. 119–120.

[37]Varina Howell Davis, *Jefferson Davis, Ex-President of the Confederate States of America: A Memoir by His Wife,* 2 vols. (New York, 1890), II, 373–376.

[38]*Ibid.*

[39]Richmond *Dispatch* April 3, 1863; John Withers to W. S. Morris, April 2, 1863, and John Withers to the Richmond Press, April 2, 1863, *O.R.,* ser. I, XVIII, 958; S. Bassett French to James A. Seddon, April 10, 1863, *O.R.,* ser. I, XVIII, 977–978; Judith W. McGuire, *Diary of a Southern Refugee during the War* (New York, 1867), p. 48.

carry army and people through to the next harvest," a Mobile mob bearing signs demanding "bread or blood" looted Dauphine Street.[40]

Distress and mob violence evoked both positive and negative responses. In Richmond the city council at first agreed with the *Whig*'s pronouncement that "violence before remonstrance is an unheard-of thing under the Southern sun. It will not be tolerated."[41] The city fathers passed a resolution blaming the April riot upon "outsiders" and "devilish and selfish motives" and offered rewards for testimony leading to the conviction of rioters. Later, however, when anarchy seemed abated, the Richmond City Council adopted a welfare program designed to identify the hungry and supply them with food at public expense. In Mobile, too, the local government took rapid steps to expand the city's "free market" and feed the hungry. Mobile citizens also founded a Confederate Association to identify speculators in foodstuffs and mete out vigilante justice to those "convicted."[42]

But efforts to alleviate want and forestall further bread riots enjoyed uneven success. In Petersburg, Virginia, a municipal supply agent traveled as far as northern Alabama in search of hogs, and thanks to his energy, conditions in Petersburg were tolerable. In Richmond, however, the sheer volume of supplies required often frustrated attempts at massive welfare. The city government eventually charged its board of supply to secure food "for the city"—not only the poor. But Richmond's supply agents were not always able to locate, purchase, and transport the quantity of food necessary.[43] Successful or not, though, the Confederate experience in local welfare programs was significant. Just as bread riots were indices of the failure of Confederate agriculture and of the tenuous nature of

[40]Mobile *Register and Advertiser*, March 25, 1863. Frank Moore, *The Rebellion Record: A Diary of American Events*, 11 vols. supp. (New York, 1861, 1868), VII, 48; VIII, 67. E. Merton Coulter, *The Confederate States of America, 1861–1865* (Baton Rouge, La., 1950), pp. 423–424.

[41]Richmond, *Whig*, April 4, 1863.

[42]Louis H. Manarin (ed.), *Richmond at War: The Minutes of the City Council, 1861–1865* (Chapel Hill, N.C., 1966), April 2 and 9, 1863; Mobile *Register and Advertiser*, September 5 and 23, 1863. See also Emory M. Thomas, "Welfare in Wartime Richmond, 1861–1865," *Virginia Cavalcade* (Summer 1972), 22–29; and William F. Zornow, "Aid for the Indigent Families of Soldiers in Virginia, 1861–1865," *Virginia Magazine of History and Biography*, LXVI (1958), 454–458.

[43]Thomas, *Confederate Richmond*, pp. 167–169, 145–147.

social solidarity in the South, so were free markets and Confederate associations indications of heightened social and economic conscience.

Paradoxically, while riot and makeshift relief schemes served notice that the nation of farmers was getting hungry, the Confederate industrial economy approached full stride. Sometime during 1863 the Confederacy achieved, by its own estimate at least, self-sufficiency in military-industrial production.

For a limited time, the government had been able to buy arms, ammunition, blankets, and such abroad. By the spring of 1863, however, it had become apparent that foreign purchases would not much longer sustain the Southern war effort. Confederate credit in Europe was overextended; Caleb Huse, the South's most active European purchasing agent, had contracted debts totaling £592,-000. And the increasingly efficient Union blockade interfered with the shipment of war supplies from Europe to the South while it impeded shipment of cotton, the Confederacy's most acceptable collateral, to European ports.[44]

In his report to the President in January 1863, War Sceretary Seddon took a sanguine view of the "increased stringency of the blockade by the enemy." The diminution of foreign supply would compel the Confederacy to rely upon its own resources and eventually to become free from dependence upon foreign purchases. Seddon's optimistic interpretation was perhaps the only one he could make in a public document.[45] In fact, however, the War Department had already generated considerable industrial activity, and encouraged by circumstances and Seddon, the supply bureaus took far longer strides during 1863.

The government, or, more specifically, the supply bureaus of the War and Navy Departments, provided impetus and direction for Confederate war industry. The War and Navy Offices made contracts with privately owned manufacturing firms such as the Tredegar Iron Works in Richmond; but Tredegar was unique, almost

---

[44]Goff, *Confederate Supply*, pp. 54–55; Frank E. Vandiver, *Ploughshares into Swords: Josiah Gorgas and Confederate Ordnance* (Austin, Tex., 1952), pp. 159, 179.

[45]Seddon to Davis, January 3, 1863; *O.R.*, ser. IV, II, 291–292. Davis underscord his war secretary's sentiments in his message to Congress: "Dependence on foreign supplies is to be deplored, and should, as far as practicable, be obviated by development and employment of internal resources." Davis to Congress, January 12, 1863, Rowland (ed.), *Jefferson Davis*, V, 413.

un-Southern, in that it was a prewar industrial plant which could readily convert to war production. The Confederate military, as soon as the illusion of a short war evaporated, had to begin generating other sources of domestic supply.[46] The effort was more or less evenly divided between encouraging private manufacturers and opening or expanding government shops.[47] Significantly, the government maintained control of the industrialization process in both the public and private economic sectors. There was too little time for a class of industrial entrepreneurs to ripen and flower "naturally." Hence the Southern war industry remained almost exclusively under government control, and because time and the South's laissez-faire heritage precluded the development of a broadly based socialized industrial economy, the Confederates centralized control and direction of war industry at the top, within the War and Navy offices.[48]

Given the magnitude of the enterprise, incredibly few men directed and managed Southern war industries. In the War Department, the bureaus of Ordnance, Quartermaster, and Nitre and Mining were responsible; the Navy Department had offices of Ordnance and Hydrography, Construction, and Provisions and Clothing. Beneath the decision-making level, however, the government employed large numbers of civilians, skilled and unskilled, white and black, slave and free, male and female. In Selma, Alabama, to cite only one example, more than 10,000 people were engaged in some form of war industry during 1863.[49]

Acts of Congress, administration policy, and "military necessity" allowed and encouraged government control of Southern war industry. In the beginning the War and Navy Departments assumed control of existing government shipyards, armories, and

[46]See Goff, *Confederate Supply*, pp. 54–55; Thomas, *Revolutionary Experience*, pp. 79–80.

[47]In a report to War Secretary Seddon in January 1863, Ordnance Bureau Chief Gorgas revealed that public and private armories would soon be producing equal numbers of small arms per month. Gorgas to Seddon, *O.R.*, ser. IV, II, 299. Except for Tredegar, public installations naturally led in production of heavier weapons and specialized items.

[48]See Raimondo Luraghi, "The Civil War and the Modernization of American Society," *Civil War History*, XVIII (1972), 230–550.

[49]John Hardy, *"Selma: Her Institutions and Her Men"* (Selma, Ala., 1879), pp. 46–48, in Malcolm C. McMillan, *The Alabama Confederate Reader* (University, Ala., 1963), pp. 288–291.

the like.[50] In general the army and in particular Josiah Gorgas of the Ordnance Bureau were most energetic at expanding the manufacturing facilities of the "old Union" and establishing new works to serve the new nation. Gorgas began early, building, refitting, and moving ordnance installations throughout the South.[51] By 1863 the other military bureaus and offices involved with the manufacture of war materials were following Gorgas' example. By this time Navy Secretary Stephen Mallory, despairing of purchasing a navy in Europe, created a construction office and began in earnest to build Southern ships in the South. The navy also assumed control of a massive gun foundry at Selma in the spring of 1863 and began to cast large guns designed by the officer in charge of naval ordnance, John M. Brooke.[52] By 1863 the Quartermaster Bureau of the War Department had set up a series of manufacturing establishments to produce uniforms, blankets, wagons, and the like. Some of the more successful of these combined the characteristics of urban and cottage industry. Quartermaster depots served as a kind of clearing house to which local women came to sell homespun thread and yard. Then other women took the thread and yarn and returned cloth. Still others took the cloth and patterns and returned clothing.[53] Significantly, during the first half of 1863 the operations of the quartermaster bureau in Mississippi, one of the South's least industrialized states in 1861, were sufficient to support a major Confederate field army at Vicksburg.[54] In April 1863 the Nitre and Mining Bureau separated from the Ordnance Bureau, and under the direction of Colonel Isaac M. St. John continued its program of extracting and refining military minerals: coal, iron, copper, nitre, and lead.[55]

In pursuit of self-sufficiency, each military agency established and operated various sorts of industrial establishments. Taken together, government-owned war industries made an enormous impact upon

[50]For case studies in state versus central government control of these installations and their products, see Vandiver, *Gorgas*, pp. 66–73.

[51]*Ibid.*, pp. 105–154.

[52]William N. Still, Jr., *Confederate Shipbuilding* (Athens, Ga., 1969), pp. 9–16; Vandiver, *Gorgas*, p. 170; Tom Henderson Wells, *The Confederate Navy: A Study in Organization* (University, Ala., 1971), pp. 53–54.

[53]Goff, *Confederate Supply*, pp. 65–76.

[54]Jackson Daily Southern Crisis, March 3, 1863, cited in John K. Bettersworth, *Mississippi in the Confederacy: As They Saw It* (Jackson, Miss., 1961), pp. 266–267.

[55]Vandiver, *Gorgas*, pp. 106–107.

the Southern economy. A portion of this impact was quantitative—
the generation of employment, production of manufactured articles, and infusion of Confederate money into the economy—but
there was a qualitative impact as well, the transformation, in terms
of war materials, of a preindustrial economy into an industrial economy.

In addition to stimulating government-owned industries, the war
also called forth activity among private manufacturers. Government
contracts, for example, allowed the Tredegar Iron Works to expand
its labor force from 700 in 1861 to 2,500 by January 1863.[56] Smaller
firms, too, such as Cook and Brother Armory of Athens, Georgia,
enjoyed increased prosperity because of government contracts.[57]
Characteristically, though, the Confederates maintained fairly stringent controls over private firms with whom the government did
business. Acts of Congress set limits (75 percent at first, later 33.3
percent) on profits gleaned from government business. Public
money subsidized creation or expansion of manufacturing establishments, but public law granted the government an option on
two-thirds of the production of industrial contractors.[58]

Confederate military supply agencies were in a position to exercise considerable control over the South's wartime economy, to the
benefit of both public and private war industries. "Military necessity" gave the government de facto power over Southern railroads,
and although priorities were often at issue and efficiency low, the
military was usually able to direct or deny transportation of raw
materials and finished products.[59] Draft laws allowed the War Department, through the Conscription Bureau, to exempt or detail

[56]Kathleen Bruce, *Virginia Iron Manufacture in the Slave Era* (New York, 1930), p.
386.

[57]Cook and Brother flourished briefly, then foundered and offered to sell out to
the government. Gorgas regretted extremely that his funds were insufficient to make
the purchase. The firm gained fame, then notoriety, for development of a double-
barreled cannon which was supposed to fire simultaneously two cannonballs linked
together with chain. The weapon looked promising—on paper. Unfortunately, when
test-fired, the cannonballs did not emerge from the twin barrels at the same time.
The result was a boomerang effect on the part of the chained balls which killed some
of the observers. Vandiver, *Gorgas*, p. 222; Charles J. Brockman, Jr., "The Confederate Armory of Cook and Brother," *Gun Digest* (1960), 74–79; and Charles J. Brockman, Jr., "A Rebel Secret Weapon," *The American Rifleman*, August 1956, 28.

[58]Coulter, *Confederate States*, p. 201.

[59]See Charles W. Ramsdell, "The Confederate Government and the Railroads,"
American Historical Review, XXII (1917), 794–810.

workers and thus channel labor into vital industries. The Impressment Act gave the military authority to seize raw and war materials and to dragoon slaves into service if necessary. Taken together these controls established the potential within the Confederacy of creating a planned industrial economy. The Confederates never realized this potential, but in terms of war industry at least, they approached it.[60]

The achievements of Southern war industrialists, both inside and outside the government, were indeed impressive. For example, during 1864 the state of Alabama produced four times more iron than any other state in the "Old Union." The gunpowder factory at Augusta, Georgia, was for its time the largest in North America. The Confederate Navy laid plans for 150 ships and before the end of the war had constructed about a third of them, including twenty-two ironclads.[61] And during 1863, Josiah Gorgas' Ordnance Bureau, the largest producer of war supplies, doubled its production of small arms from the previous year and achieved self-sufficiency. Gorgas marked the event in his diary on the third anniversary of his appointment as bureau chief:

I have succeeded beyond my utmost expectations. From being the worst supplied of the Bureaus of the War Department it [the Ordnance Bureau] is now the best. Large arsenals have been organized at Richmond, Fayetteville, Augusta, Charleston, Columbus, Macon, Atlanta, and Selma, and smaller ones at Danville, Lynchburg, and Montgomery, besides other establishments. A superb powder mill has been built at Augusta. . . . Lead smelting works were established by me at Petersburg and turned over to the Nitre and Mining Bureau. . . . A cannon foundry established at Macon for heavy guns, and bronze foundries at Macon, Columbus, Ga., and Augusta; a foundry for shot and shell at Salisbury, N.C.; a large shop for leather work at Clarksville, Va.; besides the Armories here [Richmond] and at Fayetteville, a manufactory of carbines has been built up here; a rifle factory at Asheville [transferred to Columbia, S.C.]; a new and very large armory at Macon, including a pistol factory, built up under contract here and sent to Atlanta, and thence transferred under purchase to Macon; a

[60]Luraghi, "Civil War and Modernization"; Charles W. Ramsdell, "The Control of Manufacturing by the Confederate Government," *Mississippi Valley Historical Review*, VIII (1921), 231–249; Vandiver, *Gorgas*, pp. 162–163; Lester J. Cappon, "Government and Private Industry in the Southern Confederacy," *Humanistic Studies in Honor of John Calvin Metcalf* (New York, 1941), pp. 151–189.
[61]Luraghi, "Civil War and Modernization," 244–246.

second pistol factory at Columbus, Ga. . . . Where three years ago we were not making a gun, pistol nor a sabre, no shot nor shell [except at the Tredegar Works]—a pound of powder—we now make all these in quantities to meet the demands of our large armies.[62]

The record of Southern success at war industry was indeed noteworthy, and Gorgas did not understate his accomplishments. However, there were conspicuous failures as well among Confederate efforts to produce war supplies. Some of these failures were owed to circumstances so fundamental as to be all but insurmountable. For example the South's production of pig iron never approached the capacity of Confederate ironworks to process it. The Tredegar Works was capable of handling about three times the amount of pig iron it was able to get during the war, and the Confederacy simply did not live long enough to develop its extractive industries to full potential.[63] Other failures in the South's new-found industrial effort were clearly avoidable and resulted primarily from human errors. For example neither of the quartermasters general, Abraham C. Myers and Alexander R. Lawton, who succeeded Myers in August 1863, was able to plan or organize the bureau sufficiently to achieve maximum production and distribution.[64] An example of the combination of circumstantial and human failures in Confederate war industry was the operation of the railroads. Although the military could and did preempt private use of the roads, the Confederacy never nationalized railroads. As a result no centralized planning or organization developed, and field commanders, supply agencies, and civilian shippers competed for use of Southern rolling stock.[65] Yet even had the government chosen to nationalize railroads, the Confederacy would have suffered from the basic inadequacy of the South's rail network, the attrition of wartime overuse, and the want of time and capacity to make necessary repairs.

The shortcomings in the Confederates' attempt to create instant war industry were obvious, and as the war wore on, military action

[62]Frank E. Vandiver (ed.), *The Civil War Diary of Josiah Gorgas* (University, Ala., 1947), pp. 90–91.

[63]Charles B. Dew, *Ironmaker to the Confederacy: Joseph R. Anderson and the Tredegar Iron Works* (New Haven, Conn., 1966), p. 175.

[64]Goff terms the performance of the Quartermaster Department "mixed." The department was able to produce and import but too often failed to transport and distribute. *Confederate Supply*, p. 247.

[65]Black, *Railroads of the Confederacy*, pp. 124–136.

accentuated weaknesses. When Southern armies retreated from battlefields, as they did with increased frequency during 1863 and 1864, they left behind many of the fruits of Confederate war industry. When Southern armies abandoned land area, they also exposed mines, depots, and factories to capture by the enemy and thus further limited the Confederacy's ability to conduct an industrial war. But on balance the degree of industrialization achieved by the Confederate South was phenomenal. The Confederates sustained themselves industrially better than they did agriculturally and far better than they had any reason to expect in 1861. Symbolically, in April 1865, when Lee's tired army marched and fought its way to Appomattox, the men exhausted their supply of food before they ran out of ammunition. In fact when Lee surrendered, the remnant Army of Northern Virginia had a sufficient average of seventy-five rounds of ammunition per man and adequate artillery shells.[66]

The Confederacy's military-industrial revolution was briefly successful and preeminently Southern. The relatively small group of men who managed the South's short-lived economic transformation were hardly entrepreneurs whose acquisitive instincts fit the Yankee stereotype. On the contrary, the South's war industrialists tended to be "traditional intellectuals"—schoolteachers, natural philosophers, and military scientists—as opposed to "organic intellectuals"—industrial managers, mechanical engineers, and the like.[67] And because the military maintained control of the industrialization process, the profit motive was less a factor. Joseph R. Anderson, for example, had been master of the Tredegar Iron Works since 1858, but before he had become an industrialist Anderson had been a West Point graduate, a civil engineer, and a state legislator. When the war broke out he volunteered for the artillery and rose to the rank of brigadier-general. A battle wound sustained during the Seven Days forced him to resign from the army and return to Tredegar. In 1865 he offered to give the works to the government in the hope that Tredegar might run more efficiently. Anderson's

[66]Lee to Davis, April 12, 1865, Clifford Dowdey and Louis H. Manarin (eds.), *The Wartime Papers of R. E. Lee* (New York, 1961), pp. 937–938.

[67]This distinction between types of intellectuals is fully developed in Antonio Gramsci, *Gli intellettuali e l'organizzazione della cultura* (Rome, 1971), pp. 13–32.

actions were hardly those of a model industrial capitalist. Apparently he identified with the planter-aristocratic tradition to the detriment of his entrepreneurial self-interest.[68]

Other examples deserve mention. Gorgas, for all his success at managing the Ordnance Bureau, failed at a postwar business venture in ironworks and devoted the last fourteen years of his life to higher education in the South.[69] George W. Rains, manager of ordnance operations in Augusta as a Confederate, also sought a postwar career in education. Rains taught chemistry at the Medical College of Georgia.[70] John M. Brooke, director of the naval gun works at Selma and inventor of the Brooke gun, and Matthew Fontaine Maury, who developed and produced torpedo mines and purchased naval equipment for the Confederacy, spent their postwar years at Virginia Military Institute.[71] Confederate Quartermaster General Lawton resumed law practice after the war and pursued Democratic politics.[72] These men, some of the most important and successful Confederate military industrialists, did not choose to put their wartime experiences to use during the "age of enterprise" after the war. Instead they chose more traditional Southern pursuits which had characteristically earned prestige and respectability in the ante-bellum South. It would seem from this that the war industry of the Confederate South not only sprang from a preindustrial economy but also received direction from preindustrial men.[73]

The transformation worked upon the Southern political economy was a pragmatic response to the demands of industrial war. It evidenced an unconscious recognition that the Confederacy's war effort had become total, encompassing just about every aspect of Southern national life—from the military command structure to the dearth of bread in cities and towns. In the last analysis, however, the

[68]The standard biography of Anderson and his enterprise is Dew, *Ironmaker*.

[69]Vandiver, *Gorgas*, pp. 272 ff.

[70]Mark Mayo Boatner III, *The Civil War Dictionary* (New York, 1959), pp. 676–677. See also George W. Rains, *History of the Confederate Powder Works* (Newburgh, N.Y., 1882).

[71]*Ibid.*, pp. 88, 520. See also George M. Brooke, Jr., "John Mercer Brooke," 2 vols., Ph. D. dissertation (University of North Carolina, 1955); Charles L. Lewis, *Matthew Fontaine Maury, the Pathfinder of the Seas* (Annapolis, Md., 1927); and Frances L. Williams, *Matthew Fontaine Maury: Scientist of the Sea* (Brunswick, N.M., 1963).

[72]Boatner, *Dictionary*, p. 473.

[73]Luraghi, "Civil War and Modernization," pp. 249–250.

Confederacy depended for its life upon victories on the battlefields, and as the campaigning season of 1863 began, prospects of those victories and the ultimate victory of independence appeared, to Confederates at least, bright indeed.

CHAPTER 10

The Confederate South at Full Tide

D URING the early months of 1863 the war gods seemed to smile upon the embryo Southern nation. On the first day of the new year a Confederate land force led by John B. Magruder combined with a fleet of small boats armored with cotton bales, called "cotton-clads" to recapture Galveston, Texas.[1] During February a small Southern fleet on the Mississippi managed to damage and capture the Union *Indianola,* and for a time the Confederates regained control of the river below Vicksburg.[2] In April a long-awaited Federal assault on Charleston proved abortive, thanks to the preparations of garrison commander P. G. T. Beauregard.[3] These actions, Southerners hoped, might portend coming successes in the major field campaigns of 1863.

President Davis and his generals anticipated activity on three main fronts in 1863. Ever since the previous December the enemy had threatened Vicksburg and John C. Pemberton's army. Generals U. S. Grant and William T. Sherman and Admiral David D. Porter had exhausted time, energy, and lives attempting to take this last

[1]See John B. Magruder account in Benjamin La Bree (ed.), *The Confederate Soldier in the Civil War, 1861–1865* (Louisville, Ky., 1897), pp. 408–411.

[2]James M. Merrill, *Battle Flags South: The Story of the Civil War Navies on Western Waters* (Rutherford, Vt., 1970), pp. 239–256; H. Allen Gosnell, *Guns on the Western Waters* (Baton Rouge, La., 1949), pp. 177–203; John D. Milligan, *Gunboats Down the Mississippi* (Annapolis, Md., 1965), pp. 121–130.

[3]T. Harry Williams, *P.G.T. Beauregard: Napoleon in Gray* (Baton Rouge, La., 1955), pp. 174–180.

major Southern strong point on the Mississippi from the north and west. Finally, in late March, Grant determined to move his army south of Vicksburg, cross the river, cut Pemberton's supply lines from Jackson, and advance on the city from the East. By mid-April Grant's intentions were clear to the Confederates, but Pemberton did not believe his army was strong enough to attack Grant and hold Vicksburg simultaneously.[4] At Chattanooga, meanwhile, Braxton Bragg's army confronted an enemy invasion force under William S. Rosecrans. Neither general seemed anxious to renew the combat which had concluded the previous campaigning season at Murfreesboro on the Stones River, and the war front in middle Tennessee was dormant until much later in the year.[5] On the eastern front Robert E. Lee awaited the spring campaigns from his lines at Fredericksburg. Across the Rappahannock, Union General Joseph Hooker prepared a grand stroke by which he hoped to destroy Lee's army and seize Richmond.

Although Grant's army was already in motion, the first threat in 1863 to Confederate military vitals came from Hooker. While Lee watched and waited, a large force of Federal cavalry broke through to the Confederate rear and began tearing up railroad tracks and disrupting communications between Richmond and the front. Then Hooker's army crossed the Rappahannock west of Fredericksburg and marched down the southern bank toward Lee's flank. At last Lee reacted. Leaving a small covering force commanded by Jubal A. Early at Fredericksburg, he marched with the bulk of his army to meet Hooker's columns.

The two armies collided at a crossroads called Chancellorsville on May 1. Hooker brought up reinforcements until he outnumbered Lee almost two to one, but the densely wooded terrain reduced the effect of numbers, and, more important, the Confederates discovered the Federal right flank unsecured. Stonewall Jackson and Lee plotted Hooker's annihilation on the evening of May 1, and at about six o'clock in the afternoon on May 2, after a long flank march, Jackson's entire corps fell upon the exposed Union right. Although

[4]On Vicksburg see especially Peter F. Walker, *Vicksburg: A People at War, 1860–1865* (Chapel Hill, N.C., 1960); Archer Jones, *Confederate Strategy from Shiloh to Vicksburg* (Baton Rouge, La., 1961), pp. 173–206; and Thomas L. Connelly, *Autumn of Glory: The Army of Tennessee, 1862–1865* (Baton Rouge, La., 1971), pp. 93–111.

[5]Connelly, *Autumn of Glory*, pp. 93–111.

critically outnumbered, Lee and Jackson had their enemies in a vise; Jackson knew he must maintain his momentum, and so he planned to continue his assault by moonlight. In the course of reorganizing his troop units and reconnoitering the enemy's defenses, however, he was wounded by his own men as he rode through the darkened woods. Next day J. E. B. Stuart assumed temporary command of Jackson's corps and managed to regain contact with Lee's portion of the Southern army. Hooker, acknowledging defeat, withdrew in good order back across the Rappahannock. Chancellorsville had been a brilliant battle for the Army of Northern Virginia. But a battle of annihilation it was not. And the battle cost the Confederacy the life of one of its boldest captains. Jackson died on May 10.[6]

In terms of military leadership the loss of Jackson was incalculable. Yet in death the grim Presbyterian offered the new nation a national martyr; the response was immediate and intense, not only within the South, but in Europe as well. In Richmond the news abruptly brought normal government and business activity to a halt at mid-morning on May 11. A crowd estimated as the largest ever assembled in the crowded city followed the fallen hero's coffin from the railroad station to the governor's mansion on Capitol Square. The next day a funeral procession escorted the coffin through the streets of the capitol and then returned to place the body in state at the capitol. Finally, on May 13, Jackson's body began the journey to Lexington for more ceremony at its interment. Alive, Jackson was an eccentric genius, part Southern Calvinist and part killer. Dead, this Cromwell reincarnate took first place in the pantheon of heroes in a nation of cavaliers.[7]

Victory at Chancellorsville allowed Lee some respite to reorganize the Army of Northern Virginia and come to terms with Jackson's loss. Hooker seemed content for the time being to lick his wounds north of the Rappahannock. Meanwhile, however, the threat to Vicksburg developed and demanded full attention in Richmond. On May 14, the day after Jackson's body left the Confederate capital, Grant's army occupied Jackson, Mississippi. The Federals' next

[6]The standard works on Chancellorsville are John Bigelow, *The Campaign of Chancellorsville: A Strategic and Tactical Study* (New Haven, Conn., 1910); and Edward J. Stackpole, *Chancellorsville: Lee's Greatest Battle* (Harrisburg, Pa., 1958).

[7]Frank E. Vandiver, *Mighty Stonewall* (New York, 1957), pp. 455–494; Emory M. Thomas, *The Confederate State of Richmond: A Biography of the Capital* (Austin, Tex., 1971), pp. 123–125.

move was obvious: if unmolested, Grant would move west from Jackson to Vicksburg along the railroad and lay siege to Pemberton's army in the river stronghold. The Confederate response was equally obvious—on paper at least. Joseph E. Johnston, in command of the western theater, must exert his authority, draw troops from his less-threatened commands, and attack Grant's army in concert with Pemberton. These things Jefferson Davis hoped Johnston would do. In his concern for Vicksburg, Davis tried to help; he ordered Johnston to assume personal command in Mississippi and dispatched a flurry of letters and telegrams containing advice and orders to Pemberton, Mississippi Governor J. J. Pettus, Bragg, and others. "Do not abandon Vicksburg for a single day," Davis counseled Pemberton. Johnston, who never grasped the nature and authority of his command, interpreted the President's well-meant assistance as meddling and violation of the chain of command. Pemberton felt trapped not only by Grant's army but between his commander and his commander-in-chief. Accordingly, Johnston and Pemberton failed to unite their forces and attack Grant at Jackson, and after an unsuccessful stand at Champion's Hill on May 16, Pemberton withdrew into Vicksburg. Johnston ordered Pemberton to save his army and abandon the city, but Pemberton would not or could not comply. With Vicksburg under siege and Pemberton's army inside, Johnston began collecting reinforcements with which to attempt to break Grant's hold.[8]

In Richmond the President and Secretary of War Seddon resisted grand stratagems suggested by James Longstreet and Beauregard. Independently the two generals proposed to relieve Vicksburg by concentrating all available troops in Tennessee, overwhelming Rosecrans, and marching, Beauregard to the Mississippi and Longstreet to the Ohio.[9] Although Johnston was none too sanguine about his prospects, Davis and Seddon believed he could defeat Grant—if only because the circumstance demanded it. On June 15, Johnston telegraphed, "I consider saving Vicksburg hopeless." Seddon responded on June 16, "Your telegram grieves and alarms us. Vicksburg must not be lost, at least without a struggle. The interest and honor of the Confederacy forbid it. I rely on you still to avert the loss. If better resource does not offer, you must hazard

[8]Walker, *Vicksburg*, pp. 157–166; Jones, *Confederate Strategy*, pp. 207–240.
[9]Jones, *Confederate Strategy*, 206–210.

attack. It may be made in concert with the garrison, if practicable, but otherwise without. By day or night, as you think best."[10] Beyond giving Johnston encouragement and carte blanche to fight and fail if nothing else, Davis, Seddon, and the rest of Confederate official-dom in Richmond could do little more than hope.

Meanwhile Lee and Davis had decided to take the offensive in the east. As he had done the previous fall, Lee drove his army west of his enemy, crossed the Potomac upstream, and sent widely dis-persed columns into Maryland. This time the Confederates con-tinued into Pennsylvania and posed a distinct threat to Washington and Baltimore. The invasion of Pennsylvania would not draw off troops from Vicksburg, but should Vicksburg fall, its loss would be small indeed compared to a major victory before Washington. Lee had no illusions about besieging the enemy capital immediately. He and Davis hoped to draw Hooker into another Chancellorsville; this time the ultimate prize would be Washington instead of Richmond, and this time perhaps the Southerners could achieve a battle of annihilation and at the same time a diplomatic coup.[11]

Once in Pennsylvania, Lee expanded his thinking about the cam-paign and urged that Davis collect all available troops from the Carolinas, place Beauregard in command, and order an assault on Washington from the south. The idea might have had a decisive effect upon what began as a limited offensive, but Davis believed it too complicated and too risky. Thus the President and the rest of the Confederacy contented themselves with waiting and hoping for favorable results from the campaigns already in motion.[12]

Men of the Army of Northern Virginia were not the only foreign visitors to Pennsylvania in 1863. A number of professional soldiers from Europe accompanied Lee's army during the campaign, to ob-serve for themselves the war Americans were fighting. Arthur James Lyon Fremantle of the Coldstream Guard, Captain Fitzgerald Ross of the Austrian Hussars, and Captain Justus Scheibert of the Prus-

[10]Varina Howell Davis, *Jefferson Davis: A Memoir by His Wife*, 2 vols. (New York, 1890), II, 422–423.

[11]See Douglas S. Freeman, *Lee's Lieutenants: A Study in Command*, 3 vols. (New York, 1942–1944), I, XV–XXVII; Archer Jones, "The Gettysburg Decision Reassessed," *Virginia Magazine of History and Biography*, LXXVI (1968), 64–66; and Edwin B. Cod-dington, *The Gettysburg Campaign: A Study in Command* (New York, 1968), pp. 3–25.

[12]Lee to Davis, June 22, 1863. Clifford Dowdey and Louis H. Manarin (eds.), *The Wartime Papers of R. E. Lee* (New York, 1961), pp. 527–528.

sian army all recorded impressions of their travels with the Southern army that June.[13] European civilians, too, had begun to visit the Confederacy in larger numbers to satisfy their curiosity about the Confederacy and the progress of the war.

One civilian visitor from France was Charles Girard, who afterward wrote a memoir of his travels. Girard was much impressed by what he saw; his narrative was more propaganda than anything else, but Girard caught one essential truth. "My guiding thought," he wrote, ". . . has been to give the reader a general sketch of the organization of this Government, and to show him that it is no longer a trial Government, which seated now at Richmond, but really a normal Government, the expression of popular will."

Emperor Napoleon III shared more of Girard's feelings about the Confederacy than the French traveler probably realized at the time, and during the late spring of 1863 he came as close as he ever would to translating his sympathies into actions. While Napoleon was fretting anew about his nation's need for cotton, intriguing to make the most of his Mexican conquest, and digesting reports of the Southern victory at Chancellorsville, in England John A. Roebuck announced his intention to place before Parliament a resolution supporting immediate Anglo-French recognition of the Confederacy. The Palmerston government let it be known that it opposed the project and justified its opposition on the ground that Napoleon had lost all enthusiasm for recognition. Such was not the case, though, and on June 18 the Emperor told Confederate diplomat John Slidell that he would "make a direct proposition to England for joint recognition." Even though the French cabinet cooled his ardor somewhat, the Emperor repeated his assurance of cooperation to Roebuck and his colleague John A. Lindsay in an unofficial conversation a few days later. Thus Roebuck confidently prepared to introduce his resolution on June 30, and Europe became an active front, along with Pennsylvania and Vicksburg, in the Confederate war.[14]

[13]Lee Walter Lord (ed.), *The Fremantle Diary* (New York, 1960); Fitzgerald Ross, *Cities and Camps of the Confederate States*, ed. by Richard Barksdale Harwell (Urbana, Ill., 1958); and Justus Scheibert, *Seven Months in the Rebel States during the North American War, 1863*, trans. by Joseph C. Hayes, ed. by William Stanley Hoole (Tuscaloosa, Ala., 1958).

[14]Charles A. Girard, *A Visit to the Confederate States of America in 1863: Memoir Addressed to His Majesty Napoleon III* (Tuscaloosa, Ala., 1962), p. 62; Lynn M. Case and Warren

During June of 1863 the tide of Confederate independence and nationhood probably reached its flood. Hindsight, of course, reveals that deluge followed quickly after. But at the time Southerners had a right to be optimistic, or at least hopeful, that their revolution would prevail, or at least endure. In the minds of its citizens the Confederacy was more a nation in June of 1863 than ever before or after. Thus it is appropriate to examine Southern nationality at this point and to explore the social and cultural experience of the Confederate South.

Two years of war had transformed Southern political and economic institutions and the Southern people. The Confederate experience influenced the ways in which Southerners thought and felt about themselves, related socially to each other, and expressed their relationship to God both personally and corporately. War and Confederate nationalism also conditioned Southerners' creative energies in music, art, literature, and learning. And significantly the transforming aspects of the Confederate experience did not affect only white Southerners. The black experience during wartime underwent subtle but profound metamorphosis, and slavery in the Confederate South was an unsettled institution. The end product of these Confederate alterations of ante-bellum norms was a distinctive national life behind the battle lines. Conditioned by war and revolution, that national life differed dramatically from what came before and after.[15]

In terms of their corporate self-concept, most Confederates still believed themselves to be heirs of the American Revolutionary tradition of 1776. When inaugurated on Washington's birthday in 1862, President Davis explained, "We hope to perpetuate the principles of our revolutionary fathers."[16] In 1863, Davis was still telling his fellow countrymen, "you assumed to yourselves the right, as your fathers had done before you, to declare yourselves independent."[17] In May of 1863 Congress finally settled upon a design for

F. Spencer, *The United States and France, Civil War Diplomacy* (Philadelphia, 1970), pp. 398–426; D. P. Crook, *The North, the South, and the Powers, 1861–1865* (New York, 1974), pp. 309–314, 332–339.

[15]See Emory M. Thomas, *The Confederacy as a Revolutionary Experience* (Englewood Cliffs, N.J. 1971), pp. 100–118.

[16]"Inaugural Address" in Dunbar Rowland (ed.), *Jefferson Davis, Constitutionalist: His Letters, Papers and Speeches*, 10 vols. (Jackson, Miss., 1923), V, 198.

[17]"Speech of Jefferson Davis in Richmond," *ibid.*, V, 391.

the Great Seal of the Confederate States. Appropriately the dominant feature of the design was an equestrian portrait of George Washington. Confederate postage stamps also bore likenesses of Washington and Thomas Jefferson along with those of Davis and John C. Calhoun. In the face of military reverses the Richmond *Examiner,* perhaps the most popular newspaper in the Confederacy, counseled its readers to recall their other revolutionary war:

The British ran over every high road of this country; penetrated every neighborhood, plundered every city and town to the Gulf—but lost the game. Their successors in tyranny will lose like them, unless the descendants of those who lived in the 'times that tried men's souls' have infamously degenerated.[18]

Public rhetoric and national symbols continually played upon the theme of the Confederacy as lineal descendant of the American revolutionary process. Some of this national self-image was propaganda and self-delusion designed to identify the new Southern nation with a sacred heritage and establish innocence by association. Yet, for the most part, Southerners genuinely believed that the two revolutions were comparable. Both sought separation and home rule; in each, the aim was liberation, not conquest.

Significantly, however, as the Confederacy acquired a history, Southerners began to depend less upon historical precedents and experience shared with their enemies and more upon a past which was exclusively Southern. The transition was subtle and essentially unconscious. After two years, the Confederacy had little history in terms of time, but the events of those two years were many and cataclysmic. The cause had come alive and survived; Confederate Southerners began thinking of their revolution as *sui generis* instead of a repetition of the experience of 1776.[19]

The pressure of time and the pace of events did not permit extended contemplation and sage debate by learned men about the nature of the Confederate experience. And, as might be expected, there was no universal agreement about the essence of the Confederate revolution.

George Fitzhugh, for example, believed the Confederacy to be a

[18]Richmond *Examiner,* July 28, 1863.
[19]William L. Barney, *Flawed Victory: A New Perspective on the Civil War* (New York, 1975), pp. 81–120.

counterrevolution, a correction of the liberal and democratic excesses of the American Revolution. In 1776, Fitzhugh argued, the American colonials "weaned" themselves from "Mother England," a simple and necessary biological process. "The Revolution of '76 was, in its action, an exceedingly natural and conservative affair," wrote Fitzhugh; "it was only the false and unnecessary theories invoked to justify it, that were radical, agrarian, and anarchical. . . . We now come to the Southern Revolution of 1861, which we maintain was reactionary and conservative—a rolling back of the excesses of the Reformation—of Reformation run mad—a solemn protest against the doctrines of natural liberty, human equality and the social contract, as taught by Locke and the American sages of 1776, and an equally solemn protest against the doctrines of Adam Smith, Franklin, Say, Tom Paine and the rest of the infidel political economists who maintain that the world is too much governed."[20]

Among those who perceived the Confederacy as a liberal expression and an extension of the original American Revolution, perhaps Jefferson Davis was most representative. Particularly in his speeches and messages of 1863, 1864, and 1865, Davis represented the Confederacy as an expression of national self-determination. Liberty and independence were his most often-used themes; his precedents were more often "the long and bloody war in which your country is engaged," "the history of our young Confederacy," or "a review of our history during the two years of our national existence" than any reference to the American Revolution.[21] In stressing liberty and independence as war aims in the Confederate revolution, Davis never clearly answered the questions "Liberty for whom?" and "Independence for what?" The fact that neither he nor any other Confederate, for that matter, could or did define very precisely the nature of the Confederate revolution was some index of the fluidity which characterized the experience. Most Confederate Southerners had neither the time nor the inclination to pursue philosophical speculations as did Fitzhugh. Most, like Davis, perceived their struggle as simply involving Southern self-determination. In this struggle

[20]George Fitzhugh, "The Revolutions of '76 and '61 Contrasted," *Southern Literary Messenger*, XXXVII (1863), 718, 722. See also Eugene D. Genovese, *The World the Slaveholders Made: Two Essays in Interpretation* (New York, 1969), p. 118 ff. for a dissection of Fitzhugh's thought.

[21]James D. Richardson (ed.), *A Compilation of the Messages and Papers of the Confederacy*, 2 vols. (Nashville, Tenn., 1906), I, 414, 332, 277.

they acted out, worked out in deeds, their new national character. Significantly, though, that national character grew to become more Confederate than Southern, and the process of forming and refining their nation and fighting their war for national survival created a Confederate identity. In 1861 the cause was status quo and its embodiment George Washington; by 1863 the cause had become self-determination and its hero Stonewall Jackson.

Perhaps it was no more than natural that Confederate Southerners during wartime altered their aspirations from the passive conservation of the ante-bellum status quo to the active assertion of independence. And perhaps it was also natural that during the course of the bloodiest war ever fought in the Western hemisphere, the Southern status quo underwent a metamorphosis. But that metamorphosis was important because in the process of striving for independence, the Confederates acquired a new corporate identity. No better indication of the alteration of Southerners' personal self-concept existed than the apotheosis of Stonewall Jackson.

In 1861 Southerners believed that they were heirs of the cavalier tradition. However much reality denied the cavalier myth, the fact that it was believed in made the chivalric model important.[22] Stonewall Jackson was the antithesis of much that Southerners believed about themselves. Among a people who aspired individually to the role of landed aristocrats, Jackson had been a poor boy and an eccentric college professor. Among a romantic people who prized their individualism and venerated the chivalric code, Jackson had been a grim Calvinist drillmaster who subscribed to the laws of Jehovah and Mars.[23] Yet in 1863, "Tom Fool," "Old Blue Light," "Old Jack," "Stonewall" Jackson was a war hero in the supposed struggle for cavalier values.

Some of the modifications of the Southern self-concept were obvious. The organization necessary to armies and the war government necessarily circumscribed Southerners' vaunted individualism. Confederate soldiers and bureaucrats were still individuals and still prized their assertion of self, to the exasperation of their officers

[22]See William R. Taylor, *Cavalier and Yankee: The Old South and American National Character* (New York, 1961), pp. 312–320, for a summary statement of this self-image.

[23]Vandiver (*Mighty Stonewall*, p. 494) makes a similar point. Quoting Jackson's dying words, "Let us cross over the river and rest in the shade of the trees," Vandiver asks, "Which river did he think of then—was it the Potomac or was it the Jordan?"

and government, but the discipline inherent in the organization of mass armies and the regimentation involved in governmental functions such as conscription, taxation, martial law, and impressment set some limits on the sphere within which Southerners could exercise their individuality.

Wartime dispelled some of the Southerners' provincialism as well. Farm boys who visited barber shops for the first time and Texans who fought in Virginia might not have qualified as cosmopolites, but surely the war experience broadened the horizons of many Southerners, and the reality of battle quickly disposed of naïve notions like "one Southerner can lick ten Yankees" and "Yankees are pasty-faced clerks."

Obviously the war experience confirmed Southerners' traditional hedonism. Away from the restraints of family and community, soldiers in Southern armies acted like soldiers, and because the war effort had the side effect of enlarging Southern cities, Confederate urbanites took advantage of urban anonymity and opportunities for self-indulgence. No less obviously the violent strain in Southern character fed upon the corporate violence of war.[24]

The most profound change in the Southern self-image though, involved the romantic role hitherto prescribed for Southern women. The belle had ever been more ideal than reality in Southern life, but like its male counterpart, the cavalier, popular acceptance had given substance to myth.[25] Even in 1863 and after, Confederate press and periodicals honored the ideal Southern belle on her pedestal, but Confederate reality denied both the validity and the value of woman as object and ornament.

In the beginning Southern women and girls served the cause in traditional ways. They were civilian recruiting officers for the army, shaming and inspiring men into military service by withholding or offering their affections. Once their men were off to war, Southern women vied with each other in knitting and sewing for the troops.[26] As the government matured and the war continued beyond the parade and picnic state, a few women played exceptional roles. In

[24]Thomas, *Confederacy as Revolutionary Experience*, pp. 113–114.

[25]See Anne Firor Scott, *The Southern Lady: From Pedestal to Politics, 1830–1930* (Chicago, 1970), for an extended analysis of this role.

[26]The best works on the general topic of women in the Confederacy are Mary Elizabeth Massey's *Bonnet Brigades: American Women and the Civil War* (New York, 1966); and Bell I. Wiley's *Confederate Women* (Westport, Conn., 1975).

the place-mongering of the new government, women were significant parlor and dinner party politicians. Women disguised as men
served as soldiers, and disguised as women served as spies for
Southern commanders. None of these activities were extraordinary,
although some of the women involved certainly were. Women had
sent men into battle before and knitted socks and gloves before, and
there were precedents for women being influential in politics and
spying in wartime, and precendents for women fighting in wars.
Confederate press and society did, however, pay attention and homage to some of these extraordinary women. Belle Boyd, for example, was in 1861 a plain-looking young woman of modest means and
social station; in recognition of her daring success as a spy, however,
she was "belle of the ball" in Richmond during 1862.[27] Clearly the
Confederate experience offered women traditional wartime roles
and afforded a few women opportunity to win fame and deference
by successfully usurping male roles. Such circumstances are interesting but not too unusual.

What was unusual and significant in Confederate womanhood
occurred so quietly and gradually as to escape much attention at the
time. Attended by little drama and less fanfare, Confederate women
climbed down from their romantic pedestals and began making or
extending inroads into activities traditionally dominated by males.
By default on the part of absent males and by initiative on the part
of the females involved, Confederate women became among other
things farmers, planters, nurses, and industrial workers; and in
many circumstances they became heads of households.[28]

The vast majority of Confederate soldiers came from among the
"plain-folk" farmer class of the South. When these men volunteered
or submitted to conscription, many of them left women at home to
tend their farms, and by necessity these women became farmers.
Most did not enjoy their additional responsibilities; managing crops
and livestock in addition to managing the household was not exactly
a liberating experience. For example, Georgian Mary Brooks wrote
her husband that she was "so tired for I never get any rest night or

[27]Mary Boykin Chesnut's *Diary from Dixie*, ed. by Ben Ames Williams (Boston,
1949), well chronicles the machinations of female politicians. Testimony to the fact
of female soldiers is in the *Southern Literary Messenger* XXXVII (1863), 575. Belle Boyd
wrote her own story in *Belle Boyd: In Camp and Prison* (London, 1865).

[28]See Thomas, *Confederacy as Revolutionary Experience*, pp. 105–107; and Scott, *Southern Lady*, pp. 81–102.

day, and I don't think I will last much longer, but I will try to write to you as long as you stay there, if I can raise a pen."[29] Tired or not, however, Mary Brooks and women in similar circumstances expanded their experience and maintained their families on the home front.

On larger farms and plantations, women left at home while male members of the family were away at war were spared some of the physical labor of their less well-to-do neighbors. Yet many planters' wives had to assume the responsibility for managing their plantations and the slaves. Some had the assistance of overseers or male members of the family too old or too young for military service. Nevertheless plantation women, as well as farm women, often bore the ultimate responsibility for their households. And they bore this responsibility under wartime conditions in which scarcities and the threat of military occupation or raiding added to the normal burdens of management.[30]

More burdened still were those women who undertook the life of refugees. For example, when her home fell behind enemy lines, Mrs. Roger A. Pryor lived in a hovel near Petersburg, Virginia, while her husband was in the army.[31] Mrs. Judith McGuire, whose husband was a doctor, studied to pass an arithmetic examination in order to work as a clerk in the commissary general's office in Richmond. Before she found regular employment, Mrs. McGuire and other transient women made soap to sell at a dollar per pound.[32] In these and hundreds of instances, women had to bear more responsibility and expand their skills to cope with the hardships which the war imposed upon them and their families.

Wartime also afforded Confederate women opportunities for employment in tasks which heretofore had been open only to males. The Treasury Department, for example, hired women as clerks, and when the department transferred part of its activities from Rich-

[29]Mary F. Brooks to husband, September 3, 1862, cited in Katherine M. Jones, *Heroines of Dixie* (New York, 1955), p. 172.

[30]One of the best examples of these circumstances is described in the diary of Sally Lyons Taliaferro (Mrs. William B.) of "Dunham Massie" near Gloucester, Virginia. Original diary, Swem Library, College of William and Mary; typescript, Virginia State Library, Richmond.

[31]Mrs. Roger A. Pryor, *Reminiscences of Peace and War* (New York, 1904), pp. 251–252.

[32]Judith W. McGuire, *Diary of a Southern Refugee during the War* (New York, 1867), pp. 244–251.

mond to Columbia, South Carolina, the women migrated too.[33] Confederate war industries employed women as factory workers whenever possible in order to release men for military service,[34] and women served the cause by nursing the wounded.

In traditional roles as wives and mothers, Southern women had always cared for sick and wounded men. Confederate women made the transition to caring for strangers and contributed with their sisters from the North to making nursing a profession. At first Southern physicians were extremely reluctant to expose women to the indelicacies of suffering and dying. The experience of several mass bloodlettings, however, demonstrated the need for female assistance, and by 1862 military regulations called for hospital matrons to take charge of each ward in government hospitals. In addition women administered and operated many of the private and state hospitals as well as taking wounded soldiers into their homes under emergency circumstances.[35]

The Southern women who plowed the fields and bore the responsibilities for absent men did not much enjoy their wartime roles, and probably few refugees, government employees, or nurses perceived their daily activities to be especially liberating; yet in terms of roles and models, Confederate women took a giant step away from the romantic ideal of the Southern belle. If the ante-bellum ideal of woman was only a mild corruption of the ideal of courtly love— woman as virtuous ornament and unapproachable object—the Confederate ideal was considerably more earthy. Perhaps the model Confederate female was a red-eyed nurse with unkempt hair or a war widow who succeeded as head of her household by force of will. The ante-bellum ideal of woman was one to which many aspired but

---

[33]The transfer of the "treasury ladies" effected in 1864 at the suggestion of Braxton Bragg caused a stir among some Confederates. The Richmond *Examiner* chided Bragg and Memminger, pointing out that the women were neither ducks who migrated nor soldiers. "Steady, then, Mr. Memminger. A little more brains, Captain Bragg." Richmond *Examiner*, April 25, 1864.

[34]Some of these women became casualties of the war through industrial accidents, the most notable of which occurred in March of 1863 at the ordnance laboratory on Brown's Island near Richmond. Sixty-nine workers, most of them women, were injured in an explosion accidentally set off by young Mary Ryan when she rapped an explosive device on her work bench. (Richmond *Whig*, March 14, 16, 1863).

[35]See especially Bell I. Wiley (ed.), *A Southern Woman's Story: Life in Confederate Richmond by Phoebe Yates Pember* . . . (Jackson, Tenn., 1959) and Richard B. Harwell (ed.), *Kate: The Journal of a Confederate Nurse* (Baton Rouge, La., 1960).

few approached; significant numbers of women did attain the Confederate ideal. At least, most women in the South responded in previously un-Southern ways to the challenges of war on the home front.[36]

Elsewhere on the home front the Confederate period did not seem to have inspired much in the way of culture and creativity. The great romantic flood of "lost-cause" literature had to wait for the cause to be lost; the war period itself seems to have been too brief, frenzied, and violent for much depth or innovation in Southern cultural life.

This is not to suggest that Confederate Southerners became wartime drones; they did not. Those who read books continued to do so during the war, and theaters and concert halls did a brisk business among the soliders and those who felt obliged to entertain their defenders. In the main, however, public taste was banal, and Confederates sought release and reinforcement rather than challenge from the arts. Theater companies performed Shakespeare, but minstrel shows were more popular. Patriotic airs such as "Beauregard's March" and romantic ballads such as "Lorena" were imensely popular at the time but have survived only because of their association with a people at war. *Les Misérables* was probably the Confederate best seller, but native Southern literati were conspicuously unproductive during the war years. Confederate poetry and painting, too, were excessively romantic and include no masterpieces. And, as might be expected, schools and colleges during the war either closed or counted only a few young boys among the student bodies.[37]

Thus the traditional judgment of Confederate culture as sterile is valid—as far as it goes. There was, however, creative expression and intellectual vitality in the Confederate South, more so in fact than in the periods which came before and after.[38] Those historians and

[36]Scott, *Southern Lady*, p. 102.

[37]The best summary of Confederate cultural history is Clement Eaton, *The Waning of the Old South Civilization, 1860–1880* (Athens, Ga., 1968), pp. 79–109. See also Richard Barksdale Harwell, *The Brief Candle: The Confederate Theatre* (Worcester, Mass., 1971).

[38]About the war period on both sides of Mason and Dixon's line, Edmund Wilson wrote, "The period of the American Civil War was not one in which belles lettres flourished, but it did produce a remarkable literature which mostly consists of speeches and pamphlets, private letters and diaries, personal memoirs and journalistic reports." (*Patriotic Gore: Studies in the Literature of the American Civil War* [New York,

others who have searched in vain for "culture" in the Confederacy have looked for it in the wrong places. For example the most-read novel produced in the Confederacy, Augusta Jane Evans's *Macaria or Altars of Sacrifice,* is not a fair sample of Southern writing in the sixties. The best, and indeed the most characteristic, Confederate literature was the product of periodicals and newspapers, and of the individuals who penned the letters and diaries of the era. Certainly both professional and unprofessional Southern writers produced a great deal of prose distinguished only by the authors' ability to say so little in so many tight clauses and genteel phrases, and the literature of the period contained much doggerel verse devoid of form or content or both, but the best of Confederate writing deserves rereading. War correspondents such as John Esten Cooke, for instance, sent the weekly periodical *Southern Illustrated News* vigorous, on-the-spot battlefield material which was as good as his earlier and later novels were bad.[39] Editors of the South's daily newspapers engaged in lively and literate debate on topics ranging from war strategy to turtle soup. The strength and passion of editorials by Henry Watterson of the Chattanooga *Rebel* and John M. Daniel of the Richmond *Examiner,* to cite only two of numerous examples, rendered them a worthy literature.[40]

The richest of Confederate literature was never written for publication. The letters of otherwise obscure people such as the Joneses of Georgia and the Smiths of South Carolina read like epistolary novels; and the diaries of such diverse personalities as Benny Fleet, Mary Chesnut, and Phoebe Pember rank among the best of American literature in any period.[41]

The most engaging feature of the lesser *belles-lettres* is the unromantic and articulate honesty which they display. The war experi-

1966], ix. See also Daniel Aaron, *The Unwritten War: American Writers and the Civil War* (New York, 1973). An introduction, even better than Wilson's, to this genre of Confederate literature is Douglas S. Freeman's *South to Posterity: An Introduction to the Writings of Confederate History* (New York, 1939).

[39]See Richard Barksdale Harwell, "John Esten Cooke, Civil War Correspondent," *Journal of Southern History,* XIX (1953), 501–516.

[40]Watterson wrote for the Chattanooga *Rebel,* and Daniel edited the Richmond *Examiner.*

[41]See Robert M. Meyers (ed.), *The Children of Pride: A True Story of Georgia and the Civil War* (New Haven, Conn., 1972); and Daniel E. Huger Smith, Alice R. Huger Smith, and Arney R. Childs (eds.), *The Mason Smith Family Letters, 1860–1868* (Columbia, S.C., 1950) especially pp. 96–139.

ence was real and immediate to a large percentage of Confederate Southerners. It is little wonder that their response to wartime should have been realistic instead of romantic or artificial.[42]

Other flashes of creative energy and intellectual vigor distinguished the Confederate mind, but, as was the case with wartime literature, Confederates exhibited their talents in unorthodox ways and obscure places. Southern contributions to science and technology, for example, were not displayed in academic papers or debated in centers of learning. Instead the Confederacy's "traditional" intellectuals put their talents to practical work and most often displayed them in war-related activity. Matthew Fontaine Maury's torpedo mines and John M. Brooke's ironclad ship were good examples. The maps of peacetime schoolmaster Jedediah Hotchkiss were masterpieces of cartographic art.[43] The Confederates also produced an operational submarine. The *Hunley*, after delivering a mortal blow to the *Housatonic* off Charleston in December 1863, had the bad fortune to have its enemy sink on top of it. The disaster convinced

[42]See Chesnut, *Diary;* Wiley (ed.), *Southern Women's Story;* and Betsy Fleet and John D. P. Fuller (eds.), *Green Mount, A Virginia Plantation Family during the Civil War: Being the Journal of Benjamin Robert Fleet and Letters of His Family* (Lexington, Ky., 1962). Perhaps the best single example of both the vitality and urbanity of the South's "literature of immediacy" came in response to an item in the Selma, Alabama, *Sentinel.* Jn. Haralson, an agent for the Nitre and Mining Bureau, placed an official request in the *Sentinel* asking the ladies of Selma to save the contents of their chamber pots. Haralson proposed to collect the chamber lye and use it to manufacture nitre. One of Haralson's friends, Thomas B. Wetmore, composed a poetic response to the indelicate request. The ribald rhyme concluded:

> Indeed, the thing's so very odd,
> Gunpowderlike and cranky,
> That when a lady lifts her skirt
> She shoots a horrid Yankee!

Haralson responded, in part:

> Women, yes they stoop to conquer
> And keep their virtue pure:
> It is no harm to kill a beast
> With chamber lye, I'm sure.

Haralson's and Wetmore's exchange was, of course, not great or lasting literature. It was, though, testament to the literate vibrancy of the Confederate mind; and the poems, edited by Ralph Draughon, appeared as a "Ribald Classic" in a recent issue of *Playboy* magazine (October 1973).

[43]See Archie P. McDonald, "Jedediah Hotchkiss: Confederate Map Maker," *Military Engineer*, L (1968) 121–123; and Archie P. McDonald (ed.), *Make Me a Map of the Valley: The Civil War Journal of Stonewall Jackson's Topographer* (Dallas, 1973).

the Navy Department that submarines were too risky, and the *Housa-tonic* sinking was the only triumph of the South's undersea endeav-ors.[44]

With these examples, the small triumphs of rebel ingenuity also deserve mention. Faced with a shortage of grease for the working parts of ordnance machinery, one enterprising Confederate kept his shop in production by using lard. Instead of using rubber for drive belts, Confederates were able to fabricate an acceptable substitute from bands of cotton cords.[45]

At the same time that Southerners were adjusting the ways in which they thought about themselves, both corporately and individ-ually, they also began to rethink their relationships with others. Wars, especially unsuccessful wars, have often unsettled social mores, and the Confederate war was no exception. In 1861 the planter, slaveholding class exercised aristocratic dominance of the Southern body social. That same class in its best interest led the South into the Confederacy and claimed the first places in the new nation. In 1865, when the Confederacy was a failure, Southerners for the most part resisted the temptation to repudiate the leadership of their old ruling class. The strength and staying power of the slaveholders was remarkable indeed, but the dominance of the planter class in 1861 and 1865 has obscured the considerable social ferment which characterized the intervening years.[46]

In ways both obvious and subtle the planters were unable to maintain their hegemony in the Confederate South without a fight.

[44]On the *Hunley* and other Confederate submarines see Milton F. Perry, *Infernal Machines: The Story of Confederate Submarine and Mine Warfare.* (Baton Rouge, La., 1966).

[45]See Frank E. Vandiver, "Makeshifts of Confederate Ordnance," *Journal of South-ern History* XVII (1951), 180–193.

[46]This does not discount the role of the redeemers in the New South, who, as C. Vann Woodward points out, were not necessarily part of the old aristocracy (*Origins of the New South, 1877–1913* (Baton Rouge, La., 1961), pp. 1–22). However, as William B. Hesseltine observes, "the men who led the Confederacy were still the leaders of the Southern people" after Appomattox. And "of 656 prominent Confed-erates who lived long enough to make postwar readjustments, only 71 failed to recover a substantial portion of the position and prestige they had enjoyed at the Confederacy's peak. The forgotten 71 left no records which inquisitive historians of a later day could evaluate." William B. Hesseltine, *Confederate Leaders in the New South* (Baton Rouge, La., 1950), p. 16. Jon L. Wakelyn's conclusions in *Biographical Dictio-nary of the Confederacy* (Westport, Conn., 1976) differ from Hesseltine's somewhat ("the great man of the Confederacy did not lead the New South.") Yet the continuity of aristocratic class interests seems secure.

War compelled the planters to reconfirm their pretensions to leadership under novel circumstances. Land, slaves, and *noblesse oblige* became secondary prerequisites for power and deference. The cause demanded that its advocates become soldiers, and the slaveholders vied with each other for field commands in order to defend their plantations. For the most part planters dominated the Confederate officer corps just as they had dominated in peacetime.[47]

The fortunes of war dictated that a large percentage of Southern officers did not survive. Death from battle or disease was the most absolute way in which slaveholders surrendered status. Too, many planters discovered that their command of a local militia regiment during peacetime was inadequate preparation for command in combat. By 1863 the war had winnowed out numbers of planter-officers who had been capable of supervising a militia muster of the county seat but had proven less competent on one or more battlefields.[48] Finally, the acts of Congress authorizing elections of captains and lieutenants for company-size units had a democratizing effect upon the junior level of the officer corps.[49]

At the same time death and military incompetence took their toll of aristocratic Confederates, the wartime aristocracy of military merit opened the way for "new people" By 1863 Confederate officers were not all gentlemen, and neither were all gentlemen among the Southern officers. And the unsettling ways of wartime admitted new people to the government as well. Many of these new people in army and government had wealth, but their money was new, and the war offered them social advancement and prominence beyond the status prescribed by time and family connections.[50]

The Confederate circumstance challenged the South's ante-bellum elite and shuffled its membership considerably. Nevertheless planters and planter interests, variously defined, retained control of the revolutionary South. They did so not only in the face of the external challenge offered by a war and new government but also in the face of a heightened sense of class consciousness among yeoman and laboring classes of Confederate Southerners. Food

[47]See Thomas, *Confederacy as Revolutionary Experience*, pp. 107–113.
[48]Freeman, *Lee's Lieutenants*, II, XIV–XV.
[49]Congress authorized officer elections in the winter of 1861–1862 to stimulate reenlistment and to compensate for arbitrary extension of service.
[50]Hesseltine, *Confederate Leaders in the New South*, pp.4–5.

riots and draft evasion were two indications of this social ferment. The riots may have been economic in origin, but they fed on the resentment of have-nots for the relative comfort and insulation presumably enjoyed by the haves. Nor were draft evaders simply cowards; many were farm boys who wanted no part of risking their lives for the sake of planter interests. Their slogan was the familiar description of the conflict as a rich man's war and a poor man's fight.

Efforts on the part of the yeoman class to avoid taxes and impressment were further evidence of heightened class awareness or, more precisely, identification of the planters with a government grown too meddlesome. Overt Unionism in the Confederacy, too, tended to be strongest in those subregions, mountains, and swamps inhabited almost exclusively by nonplanters. Class interest was one of the motivations behind some Southerners' decisions to enlist in the Union army or aid Federal troops when they entered the South as invaders.[51]

The degree and nature of disaffection in the wartime South and the precision with which dissenters identified the cause with planter interests inimical to their own are open to question. The masses who risked their lives in Confederate armies were of the same class as those who engaged in anti-Confederate activity. The Confederate quest for home rule never became a contest over who should rule at home. Yet the fact of disaffection and its identification with the yeoman–poor white class are empirical evidence of a quickened sense of class consciousness in the Confederate South.

Class resentment inspired disloyal activity to an unknown degree in the Confederate countryside; in the urban Confederacy, however, indications of class awareness were more direct and more easily defined. Skilled laborers were rarer in the South than in the North, and many of them realized their value in the marketplace. Working people in Southern cities at one time or another engaged in strikes, attempted collective bargaining, applied class-inspired political pressure, and on occasion, as mentioned, resorted to food riots. These actions were neither numerous nor widespread, and they

[51]The literature of disaffection and disloyalty is large. For example see Georgia L. Tatum, *Disloyalty in the Confederacy* (Chapel Hill, N.C., 1934); Harold M. Hyman, "Deceit in Dixie," *Civil War History*, III (1957), 65–82; Stephen E. Ambrose, "Yeoman Discontent in the Confederacy," *Civil War History*, VIII (1962), 259–268; Ella Lonn, *Desertion during the Civil War* (Washington, D.C., 1928); and Albert B. Moore, *Conscription and Conflict in the Confederacy* (New York, 1824).

were never completely successful. That they occurred at all in any numbers was significant.[52]

Perhaps the instance which best revealed the depth and sophistication of a nascent labor movement in the Confederacy occurred in Richmond in the fall of 1863. The Virginia General Assembly was debating a bill to fix maximum prices for items of food. State Senator for the Richmond area George W. Randolph declared that he intended to vote against the measure unless instructed otherwise by his constituents. Accordingly a mass meeting of working men convened to express their approval of statewide price controls. In the course of the meeting, on October 10, the "very large crowd" adopted a series of resolutions, one of which proclaimed:

As free men we do abhor and detest the idea that the rich must take care of the poor, because we know that without labor and production the man with his money could not exist, from the fact that he consumes all and produces nothing: and that such a dependence would tend to degrade rather than elevate the human race.[53]

This classic statement of the labor theory of value did not impress a majority of Richmond's burgers, however. In a poll taken several days later, voters rejected the price control scheme by better than a three-to-one majority.[54] The General Assembly, too, defeated the bill. The Confederacy never became a haven for the proletariat, nor was it seething with unrest among the working class. In the cities, as in the army and in the countryside, the planter class overcame challenges to its hegemony. Still there was ferment, more than there had been before or would be again for some years to come.

The most obvious reason why most white working-class Confederates were unable to take better advantage of the South's need for labor was the pressure of black Confederates. The classic example of the effect of black labor upon white occurred in a Richmond cemetery in August 1864. One morning a crew of white gravediggers went on strike against the city in hopes of getting higher wages. Almost immediately the municipal authorities hired a crew of blacks to dig the graves. When the white gravediggers learned of their replacement, they returned to the cemetery, drove the blacks away,

[52]See Thomas, *Confederacy as Revolutionary Experience*, pp. 100–102.
[53]Richmond, *Sentinel*, October 12, 1863.
[54]*Ibid.*, October 23, 1863.

and resumed digging graves. The black men had broken the strike and then absorbed the anger of the white workers, all within a single day.[55]

Black Southerners served the cause in more important ways than as scabs and whipping boys. Only because slaves remained in the fields could such a large percentage of white men fight in Southern armies. More directly, the Confederacy employed or impressed black laborers to construct fortifications, drive supply wagons, and cook for the troops. In hospitals both bonded and free blacks worked as nurses and orderlies. Just as in peacetime, wherever there was work, black Southerners were involved, and Confederate blacks were draft exempt. Accordingly Confederate, state, and local governments, as well as private enterprises, hired or impressed black workers in large numbers.[56]

Black labor was vital to the Confederacy and the black impact upon Southern life was, if anything, greater in wartime than in peacetime. Yet the converse was true as well. The Confederate experience had a profound effect upon black life in the South—so much so that by mid-1863 the Southern black experience had undergone subtle but profound metamorphoses.[57]

At the base of the slave system during the ante-bellum period was an interdependent human relationship. In relatively stable times before 1861, the institutional norm, if such a thing existed, prescribed a dependence of slaveholder upon slave for labor and deference, and a dependence of slave upon slaveholder for paternal mastery and maintenance. Within this essentially seignioral institution, the crucial equation was human.

During its early months, the Confederacy witnessed little change in the master-slave relationship. Instead, white Southerners responded to fears, at times approaching paranoia, for slavery's institutional sanctity. The hysteria which followed John Brown's raid in 1859 did not suddenly disappear, and many slaveholders perceived

[55]Richmond *Examiner*, August 5, 1864.

[56]See James H. Brewer, *The Confederate Negro: Virginia's Craftsmen and Military Laborers, 1861–1865* (Durham, N.C., 1969).

[57]The best summary of the dimensions of this development is Clarence L. Mohr, "Southern Blacks in the Civil War: A Century of Historiography," *Journal of Negro History LIX* (1974), 177–195. Mohr's yet unpublished Ph. D. dissertation (University of Georgia), "Georgia Blacks During Secession and Civil War, 1859–1865," is a masterful contribution to that historiography.

of Union armies and the threat of invasion as abolitionism reaching its violent extreme. The external threat to slavery triggered concern for its internal security. Accordingly many Confederate communities took elaborate precautions against insurrections. Slave patrols were active, and rumors of plots among slaves led in many places to mass arrests and trials by ordeal for the unfortunate accused. When white men of a community marched off to war, those whites who remained doubled their vigilance and found meaning in "shifty looks" and "downcast eyes" among blacks, but when the direst predictions of racial blood bath failed to materialize, white fears and repressive measures abated somewhat.[58]

For black Southerners did not mount any mass slave revolts during the Confederate period. An estimated 180,000 black men joined Union armies and fought the slaveholders, but Southern blacks en masse never fought the Confederacy from within. The common explanation for this has been the legendary advice given by an older slave to a younger one. The old man drew an analogy between the war and two dogs fighting over a bone. The dogs were Northern and Southern armies and the bone black people. In both cases the bone had no part in the fight. There was truth in the analogy, and for the most part Southern slaves adopted the advice and pursued a policy of wait and see. Yet, the myth of the "loyal darky" concocted by Southern whites after the war was indeed myth.[59] The black experience in the wartime South was more subtle and complex than the simplistic alternatives of mass revolt, passive "bone," or "Uncle Tom" loyalty.

The Confederate circumstance imposed strains upon the very core of Southern slavery: the master-slave relationship. In a number of ways the war experience demanded that individual slaveholders act less like masters, and in turn individual slaves acted less like slaves.

When slaveholders joined Southern armies, they left "their people" in the care and under the direction of another while they were away at war. Sometimes an elderly relative, a wife, an overseer, a neighbor, or a teen-aged son were able to fulfill the master's role. Often, however, these substitute masters failed because they did or could not furnish the paternal mastery and maintenance of the

[58] Bell I. Wiley, *Southern Negroes, 1861–1865* (New Haven, Conn. 1965), pp. 32–43.
[59] *Ibid.*, pp. 63–84.

absent master. And because whites failed as masters, blacks "failed" as slaves.[60] The experience on the Pryor farm in Georgia was exemplary. Shepard G. Pryor owned thirteen slaves in 1861 when he left his farm to fight on the Virginia front. Pryor's wife, Penelope, remained on the farm with Uncle Dick Bass, an overseer of sorts. Uncle Dick was an old man who possessed the legendary Southern "habit at command" not at all. The Pryor slaves ignored him, and Uncle Dick did little more than drink and swear. Penelope Pryor summed up her plight in October 1861: "[T]hey dont hear him at all. I believe they would do better without him, but I cant stay here without some [white] man on the place."[61] Shepard asked Penelope to, "speak to the Negroes and try to make them feel the responsibility to take care and make something."

Early in 1862, Uncle Dick and his successor overseer left the Pryor farm. Penelope was alone with her chattels. At this juncture Shepard Pryor made a crucial decision; he appointed a black overseer. "Say to Will," Pryor wrote his wife, "that he is my last overseer and he must try himself farming and take care of everything[.] You must not make him work as the rest do[.] he must look around and see that every thing goes on right[.]"[62] Pryor hoped to transmit his paternalism via the mails to his wife and through her to a black manager. The process did not work.

Shepard Pryor's chosen surrogate, Will, for a time was faithful to his charge. Then, having harvested the 1862 crop, Will began working against the slave-plantation regime by helping runaway slaves and hiding black fugitives. When Penelope Pryor informed her husband of his trustee's crimes, Shepard Pryor faced his own problem mindful of Will's dilemma. "I am truely sorry," he wrote, "that it happened with Will for I think a great deal of him. It is true that he did very wrong in denying the charges after he was caught[,] but Dear I never could blame a negro much for assisting one that was run away."[63] Thus did the Pryor family confront the quiet crisis within the slave system. When Shepard Pryor ceased to be master, Will ceased to be slave.

[60]Thomas, *Confederacy as Revolutionary Experience*, pp. 121–127.

[61]Penelope Pryor to Shepard Pryor, October 8, 1861, and October 14, 1861, Shepard Green Pryor Collection, University of Georgia, Athens.

[62]Shepard Pryor to Penelope Pryor, April 24, 1862, *ibid.*

[63]Shepard Pryor to Penelope Pryor, February 26, 1863, *ibid.*

Louticia Jackson's experience on her small holding in the Georgia Piedmont was similar to that of Penelope Pryor. Mrs. Jackson and her teen-aged son Johnny attempted to carry on when an older son left to join the army; but they had less and less success with their black work force. By 1863 she was reporting to her absent son:

They seem to feel very imdepenat [i.e. independent] as no white man comes to direct or look after them, for Willes speaks shorter to johny and orders *him* about more than any negro on the place. in consequence . . . [Johnny] seldon tells him to do anything, so sure as he does . . . Willes will make some insulting reply such as thus[:] 'what's the matter with you[,] what the reason you can't do it,' and so on, and when I ask him why he has not done certain things he will say John never told him, and says that John will tell a story in a minute. I told him he did not have to tell me so again, but he sayed he did not care what I sayed about it. a few evenings ago I asked him where he had been all the evening; he did make any reply. John then sayed 'mas talking to you.' he sayed he knew that and she's allways asking some silly question[.] he then commenced in such a loud harangue you might have heard him half a mile or more. It so excited me I left the door[,] went in the room[,] and lay down with the back ache. he does not suffer me to enquire in to anything without giving some insulting reply, though I tell them all together generally what must be done so as to avoid any difficulty with him.

He done as well as he knew how the first 6 months after you left[.] I was truly proud to see him seem to take such an intrust in the farm[.] but he got his own crop laid by[,] he then helped some in threshing the wheat, he took the fever immediately after[,] which lasted some 5 or 6 weeks in which time I attended him closely day and night[,] bathed and rubed him with my own hands fearing it would not be faithfully done [otherwise][.] in 6 months he grew w[e]ary in well doing, [and] has been a drag ever since, and we . . . can see his evil influence in most all the others that are large enough to notice him. . . . Some person must have been lecturing him I think, for he runs about a goodeal & but seldom asks for a pass and when he does he will walk up to the door and say *some of you* write me a pass,' rather in a commanding tone. . . . I believe he had got Johny afraid of him. . . . he does seem so wicked [that] if any one was to come upon him about his conduct I do not know what he would do afterwards.[64]

Will on the Pryor farm and Willes at the Jackson farm responded to the breakdown of the master-slave relationship by asserting their

[64]Mrs. Louticia Jackson to Asbury H. Jackson, August 23, 1863, Edward Harden Papers, Duke University, cited in Mohr, "Georgia Blacks," chapter 3.

own mastery. Other black Southerners in other places did the same kind of things. Still others responded by reversing the master-dependent roles; they took paternal care of their owners and their property. Mary Chesnut recorded one example of this reversal in her diary. Shortly after the war a black man told his former master, "When you 'all had de power you was good to me, and I'll protect you now. No nigger, no Yankee, shall touch you. If you want anything, call for Sambo. I mean, call for Mr. Samuel—that's my name now."[65] Mr. Samuel and those like him were neither "Uncle Toms" nor were they the stereotypical "loyal darkies" of white legends. Like Will and Willes they coped with altered racial realities imposed by wartime. Their response differed in form but not in substance. The Confederate experience offered many black Southerners a kind of first freedom even while they were still slaves.[66]

The departure of a slaveholder for the army was only one form of strain imposed upon master-slave relationships. Shortages of life's necessities also impaired the exercise of the master role, whether or not the master stayed at home. Salt was scarce throughout the Confederacy, and thus meat, too, was in short supply in many localities. These and other scarcities could and did prevent slave masters from fulfilling their maintenance responsibilities toward their bondsmen. In turn the slaves, out of resentment and/or malnourishment, were less diligent about their own responsibilities.[67]

When Union armies threatened to occupy land areas, the slaveholders involved usually fled with their slaves before the invaders. The results of "refugeeing" (a verb contributed by the Confederate experience) for blacks were unsettling. Not only was a master in flight something less than a patriachal figure, the resettlement of slaves in many cases meant the destruction of black families and plantation communities. Not surprisingly refugee blacks responded to the novel circumstance by acting less and less slavish.[68]

Impressment, too, upset the stability of the slave system. Large

[65]Chesnut, *Diary*, p. 532.
[66]Eugene D. Genovese, *Roll, Jordan, Roll: The World the Slaves Made* (New York, 1974), pp. 129–133.
[67]See Wiley, *Southern Negroes*, pp. 24–32; and Ella Lonn, *Salt as a Factor in the Confederacy* (New York, 1933).
[68]See Mary Elizabeth Massey, *Refugee Life in the Confederacy* (Baton Rouge, La., 1964); and Wiley, *Southern Negroes*, pp. 3–23.

numbers of slaves had to leave their homes and serve institutional masters when armies or cities required labor for constructing fortifications. Neither slaveholder nor slave liked the prospect. Impressment deprived the owner of his slave's services and usually meant hard labor and harsh treatment for the slave. And the impressment practice, like the enlistment of a master in the army, the flight of a plantation community before enemy troops, and the scarcities of wartime, weakened the bonds of the master-slave tie.[69]

In the urban Confederacy, as in the countryside, the war experience tended to break down traditional racial mores. Cities were small and few in the Old South, and slave populations within them had declined during the prewar years. With the advent of the Confederacy and its war, however, Southern cities experienced phenomenal growth in a short time. War industries, armies, hospitals, supply depots, and refugees contributed to the influx, and each of these items and activities brought more black Southerners to town.[70] By their very nature, cities undermined the slave system. Cities allowed, even encouraged, anonymity. Urban slaves "hired out" and "lived out" in greater numbers than rural slaves. However much municipal authorities tried, through ordinances and police vigilance, they were never able to make the city a surrogate master to resident slaves. And greater concentrations of blacks, both slave and free, made a sense of black community deeper and broader. When Southern cities swelled in size during the Confederate period, the inherent weaknesses of urban slavery increased as well.[71]

The experience of Jefferson Davis was an index of the uneasy nature of urban slavery in wartime. During the single month of January 1864, the Davises lost three slaves. The last runaway lingered long enough to start a fire in the basement of the executive mansion; only fast action on the part of the household confined the blaze and prevented the entire building from burning down. The Confederate President blamed the unfaithfulness of his slaves on

[69]See Wiley, *Southern Negroes*, pp. 110–133.

[70]On Confederate urban life see Thomas, *Confederacy as a Revolutionary Experience*, pp. 93–99; and case studies such as Emory M. Thomas, *The Confederate State of Richmond: A Biography of the Capital* (Austin, Tex., 1971); Kenneth Coleman, *Confederate Athens, 1861–1865* (Athens, Ga., 1968); Gerald M. Capers, *Occupied City: New Orleans Under the Federals, 1862–1865* (Lexington, Ky., 1965).

[71]Thomas, *Confederacy as a Revolutionary Experience*, pp. 125–127.

bribes delivered by secret agents of the enemy.[72] Perhaps Davis was correct; more likely, however, the conduct of Davis's slaves resulted more from unrest within the slave system than from external influences.

During the medieval period in western Europe, the rise of towns afforded refuge and liberation for peasants from the countryside. The process inspired the saying *"stat Luft macht frei,"* "city air makes one free." During the Confederate period in the South, for different reasons under different circumstances, city "air" often had the same effect upon black Confederates.

By mid-1863 white Southerners had already adopted some reforms toward liberalizing the institution of slavery. This process would continue and almost reach the logical extreme of emancipation.[73] But even while whites tinkered with the institution, black Southerners had begun acting out their own liberation.

Ironically, as Confederate nationality ripened and defined itself, prospects for the continued existence of the Southern nation suffered severe setbacks on three fronts. Even while Southerners were realizing their identity as Confederates, reordering their world view, and adjusting their social and racial mores, their nation trembled on two continents.

At Vicksburg, Johnston's worst fears materialized. Pemberton submitted to Grant's siege in hopes that Johnston could raise a potent enough force to relieve the city. Johnston mustered about 30,000 and marched close enough to Vicksburg to decide that his relief was too little and too late. The garrison surrendered on July 4; Pemberton's entire army were prisoners, and the Mississippi was open to the enemy all the way to its mouth.[74]

In Pennsylvania, Lee's campaign came to grief at Gettysburg. The battle which Lee hoped would be another Chancellorsville began on July 1 as the two armies concentrated. On June 28, General George G. Meade had replaced Hooker as commander of the Army of the

[72]Thomas, *Confederate Richmond,* pp. 155–156.

[73]See Wiley *Southern Negroes,* pp. 163–172; Robert F. Durden, *The Gray and the Black: the Confederate Debate on Emancipation* (Baton Rouge, La., 1972); and Bell I. Wiley, "The Movement to Humanize the Institution & Slavery during the Confederacy," *Emory University Quarterly,* V (1949), 207–220.

[74]Walker, *Vicksburg,* pp. 166–200; Jones, *Confederate Strategy,* 219–240; cf. Thomas L. Connelly, "Vicksburg: Strategic Point or Propaganda Drive?" *Military Affairs,* XXXIV (1970), 49–53, which argues that the fall was overrated.

Potomac. When Lee reached the field, he found that his troops held the town of Gettysburg, but that Meade's Federals were fortifying Cemetery Hill and the ridge line extending south to two domelike hills known as Big Round Top and Little Round Top. Next day Lee ordered Longstreet's corps to attack the Round Tops and Richard S. Ewell's corps to extend the Southern line around Cemetery Hill. Neither attack enabled the Confederates to dislodge their enemies from the heights. Finally on July 3, Lee determined to have a showdown. Meade's reinforcements kept arriving to strengthen his position, but Lee believed his men could breach Meade's center and felt that victory was worth the risk involved in a frontal assault. "Pickett's Charge," the attack on the Union center, was a gallant disaster. In a way it was the entire Confederate war in microcosm—a gathering of clans instead of military organizations led by an officer corps distinguished by its individual eccentricities, marching forth with bands playing and flags flying to take a gamble justified largely by the size of the stakes. Lee risked all and lost. After a day spent burying his dead and restoring organization to his army, Lee put his troops on the road south, back to Virginia.[75]

The third Confederate disaster of summer 1863 occurred in Europe. On June 30, Roebuck introduced his resolution to recognize the Southern nation in concert with France in the House of Commons. Amid debate on the resolution, he revealed the substance of his conversations with the French Emperor. Commons was incensed at Roebuck's and Lindsay's free-lance diplomacy, and Roebuck withdrew his resolution. Roebuck's *faux pas* deepened the English chill, and Napoleon III, after learning of the results at Vicksburg and Gettysburg, resisted the notion of recognizing the Confederacy unilaterally. France needed a strong New World ally.[76]

Vicksburg's defenders had numbered 30,000. Gettysburg had cost nearly as many in killed, wounded, and missing. The Confederacy had lost France as well, and in the aftermath of debacle, the Confederates suffered a severe loss of confidence in themselves.

Johnston blamed Vicksburg first upon Pemberton's failure to fol-

[75]The best account of the campaign and battle is Coddington, *Gettysburg.*

[76]Case and Spencer, *The United States and France,* pp. 398–426. Crook, *The North, the South, and the Powers,* pp. 309–315. See also Alfred J. Hanna and Kathryn A. Hanna, *Napoleon III and Mexico: American Triumph over Monarchy* (Chapel Hill, N.C., 1971); and Nancy Nichols Barker, "France, Austria, and the Mexican Venture, 1861–1864," *French Historical Studies,* III (1963), 224–245.

low orders and then upon Davis' interference.[77] Davis, when Josiah Gorgas lamely remarked that Vicksburg had fallen for want of supplies, snapped, "Yes, from want of provisions inside, and a general outside who wouldn't fight."[78]

Lee blamed himself for Gettysburg. When others did likewise in print, Lee offered his resignation and urged the President to fill his place with someone who could inspire more confidence among the public.[79]

Davis rejected Lee's resignation and eventually entrusted Johnston with another crucial command, but the evidence of Southern vincibility was very real in the summer of 1863. Once again Davis spoke of the "darkest hour of our political existence,"[80] but Gorgas best bespoke the mood. "Yesterday," he wrote in his diary, "we rode on the pinnacle of success. Today absolute ruin seems our portion. The Confederacy totters to its destruction."[81]

[77]The quarrel is well summarized in Varina Davis, *Jefferson Davis*, II, pp. 412–440, and in Johnston's, *Narrative of Military Operations . . . during the Late War Between the States*, new edition, Frank E. Vandiver (ed.), Urbana, Ill., 1959), pp. 205–252.

[78]Frank E. Vandiver, (ed.), *The Civil War Diary of General Josiah Gorgas* (University, Ala., 1947), p. 50.

[79]Lee to Davis, August 8, 1863, in Dowdey and Manarin (eds.), *Wartime Papers of R. E. Lee*, pp. 589–590.

[80]Davis to General E. K. Smith, July 14, 1863, in Rowland (ed.), *Jefferson Davis . . . Letters, Papers and Speeches*, pp. 552–554.

[81]Vandiver (ed.), *Gorgas Diary*, p. 55.

CHAPTER 11

The Disintegration of Southern Nationalism

FRIDAY, August 21, 1863, was by proclamation of Jefferson Davis a day of "fasting, humiliation, and prayer" in the Confederate States. On this day the President invited his countrymen to go to their "respective places of public worship" and to pray for divine favor "on our suffering country."[1]

Throughout the war Davis periodically proclaimed days of fasting and public prayer either in thanksgiving for a recent victory or in penance for defeats. In May 1862, the President had been baptized and confirmed in St. Paul's Episcopal Church in Richmond, and he realized as a matter of personal piety and public policy that the Confederate cause required God on the Southern side.[2]

Regardless of God's preference, Southern churches ever served as staunch boosters of Confederate morale. Clerical fire-eaters like South Carolina Presbyterian James H. Thornwell and Louisianan Benjamin M. Palmer were among the most enthusiastic advocates of secession, and most Southern Protestant denominations made ecclesiastical secessions from their Northern brethren before the political schism in 1860 and 1861. Then, from the beginning of the war, Southern churches of all sorts with few exceptions promoted

[1]The proclamation and others like it exhorting either humiliation or thanksgiving is in James D. Richardson (ed.), *Messages and Papers of the Confederacy*, 2 vols. (Nashville, Tenn., 1906) I, 328.
[2]See Frank E. Vandiver, *Ploughshares into Swords: Josiah Gorgas and Confederate Ordnance* (Austin, Tex. 1952), pp. 128–129; and Hudson Strode, *Jefferson Davis*, 3 vols. (New York, 1955–1964), II, 242–244.

the cause militant. Clergymen served the Southern army as chaplains, and a few, such as Episcopal Bishop of Louisiana Leonidas Polk, undertook combat service.[3]

Behind the battle lines religious organizations and presses prepared and distributed tracts and portions of scripture for the moral and spiritual uplift of the army and nation.[4] Presbyterian pastor Moses D. Hoge personally shepherded more than 300,000 Bibles from England through the blockade in 1862,[5] and throughout the Confederacy clergymen regularly delivered patriotic sermons to stir the blood of the faithful. Southerners were the "chosen people" in these orations; Yankees were Philistines whom Jehovah would surely destroy in His time. In times of victory Southern arms were like those of Joshua; in the wake of defeats God was chastising and cleansing Confederates to prepare them for eventual triumph.

When not resounding with the prophecy of Southern patriotism, Confederate churches were centers of volunteer action in support of the war effort. Moreover, by donations of everything from pew cushions to brass bells, Southern churches gave direct material aid to the cause. Among all the institutions in Southern life, perhaps the church most faithfully served the Confederate army and nation. The press was often fractious on policy and tactics; the schools weakened or closed; but the church usually remained constant and seemed to thrive on the emotional and physical sacrifices of wartime.[6]

[3] The best general study of the Confederate church is James W. Silver, *Confederate Morale and Church Propaganda*, Norton edition (New York, 1967). A number of Articles by W. Harrison Daniel add solid detail. See for example Daniel's "Southern Protestantism—1861 and After," *Civil War History* V (1959), 276–282; "Virginia Baptists, 1861–1865," *Virginia Magazine of History and Biography* LXXII (1964), 94–114; and "Southern Presbyterians in the Confederacy," *North Carolina Historical Review*, XLIV (1967), 231–255. See also Benjamin J. Blied, *Catholics and the Civil War* (Milwaukee, 1945); and Bertram W. Korn, "The Jews of the Confederacy," *American Jewish Archives*, XIII (1961), 3–90. Significantly religious thinking inspired anti-Confederate activities among Quakers, Unitarians, and other sects. See Samuel Horst, *Mennonites in the Confederacy: A Study in Civil War Pacificism* (Scottsdale, Pa., 1967). On Bishop Polk the standard biography is Joseph H. Parks, *General Leonidas Polk, C.S.A.: The Fighting Bishop* (Baton Rouge, La., 1962).

[4] For titles and locations see Marjorie Lyle Crandall, *Confederate Imprints: A Check List Based Principally on the Collection of the Boston Athenaeum*, 2 vols. (Boston, 1955); and Richard Harwell, *More Confederate Imprints*, 2 vols. (Richmond, Va., 1957) II.

[5] Emory M. Thomas, *The Confederate State of Richmond: A Biography of the Capital* (Austin, Tex., 1971), p. 131.

[6] Silver, *Church Propaganda*, pp. 93–101; Emory M. Thomas, *The Confederacy as a Revolutionary Experience* (Englewood Cliffs, N. J., 1971), pp. 116–117.

Thus in the midst of the national depression stemming from military reverses in the summer of 1863, President Davis directed his fellow Southerners to their places of worship. Although some Confederates were asking with more cynicism than humor what made a fast day different from any other, religious leaders responded as usual and counseled congregations to renew their hopes and amend their lives for the sake of victory.

Some Southerners, though, did not go to church on August 21, 1863. While many sought new strength for their souls and salve for their bruised morale, some took more direct action in the Southern crusade. At about five o'clock in the morning approximately 450 Southern rebels under the command of William Clarke Quantrill thundered down upon Lawrence, Kansas. Four hours later the raiders clattered away and left the town a smoking shambles, 150 of its inhabitants dead and thirty more wounded.[7]

Quantrill styled himself a colonel in the Confederate army and insisted that his tactics served the cause. In December 1862, he had visited Secretary of War James A. Seddon in Richmond to secure his commission and press upon Seddon the need for a "no-quarter" fight to the finish in the Confederate west. Seddon termed Quantrill's notions of war "barbarism" and denied him his commission. When Quantrill returned to Missouri, he claimed a colonelcy anyway and carried on guerrilla warfare in precisely the manner he had outlined to Seddon.[8]

The war in western Missouri and eastern Kansas was indeed "mean," a continuation of the raiding and bushwhacking which had been going on there since the mid-1850s. Conditioned by such circumstances and driven by a compulsion to "be somebody," Quantrill had won considerable notice, or notoriety, even before his raid on Lawrence. He attracted to his band of partisans and outlaws some men who doubtless believed they served a cause larger than themselves. Others, however, joined Quantrill only to indulge their lust for blood and booty.[9]

The affair at Lawrence was revealing. Long a center of abolitionism and unionism, Lawrence was a natural but ambitious target for

[7]The best work on Quantrill and his raid is Albert Castel, *William Clarke Quantrill: His Life and Times* (New York, 1962).
[8]Castel, *Quantrill*, pp. 101–103.
[9]*Ibid.*, pp. 103–121.

the bushwhackers. As soon as the raiders overwhelmed the small body of Federal troops in the town and one of them tied an American flag to the tail of his horse, the raid degenerated into a series of murders, robberies, and burnings directed against unarmed civilians, though women and children went unharmed. Quantrill's band broke into fragments of undisciplined, brutal individuals. Only one of Quantrill's followers was a casualty and only because he had become too drunk to ride out of Lawrence with the rest. Apologists for Quantrill later emphasized the symbolism of Lawrence, the savage nature of border warfare, and the raiders' respect for women and children. Nevertheless the affair was never so much a military action as it was the simple massacre of all but defenseless civilians. And for his leadership in such activities Quantrill earned considerably more infamy than fame.[10]

The paradox of August 21, 1863, was striking. At the same time that Southern pulpits rang with the rhetoric of righteousness and prayers for the cause, one of Quantrill's bushwhackers was screaming at the widow whose husband and brother-in-law he had just helped murder, "We are fiends from hell!"[11] To complete the irony, the most often played theme in public pronouncements of members of the Confederate government during the summer of 1863 concerned the numbers and severity of atrocities committed by the enemy.[12]

Perhaps there was significance in the fact that the vicious actions of 450 guerrillas produced at least a limited victory while the prayers of many times that number yielded considerably less. Because they sought to defend their homes from invasion, the Confederates had quite naturally chosen to fight a conventional war for the control of land areas. Precedent existed for an unconventional conflict of bushwhacking bands and guerrilla forces, yet as long as partisan activity threatened Southerners' commitment to people and place,

[10]*Ibid.*, pp. 122–143. See also Richard S. Brownlee, *Gray Ghosts of the Confederacy: Guerrilla Warfare in the West, 1861–1865* (Baton Rouge, La., 1958), 110–141, for a discussion of Quantrill, the raid, and its implications for the Confederacy.

[11]Castel, *Quantrill*, p. 131.

[12]During July Vice-President Stephens went to Washington to deliver a letter from Davis to Lincoln complaining of United States troops "who violate all the rules of war by carrying on hostilities . . . against noncombatants, aged men, women and children . . . [and who] destroy all private property within their reach. . . ." Richardson (ed.), *Messages and Papers*, II, 343. See also James Z. Rabun (ed.), *A Letter for Posterity: Alexander Stephens to His Brother Linton, June 3, 1864* (Athens, Ga., 1954).

invited reprisals from the enemy, and precluded the maintenance of racial subordination in slavery, the Confederates eschewed guerrilla warfare.[13]

To be sure there had been some bushwhacking, and there were a few cavalry units organized in accord with the act of Congress authorizing "partisan rangers." The audacious exploits of John S. Mosby's men behind enemy lines, like John Hunt Morgan's daring raids into Kentucky, Indiana, and Ohio, fired the Southern imagination during the summer of 1863.[14] However, in the broader scope of the Confederate war effort, the efforts of Morgan and Mosby were more or less side shows. The President and his generals tolerated the irregulars because their exploits had a beneficial effect on public morale, their activities usually complemented those of conventional forces, and the individuals involved would serve the cause in no other way. And Morgan's and Mosby's troopers, if not Quantrill's, adhered to a mild mutation of the "civilized" code of warfare.[15]

By the summer of 1863 guerrilla warfare had become a more viable option for Confederate strategists than it had been in 1861. Large chunks of Southern soil had fallen into the hands of the enemy, and the prospect of winning back this territory by conventional means seemed tenuous at best in the near future. Thus the possibility for a large-scale partisan effort existed if the Confederates were willing to endure reprisals from the enemy, surrender control of black Southerners, and give themselves over to the rootless barbarism prescribed by Quantrill. Southerners recognized to their chagrin that their war had become "mean," and they began, perhaps for the first time, actually to fear for their success by conventional military operations. But for the most part they rejected the guerrilla alternative and prayed for divine intervention by con-

[13]On this issue see especially Albert Castel, "The Guerrilla War," *Civil War Times Illustrated* (special issue, 1974); and William L. Barney, *Flawed Victory: A New Perspective on the Civil War* (New York, 1975), pp. 18–19.

[14]On Mosby see Charles W. Russell (ed.), *The Memoirs of Colonel John S. Mosby* (Boston, 1917); and *Mosby's War Reminiscences and Stuart's Cavalry Campaigns* (Boston, 1887). On Morgan see Cecil F. Holland, *Morgan and his Raiders: A Biography of the Confederate General* (New York, 1942); and Howard Swiggett, *The Rebel Raider: A Life of John Hunt Morgan* (Indianapolis, Ind., 1937).

[15]Mosby, for example, according to legend permitted no profanity among his troopers with one exception. Upon bidding an enemy to surrender, the Confederate might command, "Surrender, you Yankee Son-of-a-bitch!" J. Bryan III, *Sword over the Mantle: The Civil War and I* (New York, 1960), p. 27.

ventional means. God, though, appeared to be on the side with the strongest battalions.[16]

Thus the resort of Southerners to the extremes of prayer and savagery on August 21 was in itself an index of failing Confederate fortunes. Confederates had adopted a traditional nineteenth-century mode of warfare that demanded that Southerners fight their war on the enemy's terms: with masses of men supported by an integrated logistical economy. Accordingly, the Confederacy had husbanded its resources as best it could and had sacrificed significant portions of the Southern ideological soul in an effort to create and sustain the war. Though the Southern war machine had never been exactly well oiled or efficient, it had functioned well enough. Late in the campaigning season of 1863, however, it displayed unmistakable signs of disintegration and decay. And as the war went badly, the fabric of Southern national life began to unravel. Predictably, military disintegration and national unraveling fed upon each other. The Confederacy survived for a year and a half longer, and during that period Southerners continued to husband and to sacrifice. By degrees, though, the creative national response to the challenge of war turned desperate; and by the time the war wound down, the South was exhausted, and the Southern nation was no more.

Pressure from the enemy mounted during the fall of 1863. While Grant consolidated his victory over Pemberton and Johnston at Vicksburg and Meade probed South in an effort to renew his battle with Lee, Rosecrans finally moved on Chattanooga and Bragg's Southern army.

In the vicinity of Murfreesboro, Rosecran's base, the two armies had sparred with each other. Bragg of necessity remained on the defensive as he dispatched troop units to Vicksburg and thereby increased his numerical inferiority. By the time Vicksburg fell, the enemy at Murfreesboro outnumbered Bragg's Confederates by about a three to two ratio. Clearly, in Bragg's mind at least, Rosecrans had the initiative and eventually he chose to exercise it.[17]

On June 26, Rosecrans put his army in motion. By a series of

[16]See Raimondo Luraghi, "The Civil War and the Modernization of American Society: Social Structure and Industrial Revolution in the Old South before and during the War," *Civil War History*, XVIII (1972), 246–248.

[17]Thomas L. Connelly, *Autumn of Glory: The Army of Tennessee, 1862–1865* (Baton Rouge, La., 1971), pp. 69–111.

sharp skirmishes and astute maneuvers, the Federals advanced on Bragg's Confederates and in nine days drove them back across the Tennessee River and into Chattanooga. On July 4, while Pemberton was surrendering Vicksburg and Lee was deciding to retreat from the catharsis at Gettysburg, Bragg's Army of Tennessee marched into Chattanooga and began preparations for a showdown stand in the Confederate heartland.

Chattanooga was important symbolically and substantively. If the enemy could seize the city, they might destroy the Army of Tennessee in the process. In terms of both political and military logistics Chattanooga was a significant rail link between Richmond and the seaboard Confederacy and the Southern hinterland between the Appalachians and the Mississippi. Chattanooga was the last defensible strong point left to the Confederacy in Tennessee. And, finally, Chattanooga was important because Bragg and the Southern military hierarchy made it so; the Confederates chose to stand and fight there, and thus the resultant campaign, like the campaigns at Vicksburg and Gettysburg, possessed a significance which transcended factors more immediate and mundane.[18]

The opening round in the battle for Chattanooga was time-consuming and inconclusive. After his lightninglike advance to the Tennessee, Rosecrans hesitated. For a month and a half the Union commander delayed, and both armies girded for the fight. The Confederates in Chattanooga depended upon the Western and Atlantic Railroad from Atlanta for supplies. To occupy the city after the enemy cut this supply line would be worse than folly; it would almost inevitably result in the loss of both army and city. Accordingly Rosecrans elected to try to bypass Chattanooga, cross the Tennessee, and seize the rail line at some point behind the Confederates. Bragg, still on the defensive, attempted to guess where the Federals would try to cross the river and to prevent the crossing. Bragg's guess was wrong. The Union army on August 16 made a feint at the river northeast of Chattanooga and then moved in strength to a crossing at Caperton's Ferry, southwest of the city. When Bragg realized what was happening, he had no choice but to abandon Chattanooga and attempt a stand farther south.[19]

[18]*Ibid.*, pp. 112–134; and Fairfax Downey, *Storming the Gateway: Chattanooga, 1863* (New York, 1960), pp. 66–74.
[19]Connelly, *Autumn of Glory*, pp. 137–165.

By the end of the first week in September the situation was again in flux. The Army of Tennessee was dispersed but intact in the rugged mountainous region of northwest Georgia. Rosecrans had maneuvered Bragg out of Tennessee at small cost to himself, but neither had the Confederates suffered significantly. Bragg hoped that when Rosecrans divided his forces to track down the Confederates, the hunted might become the hunters and destroy the Federals piecemeal. Reinforcements encouraged Bragg's hope; a division from Johnston's army and Longstreet's entire corps from the Army of Northern Virginia were on the way. Bragg's first attempts to seize the initiative, however, proved frustrating. Even though the enemy did just about what Bragg hoped they would do—divide themselves in the mountains—the recently reorganized Army of Tennessee was unable to capitalize upon the circumstance.

At last, on September 20, Bragg had his day. Federal troop units were scattered due south of Chattanooga along a line parallel to the Lafayette Road, which ran into the city. Bragg's army was able to cross Chickamauga Creek, which also roughly paralleled the Lafayette Road, and advance in fairly good order upon the enemy. If the Confederates could seize and hold any portion of the road between elements of Rosecrans' army and Chattanooga, then the Federals would be cut off from their base of supply and ripe for destruction.[20]

The Confederates attacked early on the morning of the twentieth. The assaults were uncoordinated, and Rosecrans was able to concentrate his army to meet them, but just at the moment when Longstreet's veterans swept forward at 11:30, a Union division commander misinterpreted his confused orders from Rosecrans and withdrew his troops from the Federal front. Longstreet's Confederates poured through the gap, and Union resistance seemed about to crumble. Rosecrans was convinced he had been beaten, and he led the hasty retreat to Chattanooga himself. Bragg, however, did not press his advantage. He failed to maintain the momentum of his advance by committing reserve troops to the critical part of the battlefield. As a result the Southern assaults faltered before the determined stand made by George H. Thomas' Union corps. With justice Bragg claimed victory at Chickamauga, but Bragg had won

[20]*Ibid.*, pp. 166–200.

a battle when he might have won an entire campaign.[21]

The Union army re-formed at Chattanooga, and Bragg chose to lay siege to the city. The Confederates fortified the high ground on Lookout Mountain and Missionary Ridge, which dominated the city. Then Bragg sent Joseph Wheeler's cavalry on a raid to sever Union supply lines. Wheeler's efforts and rain, which made bad roads worse, took a significant toll, and Rosecrans' army was in pitiful shape by mid-October. Again, though, Bragg did not press his advantage. On the contrary he detached Longstreet's corps and sent it to attack Knoxville. Longstreet conducted a campaign at Knoxville similar to the one Bragg was conducting at Chattanooga. Both Confederate commanders informed Richmond that they had their enemy at bay, but neither general attempted a *coup de grâce.*

While Bragg and his Army of Tennessee were content and confident, their enemies were active. Washington made Grant commander of a western theater from the mountains to the Mississippi, an imitation of Johnston's charge from Richmond almost a year earlier. Perhaps because Grant learned from Johnston's experience, but more likely because Grant was a more aggressive general, the Union theater command fulfilled most of the hopes which Davis had had for his version of the concept. Grant replaced Rosecrans with Thomas and came to Chattanooga himself to oversee the continuation of the campaign. Too, the Washington War Office dispatched Hooker's corps from Meade's army to counter Richmond's transfer of Longstreet's corps, and two more corps commanded by Sherman began a transit from Vicksburg to reinforce the Chattanooga position still further. As reinforcements swelled the enemy force, Thomas was able to open newer and shorter supply routes into the "besieged" city.

Unaccountably Bragg failed to appreciate the significance of the activity going on beneath him during October and November. His position, he believed, was impregnable, and winter would soon end the campaigning season of 1863. Thus the Southern army watched and waited for the most part while the enemy gathered strength.[22]

On November 24 the Federals struck. Hooker and three divisions seized the low ground between Lookout Mountain and the Tennes-

[21] *Ibid.,* pp. 201–234; Glen Tucker, "The Battle of Chickamauga," *Civil War Times Illustrated,* VIII (1969), 4–46. Downey, *Storming the Gateway,* pp. 93–129.
[22] Connelly, *Autumn of Glory,* pp. 235–272.

see River and threatened to isolate the Southerners on Lookout Mountain from those on Missionary Ridge. Sherman attacked the northern end of the Confederate position on the ridge line at Tunnel Hill. Bragg responded by withdrawing his troops from Lookout Mountain and concentrating on the Missionary Ridge line. He still had reason to be confident that the Federals' attack would result in their wholesale slaughter.

Next day, November 25, Grant ordered Hooker and Sherman to assult the Confederate flanks. Thomas' troops were supposed to try to take the first of three ranks of rifle pits in the center of Bragg's line. Hooker was slow, and Patrick Cleburne's Confederates thwarted Sherman's attack. In the center, however, Thomas' Federals accomplished what Pickett's charge failed to achieve at Gettysburg; they broke through the middle of the entrenched Confederates on Missionary Ridge. Once in possession of the first line of rifle pits, the Federals renewed their charge and in less than an hour carried the top of the ridge. Whether they acted out of courage or out of fear for their exposed position at the base of the ridge was immaterial; Bragg's line was broken.

Bragg's army also broke. The troops, for the first and only significant time in the life of the Army of Tennessee, fled in panic down the back side of Missionary Ridge. Only nightfall, confusion in the ranks of the enemy, and a rear guard action fought mainly by Cleburne's division, saved Bragg's army from annihilation. The campaign for Chattanooga had ended in disaster. Bragg took his shattered command into winter quarters at Dalton, Georgia, and blamed his debacle on drunken officers, cowardly soldiers—everyone save himself. Bragg's subordinates responded naturally to failures in leadership. His officers divided into hostile camps, and his men deserted in alarming numbers. By the end of the year, one of the Confederacy's two major field armies seemed to be on the verge of disintegration.[23]

The Confederacy's other major field army, Lee's Army of Northern Virginia, spent the second half of the 1863 campaigning season in northern Virginia. Lee was anxious to atone for Gettysburg, and Meade was equally anxious to atone for his own failure to follow up the great battle by destroying the Southern army. Nevertheless the

[23]*Ibid.*, pp. 272–278; Downey, *Storming the Gateway*, pp. 156–195.

campaigns of late 1863 in the east were inconclusive.

In mid-September Meade's army advanced on Lee's position at Culpeper Court House. Then, just as the two armies were about to join battle, Meade lost two corps sent to reinforce Rosecrans after Chickamauga. It then became Lee's turn to advance as Meade withdrew to Centreville. Lee's attempt to flank Meade and interpose the Army of Northern Virginia between Meade and Washington came to grief at Bristoe Station on October 14. So in November Lee took his army back across the Rappahannock and prepared to go into winter quarters.

Meade, however, tried one last time to flank the Confederates and defeat Lee. The Federals crossed the Rapidan River in strength and attempted to do what Hooker had tried to do, very near to where he had tried to do it. About ten miles west of Chancellorsville the Army of the Potomac found the Confederates in a strong defensive position along Mine Run, a creek which flows north into the Rapidan. What Lee hoped to do was hold Meade's attacking units in check with the aid of trenches and Hill's corps. Then Ewell's corps would emulate Jackson's action at Chancellorsville by striking the enemy's exposed southern flank. Meade unwittingly foiled the scheme. Believing the Confederate position too strong for a frontal assault, the Union general withdrew back across the Rapidan. Thus when Ewell's troops surged forward on December 2, they found only trees in their way. At this point both armies went into winter quarters and accepted stalemate on the Rapidan.[24]

In terms of lines and symbols on maps, the Confederacy was not much worse off when the military campaigns of 1863 ended than it had been before they began. On the Virginia front Lee and Meade were just about where Lee and Burnside had been a year earlier. In the "near west" Chattanooga was lost, but the battle front had moved less than ninety miles during the year—from Murfreesboro to Chattanooga, five days march in 365 days. Farther west, Vicksburg too was gone, but the enemy could never hope to interdict absolutely passage across the Mississippi.

The trans-Mississippi region was still in flux, but then it had ever been in flux. At least by the end of 1863 the Southern War Office

[24]See Douglas S. Freeman, *Lee's Lieutenants: A Study in Command,* 3 vols. (New York, 1942–1944), III, 206–279; and Jay Luvaas and Wilbur S. Nye, "The Campaign that History Forgot! Mine Run," *Civil War Times Illustrated,* VIII (1969), 11–36.

had imposed unity of command out there, in the person of Edmund Kirby Smith. Davis and Seddon had selected Smith the previous spring and let him know that he was all but independent within his enlarged department. When Vicksburg fell Smith's responsibilities grew still more, but although he complained a lot, he was establishing himself as the Confederacy incarnate west of the river.[25]

Lines and symbols on maps, however, were not flesh and blood. Southerners still could find reason to be sanguine; but from Jefferson Davis on down the South's status pyramid, Confederates realized all too well that the Southern nation was sick. Indices were available with which to chart the Confederacy's failing health, and the nation's vital signs did not offer a happy long-range prognosis. The Army of Northern Virginia had realized its vincibility during 1863. The Army of Tennessee under Bragg was a shattered shell. In the early months of 1863 many Southerners had had confidence in victory and independence before the year was out. By December the same Southerners were hoping to stave off defeat.[26]

Moreover the Southerners now realized that they would have to stave off defeat by themselves. Failure to secure French mediation-/intervention in July of 1863 only began the final decline in the Confederacy's quasi relations with the European powers. In a fit of pique and despair Benjamin, in August, ordered Mason in London to conclude his efforts and abandon the pretended mission. Then in October Benjamin expelled British consuls from the Confederacy, claiming that they were harboring British-born draft evaders.[27] Benjamin also recalled DeLeon from his propaganda duties in France. DeLeon had had the misfortune of seeing one of his letters to Davis, in which he complained of Slidell and French journalists, intercepted and published in New York newspapers.[28] Congress completed the Confederacy's diplomatic retrenchment in December when the Senate refused to confirm L. Q. C. Lamar's projected

[25]Robert L. Kerby, *Kirby Smith's Confederacy: The Trans-Mississippi South, 1863–1865* (New York, 1972), pp. 51–54, 209–281.

[26]See Bell I. Wiley, *The Road to Appomattox,* Atheneum edition (New York, 1968), pp. 61–70.

[27]Frank L. Owsley, *King Cotton Diplomacy: Foreign Relations of the Confederate States of America,* second edition (Chicago, 1959), pp. 467–494; D. P. Crook, *The North, the South, and the Powers, 1861–1865* (New York, 1974), pp. 330–332.

[28]Charles P. Cullop, *Confederate Propaganda in Europe: 1861–1865,* (Coral Gables, Fla., 1969), pp. 77–84.

mission to Russia.[29] Obviously, if the Confederacy sought entry into the family of nations, the South would have to gain it alone by right of conquest and endurance, but perhaps this had always been the case.

Military and diplomatic circumstances were reflected in the Confederacy's marketplaces. A gold dollar, which had cost three dollars in Confederate paper in January 1863, cost eighteen to twenty dollars by December. Secretary of the Treasury Memminger estimated in December that more than $700 million worth of notes were circulating in an economy capable of absorbing $200 million.[30] Too, as the Union blockade tightened and the South's capacity to produce and transport consumer goods declined, scarcity increased on the home front.[31] Finally, there had been failures in the South's war production which became in turn cause and effect of further failure. The loss of the copper mines at Ducktown, Tennessee, was a good case in point. The mines were lost to the Confederacy as a result of the Chattanooga campaign. Copper was essential to the manufacture of friction primers which in turn were essential to the operation of small arms and artillery. Theoretically, at least, without copper Confederate soldiers would be unable to fire their weapons at all. The blockade removed the possibility of importing sufficient quantities of copper after the loss of the Ducktown supply. The Nitre and Mining Bureau made up the shortage by impressing copper coils from North Carolina stills—an expedient hardly calculated to raise morale in North Carolina.[32] As Southern armies became less able to defend Southern territory, the Confederacy lost the resources of that territory and so the armies became weaker still. And as civilian morale drooped with each defeat, resultant sacrifices seemed all the more intolerable.

During the fall of 1863 Confederate citizens were able to express their frustration politically in the Congressional elections. Not surprisingly the returns reflected a decline in national morale and less than confidence in the Davis administration's ability to manage the war, foreign relations, and the South's political economy. Because

[29]Owsley, *King Cotton Diplomacy*, pp. 489–490.
[30]Richard Cecil Todd, *Confederate Finance* (Athens, Ga., 1954), pp. 197, 111–112.
[31]See Mary Elizabeth Massey, *Ersatz in the Confederacy* (Columbia, S.C., 1952), pp. 3–31, 159–173.
[32]Vandiver, *Ploughshares into Swords*, pp. 201–202.

Confederate politics lacked the relative consistency and order of party structure, no one knew precisely to what degree the administration's strength eroded at the polls in 1863. There were other ambiguities as well. Opposition to Davis and his government did not necessarily go with defeatism, although sometimes it did. Candidates who stood for election and against the administration usually went to great pains to prove their patriotism. They simply argued that they would find alternative means for achieving the common end of independence. Adding to the obscurity was the fact that much or most of Arkansas, Louisiana, Mississippi, Missouri, Kentucky, and Tennessee were under the control of the enemy. Thus elections in those states did not exactly reflect the will of Confederate voters, only Confederates in exile. However calculated, though, the returns from the Congressional elections in 1863 did indicate failing confidence in the Davis administration.

Off-year elections in American politics have more often than not injured incumbent administrations, but Davis' was a war government in peril, and the President hardly needed troubles with domestic politics. Troubles he had, though, when the Confederacy's Second Congress convened in May, 1864. The number of openly antiadministration members rose in the House from twenty-six to forty-one, out of 106 districts, and in the Senate from eleven to twelve, out of twenty-six members. These numbers were imprecise in that they identified only open antagonists as antiadministration, and they reflected only a fraction of the difficulty Davis had making his programs palatable to the Second Congress. Nevertheless Davis prevailed and, however much chastened, his administration remained in control of the Confederate destiny.[33]

The President—and indeed just about every other Confederate—realized that the South's national destiny required some fundamental decisions to be made quickly and correctly. Something had to be done about matters no less vital than the economy of the country, the strategy of the war, and renewed resources with which to fight the war. Those most responsible were the administration, the military, and the Congress.

[33]Wilfred Buck Yearns, *The Confederate Congress* (Athens, Ga., 1960), pp. 58–59; Thomas B. Alexander and Richard E. Beringer, *The Anatomy of the Confederate Congress: A Study of the Influences of Member Characteristics on Legislative Voting Behavior, 1861–1865* (Nashville, Tenn., 1972), pp. 44–45.

The Commander-in-Chief dealt with the most immediate problem first: Bragg and his army. It was clear, even to Bragg and to his friend Davis, that Bragg could no longer command the Army of Tennessee. Accordingly Bragg offered his resignation, and on November 30 the President accepted it. For two weeks Davis pondered a replacement. He discussed with Lee the possibility of sending him west. Lee was hardly eager to leave his familiar command in familiar territory, but he was willing to go and believed for a while that Davis planned to send him. Davis also considered Beauregard, but finally he chose Johnston on December 16. The choice was revealing. It showed the degree of the President's magnanimity toward a general with whom he had quarreled often and bitterly since 1861 but in whom he still had confidence. More important, the selection of Johnston over Beauregard was a rejection of Beauregard's strategic ideas in favor of Johnston's, which were more in accord with the President's. Beauregard had long contended that the west, not the east, was the crucial front in the war. Thus Beauregard periodically proposed a grand concentration in the west at the expense of a holding action in Virginia. Davis favored a division of labor and energy and believed at worst that Virginia was untenable with fewer troops and resources and at best that victorious campaigns were possible on both fronts. Johnston, by accepting command of the Army of Tennessee, in effect accepted Davis' strategic concept, and in reality he had already acted out a rejection of grand concentration in the west during his tenure as theater commander in 1863.[34]

Thus Lee would remain with the Army of Northern Virginia and necessarily compete with Johnston for manpower and resources with which to conduct the campaigns of 1864. When Johnston joined the Army of Tennessee at Dalton, he found that he had begun the competition at a significant disadvantage. Although Davis had assured him that his new command was in fine fighting trim, Johnston

[34]Lee made plain his reluctance to undertake command of the Army of Tennessee in a letter to Davis on December 7. (Clifford Dowdey and Louis H. Manarin [eds.], *The Wartime Papers of R. E. Lee* [New York, 1961], p. 642.) However on December 9 the general indicated in a letter to J. E. B. Stuart the strong possibility of his departure. "I am called to Richmond this morning by the President. I presume the rest will follow. My heart and thought will always be with the army." See Connelly, *Autumn of Glory*, pp. 281–288; Thomas Lawrence Connelly and Archer Jones, *The Politics of Command: Factions and Ideas in Confederate Strategy* (Baton Rouge, La., 1973), pp. 141–143; and Gilbert E. Govan and James W. Livingood, *A Different Valor: The Story of General Joseph E. Johnston, C.S.A.* (New York, 1956), pp. 235–239.

found out otherwise. Bragg's old subordinates were still divided into hostile camps along pro- and anti-Bragg lines, and the troops were in pitiful condition physically and mentally. Johnston met this challenge characteristically. He complained to Davis and about Davis to others; but he also began putting an army together at Dalton. He offered amnesty to deserters and furloughs to the faithful in the ranks. He occupied his subordinates constructively with the collection and movement of much-needed supplies and with the reinstitution of order and discipline. Before long, members of the Army of Tennessee were again fighting among themselves—this time however with snowballs and renewed *esprit.* [35]

Meanwhile in Richmond Davis addressed the more basic problem of expanding the ranks for the 1864 campaigning season. When Congress assembled on December 7, 1863, Davis urged immediate attention to measures designed to swell the draft. He also urged passage of a law to employ free blacks and slaves in noncombatant military duties formerly performed by soldiers. Eventually the Congress did authorize use of 20,000 black Confederates as cooks, teamsters, laborers, nurses, and the like,[36]and eventually Congress revised significantly the Conscription Act. At Davis' request the new law, passed February 17, 1864, severely limited the number of draft exempt categories and expanded the military age limits from eighteen to forty-five to seventeen to fifty. The most significant feature of the new act, however, was the vast prerogatives it gave the President and War Department to control the South's labor pool. By cutting drastically the number of legal exemptions from the military, the Congress gave the administration power to allocate manpower through the system of military details. In effect the law said that if the War Office deemed a man's contribution to the economy worth more than his service as a soldier, the government could draft him and send him back to his work or farm as a soldier on special assignment. In theory at least the law gave to the administration the power to manage totally the Southern economy as it related to labor.[37]

[35]Connelly, *Autumn of Glory,* pp. 289–292; Govan and Livingood, *Different Valor,* pp. 240–260.

[36]Richardson, *Messages and Papers,* I, 370; James A. Seddon to Jefferson Davis, November 26, 1863, *War of the Rebellion: A Compilation of the Official Records of the Union and Confederate Armies,* 70 vols. in 127 (Washington, D.C., 1880–1901), ser. IV, II, 998–999; *ibid.,* III, 208.

[37]Albert Burton Moore, *Conscription and Conflict in the Confederacy* (New York, 1927), pp. 308–312.

In practice the Conscription Act of 1864 came to quite a bit less. The fact was that the South's manpower reserve was fairly well depleted, and many of those who remained subject to the draft resisted conscription to the point of violence. Despite renewed efforts on the part of the Conscription Bureau, inefficiency characterized its operations and undermined still more the confidence of Confederates in their government. Thus the results of the new law were disappointing. An estimated 15,820 conscripts joined the South's armies between January 1 and April 1, 1864. About as many volunteered during that period in indirect response to the conscription program. Yet during the same time the Conscript Bureau exempted 26,000 and detailed 13,000 more—generating a net loss for the military. Most significant was the fact that on June 30, 1864, the sum total of the present-for-duty strength in all Confederate armies was no more than 200,000. That figure was 30,000 to 40,000 less than the total strength at the end of 1863 and perhaps 100,000 less than Confederate strength a year earlier. And the Southern total was roughly one-third that of the enemy's.[38]

Mercifully, these depressing figures and ratios were unknown to Confederates in the winter of 1863–1864. But many Southerners had a pretty good intuitive grasp of the numerical odds against them, and those in the armies had first-hand experience with the growing disparity in strength. During December of 1863 one Southern officer, especially, subjected the dilemma to searching analysis and proposed a radical solution. That officer was Patrick Cleburne, a division commander in the Army of Tennessee. A native of Ireland, Cleburne had emigrated to the United States in 1849. He settled in Helena, Arkansas, and by 1856 was an established local lawyer. He began his Confederate military career as captain of the "Yell Rifles" and advanced on the strength of aggressive achievement to major general in command of a division. "The Stonewall Jackson of the West," as his admirers described him, was a bold fighter, and in December 1863, Cleburne proved himself an equally bold thinker.[39]

On the evening of January 2, 1864, at a meeting of general officers

[38] *Ibid.*, pp. 312–317.
[39] On Cleburne, Howell and Elizabeth Purdue's *Pat Cleburne, Confederate General: A Definitive Biography* (Hillsboro, Tex., 1973) does not justify the subtitle. Probably the best source on the man is still Irving A. Buck, *Cleburne and His Command* (Thomas Robson Hay [ed.], Jackson, Tenn., 1958).

of the Army of Tennessee, Cleburne presented his prepared brief. He began by painting a vivid, gloomy picture of his country's position and prospects. Southerners had poured out blood and treasure for nearly three years in what appeared to be a losing cause. Defeat alone loomed, and defeat would mean destruction of everything sacred to Southerners including the very memory of their struggle and sacrifice. Three factors were most influential in producing the South's sad circumstance: the Confederacy lacked soldiers, the South lacked supplies, and "slavery, from being one of our chief sources of strength at the commencement of the war, has now become, in a military point of view, one of our chief sources of weakness." To remedy these deficiencies at one stroke, Cleburne proposed "that we immediately commence training a large reserve of the most courageous of our slaves, and further that we guarantee freedom within a reasonable time to every slave in the South who shall remain true to the Confederacy in this war." Cleburne continued for some pages to justify his solution in terms of military, economic, propaganda, and moral values. He asserted, "As between the loss of independence and the loss of slavery, we assume that every patriot will freely give up the latter—give up the Negro slave rather than be a slave himself."[40]

"Cleburne's Memorial" was not the first suggestion by a Confederate to arm Southern slaves. In fact, during 1861 several groups of free black Southerners offered themselves as soldiers to the Confederate War Department, and although the War Office rejected each of these applications, some blacks did serve in the Southern armies. Already in 1863 a number of individual Confederates and the Alabama legislature had recommended to the Richmond government enlistment of slave soldiers.[41] Before Cleburne, however, no one had advanced so comprehensive a plan, and no one had seriously proposed universal emancipation as Confederate policy. Cleburne was not, however, an isolated farmer; he was a respected general officer with more than enough combat and administrative experience to lend credence to his military judgments.

[40]The text of "Cleburne's Memorial" is in *O. R.*, ser. I, LII, pt. 2, 586–592; and Robert F. Durden, *The Gray and the Black, the Confederate Debate on Emancipation* (Baton Rouge, La., 1972), pp. 53–63. See also Irving A. Buck, "Negroes in Our Army," *Southern Historical Society Papers* XXXI (1903), 215.

[41]*O.R.*, ser. IV, I, 1020; XV, 556–557, 559; II, 767, 947.

Predictably, as soon as Cleburne concluded reading his paper a heated debate ensued among his colleagues. The debate was inconclusive, and Johnston, the commanding general, made it more so by deciding not to forward Cleburne's Memorial through channels to Richmond. One of Cleburne's severest critics, however, Georgian general W. H. T. Walker, did request a copy of the "incendiary" document from the author and sent it directly to the President with a letter expressing appropriate outrage. Meanwhile Cleburne's proposition remained for a time an open, substantive question among the officer corps in the Army of Tennessee. Unfortunately it then became a political question, and Cleburne's "brother officers" tended to divide over the issue in rough accord with the old pro- and anti-Bragg factionalism.[42]

Davis received Walker's letter and a copy of Cleburne's Memorial on January 28 and immediately decided to close the debate. Next day War Secretary Seddon wrote Johnston to order "suppression, not only of the memorial itself, but likewise of all discussion and controversy respecting or growing out of it." Seddon and Davis had "no doubt . . . of the patriotic intents of its gallant author," but "the agitation and controversy which must spring from the presentation of such views by officers high in public confidence are to be deeply deprecated." From this point Cleburne's proposal inspired little or no discussion of its merits. The controversy survived, however, in *ad hominem* attacks and counterattacks among officers of the Army of Tennessee. Although Cleburne scrupulously remained a noncombatant in this rancorous campaign, he suffered from it. Three times within the next eight months Cleburne was passed over for command of an army corps and promotion to lieutenant general. In each case less distinguished, less controversial men received the honors.[43]

Cleburne's ideas, however, persisted. Even though Davis dismissed Cleburne's radical suggestion in January of 1864, he could not avoid the fundamental question it raised. If choice were necessary, would Southerners choose slavery or independence? For the

[42]Buck, "Negroes in Our Army," 216; Buck, *Cleburne*, pp. 189–190; Walker to Davis, January 12, 1864, *O.R.*, ser. I, LII, pt. 2, 595; Connelly, *Autumn of Glory*, pp. 318–321.

[43]Seddon to Johnston, January 24, 1864, *O.R.*, ser. 1, LII, pt. 2, 606–607; Connelly, *Autumn of Glory*, pp. 320–321.

moment, the President and others hoped never to have to make the choice, but having already sacrificed much of that which had called the Confederacy into being, Davis and other Southerners had now to wonder about the limits of sacrifice and the goal of national independence.

Even while Cleburne pondered what for Southerners might be the ultimate sacrifice, the President and his Congress were attempting to sustain and extend corporate sacrifices already made. From a considerable wringing of hands and gnashing of teeth during the winter session of 1863–1864 emerged four significant pieces of legislation in addition to the new Conscription Act.

With less difficulty than he expected Davis got a new law authorizing suspension of habeas corpus. The authority which had lain in limbo for almost a year conferred upon the President, the Secretary of War, and the commanding general of the Trans-Mississippi Department power to detain traitors and to refuse to deliver their prisoners to civil authorities. Thus the centralizing and nationalizing tendencies of the Richmond government were again upheld at the expense of individual liberties and state rights.[44]

As expected, Congress paid much attention to the Confederacy's economic peril. On February 17, 1864, a new tax bill became law. The new levy was especially severe regarding personalty and provided some relief to agricultural interests by allowing the 5 percent tax on arable land to be deducted from the tax in kind. For the most part, however, the tax law merely extended the program enacted in 1863 and called forth further material sacrifice from Confederates in order to maintain the war effort.[45]

On the same day that the new tax law passed, Congress responded at Treasury Secretary Memminger's urging to the deepening currency crisis in the nation. The plain fact was that despite inducements, Confederates were not exchanging treasury notes for interest-paying, noncirculating bonds. Accordingly the notes continued to circulate, and paper money threatened to flood the country as the government's printing presses continued to roll. The

[44]Davis made a special plea to Congress on February 3, 1864 (Richardson [ed.], *Messages and Papers*, I, 395–400). Congress responded with the suspension law on February 15. When the act expired on July 31, Davis was unwilling or unable to renew it. See Yearns, *Confederate Congress*, pp. 156–160; and John B. Robbins, "The Confederacy and the Writ of Habeas Corpus," *Georgia Historical Quarterly* LV (1971), 83–101.

[45]Todd, *Confederate Finance*, pp. 148–153.

solution, Memminger believed, was to force the exchange of notes for bonds in order to reduce the amount of paper in circulation. Congress agreed and on February 17 enacted a "Compulsory Funding Measure." The law said in effect that note holders who failed to exchange treasury paper for bonds would suffer devaluation by as much as one-third of the face value of their notes. By this means Memminger and Congress hoped to reduce the amount of currency in circulation by as much as two-thirds. The scheme failed. It failed because Southerners did not exchange their paper, because a new issue of notes designed to prevent too rapid a deflation only renewed the inflationary spiral, and because these fiscal manipulations only served to undermine further the confidence of the people in their government.[46]

The final piece of legislation in response to the new realities of national life was a law to regulate further the economy. As the blockade tightened, the administration became increasingly alarmed over nonessential cargoes "run in." The Confederate cause seemed to demand that every hard-won import contribute to the war effort and not to private enrichment or consumer tastes. Consequently on February 6, 1864, Congress passed a law requiring that anyone exporting cotton, tobacco, or any other element of the South's staple wealth do so only under the President's direction, and Davis immediately required every vessel to surrender at least half its cargo space to government shipments. As a result the government in effect conducted the Confederacy's foreign commerce during the final year of its life. Using impressed cotton and the congressional authority over blockade running, the supply agencies of the War Department practiced the nearest thing to state socialism to appear in the nineteenth century.[47]

The new draft, habeas corpus law, tax levy, currency-reduction legislation, and governmental blockade-running monopoly were rather drastic measures. Congress and the administration resorted to these expedients in answer to what they perceived as a crisis in the national fate. Taken together, they seem to have been acts of

[46]*Ibid.*, pp. 111–114. Public opinion was generally favorable toward currency reduction, at least in its early stages. For example, Whiggish editor E. H. Cushing in the Houston *Daily Telegraph* applauded congressional fiscal courage and added, "if it be done, best be done quickly" (March 21, 1864).

[47]See Louis B. Hill, *State Socialism in the Confederate States of America* (Charlottesville, Va., 1936).

creative desperation. The hard truth was that law and policy could not tap resources which did not exist, and even had the Confederates been able to commit 100 percent of themselves and their property to the war effort, in 1864 this would probably not have been enough. Perhaps Congress and country could congratulate themselves as winter turned to spring in 1864 that they had made every reasonable sacrifice and sold almost every nonessential portion of the Southern soul in the name of national salvation, but many wondered with reason if even this much would be enough.[48]

Confederates believed that they were as prepared as they could be for the renewal of large-scale combat in the spring of 1864. The President and Secretary of War realized that the South's military situation was precarious but continued their attempt to focus upon two fronts at the same time. Davis brought Bragg to Richmond to be a kind of chief of staff and personal advisor. Longstreet and his corps returned to Lee's army in early April. Eventually, on May 15, Beauregard and the bulk of Confederate troops in the Carolinas concentrated also in Virginia. In late April, Davis reaffirmed Smith's "full authority" in the trans-Mississippi over matters military and civil. Thus did Davis narrow his vision to his two remaining field armies, Lee's and Johnston's, and assemble his clans for a last campaign. Yet even with the concentration Davis was able to effect, the Army of Tennessee and the Army of Northern Virginia were each outnumbered by roughly two to one.[49]

During the winter the Union, too, had made changes in command and organization. Lincoln had finally found a general who shared his instincts, and so the Union President made Grant commander of all his armies. Grant in turn placed his old associate Sherman in command at Chattanooga. Meade retained command of the Army of the Potomac, but Grant joined that army, pitched his tent next to Meade's, and prepared to confront Lee. Grant accepted an essentially two-front war, in Georgia and in Virginia. He might have strained the Confederacy more had he opened still more fronts; he

[48]For extended statements of this thesis see Frank E. Vandiver, *Rebel Brass* (Baton Rouge, La., 1956), pp. 18–23; and Charles W. Ramsdell, *Behind the Lines in the Southern Confederacy* (Baton Rouge, La., 1944), pp. 113–120. Certainly significant to the Confederacy's last year is Vandiver's contention (*Basic History of the Confederacy* [Princeton, 1962], p. 96) that, "The Confederate States was first exhausted, then defeated."

[49]For a good general statement of the Confederacy's circumstance and prospects in the spring of 1864 see Alan Nevins, *The War for Union*, IV, *The Organized War to Victory, 1864–1865*, 4 vols. (New York, 1959–1971), 1–18.

decided to maintain as much pressure as possible elsewhere but to concentrate upon the destruction of the South's two field armies. He ordered simultaneous drives on Johnston in Georgia and on Lee in Virginia, both to commence during the first week of May.[50]

The twin assaults began first at the Rapidan. On May 4 the Army of the Potomac surged across the river and plunged into the Wilderness, an area of thick undergrowth and second-growth timber between Chancellorsville and Mine Run. Lee chose not to contest the crossing. Southern troops did challenge Grant's exodus through the Wilderness, however, in strength. The tangled growth minimized the weight of numbers and thus favored the Confederates, who thwarted their enemies at the two major roads and at hundreds of isolated clearings. Battle raged for two days and ended with the Southern lines intact. Previously Hooker had withdrawn after a similar blood bath at Chancellorsville, and Meade had not risked battle (Mine Run). Grant, however, determined to press the issue.

Lee felt more than knew that "those people" would try to flank his right. Thus began a race to Spotsylvania Court House, where the bloody process at Wilderness repeated itself with like results. After fighting from May 8 to 21, the Army of Northern Virginia still held the crucial road junction leading south to Richmond. Again, however, the enemy sidestepped east and pressed forward.[51]

Meanwhile the Federals had mounted a cavalry raid on Richmond. J. E. B. Stuart's Confederates had ridden to the rescue and intercepted the blue horsemen. But the action at Yellow Tavern cost the South Stuart, who received a mortal wound in the aftermath of the battle. Throughout Southern armies the cavalry had deteriorated, owing primarily to the decline in the quality of Confederate horseflesh. At Yellow Tavern, the loss of the flamboyant Stuart compounded the South's problems; in the cavalry and elsewhere many talented leaders were dead, and they were more difficult to replace than cavalry mounts.[52]

[50]See Bruce Catton, *Grant Takes Command* (Boston, 1968), pp. 104–178.

[51]Clifford Dowdey, *Lee's Last Campaign* (Boston, 1960); Edward Steere, *The Wilderness Campaign* (Harrisburg, Pa., 1960); and Freeman, *Lee's Lieutenants*, III, 342–410.

[52]On Stuart's death see John W. Thomason, Jr., *Jeb Stuart* (New York, 1930), pp. 498–501. Freeman maintains that deaths of talented commanders were crucial and that because of the attrition by June of 1864 "Lee did not have a sufficient number of qualified subordinates to maintain the discipline and to direct the operations of any Army." (*Lee's Lieutenants*, III, XIV). See also Charles W. Ramsdell, "General Robert E. Lee's Horse Supply, 1862–1865," *American Historical Review* XXXV (1930), 758–777.

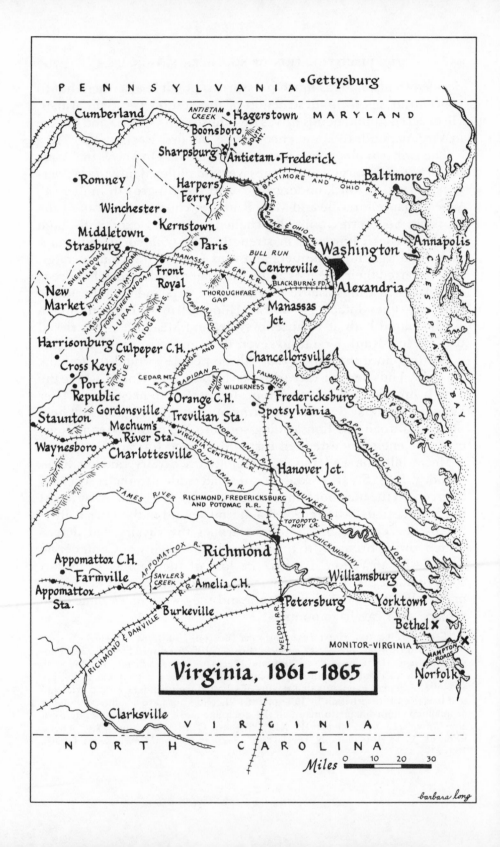

Virginia, 1861–1865

barbara long

Grant and Lee collided again at the tiny crossroads of Cold Harbor. The area had been a battlefield before, during McClellan's peninsula campaign in 1862, and in itself Second Cold Harbor was no more decisive than First Cold Harbor. This time the Federals came head on at entrenched Confederates. Fifteen minutes on June 1 essentially decided the action; men could not live on open ground in the face of men in trenches. Again the Army of Northern Virginia stoutly barred the way to Richmond, but Lee's army had been marching and fighting almost constantly for a month. The Confederates had inflicted 60,000 casualties upon their enemies, 2,000 per day, almost as many casualties as the total Southern strength. Still "those people" did not relent.

For a crucial few days Lee lost his opponent. Perhaps Stuart could have found Grant's army and discerned its intentions; perhaps not. Federal cavalry blocked all attempts on the part of Lee's horsemen to sense their enemies. Then suddenly Grant's purpose became clear. The bulk of the Federal force was crossing the James River and heading for Petersburg. Lee was not surprised; he had feared McClellan would do the same thing in 1862. Nevertheless the situation was critical, and the Army of Northern Virginia was unprepared. Petersburg was about twenty to twenty-five miles south of Richmond; should Grant be able to capture the town, he would have the Confederate capital and Lee's base of supply in a state of semi-siege. Without Petersburg, Lee and Richmond would have only one railroad in and out of the capital, and it would be a mere matter of time before Grant's host cut those tracks, too.

Lee moved troops as rapidly as possible to meet the threat to Petersburg. Beauregard was closest and on June 15 fortified the town with just 2,400 troops. On June 16, only 4,000 Confederates held out against 48,000 attackers. The numbers increased on both sides during the next two days. The Confederates held. Then Grant settled down to siege operations against Petersburg which would consume the armies on the Virginia front for almost the duration of the war. Lee had no choice but to accept the siege.[53]

In 1862, when the threat of siege was imminent, both Davis and Lee were prepared to abandon the capital in order to save the army. Now, however, the army had no hope of survival in open country;

[53]Freeman, *Lee's Lieutenants*, III, 434–514, 528–538.

the Confederates had to have trenches to offset the superior numbers against them. The Confederates had to remain in one place in
order to have logistical support; Southern supply and transportation facilities were no longer able to sustain a maneuvering field
army of any size, and Richmond had become more than a political
objective. The capital was crucial, not only as a center of war industry and a base of supply for the army, but also as the last hope for
faltering Southern national morale. Richmond had served as a military magnet before, luring enemy armies onto killing grounds in
1861, 1862, and 1863. In 1864, though, Richmond was a military
millstone around Lee's neck. The Army of Northern Virginia and
indeed the Confederacy could not live without the city. But every
day the Confederates remained in their trenches, they were accepting a war of attrition—and such a war they could not hope to win.[54]

By the time Lee and Grant settled into siege operations before
Petersburg, the campaign in the west had developed a similar pattern which, unfortunately for the Confederacy, promised similar
results. Sherman put his vast force in motion on May 7 and attempted to occupy Johnston's attention in the mountain passes
between Chattanooga and Dalton while slipping a flanking army
into the Confederate rear at Resaca. The Army of Tennessee was
dependent upon Atlanta as a base of supply and upon the Western
and Atlantic (W & A) Railroad for the transport of those supplies.
Thus Sherman and Johnston both knew that the Confederates
would have to respond to any Federal threat to the W & A and that
if the response were unsuccessful, the Army of Tennessee would
quickly become impotent. This time Johnston was too clever for
Sherman; when the Federals reached Resaca on May 14 they found
entrenched Southern troops ready to meet them.

Sherman tried again, and again Johnston was ready, at Cassville.
Then it was Johnston's turn. The Confederate general sent Polk's
corps off into the Southwest hoping to make Sherman believe that
Polk's dust represented the entire Army of Tennessee. Johnston
then entrenched his remaining corps (John Bell Hood's and William
J. Hardee's) along the route of march down the W & A tracks.
Sherman was deceived, sending Thomas and James B. McPherson

[54]Thomas, *Confederate State of Richmond*, pp. 176–178, 190–191.

after Polk's dust and leaving John M. Schofield's Army of the Ohio to continue the march down the W & A and into Johnston's trap. The Southerners had a golden opportunity to annihilate a Union army of about 17,000 men, but at the crucial juncture Hood believed the enemy was about to flank his troops and revealed his position and strength. Accordingly Sherman again concentrated his forces, and Johnston had to fall back once more.

Next Sherman abandoned the rail line and pressed his entire army westward in an effort to flank the Confederates. Once again Johnston was too quick and the armies collided at New Hope Church. The battle was inconclusive, and Sherman then fought his way back to the railroad. Finally, after days of June rains and close-quarter fighting, the Federals pushed the Southerners back to Kennesaw Mountain. On June 27, Sherman repeated Grant's mistake at Cold Harbor; he attempted to run over entrenched Confederates. The Southerners stood firm and after a bloody morning Sherman called a halt to the slaughter.[55]

Toward the middle of July, Sherman began again to test the Confederates with wide flanking movements. This time when Johnston withdrew he crossed the Chattahoochee River and formed his defensive line along Peachtree Creek on the outskirts of Atlanta. To reach this point the enemy had taken seventy-four days and suffered 25,000 casualties. As a withdrawal and delaying action, Johnston's campaign was brilliant. Yet Jefferson Davis wanted more than delay and retreat from Johnston. The President hoped for an offensive, and he did not want to lose Atlanta, the last major rail link between Richmond and the gulf South. Davis, therefore, sent Bragg as his personal representative to find out what Johnston intended to do next. Sending Bragg to inspect his old army was a bad idea, and asking Johnston for his plans only rekindled the general's suspicions of his President. The meeting between Bragg and Johnston was formally cordial but less than encouraging. Johnston was reluctant to reveal his strategy to anyone, much less to Bragg. Hence Davis decided to make a change in commanders. On July 17, Johnston received a curt telegram informing him that he was no

[55]Connelly, *Autumn of Glory*, pp. 326–360; Govan and Livingood, *A Different Valor*, pp. 261–295; Joseph E. Johnston, *Narrative of Military Operations*, ed. by Frank E. Vandiver (Bloomington, Ind., 1959), pp. 262–344.

longer in command; Johnston's replacement was Hood.[56]

John Bell Hood was a fighting general; few men questioned that. Yet many, including Lee, questioned Hood's judgment. Furthermore Hood was by this time a physical wreck. Having lost the use of both an arm and a leg, he was often in pain and had to be tied to his horse in order to ride. But Hood accepted command of the Army of Tennessee and accepted also an obvious mandate from the President for offensive action. He determined to give Davis a fight; probably he also fought to prove himself to himself and to his young love in Richmond, Sally "Buck" Preston.[57]

Just forty-eight hours after assuming command, Hood hurled his army into action. On July 20 the Confederates attempted to destroy Thomas' force as it crossed Peachtree Creek. The battle was inconclusive. Next day Hood turned about and struck McPherson's Federals as they pressed in upon Atlanta from the east. The Confederates killed McPherson, but again the battle was inconclusive. On July 28 the Southerners attacked once more, at Ezra Church, but again to no lasting effect.

After this week of furious fighting the campaign became a siege. Hood's battered troops took up positions in Atlanta's trenches, and Sherman's men began moving on the railroads which led into the city. The siege continued for a month. On August 28, Hood became aware that Sherman was about to capture the Macon Railroad line. Characteristically he led his army forth to battle; he lost at Jonesboro, and on September 2 the Federals took possession of Atlanta.[58]

[56]Connelly *Autumn of Glory*, pp. 361–416; Govan and Livingood, *A Different Valor*, pp. 295–322.

[57]Lee summarized his opinion of the situation by telegraph in four sentences: "It is a bad time to release the commander of an army situated as that of Tennessee. We may lose Atlanta and the army too. Hood is a bold fighter. I am doubtful as to other qualities necessary." Lee to Davis telegram, July 12, 1864, in Clifford Dowdey and Louis H. Manarin (eds.), *The Wartime Papers of R. E. Lee* (New York, 1961), p. 821; Connelly, *Autumn of Glory*, pp. 417–426; biographies of Hood include Richard O'Connor, *Hood: Cavalier General* (New York, 1949); and John P. Dyes, *The Gallant Hood* (Indianapolis, Ind., 1950). A recent, somewhat more charitable than traditional, interpretation of Hood's command before Atlanta is in Lt. Col. Joseph P. Mitchell's *Military Leaders of the Civil War* (New York, 1972), pp. 193–214. Hood's own story is in his memoir *Advance and Retreat*, ed. by Richard N. Current (Bloomington, Ind., 1959).

[58]Connelly, *Autumn of Glory*, pp. 429–469; Hood, *Advance and Retreat*, pp. 161–217; and Errol MacGregor Clauss, "The Atlanta Campaign 18 July–2 September, 1864," Ph.D. dissertation (Emory University, 1965).

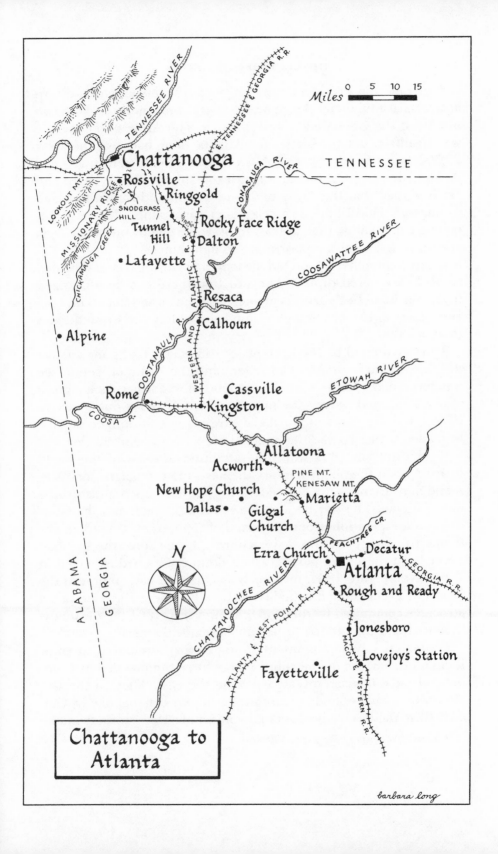

Miles
0 5 10 15

TENNESSEE RIVER

E. TENNESSEE & GEORGIA R.R.

Chattanooga

TENNESSEE

•Rossville

CONASAUGA RIVER

•Ringgold

LOOKOUT MT.

MISSIONARY RIDGE

SNODGRASS HILL

Rocky Face Ridge

Tunnel Hill

CHICKAMAUGA CREEK

•Dalton

COOSAWATTEE RIVER

ATLANTIC R.R.

•Lafayette

Resaca

•Calhoun

OOSTANAULA R.

•Alpine

WESTERN AND ATLANTIC R.R.

ETOWAH RIVER

•Cassville

Rome

•Kingston

COOSA R.

•Allatoona

Acworth

PINE MT.

KENESAW MT.

New Hope Church

Dallas•

•Marietta

Gilgal Church

PEACHTREE CR.

N

Ezra Church

•Decatur

Atlanta

GEORGIA R.R.

ALABAMA

GEORGIA

Rough and Ready

CHATTAHOOCHEE RIVER

ATLANTA & WEST POINT R.R.

•Jonesboro

•Lovejoy's Station

MACON & WESTERN R.R.

Fayetteville

Chattanooga to Atlanta

barbara long

This time the President came in person to inspect his western army. Davis found Hood prepared to fight some more, and the two discussed the Confederacy's next move. The Army of Tennessee was steadfast, but the battles for Atlanta alone had cost the army 27,500 casualties, and both Johnston's and Hood's campaigns had demonstrated that Sherman was just too strong. Hence Hood and Davis agreed that the Army of Tennessee should return home to Tennessee. Hood hoped to seize Sherman's supply line at Chattanooga and, failing that, at least to draw the enemy out of Georgia and await a favorable opportunity to fight him.[59]

In late September, Hood led the march north, and Davis returned to his beleaguered capital. The situation there was little changed from mid-June. Lee's army remained in its holes and hoped that the enemy would tire or commit a blunder enabling the Confederates to attack him.

Thus by the fall of 1864 the major campaigns had gone against the Confederacy. Atlanta had fallen, and the Army of Tennessee wandered back over the familiar ground of its former campaigns a much weakened force. Richmond survived and would survive longer, but the Army of Northern Virginia was no longer capable of maneuvering against the enemy except, in the end, to flee.

Significantly in 1864 while the attention of most of the world focused upon the major military themes—the campaigns for Richmond and Atlanta—the Confederate's war developed a disturbing minor theme. The war became base and desperate, and the baseness and desperation produced a kind of counterpoint, a sad, minor theme to accompany the major chords. To be sure, the war had never been the grand parade which Southerners had expected in 1861. Even before 1864, men such as Quantrill had embraced the aspect of premeditated brutality even as President Davis bewailed atrocities committed by the North. However in 1864 the meanness mounted and threatened to become a major theme.

On March 1 two columns of Union cavalry attempted to enter Richmond. Early in the morning a large force commanded by Colonel Judson Kilpatrick threatened from the east. Then in the late afternoon a smaller body of mounted troopers commanded by Colonel Ulric Dahlgren advanced in the midst of a sleet storm from the

[59]Connelly, *Autumn of Glory*, pp. 470–480.

west. On both occasions contingents of "home guards" drove off the raiders. The two thrusts at the city were designed to be simultaneous, and the Confederates rejoiced at their enemies' lack of coordination. A short time later more home-guard units ambushed Dahlgren's column as it attempted to reach Union lines on the peninsula. Dahlgren was killed in the first volley from the ambushers, and a small boy named William Littlepage ran from his hiding place to rifle the dead Colonel's pockets. Littlepage was looking for a pocket watch. He found none but did take Dahlgren's cigar case. When Littlepage opened the case, he discovered what appeared to be the draft of a speech from Dahlgren to his men.

We hope to release the prisoners from Belle Island [prison camp at Richmond] first, and having seen them fairly started, we will cross the James River into Richmond, destroying the bridges after us, and exhorting the released prisoners to destroy and burn the hateful city, and do not allow the Rebel leader, Davis, and his traitorous crew to escape.[60]

Richmond responded to Littlepage's discovery with righteous indignation. Newspaper editors proposed hanging the captives from Dahlgren's unit. Lee termed the raid a "barbarous and inhuman plot" and demanded an explanation from Meade. The Union general called the entire incident a hoax and protested that his army did not wage war on civilians.

On April 12, Nathan Bedford Forrest and 1,500 cavalrymen attacked 557 Federals at Fort Pillow, an earthen fort on the east bank of the Mississippi about forty miles north of Memphis. The assault easily carried the works. The Southern horsemen found that about half of the garrison force were black, and most of the other half were Tennessee Unionists. Union casualties in the action were 331, compared to 100 Confederate. Major William F. Bradford, the Federal commander, charged that the Southerners had cut down unarmed Union soldiers while they were trying to surrender. Forrest contended that those shot in the aftermath of his assault were still resisting. Whatever the precise truth of the matter, the "Fort Pillow Massacre" like Dahlgren's raid, brought

[60]Thomas, *Confederate State of Richmond*, pp. 157–160; Virgil Carrington Jones, *Eight Hours before Richmond* (New York, 1957); and J. William Jones (comp.), "The Kilpatrick-Dahlgen Raid against Richmond," *Southern Historical Society Papers*, XIII (January–December 1955), 546–560.

the war closer to the reality of "no quarter."[61]

On July 30 cavalry units of Jubal Early's command rode into Chambersburg, Pennsylvania. Early and a small army of 12,000 men had left Lee's lines in early July to attempt to duplicate Jackson's successes in the Shenandoah Valley in 1862. The Confederates were able to raise a siege at Lynchburg, march down the valley, cross into Maryland, and briefly threaten Washington. Then Early had to abandon his bluff and retreat. At Chambersburg one of Early's Confederate cavalry commanders assembled the town fathers and demanded $500,000 in currency or $100,000 in gold to settle claims against the Union for property destroyed in the Shenandoah Valley. When the residents of Chambersburg failed to raise the money, the Southerners burned the town in retaliation.[62]

On September 7, Sherman ordered all remaining residents of Atlanta to leave the city. In all, the Federals evicted about 1,600 people. Hood protested, and Confederates everywhere were indignant. Sherman replied, "If the people raise a howl against my barbarity and cruelty, I will answer that war is war and not popularity-seeking."[63]

On October 2 an outnumbered band of Confederate soldiers conducted a "miraculous" defense of the critical salt mines at Saltville in southwest Virginia. When the battle ended, however, the Southerners murdered their one hundred Federal prisoners, most of whom were black and some of whom were wounded.[64]

Perhaps, after all, Quantrill had been right—or at least prophetic

[61]On Forrest himself see Robert S. Henry, *"First with the most" Forrest* (Indianapolis, Ind., 1944); John A. Wyeth, *Life of General Nathan Bedford Forrest*, new edition (Dayton, Ohio, 1975); and Andrew N. Lytle, *Bedford Forrest and His Critter Company* (New York, 1931). On Fort Pillow see Ronald K. Hugh, "Fort Pillow Massacre: Aftermath of Paducah," *Illinois State Historical Society Journal*, LXVI (1973), 62–70; and George Bodnia (ed.), "Fort Pillow 'Massacre,' Observations of a Minnesotan," *Minnesota History*, 1973, 186–190.

[62]Jubal Anderson Early, *War Memoirs: Autobiographical Sketch and Narrative of the War between the States*, ed. by Frank Vandiver (Bloomington, Ind., 1960), pp. 401–405; and Liva Baker, "The Burning of Chambersburg," *American Heritage*, XXIV (1973), 36–39, 97.

[63]William T. Sherman, *Memoirs of General Sherman*, 2 vols. (New York, 1875), II, 111; for details of another forced evacuation see Charles R. Mink, "General Orders, No. 11: The Forced Evacuation of Civilians during the Civil War," *Military Affairs* XXXIV (1970), 132–136; and Ann Davis Niepman, "General Orders 11 and Border Warfare during the Civil War," *Missouri Historical Review* LXVI (1973), 185–210.

[64]William C. Davis, "Massacre of Saltville," *Civil War Times Illustrated*, IX (1971), X, 4–11.

—when he argued with Secretary Seddon about raising the "black flag" and proclaiming "no quarter." The "modern" war had all but eradicated the antique notions of honor and chivalry with which many Southerners entered the conflict. Yet the volume of outrage which greeted each new atrocity tale was evidence that antique notions prevailed on both sides of the Potomac.

In the South, Confederates confounded the new barbarism which marked the war in 1864; at the same time the war became most "mean," a wave of religious revivals swept Confederate armies.[65] As their young country crumbled, Confederates revealed their desperation. They seemed to seek refuge in extremes—in the brutal license of war and in the peace and righteousness which was not of their world but the next. The Southern nation and its people were coming apart.

[65]See J. William Jones, *Christ in the Camp or Religion in the Confederate Army* (Atlanta, Ga., 1904).

CHAPTER 12

Death of the Nation

THE *Alabama* was all but worn out. Its bottom was fouled, its powder indifferent, and its engines prematurely old. Raphael Semmes had taken his famous raider into port at Cherbourg for badly needed refitting in June of 1864. Before the major work could begin, however, the U.S.S. *Kearsarge* appeared at the mouth of the harbor. Semmes pondered his alternatives and decided to leave the sanctuary of his neutral port and give battle immediately. Perhaps he realized that he stood a better chance fighting one Federal ship than he would against the squadron sure to follow the *Kearsarge*. Perhaps he had a kind of romantic death wish and chose quite literally to go down in flames rather than rot at anchor in port. He wrote later that at the time he believed the two ships to be evenly matched, and thus he fought because he thought he had a good chance to win. In any event, at 9:00 A.M. on June 19 the *Alabama* steamed into the channel to challenge its enemy.

As the battle revealed, the ships were anything but evenly matched; the *Alabama* was much inferior. Moreover Captain John A. Winslow, in command of the *Kearsarge,* had installed a heavy cable-chain matting on either side of his ship to protect her vitals amidships. Semmes attempted to stay at long range, but Winslow closed on him. Southern shot bounced off the *Kearsarge*'s cable-chain armament as though the Union ship were ironclad. A shell from one of the *Alabama*'s big guns did land on the *Kearsarge*'s deck but failed to explode. All the while the enemy's fire had telling effect. In an hour it was all over. The *Alabama* began to sink. Semmes struck his colors and ordered his crew over the side. He drew his sword, hurled it defiantly into the channel, and then dove into the water himself.[1]

Early in August 1864, on Mobile Bay, Franklin Buchanan emulated Semmes' gallantry with similar results. Buchanan commanded the defenses of Mobile Bay against an invading fleet led by David Farragut. The Confederates at Mobile depended upon a series of land fortifications, a field of torpedo mines, and the ironclad ram *Tennessee* to defend themselves and the bay. On August 5, Farragut's Federals ran this gauntlet and by noon seventeen Union warships were at anchor inside Mobile Bay. Buchanan, aboard the *Tennessee*, watched the parade of enemy vessels steam through the channel amid a hail of Southern shot and shell. He reflected briefly and then ordered the *Tennessee* to charge the Union fleet. The lone Southern ship made a noble fight, but after Buchanan suffered a wound in the leg, the *Tennessee*'s smokestack lay on its deck and its steam pressure was falling rapidly. When a Union shell severed the *Tennessee*'s rudder chain and it no longer responded to the helm, the ship's captain, J. D. Johnston, raised the white flag of surrender. Buchanan, too, had gone down in flames rather than forestall inevitable defeat.[2]

Buchanan refused to meet the victorious Farragut and nursed his wound and pride aboard the *Tennessee* until the Federals moved him to a military hospital at Pensacola. Semmes was more fortunate. He was pulled from the channel by the crew from a British yacht and so escaped capture. Eventually he made his way back to Richmond in early 1865 to become an admiral with virtually no fleet. By then the South's blue-water navy consisted of one cruiser, the *Shenandoah*, which put to sea on October 8, 1864. The last significant Confederate ironclad, the *Albemarle*, went down on the night of October 27, 1864, at Plymouth, North Carolina, victim of sneak

[1]Raphael Semmes, *Service Afloat, or, The Remarkable Career of the Confederate Cruisers, Sumter and Alabama, during the War Between the States* (Baltimore, 1887), pp. 750–769; William M. Robinson, Jr., "The *Alabama-Kearsarge* Battle: A Study in Original Sources," *Essex Institute Historical Collections*, XL (1924), 97–120, 209–218; and William M. Leary, Jr., "*Alabama* versus *Kearsarge*: A Diplomatic View," *American Neptune*, XXIX (1969), 167–173. The chapter on the *Alabama-Kearsarge* battle in Norman C. Delaney, *John McIntosh Kell of the Raider* Alabama (University, Ala., 1973) is a superb account.

[2]Emory M. Thomas, "Damn the Torpedoes . . . : The Battle for Mobile Bay," *Civil War Times Illustrated*, XVI (April 1977), 5–10, 43–45.

attack by a Union torpedo launch. When Semmes assumed command of the entire Confederate Navy on February, 18, 1865, it numbered eight ships.[3]

The Confederacy, too, was sinking but still defiant. Nor was the nation's defiance limited to noble gestures. Like Semmes and Buchanan, the South as a whole seemed determined to fight its war to a conclusion—even though rational Southerners could find little reason, after the summer of 1864, to doubt that that conclusion would be defeat.

The land war went no better than the war at sea during the fall and winter. When Hood led the Army of Tennessee west into Alabama, then north into Tennessee in late September, Sherman's host followed for a time. Then on October 28 the Union commander decided to quit the chase. Ordering Thomas, whose army was at Nashville, to deal with Hood, Sherman returned with his own army of 60,000 to Atlanta, and from there on November 16 set out for the sea. He divided his force into three columns, cut his lines of communication and supply, and took the war to the people of Georgia. His troops lived off the country and destroyed just about everything of value which happened in their path—the 1864 harvest and the South's economic resources between Atlanta and Savannah. Local militia and home guards proved less than annoyances to Sherman's runaway army. Not only did Southern civilians suffer. Letters from soldiers' families who had been in Sherman's path had a profoundly demoralizing effect upon the troops of Hood's and Lee's armies. Desertions increased as men headed home to protect and feed their families.[4]

Sherman reached Savannah on December 10; the city's less than 18,000 defenders under William J. Hardee had little prospect of holding the place. Hardee did compel Sherman to fight for his supplies; the Confederates flooded the rice fields between Sherman and the sea, blocking the Federals' access to their supply ships offshore. However, on December 13 the enemy captured Fort McAllister and opened a channel for resupply through the Ogeechee

---

[3]Semmes, *Service Afloat,* pp. 799–808; J. T. Scharf, *History of the Confederate Navy* (New York, 1877), pp. 809–812; Frank J. Merli, *Great Britain and the Confederate Navy, 1861–1865* (Bloomington, Ind., 1970), 226–234; 250–259.

[4]Thomas L. Connelly, *Autumn of Glory: The Army of Tennessee, 1862–1865* (Baton Rouge, La., 1971), pp. 470–484; James F. Rhodes, "Sherman's March to the Sea," *American Historical Review,* VI (1901), 466–474.

River south of Savannah. When Sherman next threatened to close off Hardee's escape route from the city, the Confederate army abandoned Savannah and headed north. Hardee and the War Office in Richmond hoped to concentrate as many Southern troops as possible and make a stand against Sherman in the Carolinas. The hope was illusory.[5]

Meanwhile in Tennessee, Hood's troubles mounted. After Sherman returned to Georgia, the Army of Tennessee, numbering about 39,000, enjoyed initial success maneuvering in its home state against smaller contingents of Thomas' army. Hood hoped to attack and destroy elements of Thomas' force before they could concentrate at Nashville. The Confederates, however, lost a splendid opportunity to cut off and destroy Schofield's oversized corps of 34,-000 at the Battle of Spring Hill on November 29, 1864. Then Hood followed Schofield to Franklin, Tennessee, and decided that, since maneuver had failed to trap his enemies, he would launch a frontal assault and attempt to overrun them. The Union force was slightly smaller than Hood's, but it was entrenched and ready. On November 30, Hood's Southern infantry charged the Union trenches across a mile of open ground with no artillery preparation. The Battle of Franklin was slaughter; the Confederates suffered more than 6,000 casualties, including twelve general officers. In the aftermath of battle the bodies of five Southern generals, including Patrick Cleburne, lay on a single front porch, and Hood's troops had lost almost all confidence in their commander.

Nevertheless Hood, with about 31,000 survivors of Franklin, advanced on Nashville, where Thomas waited with nearly 50,000 Federals. The Confederate general hoped this time to stand on the defense, lure his enemies out of Nashville, and destroy them. Hood's hopes continued unfullfilled. Thomas took his time in preparation and then on December 15 and 16 he enveloped Hood's left flank and all but annihilated the Army of Tennessee.[6]

In mid-January 1865, Davis acceded to Hood's request to be relieved of his command. After the Battle of Nashville, however, the

[5]N. C. Hughes, Jr., "Hardee's Defense of Savannah," *Georgia Historical Quarterly*, XLVII (1963), 43–67.

[6]Connelly, *Autumn of Glory*, pp. 484–514; Stanley F. Horn, *The Decisive Battle of Nashville* (Baton Rouge, La., 1956); Thomas R. Hay, *Hood's Tennessee Campaign* (New York, 1929).

Army of Tennessee offered little in the way of resistance to further Federal conquest. About 5,000 veterans did make their way across the mountains to join the Confederates attempting to block Sherman's drive. As this remnant army marched, some of their number summarized their mood in song; to the tune of "Yellow Rose of Texas," they sang:

> And now I'm going southward;
> My heart is full of woe.
> I'm going back to Georgia
> To see my Uncle Joe.
>
> You may talk about your Beauregard
> And sing of General Lee,
> But the Gallant Hood of Texas
> Played Hell in Tennessee.[7]

"Uncle Joe" Johnston returned to command, at the behest of Lee, whom Congress made commanding general of all Confederate armies on February 6, 1865. The appointment was testimony to faith in Lee's ability and also was tantamount to a vote of no confidence in the President's capacity to fill the role of commander-in-chief. Davis had tried to unify military command in himself, and although he had done so to a greater degree than his enemies, the Southern President had failed as war leader, if only because he was losing the war. Congress, therefore, tried to buoy Southern morale and unify command at the same time by making Lee a supreme commander. Too late—"Uncle Joe" was not in Georgia now; Johnston's command numbered only 17,000, and it confronted Sherman's 60,000 in the Carolinas. On February 22, 1865, the same day Johnston received orders, the Confederacy's last major port, Wilmington, North Carolina, fell. By this time Charleston was gone and Columbia was a smoldering ruin; both had fallen on the seventeenth. Johnston resumed command against Sherman on February 25 and promised little. He suggested that Lee send half his army in an attempt to strike a decisive blow against Sherman, but Lee pointed out that the remaining half of the Army of Northern Virginia would then be defenseless against Grant. Both Lee and Johnston hoped for a concentration against Sherman later on; but considerations of

[7]Stanley F. Horn, *The Army of Tennessee* (Norman, Okla., 1953), p. 418.

grand strategy seemed more and more to be merely dictated responses to the Federal initiative. Consequently Johnston continued only to harass Sherman as best he could while the Confederacy shrank before the Union advance.[8]

Still, Lee's Army of Northern Virginia maintained its precarious perimeter around Richmond and Petersburg. Life in the trenches was hard enough in summer when the sun baked the inhabitants; in winter rain, cold, and hunger made the ordeal much harder. Battle action compounded the difficulty while sharpshooters and artillery barrages reduced death to an impersonal affair of fate. Lieutenant Fred Fleet wrote his sister in late December from his "bombproof," in which water stood "an inch or two deep on the floor." He wrote of a comrade who, like himself, "had just written a letter to his sister." He "sealed it up, when, as he was standing in his tent a ball came through and entered his head just behind his left ear and came out at his right eye, killing him instantly. . . . Ah! we soon become hardened to such scenes. Scarcely a day passes that some one in this Brigade is not killed or wounded."[9]

Throughout the weary months from the summer of 1864 to the spring of 1865 the two armies probed and patroled. All-out assaults upon isolated sectors of the trench lines sometimes advanced the attackers a few hundred yards if successful and often inspired counterattacks which restored the original positions. Eventually the trench networks extended for fifty miles around Petersburg and continued north of the James as a series of earthen forts east of Richmond. For the most part Lee's army endured. Yet misery, hunger, death, and plaintive letters from home drove many to abandon the cause and desert. During one five-week period almost 8 percent (2,934) of the army's effective total disappeared. And all the while Grant's relentless pressure stretched the thin line of Southern earth and men ever thinner.[10]

In the Shenandoah Valley, Jubal Early had more than his share of

[8]John G. Barrett, *Sherman's March Through the Carolinas* (Chapel Hill, N.C., 1956); Connelly, *Autumn of Glory*, pp. 517–526; Allan Nevins, *The War for the Union; The Organized War to Victory, 1864–1865* (New York, 1971), pp. 261–262.

[9]Betsy Fleet and John D. P. Fuller (eds.), *Green Mount: A Virginia Plantation Family during the Civil War*, (Lexington, Ky., 1962), p. 351.

[10]Douglas S. Freeman, *Lee's Lieutenants: A Study in Command*, 3 vols. (New York, 1942–1944), III, 528–546, 588–636; Joseph P. Cullen, "The Siege of Petersburg," *Civil War Times Illustrated*, IX (August 1970), 26.

troubles upon his return from the raid on Washington. Union General Phillip Sheridan's reinforced cavalry first chased Early's small army, then at Cedar Creek on October 19 fought and all but annihilated the Confederates. Sheridan, in the fall of 1864, conducted in the Valley the same kind of inverse "scorched-earth" campaign that Sherman employed in Georgia. The Federals burned the recent harvest and hanged local bushwhackers who dared oppose their activities. Sheridan's tactics, like Sherman's, produced bitterness and hatred among the Southern victims. The tactics of "total war" also produced despair and weakened the Southern will to continue the struggle to be a nation.[11]

Clearly the Confederacy was losing its war. And behind the battle lines the Southern nation underwent a disintegration parallel to that taking place on its battlefields.

With good reason the Southern people despaired: their sacrifices of blood and treasure seemed to have yielded only disaster. In ever growing numbers in 1864 the Confederates reconciled themselves to defeat and reunion with their Northern enemies. Nor was this a mental and emotional process only; during the fall and winter of 1864 many Confederate Southerners expressed their defeatism in deeds. Soldiers in increasing numbers deserted the colors and returned home. The Conscript Bureau was unable to find replacements for them and in early 1865 Congress abolished the bureau altogether. The peoples' loss of faith in the nation was also reflected in their declining faith in the national currency. Between January 1864 and January 1865 the price of gold more than doubled, and by March 1865 a gold dollar was worth up to seventy dollars in Confederate script. In Richmond the collapse of civilian morale found tangible expression in a mood of "eat, drink, and be merry." Citizens of the capital prepared for the coming deluge with a frenzy of merrymaking. To the dismay of the city's more sober-sided residents, the number of parties and marriages seemed to increase in direct proportion to the decline in the nation's military fortunes. Outside of the capital Southerners expressed their despair by resisting taxes, hiding their livestock and produce from im-

[11]Freeman, *Lee's Lieutenants*, III, 557–587, 595–612. See also Richard H. O'Connor, *Sheridan the Inevitable* (Indianapolis, Ind., 1953); Edward J. Stackpole, *Sheridan in the Shenandoah: Jubal Early's Nemesis* (Harrisburg, Pa. 1961).

pressment officers and tax-in-kind collectors, and damning the government which had led them into such folly.[12]

The activities of the Confederate government, too, became both cause and effect of the South's impending national doom. President Davis responded to the growing crisis by making optimistic public statements and by adopting a studied business-as-usual approach to governmental affairs. Davis also convinced himself and tried to convince others that the Confederacy needed no stable land base and that even should Federal troops overrun all his armies, the Southern nation would prevail in the continued resistance of its people.[13]

More and more, however, through enemy action and through the disaffection of the Southern people, the Confederacy fragmented. Increasingly Richmond became a kind of city-state polis, isolated even from portions of the Southland not yet in enemy hands. The trans-Mississippi had for some time been outside Richmond's direct sphere of influence. Edmund Kirby Smith all but administered the region civilly and militarily as Roman provincial governor. The loss of Chattanooga and Atlanta further fragmented the South, not only from a military perspective, but also from the standpoint of governmental administration. Then when Sherman marched to the sea and began to move northward through South Carolina, the Confederacy contracted still further. Senators and congressmen without constituencies met in Richmond and lived as exiles from their homes. The government survived in an unreal isolation from the nation it supposedly served.[14]

[12]Bell I. Wiley, *The Road to Appomattox*, Atheneum edition (New York, 1968), pp. 70–75; Albert Burton Moore, *Conscription and Conflict in the Confederacy* (New York, 1924), pp. 336–353; Emory M. Thomas, *The Confederate State of Richmond: A Biography of the Capital* (Austin, Tex., 1971), pp. 181–187; Richard Cecil Todd, *Confederate Finance* (Athens, Ga., 1954), p. 197; Ella Lonn, *Desertion During the Civil War* (New York, 1928).

[13]To Congress Davis said on November 7, 1864, "The truth so patent to us must ere long be forced upon the reluctant Northern mind. There are no vital points on the preservation of which the continued existence of the Confederacy depends. There is no military success of the enemy which can accomplish its [the Confederacy's] destruction. Not the fall at Richmond, nor Wilmington, nor Charleston, nor Savannah, nor Mobile, nor of all combined, can save the enemy from the constant and exhaustive drain of blood and treasure which must continue until he shall discover that no peace is attainable unless based on the recognition of our indefeasible rights." James D. Richardson (ed.), *A Compilation of the Messages and Papers of the Confederacy*, 2 vols. (Nashville, Tenn., 1906), I, 484–485.

[14]Thomas, *Confederate State of Richmond*, p. 191.

Congress held two sessions during the Confederacy's final months of life. In the midst of crisis, however, the solons often wrangled over petty matters and seemed powerless to consider remedies for their nation's crisis. Texas Senator Wigfall, for example, bent much of his energies to the task of humbling President Davis. Wigfall and his opposition thwarted Davis for the sake of thwarting him, and their finest hour came on January 31, 1865, when they finally overrode a Presidential veto. The bill was almost inconsequential—it permitted newspapers to send their editions to soldiers free of charge—but Wigfall had had his triumph.

Representative Henry S. Foote from Tennessee decided during the last session of Congress to make his own separate peace with the enemy. Foote set out for Washington but suffered the ignominy of capture and return. Then Congress suffered the ignominy of censuring one of its members for attempting to flee to the enemy.[15]

The President's cabinet was not much more stable than the Congress. Memminger left the Treasury Office in July 1864, to be replaced by another South Carolinian, George Trenholm. The new secretary advocated ever more stringent taxes and used his background and connections in the import-export firm of Frazier and Trenholm to open negotiations for a foreign loan. Nevertheless Trenholm faced an impossible task, and his efforts were no more successful than Memminger's had been.[16]

Late in January 1865, War Secretary Seddon resigned under pressure. Foote had accused Seddon of war profiteering on sales of grain to the government; the charges were false, but the episode did not bolster Seddon's reputation. Since Bragg had come to Richmond, Seddon's influence with Davis had declined apace, and Seddon, too, from his vantage point in the War Office, was fully aware of the desperate straits in which the Confederacy found itself. The final straw in Seddon's resolve snapped when a delegation from the Virginia General Assembly requested Davis to ask his entire cabinet to resign in an effort to restore some of the nation's morale. Seddon

[15]Alvy L. King, *Louis T. Wigfall: Southern Fire-Eater* (Baton Rouge, La., 1920), pp. 200–202; Wilfred Buck Yearns, *The Confederate Congress* (Athens, Ga., 1960), p. 182; *Journal of the Congress of the Confederate States of America, 1861–1865,* 7 vols. (Washington, D.C., 1904–1905), VII, 458, 465, 466, 490–492.

[16]Rembert W. Patrick, *Jefferson Davis and His Cabinet* (Baton Rouge, La., 1944), pp. 234–243; B. S. Baruc to Trenholm, December 9, 1864, and Trenholm to Baruc, December 13, 1864, Trenholm Papers, Library of Congress, Washington, D.C.

chose to make an issue of the request and view the no-confidence action on the part of his own state's legislature as a personal affront.[17]

On February 6, 1865, Davis nominated John C. Breckinridge to replace Seddon. Breckinridge came to the War Office from field command. When from the inside he discovered the sad state of the department, the armies, and the government, the new secretary of war began to advocate peace. Breckinridge presided faithfully over his department until the end; his own advice, though, was immediate surrender.

With Wigfall in the lead, Congress now sought to save the country by trying to limit the President's prerogative; part of this tactic involved attacks upon Davis' advisors. In the face of the pressure, cabinet members slipped into deeper despondency. Judah Benjamin offered to resign if Davis believed the resignation would improve the administration's political posture; Davis did not, so Benjamin, too, remained to the end.[18]

Even before the fall of 1864, it was apparent to most Southerners that the Confederacy was fatally ill. The navy was merely a token force. Hood had wasted an army which had little or no chance of victory anyway. Neither Johnston nor anyone else believed he could impede Sherman's advance through the Carolinas. Lee's army persisted but grew weaker as the enemy grew stronger. Sherman and Sheridan had laid waste some of the South's finest farmland and imposed submission wherever their armies marched. Civilian morale and support for the nation was collapsing irrevocably, and the government was unable to govern most of the area over which it still claimed sovereignty. In this crisis Congress turned its wrath, not upon the enemy, but upon the Davis administration. The President himself remained steadfast; but as the cabinet, Congress, army, navy, and country crumbled, the Confederacy was clearly half dead.

Yet, even though they were engaged in campaigns which hindsight reveals lost the war, Confederate soldiers still distinguished themselves during that final season of combat. Although many succumbed to defeatism and deserted, many more remained dutifully at their posts, and those who did remain quite often carried on the war with courage and even with some success.

[17]Patrick, *Davis and His Cabinet,* pp. 145–149.
[18]*Ibid.,* pp. 149–154, 199–200.

In the trans-Mississippi, for example, the Confederates foiled the major Federal campaign in the region in 1864. In March Union General Nathaniel Banks had attempted to press a massive amphibious force up the Red River into northern Louisiana. Southern troops under the command of Richard Taylor defeated Bank's army at the battles of Sabine Crossroads and Pleasant Hill on April 8 and 9 and drove them into headlong retreat. Even so, Taylor was not satisfied and complained that had departmental commander Smith been willing to concentrate his forces, the victory would have become an annihilation.[19] Johnston's withdrawal in North Georgia, Lee's battles in the Wilderness and at Spotsylvania Court House, and Beauregard's defense of Petersburg were further examples of skill and resourcefulness. More such examples came from the record of Nathan Bedford Forrest's cavalry, which won some of its greatest victories during the Confederacy's darkest hours. Forrest and his troopers fought and raided with spirit and success throughout this period of general gloom and in so doing tied down Union forces many times their size attempting to trap "that devil Forrest." At Johnsonville, Tennessee, on November 4, for example, Forrest's naval-cavalry (they had a captured gunboat in tow) shelled a Federal supply depot on the Tennessee River and destroyed an estimated $6.7 million worth of war materiel en route to Thomas' army at Nashville. Although the troopers had to abandon their gunboat, Forrest led them away unscathed to join Hood's army for the ill-fated Tennessee campaign.[20] In the east, John Mosby's rangers continued their partisan tactics in northern Virginia. On October 14, even as Sheridan was preparing to subdue "Mosby's Confederacy," the Southern irregulars swooped down upon a United States mail train at Duffield Station near Harpers Ferry. Mosby and his men destroyed the train and relieved the Union paymasters aboard of $168,000 in greenbacks. Through the fall and winter Mosby's band continued to be a thorn in the side of the invading army.[21]

In Lee's army, too, the final months had their moments of glory.

[19]See Ludwell H. Johnson, *Red River Campaign: Politics and Cotton in the Civil War* (Baltimore, 1958).

[20]Robert S. Henry, *"First With the Most" Forrest* (Indianapolis, Ind., 1944), pp. 366-381.

[21]John S. Mosby, *The Memoirs of Colonel John S. Mosby*, ed. by Charles W. Russell (Boston, 1917); Major John Scott, *Partisan Life with Col. John S. Mosby* (New York, 1867), pp. 334-339.

The Confederates not only held out against an enemy with twice their numbers; as late as March 25, 1865, they were able to mount an attack which for a few hours cleared the enemy trench line for a space of three-quarters of a mile. And even as Lee's cavalry grew smaller in numbers and weaker in quality horseflesh, Wade Hampton's troopers, on September 16, 1864, conducted the "great beefsteak raid." The Southerners attacked a well-defended Union camp and drove 2,500 cattle back into Confederate lines to help feed their comrades.[22]

At Fort Fisher, which guarded the entrance to the Cape Fear River and the port of Wilmington, five hundred Confederates beat off a massive Federal assault force composed of sixty ships and a field army in late December 1864. When the Federals finally did capture the fort on January 15, 1865, one Virginian planter-doctor remarked that the fall of Wilmington would be "of signal benefit." Blockade running, Dr. Benjamin Fleet believed, had drained too much gold from the Confederacy. "When all our seaport towns are taken," he asserted, "I presume the war will have begun in real earnest."[23]

The Army of Tennessee under Johnston even won a final victory against Sherman. At Bentonville, North Carolina, in late March 1865, these Confederates, in their last major battle, were able to break the enemy line and stop most of Sherman's army in its tracks for three days.[24]

If removed from the context of ultimate defeat, these actions might rank among the finest hours of Southern arms. Though the Confederacy was losing the war during 1864 and 1865, Southern commanders were still resourceful, and Southern soldiers still won victories. And on the home front, as well as on the battlefield, the Confederacy threw off sparks of life to the end. Amid disintegration and declining morale, Confederates still attempted to cope with their fate and to respond positively to the deepening crisis. Behind the ever-contracting battle lines the Southern nation was half alive.

[22]Freeman, *Lee's Lieutenants*, III, 637–654; 590 and n.

[23]Pa to Fred, January 19, 1865, in Fleet and Fuller (eds.), *Green Mount*, p. 356; Charles L. Price and Claude C. Sturgill, "Shock and Assault in the First Battle of Fort Fisher," *North Carolina Historical Review*, XLVII (1970), 24–39.

[24]Connelly, *Autumn of Glory*, pp. 526–529; Wade Hampton, "The Battle of Bentonville," Clarence C. Buel and Robert U. Johnson (eds.), *Battles and Leaders of the Civil War*, 4 vols. (New York, 1881–1883), pp. 701–705.

When Jefferson Davis opened the final session of the Confederate Congress on November 7, 1864, his message contained much that the members expected to hear. He made the best of the military situation and asked for more troops. As anticipated, he asked for revisions in the tax law and remedies to the inflationary spiral in Confederate money. Yet to his Congress the President offered one program which took it by complete surprise and with good reason. Davis proposed nothing less radical than a limited form of emancipation for Southern blacks.[25]

The President prefaced his proposal with the observation that congressional authorization to employ slaves in noncombatant military services had been less successful than anticipated. Rather than tinker with the act to try to improve it, Davis now suggested "a radical modification in the theory of law." The President pointed out that slaves "viewed merely as property" were and had been subject to impressment for short periods of labor in the construction of field fortifications. Then he went to the core of his argument: "The slave," he said, "bears another relation to the State—that of a person." What the Confederacy now needed, Davis contended, was the service of the slave as person. The military duties, although noncombatant, required instruction and extended terms of service. Because of the hazards involved those duties also demanded "loyalty and zeal." Thus, the President concluded, "the relation of person predominates . . . and it would seem proper to acquire for the public service the entire property in the slave, and to pay therefor due compensation rather than to impress his labor for short terms."

If the government bought these slaves, how should it own them? "Should he the slave be retained in servitude, or should his emancipation be held out to him as a reward for faithful service, or should it be granted at once on the promise of such service?" The President favored what he described as the middle ground. "The policy of engaging to liberate the negro on his discharge after service faithfully rendered seems to me preferable to that of granting immediate manumission, or that of retaining him in servitude."[26]

Davis asked therefore that Congress authorize the government to purchase 40,000 slaves under the terms he outlined. In effect he was

[25]Davis to Congress, November 7, 1864, Richardson (ed.), *Messages and Papers*, pp. 482–498.
[26]*Ibid.*, pp. 493–496.

requesting, not only a military work force, but also permission to embark upon a program of compensated emancipation. For the moment the President shrank from asking for authorization to employ blacks as soldiers, but he did not rule out that possibility. "Until our white population shall prove insufficient for the armies we require and can afford to keep in the field, to employ as a soldier the negro . . . would scarcely be deemed wise or advantageous. . . . But should the alternative ever be presented of subjugation or of the employment of the slave as soldier, there seems no reason to doubt what should then be our decision."[27]

However practical and expedient Davis' suggestions sounded, they threatened to undermine the remaining remnant of the antebellum Southern ideology. Already the Confederate experience had compelled Southerners to compromise and discard much of their cherished way of life. Now the President asked for a sizable chip of what many Southerners regarded as the cornerstone of their national culture. Davis wanted Confederate Southerners to compromise and perhaps eventually sacrifice their peculiar institution for the sake of national survival. The President's request was the opening round of a national debate within the Confederacy on the proposition of emancipation versus independence. The debate was destined to continue until the Confederacy was no more. Thus while dying, the Southern nation persisted in trying to define its national life.[28]

Davis' request to Congress was not exactly a trial balloon dispatched to test the sentiment of the country. Already the issue of arming and emancipating Southern slaves had received considerable publicity. In September 1864, Northern newspapers had published a captured letter from Louisiana Governor Henry W. Allen in which Allen stated, "The time has come for us to put into the army every able-bodied negro man as a soldier."[29] A month later the powerful Richmond *Enquirer* called in strident terms for the use of black troops. "We believe," the editor explained, "that the negroes, identified with us by interest, and fighting for their free-

27 *Ibid.*

28 The existence and significance of this debate are the themes of Robert F. Durden, *The Gray and the Black: The Confederate Debate on Emancipation* (Baton Rouge, La., 1972). See especially vii–viii.

29 Henry W. Allen to James A. Seddon, September 26, 1864, cited in Durden, *Gray and the Black*, p. 74.

dom here, would be faithful and reliable soldiers."[30] In the days which followed, the Lynchburg *Virginian* and the Mobile *Register* endorsed the *Enquirer*'s proposal. That same month governors of Virginia, North Carolina, South Carolina, Georgia, Alabama, and Mississippi met in Augusta and adopted a resolution calling for a "change of policy" regarding the use of slaves in the "public service." These indications of public opinion and some negative response—most notably from the Charleston *Mercury* and William W. Holden's *North Carolina Standard*—served as prologue to Davis' action when Congress convened.[31]

Earlier in the year Davis had muzzled Cleburne's Memorial and shut off debate within the army on the topic of arming and freeing the slaves. Now amid a growing volume of rhetoric on the same subject, the Confederate President acted. He made a tentative beginning at becoming "the great emancipator" for Southern blacks.

For the moment the President's bid was in vain. The Confederate Congress effectively buried President Davis' military labor and emancipation proposal by the evasive device of patching up the original Military Laborers Act of February 17, 1864. In the meantime, however, the debate swept past the merits of Davis' November 7 suggestion. The immediate issue quickly became whether or not to arm the slaves, and every new indication of the South's military decline during the fall and winter of 1864–1865 impelled Confederates to confront that issue. Beyond the immediate matter of tapping the South's last source of military manpower, however, lay a more fundamental question. If black men could be soldiers in the South, then they could never again be considered less than men; they could never again be slaves. At base the debate over arming the slaves was a debate over the South's entire racial attitude.

Howell Cobb said it best. He had had a frustrating Confederate career as—more or less—a "political general." Now commander of Georgia's reserve forces, he wrote to War Secretary Seddon in early January 1865 pleading with the administration to abandon the effort to arm the slaves. "The day you make soldiers of them," Cobb insisted, "is the beginning of the end of the revolution. If slaves will make good soldiers our whole theory of slavery is wrong." Cobb did not believe that slaves could make good soldiers and advised Sed-

[30]Cited in *ibid.*, p. 75.
[31]*Ibid.*, pp. 75–100.

don to "purchase" the aid of England and France by emancipation before resorting to black troops.[32]

However wrong Cobb was in his racial preconceptions, he perceived the real issue. Nor was he the only Southerner to see that the Confederacy was debating far more than a military expedient. Confederates divided on the issue in rough accord with their response to the Confederate experience. Those who had most resisted expedient change in the wartime South lined up on the side of the racial status quo. Those most caught up in the positive aspects of the Confederate experience were also most ready to alter the South's racial mores in the hope of independence.

The emancipation debate raged publicly in newspaper editorials and correspondence, in legislative debates, at mass meetings of concerned citizens, and in political speeches. The immediate response to Davis' November 7 address to Congress was a barrage of heavy attacks in the columns of some of the Confederacy's most influential newspapers. In Richmond the *Examiner* led the charge, followed closely by the *Whig* and the *Dispatch;* in Charleston, both the *Mercury* and the *Courier* opposed the direction of the President's policy. Yet the proposal attracted vigorous defenders, too; the Richmond *Enquirer* supported the measure, as did the Richmond *Sentinel,* the Mobile *Register,* and the Wilmington *Journal.*[33]

The issue divided Confederate leaders as well. Cabinet members, with Benjamin in the lead, generally favored arming the slaves, although Seddon was less than enthusiastic. They were joined by Governors Allen of Louisiana and William Smith of Virginia. Among more vocal opponents of the ploy were powerful Governors Joe Brown of Georgia and Zebulon Vance of North Carolina. Perhaps most formidable in the opposition was R. M. T. Hunter, senator from Virginia and president pro tem. of the Confederate Senate. Sooner or later the issue would require congressional action, and Hunter was a powerful obstacle to that action.[34]

The debate continued on hypothetical and theoretical levels during the last two months of 1864. Then, with the fall of Savannah and Hood's failure in Tennessee, the nation's military position went

[32]Howell Cobb to James A. Seddon, January 8, 1865, cited in *ibid.,* pp. 183–185.
[33]*Ibid.,* 106–161.
[34]*Ibid.,* 181–183, 193–195, 74, 253, 143–146, 183–185, 250–253, 138, 202–203, 206–207, 242–249; Yearns, *Confederate Congress* 95–99.

from grave to desperate, and President Davis determined to take personal action. Late in December he called in Louisiana Congressman Duncan F. Kenner, who for some time had tried to convince the President that slavery was the major stumbling block in the way of Southern independence. Now that Davis had converted to Kenner's view, he asked the Louisianian to undertake a secret mission to Britain and France. Kenner would propose emancipation to the powers in exchange for their recognition. Kenner agreed and traveled to Wilmington in time to witness the fall of Fort Fisher and the closing of the port. Undaunted, he slipped through the battle lines and sailed to Europe from New York in late January.

In Paris, Kenner delivered his message indirectly to Napoleon III, and the Emperor responded that he would follow the lead of England. In London, Kenner's offer received a firm rebuff; again by indirect communication, Palmerston informed the Confederate that Great Britain would under no circumstances recognize the South as a nation. The Kenner mission was a desperate hope; there was no reason to expect anything from it. The mission did reveal, however, the state of Davis' and Benjamin's thinking at the time regarding the primacy of independence over all other considerations.[35]

Hints of the secret mission on which Kenner had embarked stimulated the emancipation debate in the South during January. Then in early February an event unrelated to the substance of the debate triggered the Confederates' decision on the matter.

Many of those Southerners who believed that emancipation was too radical a departure from the Southern status quo had pinned their hopes and arguments upon the possibility of a negotiated peace with the United States. Such a peace, they hoped without rational basis, might preserve the South's national identity and slavery as well. In all probability Jefferson Davis realized the futility of attempting to negotiate peace with an all but victorious enemy. Nevertheless he decided to try—perhaps in the same way that he decided to try the Kenner mission.

Through the good offices of Francis Preston Blair, Sr., scion of a Maryland political family, Davis and Lincoln agreed to a discussion of peace on February 3 aboard the steamboat *River Queen* in Hampton Roads. Blair spoke to Davis of a military alliance between North

[35]Durden, *Gray and the Black*, pp. 147–156; D. P. Crook, *The North, the South, and the Powers 1861–1865* (New York, 1974), pp. 356–358.

and South to uphold the Monroe Doctrine against France in Mexico; Lincoln, although he must have known Blair was trying to arrange a peace conference, surely had no knowledge of the Mexican scheme. Lincoln attended the conference in person accompanied by Secretary of State Seward. Significantly Davis did not attend; instead he sent Vice-President Stephens, Senator Hunter, and former supreme court justice from Alabama John A. Campbell. Stephens and Hunter were Davis' political opponents. Campbell was assistant secretary of war in addition to being a would-be peacemaker. Did Davis choose his representatives because he wished them to realize the folly of believing the war might end short of independence or unconditional surrender? Perhaps. At any rate the President made independence his only demand. Lincoln's demand was reunion; and the Hampton Roads Conference quickly reached an impasse. The five men met for some time, and discussions were cordial. Yet they never could surmount the fundamental barrier erected by the two presidents.[36]

Reaction to the failure of the Hampton Roads Conference in the South revealed the depth of many Confederates' faith in a negotiated peace. When the peace conference shattered that faith by demonstrating the lack of anything to negotiate, Southerners responded with a final surge of national fervor. Mass meetings held in Richmond, Mobile, Lynchburg, and elsewhere stirred a renewed patriotism. And one of the chief measures advocated at these mass meetings was arming the slaves for the salvation of the war effort.[37]

At this juncture the administration decided the time was right for Congressional action. Davis had proposed a halfway measure in November, then acted covertly in dispatching Kenner to Europe in December. On February 10, Congressman Ethelbert Barksdale of Mississippi introduced what became the administration bill to arm the slaves. The Virginia legislature was considering similar action, and from a military perspective the time seemed now or never.[38]

A few days earlier Congress had taken some pride in providing a new command for Robert E. Lee, commanding general of all

[36]See Ludwell H. Johnson, "Lincoln's Solution to the Problem of Peace Terms, 1864–1865," *Journal of Southern History*, XXXIV (1968), 576–586; Paul J. Zingg, "John Archibald Campbell and the Hampton Roads Conference: Quixotic Diplomacy, 1865," *Alabama Historical Quarterly*, XXXVI (1974), 21–34.
[37]Durden, *Gray and the Black*, pp. 187–198.
[38]*Ibid.*, pp. 202–203.

Confederate armies. Naturally, when the bill to authorize black troops came before Congress, Lee's opinion was crucial. Indeed for some time both proponents and opponents of the measure had sought guidance from Lee. To this point, however, the General had believed that he should remain silent on a question of politics.

Mounting pressure and his new responsibilities now drove Lee into the open. First privately, then publicly, he endorsed the measure; in a more or less open letter to Congress addressed to Barksdale on February 18, Lee asserted that blacks would make "efficient" soldiers and expressed his opinion that they should fight as free men, not slaves.[39]

From officers and men in Lee's army came other endorsements of the plan to arm the slaves. Virginia Military Institute (VMI) offered to help train black recruits, and in the face of such approval in the army, the *Examiner* and *Whig* newspapers changed their editorial stance. Still Congress delayed action. Not until March 13 did Congress pass the Act to Increase the Military Force of the Confederate States, and even that action was equivocal. The final section included the provision "that nothing in this act shall be construed to authorize a change in the relation which the said slaves shall bear toward their owners." The Confederate Congress agreed to arm the slaves (by one vote in the Senate) but not to emancipate them.[40]

Virginia's General Assembly had already endorsed the measure on March 4 and 5 and resolved to offer slaves in the state to the army, but again, the legislators did not endorse emancipation. It was left to President Davis and his War Office to close the emancipation debate; they did so by bureaucratic fiat. General Order Number Fourteen was the adjutant and inspector general's implementation of Congress' law, and that directive contained two crucial sentences which transformed an ambiguous public law into a radical public policy. "No slave will be accepted as a recruit unless with his own consent and with the approbation of his master by a written instrument conferring, as far as he may, the rights of a freedman." Black troops in Confederate armies would serve not as slaves or even with the hope of future emancipation; they were to serve as free men. And more, "All officers . . . are enjoined to a provident, considerate, and humane attention to whatever concerns the health, comfort,

[39] *Ibid.*, pp. 204–209.
[40] *Ibid.*, pp. 199–202, 215–224.

instruction, and discipline of these troops, and to the uniform ob-
servance of kindness, forbearance, and indulgence in their treatment of them, and especially that they will protect them from injus-
tice and oppression." However paternalistic was the tone of this
provision, it prescribed equal treatment for black soldiers.[41]

By March 23, 1865, when the War Office issued General Order
Number Fourteen, the Confederacy had little time left to live.
Nevertheless the recruiting and training of black Confederates went
forward, and on March 25 newspapers in Richmond reported the
formation of the first black company under the new law. The *Dispatch* with "no hesitation" stated that black troops displayed at drill
"as much aptness and proficiency . . . as is usually shown by any
white troops we have ever seen."[42] At this point Richmond had just
over one week of life as the Confederate capital. Like many other
Confederate concessions to reality, Southern leaders made the decision to recruit black soldiers too late. The wonder was, however,
that the Confederates made the decision at all.[43]

During the South's last several months of national existence, the
Confederacy hovered between life and death. In a very real sense
Southerners were undergoing a final fling at defining themselves as
a people. Both those who accepted the South's death as a nation and
those who persisted in clinging to national life contributed to this
process of Southern self-discovery. In so doing they simply carried
to conclusion the search for Southern identity which had already
characterized much of the Confederate experience.

In the beginning the Confederate South was a cause, the sanctifi-
cation of the Old South status quo. Because the South began as a
section instead of a nation, the cause of Southern nationalism most
often found negative expression within the United States. In 1861,
however, the cause was incarnate. The Confederacy was the political
expression of Southern nationalism and the logical extension of
ante-bellum Southern ideology. At that point the process of positive
identification began.

At first, while the South's political leaders formed a national government and girded for a war of national survival, the Confederacy

[41]*Ibid.*, pp. 249–250, 268–269.
[42]*Ibid.*, pp. 274–275; Thomas, *Confederate State of Richmond*, pp. 189–190.
[43]Robert Durden's conclusion (*Gray and the Black*, pp. 289–290) is at some variance
with the view expressed here and drawn much from his evidence.

was essentially a national replica of the sectional status quo. And in July of 1861 the Confederates confirmed their static self-image at the First Battle of Manassas. Up to that point the Confederate South was a republic of slaveholders, a "peculiar people" whose political economy and whose social and cultural mores had been grafted to the superstructure of a nation.

During the months which followed the triumph at Manassas, however, the war experience began to test and temper the new nation. By the spring of 1862 the Confederacy had been tried and found wanting. The Southern nation had suffered a series of shocks and setbacks which threatened its continued existence. Then, when their national experiment seemed almost a failure, Confederate Southerners began to respond to their circumstance by redefining themselves—or, more precisely, by defining themselves as a national people. The war did not permit sage debate by learned men about the Southern soul; the pressure of time and the pace of events demanded that Confederate Southerners define themselves in deeds. Accordingly the Confederacy acted out its national identity.

In many respects the Southern nationalism of the Confederacy resembled that of the United States from which the Southerners were trying so desperately to separate. The administration of Jefferson Davis reversed the state rights political philosophy which had called it into being and bade fair to make the Confederacy a centralized, national state. Draft laws, impressment, confiscatory taxation, habeas corpus suspension, economic management, and more affronted the South's state rights tradition.

Southerners entered the Confederacy asserting that cotton was king. Before long they began to wonder with the editor of the *Southern Literary Messenger,* "Yes, Cotton is King, but I often times fear the King he resembles is possibly—Lear."[44] The demands of "modern" war dethroned not only King Cotton but a great deal of the South's agrarian enthusiasm as well. The Confederacy's economic emphasis was industrial and centrally organized from the top, the War Department. Confederate war industry sustained the South's war effort. Agriculture not only lost priority in the Confederate mind; it failed the test of war. For a number of reasons rebel armies usually ran out of butter before they ran out of guns.

[44]*Southern Literary Messenger,* XXXVII (1863), 286.

The Confederate experience upset many of the old saws about class and hierarchy in the South. The so-called solid South came unhinged amid bread riots, strikes, and dissent. War compelled the planters to reconfirm their pretensions to social leadership and forced the slaveholding class to assert its leadership on the field as well as in the fields. Too, the unsettling ways of war brought many "new people" to the fore who might have remained anonymous in peacetime.

Even though the "work ethic" held little sway among the rebels, certainly the Confederate South was not leisured. Romanticism came hard to a people involved in the reality of war. Drill sergeants and bureaucrats at least circumscribed Southerns' vaunted individualism. Southern belles came off their pedestals and labored in hospitals and factories for the cause. In short Confederate Southerners gave up, in one way or another, most of those characteristics that they had called the Confederacy into being to protect.

By the fall of 1864 little was left to sacrifice, and many Southerners despaired. Yet even as the nation came apart and some Southerners ceased to resist their enemies, the Confederacy lived on in the steadfastness of its soldiers and the energy of national debate over slavery. In the end Southerners themselves decided for emancipation in the vain hope of national survival. Like so many other creative decisions which the Confederates made or to which they assented, the decision to arm and free black Confederates is open to more than one interpretation. Both then and now, many have said that Confederate emancipation was the desperate measure of a dying people. Like the other transforming aspects of the Confederate experience—political, economic, social, and cultural—the emancipation debate in the Confederate South is analogous to an eight-ounce glass in which there are four ounces of liquid. Of course the glass is half empty—the Confederacy was doomed from the outset by its archaic polity, society, economy, and "peculiar institution." But the glass is also half full—the Confederate experience was a positive attempt to transcend a "peculiar" past in order to achieve Southern self-determination.

In April 1865, the Confederate struggle had but one goal: independence, the ability to exist as a people. As long as Richmond survived as a kind of embattled city-state the cause endured.

On April 2, 1865, however, Lee pronounced the capital no longer tenable. At a country crossroads appropriately named Five Forks, southwest of Petersburg, on April 1, George E. Pickett lost his division and Lee's flank while attending a shad bake nearby. The Federals were within reach of the last rail line into the capital and were nearly astride the only escape route open to the Southern government and Lee's army. Lee acted decisively.[45]

The fateful message from the front reached the telegraph room of the War Department on Sunday morning April 2 while Jefferson Davis worshiped at St. Paul's Church a few blocks away. When the church sexton interrupted the President's participation in the antecommunion service, the incident caused little alarm; Davis frequently had had to attend to government business on short notice. Davis left the church quietly and quickly. Then other members of the government began receiving messages, and before the service concluded most of the worshipers had guessed the reason. The Confederacy was about to evacuate its capital; Lee's army was in flight.

Richmond began a difficult twenty-four hours. Davis and his government departed by train for Danville, Virginia. The Army of Northern Virginia was marching pell-mell toward the west. Lee hoped to outdistance the Federals and join Johnston for a last stand in the field. Meanwhile the capital endured chaos, riot, and fire. The chaos was perhaps natural. The riot began when hungry people broke into the government commissary to find food and when thirsty people took offense at the barrels of liquor being poured into the streets by Virginia militia. The fire was an outgrowth of chaos, riot, and the exploding shells from the armory burned by the retreating Confederates. Next morning, on April 3, Joseph Mayo, the same mayor who swore in 1862 never to give up the city, rode out in a carriage to find a Union officer to whom he might surrender.[46]

Meanwhile Lee's troops forced their way west in the hopes of securing time, supplies, and a route South. Davis and his government on wheels reached Danville, and on April 4 the President issued what would be his last proclamation to the Confederate people. His thinking about such a contingency had developed since November when he had assured Congress that the nation would

[45]Freeman, *Lee's Lieutenants*, III, 655–681.

[46]Thomas, *Confederate State of Richmond*, pp. 194–197; Rembert W. Patrick, *The Fall of Richmond* (Baton Rouge, La., 1960).

survive with or without a land base. The war would continue, Davis told his fellow Southerners.

We have now entered upon a new phase of a struggle the memory of which is to endure for all ages. . . . Relieved from the necessity of guarding cities and particular points, important but not vital to our defense, with an army free to move from point to point and strike in detail detachments and garrisons of the enemy, operating on the interior of our own country, where supplies are more accessible, and where the foe will be far removed from his own base and cut off from all succor in case of reverse, nothing is now needed to render our triumph certain but the exhibition of our own unquenchable resolve. Let us but will it, and we are free.[47]

The "new phase" of which the President spoke was a guerrilla phase. Davis proposed to fight on from the hills or wherever Confederates kept the faith.

Even though Davis' ideas reversed the normal pattern of guerrilla operations and envisioned a transition from regular forces to partisans instead of the other way around, the President had some precedent for his "new-phase" strategy. The Spanish in 1807 had frustrated Napoleon and with help from the outside had thrown off their French conquerors. Davis was relying, too, upon the tradition of bushwhacking already present in the Confederate war. And there were other Southerners who shared the President's dream.

For example Wade Hampton, successor to Stuart as commander of Lee's cavalry, wrote to Davis:

The main reason urged for negotiation [for peace] is to spare the infliction of any further suffering on the people. Nothing can be more fallacious than this reasoning. *No* suffering which can be inflicted by the passage over our country of the Yankee armies can equal what would fall on us if we return to the Union.[48]

In a more direct vein, another cavalry general, Thomas T. Mumford, wrote orders to his dispersed brigade.

We still have a country, a flag, an army, a Government. Then to horse! . . . Let us who struck the last blow as an organized part of the Army of

[47]Davis to People, April 4, 1865, Dunbar Rowland (ed.), *Jefferson Davis, Constitutionalist: His Letters, Papers, and Speeches*, 10 vols. (Jackson, Miss., 1923), VI, 529–531.

[48]Hampton to Davis, April 19, 1865, cited in Hudson Strode (ed.), *Jefferson Davis: Private Letters, 1823–1889* (New York, 1966), pp. 154–155.

Northern Virginia strike the first with that victorious army which, by the blessings of our gracious God, will yet come to redeem her hallowed soil.[49]

Yet Davis, Hampton, and Mumford were among a tiny minority of Southerners who embraced a new war "to the knife."

While the President and his party fled farther South into North Carolina, Lee's army sought safety. As the troops marched they diminished in number. Some were captured; some were cut off from the main army; some simply went home. The crisis came at Appomattox, where, of the approximately 60,000 soldiers who had marched out of the trenches around Richmond and Petersburg, less than 8,000 remained. The Federals were in front of them and behind them in strength. Lee needed to make a decision.[50]

While the General pondered, an artillery staff officer offered the sort of advice Davis would have given had he been present: Let the men take to the hills, let the Confederate army become like "rabbits and partridges" in order to fight on against their enemies.

Lee was patient with the staff officer, but he had obviously considered and rejected this counsel. Partisan war was not possible, Lee maintained. "The men would not fight that way. Their homes have been overrun, and many would go to look after their families," he said. Even more important, Lee continued:

We must consider its effect on the country as a whole. Already it is demoralized by four years of war. If I took your advice the men would be without rations and under no control of officers. They would be compelled to rob and steal in order to live. They would become mere bands of marauders, and the enemy's cavalry would pursue them and overrun many sections they may never have occasion to visit.[51]

In the face of this alternative, this kind of independence, Lee preferred peace.

On April 9, the General met with Grant at Wilbur McLean's house and surrendered the Army of Northern Virginia. McLean had

[49]Mumford to soldiers, April 21, 1865, *War of the Rebellion: A Compilation of the Official Records of the Union and Confederate Armies*, 70 vols. in 127 (Washington, D.C., 1880–1901), ser. I, XLVI, pt. 3, 1395.

[50]Freeman, *Lee's Lieutenants*, III, 712–730; Burke Davis, *To Appomattox: Nine April Days*, 1865 (New York, 1959); Philip Van Doren Stern, *An End to Valor: The Last Days of the Civil War* (Boston, 1958).

[51]Cited in Douglas S. Freeman, *R. E. Lee: A Biography*, 4 vols. (New York, 1934–1935), IV, 123.

moved from Manassas because the war was disruptive, and he was tired of having his home used as a headquarters. Now peace came to McLean's parlor, although in the aftermath of surrender enemy officers took away pieces of furniture from the historic room. No matter; for McLean and Lee's army the war was over.

Ironically it was a Northern officer who best described the Army of Northern Virginia's final parade, the march into Appomattox to stack arms. General Joshua Chamberlain, who received the formal surrender on behalf of Grant, recalled the procession which took place on April 12:

Before us in proud humiliation stood the embodiment of manhood: men whom neither toils and sufferings, nor the fact of death, nor disaster, nor hopelessness could bend from their resolve; standing before us now, thin, worn, and famished, but erect, and with eyes looking level into ours, waking memories that bound us together as no other bond. . . .

Instruction had been given; and when the head of each division column comes opposite our group, our bugle sounds the signal and instantly our whole line from right to left, regiment by regiment in succession, gives the soldier's salutation, from the "order arms" to the old "carry"—the marching salute. Gordon [General John B.] at the head of the column, riding with heavy spirit and downcast face, catches the sound of shifting arms, looks up, and, taking the meaning, wheels superbly, making with himself and his horse one uplifted figure, with profound salutation as he drops the point of his sword to the boot toe; then facing to his own command, gives word for his successive brigades to pass us with the same position of the manual, —honor answering honor. On our part not a sound of trumpet, nor roll of drum; not a cheer nor word, nor whisper of vaingloring, nor motion of man standing again at the order, but an awed stillness rather, a breath-holding, as if it were the passing of the dead![52]

The Confederacy lived on, though, in the person of Jefferson Davis, and Lee dutifully reported his surrender shortly after the fact. Later, on April 20 the General wrote Davis more details of that last nightmarish week between the evacuation of Richmond and his surrender. He took some pains to speak to the issue of a "new phase" of war. "A partisan war may be continued," Lee wrote, "and hostilities protracted causing individual suffering and the devasta-

[52]Joshua Lawrence Chamberlain, *The Passing of the Armies* (New York, 1915) quoted in Henry Steele Commager (ed.), *The Blue and the Gray* (Indianapolis, Ind., 1950), pp. 142–143.

tion of the country, but I see no prospect by that means of achieving a separate independence."[53] What Lee meant by "a separate independence" was independence within a defined place with stable relationships among people. The independence for which Davis grasped was that of a guerrilla nomad who might have to conduct reprisals against his own people. What Davis now asked was that Southerners make the ultimate sacrifice: that of themselves and their fundamental attachment to people and place. The overwhelming majority of Southerners would have none of it.

A few days after Lee explained his rejection of the partisan option, on April 25, the President ordered Joe Johnston to begin the war's new phase. Johnston, who had conferred with Davis earlier and made clear the hopelessness of his army's situation, received the President's order by telegraph on the morning of April 26. Davis ordered Johnston to disband his infantry and appoint a future rendezvous for the men in order that they might continue the fight as partisans. Johnston himself was to join Davis with as many mounted troops as he could muster.[54] Johnston refused. Later he explained that Davis' order threatened the safety of the army and the people in order to secure a limited protection for the government. Like Lee, Johnston chose surrender, on April 29, instead of partisan war, and he did so in the face of a direct order to the contrary.[55]

Even Forrest, for whom Sherman was convinced "nothing is left . . . but death or highway robbery" as a guerrilla chieftain, determined to go home in peace. To his troops on May 9 Forrest pronounced the cause "hopeless" and the Confederate government "at an end." "That we are beaten," he stated, "is a self-evident fact, and any further resistance on our part would be justly regarded as the very height of folly and rashness."[56]

Thus Davis continued his flight alone, virtually an exile in his own country. Southerners as a people had had enough of fighting; they accepted defeat. And in so doing they affirmed that culture of the folk—the primacy of people and place—that perhaps best defined

[53]Lee to Davis, April 20, 1865, Clifford Dowdey and Louis H. Manarin (eds.), *The Wartime Papers of R. E. Lee* (New York 1961), p. 939.
[54]Davis to Johnston, April 25, 1865, cited in Joseph E. Johnston, *Narrative of Military Operation*, ed. by Frank E. Vandiver (Bloomington, Ind., 1959), p. 411.
[55]*Ibid.*, pp. 411–412.
[56]Henry, *Forrest*, pp. 436–438.

them as a people. Having sacrificed or been willing to sacrifice most of the ideological tenets they went to war to defend, ultimately Confederate Southerners were willing to lose their national life in order to save life itself.[57]

Davis did not understand. He fled until on May 10 a small force of Union cavalry captured him at Irwinville, Georgia. Davis endured imprisonment, the threat of a trial for treason, and the stigma of defeat. He never gave up. To the end of his life, he continued to champion a cause which was long since lost. More than twenty years later he wrote in his memoir, *The Rise and Fall of the Confederate Government,* "that the war was, on the part of the United States Government, one of aggression and usurpation, and, on the part of the South, was for the defense of an inherent, unalienable right."[58]

Nor did Edmund Ruffin surrender. Unlike Davis, however, Ruffin realized that the cause was lost. And Ruffin had neither the will to adapt to the ways of the victors nor the temperament to live with defeat.

On June 17, 1865, he closed his diary:

I here declare my unmitigated hatred to Yankee rule—to all political, social and business connections with the Yankees and to the Yankee race. Would that I could impress these sentiments, in their full force, on every living Southerner and bequeath them to every one yet to be born! May such sentiments be held universally in the outraged and down-trodden South, though in silence and stillness, until the now far-distant day shall arrive for just retribution for Yankee usurpation, oppression and atrocious outrages, and for deliverance and vengeance for the now ruined, subjugated and enslaved Southern States! . . . And now with my latest writing and utterance, and with what will be near my latest breath, I here repeat and would willingly proclaim my unmitigated hatred to Yankee rule—to all political, social and business connections with Yankees, and the perfidious malignant and vile Yankee race.[59]

Then Ruffin sat straight in his chair and placed the muzzle of his silver-mounted gun in his mouth. With a forked stick he pushed

[57]See David M. Potter, "The Enigma of the South," in *The South and the Sectional Conflict* (Baton Rouge, La., 1968), pp. 3–16.

[58]See Hudson Strode, *Jefferson Davis,* 3 vols. (New York, 1955–1964), III, 227 ff.; Jefferson Davis, *The Rise and Fall of the Confederate Government,* 2 vols. (New York, 1881, Collier edition, New York, 1961), p. 562.

[59]Edmund Ruffin Diary, June 17, 1865, Library of Congress, Washington.

the trigger and joined the Confederacy in violent death.[60]

Most Southerners, of course, did not follow the example of Davis or Ruffin. Rather, they turned to the model of Lee for inspiration and set out to rebuild their land and lives. But Reconstruction in the postwar South could not be resurrection of the ante-bellum South, and ex-Confederates who accepted defeat and reunion were often unable to accept the consequences of being a vanquished people. Thus has the "Lost Cause" lingered in the Southern soul. Thus has the Confederacy, real and imagined, as experience and myth, since defined Southern identity and made of Southerners a peculiar people. And thus could the first unquestionably Southern President of the United States since 1865 state that his favorite motion picture was *Gone with the Wind*. Jimmy Carter then added that he may have seen a "different version" of the film in his native Georgia. "My favorite scene was the burning of Schenectady, N.Y., and President Grant surrendering to Robert E. Lee."[61]

[60]Edmund Ruffin, Jr., to his sons, June 20, 1865, in "Death of Edmund Ruffin," *Tyler's Quarterly Historical and Genealogical Magazine*, V (1924), 193.
[61]See Emory M. Thomas, *Honest to Clio: The New History of the Old South* (Macon, Ga., 1973). The Carter quote is from *Newsweek*, November 28, 1977, 85.

APPENDIX

The Constitution of the Confederate States of America, March 11, 1861

We, the people of the Confederate States, each State acting in its sovereign and independent character, in order to form a permanent government, establish justice, insure domestic tranquillity, and secure the blessings of liberty to ourselves and our posterity—invoking the favor and guidance of Almighty God—do ordain and establish this Constitution for the Confederate States of America.

Art. I

Sec. 1.—All legislative powers herein delegated shall be vested in a Congress of the Confederate States, which shall consist of a Senate and House of Representatives.

Sec. 2. (1) The House of Representatives shall be . . . chosen every second year by the people of the several States; and the electors in each State shall be citizens of the Confederate States, and have the qualifications requisite for electors of the most numerous branch of the State Legislature; but no person of foreign birth, not a citizen of the Confederate States, shall be allowed to vote for any officer, civil or political, State or Federal.

(2) No person shall be a Representative who shall not have attained the age of twenty-five years, and be a citizen of the Confeder-

James M. Matthews, ed., *Statutes at Large of the Provisional Government of the Confederate States of America* (Richmond, 1864), pp. 11–23.

ate States, and who shall not, when elected, be an inhabitant of that State in which he shall be chosen.

(3) Representatives and direct taxes shall be apportioned among the several States which may be included within this Confederacy, according to their respective numbers, which shall be determined by adding to the whole number of free persons, including those bound to service for a term of years, and excluding Indians not taxed, three-fifths of all slaves. The actual enumeration shall be made within three years after the first meeting of the Congress of the Confederate States, and within every subsequent term of ten years, in such manner as they shall by law direct. The number of Representatives shall not exceed one for every fifty thousand, but each State shall have at least one Representative; and until such enumeration shall be made the State of South Carolina shall be entitled to choose six; the State of Georgia ten; the State of Alabama nine; the State of Florida two; the State of Mississippi seven; the State of Louisiana six; and the State of Texas six.

(4) When vacancies happen in the representation of any State, the Executive authority thereof shall issue writs of election to fill such vacancies.

(5) The House of Representatives shall choose their Speaker and other officers; and shall have the sole power of impeachment; except that any judicial or other federal officer resident and acting solely within the limits of any State, may be impeached by a vote of two-thirds of both branches of the Legislature thereof.

SEC. 3. (1) The Senate of the Confederate States shall be composed of two Senators from each State, chosen for six years by the Legislature thereof, at the regular session next immediately preceding the commencement of the term of service; and each Senator shall have one vote.

(2) Immediately after they shall be assembled, in consequence of the first election, they shall be divided as equally as may be into three classes. The seats of the Senators of the first class shall be vacated at the expiration of the second year; of the second class at the expiration of the fourth year; and of the third class at the expiration of the sixth year; so that one-third may be chosen every second year; and if vacancies happen by resignation or otherwise during the recess of the Legislature of any State, the Executive thereof may make temporary appointments

until the next meeting of the Legislature, which shall then fill such vacancies.

(3) No person shall be a Senator, who shall not have attained the age of thirty years, and be a citizen of the Confederate States; and who shall not, when elected, be an inhabitant of the State for which he shall be chosen.

(4) The Vice-President of the Confederate States shall be President of the Senate, but shall have no vote, unless they be equally divided.

(5) The Senate shall choose their other officers, and also a President pro tempore, in the absence of the Vice-President, or when he shall exercise the office of President of the Confederate States.

(6) The Senate shall have sole power to try all impeachments. When sitting for that purpose they shall be on oath or affirmation. When the President of the Confederate States is tried, the Chief Justice shall preside; and no person shall be convicted without the concurrence of two-thirds of the members present.

(7) Judgment in cases of impeachment shall not extend further than removal from office, and disqualification to hold and enjoy any office of honor, trust, or profit, under the Confederate States; but the party convicted shall, nevertheless, be liable and subject to indictment, trial, judgment, and punishment according to law.

SEC. 4. (1) The times, places, and manner of holding elections for Senators and Representatives, shall be prescribed in each State by the Legislature thereof, subject to the provisions of this Constitution; but the Congress may, at any time, by law, make or alter such regulations, except as to the times and places of choosing Senators.

(2) The Congress shall assemble at least once in every year; and such meeting shall be on the first Monday in December, unless they shall, by law, appoint a different day.

SEC. 5. (1) Each House shall be the judge of the elections, returns, and qualifications of its own members, and a majority of each shall constitute a quorum to do business; but a smaller number may adjourn from day to day, and may be authorized to compel the attendance of absent members, in such manner and under such penalties as each House may provide.

(2) Each House may determine the rules of its proceedings, punish its members for disorderly behavior, and, with the concurrence of two-thirds of the whole number, expel a member.

(3) Each House shall keep a journal of its proceedings, and from time to time publish the same, excepting such parts as may in their judgment require secrecy, and the ayes and nays of the members of either House, on any question, shall, at the desire of one-fifth of those present, be entered on the journal.

(4) Neither House, during the session of Congress, shall, without the consent of the other, adjourn for more than three days, nor to any other place than that in which the two Houses shall be sitting.

Sec. 6. (1) The Senators and Representatives shall receive a compensation for their services, to be ascertained by law, and paid out of the Treasury of the Confederate States. They shall, in all cases except treason and breach of the peace, be privileged from arrest during their attendance at the session of their respective Houses, and in going to and returning from the same; and for any speech or debate in either House, they shall not be questioned in any other place.

(2) No Senator or Representative shall, during the time for which he was elected, be appointed to any civil office under the authority of the Confederate States, which shall have been created, or the emoluments whereof shall have been increased during such time; and no person holding any office under the Confederate States shall be a member of either House during his continuance in office. But Congress may, by law, grant to the principal officer in each of the Executive Departments a seat upon the floor of either House, with the privilege of discussing any measure appertaining to his department.

Sec. 7. (1) All bills for raising revenue shall originate in the House of Representatives; but the Senate may propose or concur with amendments as on other bills.

(2) Every bill which shall have passed both Houses shall, before it becomes a law, be presented to the President of the Confederate States; if he approve he shall sign it; but if not, he shall return it with his objections to that House in which it shall have originated, who shall enter the objections at large on their journal, and proceed to reconsider it. If, after such reconsideration, two-thirds of that House shall agree to pass the bill, it shall be sent, together with the objections, to the other House, by which it shall likewise be reconsidered, and if approved by two-thirds of that House, it shall become a law. But in all such cases, the votes of both Houses shall be

determined by yeas and nays, and the names of the persons voting for and against the bill shall be entered on the journal of each House respectively. If any bill shall not be returned by the President within ten days (Sundays excepted) after it shall have been presented to him, the same shall be a law, in like manner as if he had signed it, unless the Congress, by their adjournment, prevent its return; in which case it shall not be a law. The President may approve any appropriation and disapprove any other appropriation in the same bill. In such case he shall, in signing the bill, designate the appropriations disapproved; and shall return a copy of such appropriations, with his objections, to the House in which the bill shall have originated; and the same proceedings shall then be had as in case of other bills disapproved by the President.

(3) Every order, resolution, or vote, to which the concurrence of both Houses may be necessary (except on a question of adjournment) shall be presented to the President of the Confederate States; and before the same shall take effect shall be approved by him; or being disapproved by him, shall be repassed by two-thirds of both Houses, according to the rules and limitations prescribed in case of a bill.

SEC. 8.—The Congress shall have power—(1) To lay and collect taxes, duties, imposts, and excises, for revenue necessary to pay the debts, provide for the common defence, and carry on the Government of the Confederate States; but no bounties shall be granted from the treasury; nor shall any duties or taxes on importations from foreign nations be laid to promote or foster any branch of industry; and all duties, imposts, and excises shall be uniform throughout the Confederate States.

(2) To borrow money on the credit of the Confederate States.

(3) To regulate commerce with foreign nations, and among the several States, and with the Indian tribes; but neither this nor any other clause contained in the Constitution shall be construed to delegate the power to Congress to appropriate money for any internal improvement intended to facilitate commerce; except for the purpose of furnishing lights, beacons, and buoys, and other aids to navigation upon the coasts, and the improvement of harbors, and the removing of obstructions in river navigation, in all which cases, such duties shall be laid on the navigation facilitated thereby, as may be necessary to pay the costs and expenses thereof.

(4) To establish uniform laws of naturalization, and uniform laws on the subject of bankruptcies throughout the Confederate States, but no law of Congress shall discharge any debt contracted before the passage of the same.

(5) To coin money, regulate the value thereof, and of foreign coin, and fix the standard of weights and measures.

(6) To provide for the punishment of counterfeiting the securities and current coin of the Confederate States.

(7) To establish post-offices and post-routes; but the expenses of the Post-office Department, after the first day of March, in the year of our Lord eighteen hundred and sixty-three, shall be paid out of its own revenues.

(8) To promote the progress of science and useful arts, by securing for limited times to authors and inventors the exclusive right to their respective writings and discoveries.

(9) To constitute tribunals inferior to the Supreme Court.

(10) To define and punish piracies and felonies committed on the high seas, and offences against the law of nations.

(11) To declare war, grant letters of marque and reprisal, and make rules concerning captures on land and water.

(12) To raise and support armies; but no appropriation of money to that use shall be for a longer term than two years.

(13) To provide and maintain a navy.

(14) To make rules for government and regulation of the land and naval forces.

(15) To provide for calling forth the militia to execute the laws of the Confederate States; suppress insurrections, and repel invasions.

(16) To provide for organizing, arming, and disciplining the militia, and for governing such part of them as may be employed in the service of the Confederate States; reserving to the States, respectively, the appointment of the officers, and the authority of training the militia according to the discipline prescribed by Congress.

(17) To exercise exclusive legislation, in all cases whatsoever, over such district (not exceeding ten miles square) as may, by cession of one or more States, and the acceptance of Congress, become the seat of the Government of the Confederate States; and to exercise a like authority over all places purchased by the consent of the Legislature of the State in which the same shall be, for the erection

of forts, magazines, arsenals, dock-yards, and other needful buildings, and

(18) To make all laws which shall be necessary and proper for carrying into execution the foregoing powers, and all other powers vested by this Constitution in the Government of the Confederate States, or in any department or officer thereof.

SEC. 9. (1) The importation of negroes of the African race, from any foreign country, other than the slaveholding States or Territories of the United States of America, is hereby forbidden; and Congress is required to pass such laws as shall effectually prevent the same.

(2) Congress shall also have power to prohibit the introduction of slaves from any State not a member of, or Territory not belonging to, this Confederacy.

(3) The privilege of the writ of habeas corpus shall not be suspended, unless when in cases of rebellion or invasion the public safety may require it.

(4) No bill of attainder, ex post facto law, or law denying or impairing the right of property in negro slaves shall be passed.

(5) No capitation or other direct tax shall be laid unless in proportion to the census or enumeration hereinbefore directed to be taken.

(6) No tax or duty shall be laid on articles exported from any State, except by a vote of two-thirds of both Houses.

(7) No preference shall be given by any regulation of commerce or revenue to the ports of one State over those of another.

(8) No money shall be drawn from the treasury but in consequence of appropriations made by law; and a regular statement and account of the receipts and expenditures of all public money shall be published from time to time.

(9) Congress shall appropriate no money from the treasury except by a vote of two-thirds of both Houses, taken by yeas and nays, unless it be asked and estimated for by some one of the heads of departments, and submitted to Congress by the President; or for the purpose of paying its own expenses and contingencies; or for the payment of claims against the Confederate States, the justice of which shall have been judicially declared by a tribunal for the investigation of claims against the Government, which it is hereby made the duty of Congress to establish.

(10) All bills appropriating money shall specify in federal currency the exact amount of each appropriation and the purposes for which it is made; and Congress shall grant no extra compensation to any public contractor, officer, agent, or servant, after such contract shall have been made or such service rendered.

(11) No title of nobility shall be granted by the Confederate States; and no person holding any office of profit or trust under them shall, without the consent of the Congress, accept of any present, emolument, office, or title of any kind whatever, from any king, prince, or foreign state.

(12) Congress shall make no law respecting an establishment of religion, or prohibiting the free exercise thereof; or abridging the freedom of speech or of the press; or the right of the people peaceably to assemble and petition the Government for a redress of grievances.

(13) A well-regulated militia being necessary to the security of a free State, the right of the people to keep and bear arms shall not be infringed.

(14) No soldier shall, in time of peace, be quartered in any house without the consent of the owner; nor in time of war, but in a manner to be prescribed by law.

(15) The right of the people to be secure in their persons, houses, papers, and effects, against unreasonable searches and seizures, shall not be violated; and no warrant shall issue but upon probable cause, supported by oath or affirmation, and particularly describing the place to be searched, and the person or things to be seized.

(16) No person shall be held to answer for a capital or otherwise infamous crime, unless on a presentment or indictment of a grand jury, except in cases arising in the land or naval forces, or in the militia, when in actual service, in time of war, or public danger; nor shall any person be subject for the same offence to be twice put in jeopardy of life or limb; nor be compelled in any criminal case to be a witness against himself; nor be deprived of life, liberty, or property, without due process of law; nor shall private property be taken for public use without just compensation.

(17) In all criminal prosecutions the accused shall enjoy the right to a speedy and public trial, by an impartial jury of the State and district wherein the crime shall have been committed, which district shall have been previously ascertained by law, and to be informed

of the nature and cause of the accusation; to be confronted with the witnesses against him; to have compulsory process for obtaining witnesses in his favor; and to have the assistance of counsel for his defence.

(18) In suits at common law, where the value in controversy shall exceed twenty dollars, the right of trial by jury shall be preserved; and no fact so tried by a jury shall be otherwise reexamined in any court of the Confederacy, than according to the rules of common law.

(19) Excessive bail shall not be required, nor excessive fines imposed, nor cruel and unusual punishment inflicted.

(20) Every law, or resolution having the force of law, shall relate to but one subject, and that shall be expressed in the title.

SEC. 10. (1) No State shall enter into any treaty, alliance, or confederation; grant letters of marque and reprisal; coin money; make any thing but gold and silver coin a tender in payment of debts; pass any bill of attainder, or ex post facto law, or law impairing the obligation of contracts; or grant any title of nobility.

(2) No State shall, without the consent of Congress, lay any imposts or duties on imports or exports, except what may be absolutely necessary for executing its inspection laws; and the net produce of all duties and imposts, laid by any State on imports or exports, shall be for the use of the Treasury of the Confederate States; and all such laws shall be subject to the revision and control of Congress.

(3) No State shall, without the consent of Congress, lay any duty on tonnage, except on sea-going vessels, for the improvement of its rivers and harbors navigated by the said vessels; but such duties shall not conflict with any treaties of the Confederate States with foreign nations; and any surplus revenue, thus derived, shall, after making such improvement, be paid into the common treasury; nor shall any State keep troops or ships of war in time of peace, enter into any agreement or compact with another State, or with a foreign power, or engage in war, unless actually invaded, or in such imminent danger as will not admit of delay. But when any river divides or flows through two or more States, they may enter into compacts with each other to improve the navigation thereof.

ART. II

SEC. 1. (1) The Executive power shall be vested in a President of the Confederate States of America. He and the Vice-President shall hold their offices for the term of six years; but the President shall not be reeligible. The President and Vice-President shall be elected as follows:

(2) Each State shall appoint, in such manner as the Legislature thereof may direct, a number of electors equal to the whole number of Senators and Representatives to which the State may be entitled in the Congress; but no Senator or Representative, or person holding an office of trust or profit under the Confederate States, shall be appointed an elector.

(3) The electors shall meet in their respective States and vote by ballot for President and Vice-President, one of whom, at least shall not be an inhabitant of the same State with themselves; they shall name in their ballots the person voted for as President, and in distinct ballots the person voted for as Vice-President, and they shall make distinct lists of all persons voted for as President, and of all persons voted for as Vice-President, and of the number of votes for each; which list they shall sign, and certify, and transmit, sealed, to the . . . government of the Confederate States, directed to the President of the Senate. The President of the Senate shall, in the presence of the Senate and House of Representatives, open all the certificates, and the votes shall then be counted; the person having the greatest number of votes. for President shall be the President, if such number be a majority of the whole number of electors appointed; and if no person shall have such a majority, then, from the persons having the highest numbers, not exceeding three, on the list of those voted for as President, the House of Representatives shall choose immediately, by ballot, the President. But, in choosing the President, the votes shall be taken by States, the representation from each State having one vote; a quorum for this purpose shall consist of a member or members from two-thirds of the States, and a majority of all the States shall be necessary to a choice. And if the House of Representatives shall not choose a President, whenever the right of choice shall devolve upon them, before the fourth day of March next following, then the Vice-President shall act as Presi-

dent, as in case of the death, or other constitutional disability of the President.

(4) The person having the greatest number of votes as Vice-President shall be the Vice-President, if such number be a majority of the whole number of electors appointed; and if no person have a majority, then from the two highest numbers on the list, the Senate shall choose the Vice-President; a quorum for the purpose shall consist of two-thirds of the whole number of Senators, and a majority of the whole number shall be necessary for a choice.

(5) But no person constitutionally ineligible to the office of President shall be eligible to that of Vice-President of the Confederate States.

(6) The Congress may determine the time of choosing the electors, and the day on which they shall give their votes; which day shall be the same throughout the Confederate States.

(7) No person except a natural born citizen of the Confederate States, or a citizen thereof, at the time of the adoption of this Constitution, or a citizen thereof born in the United States prior to the 20th of December, 1860, shall be eligible to the office of President; neither shall any person be eligible to that office who shall not have attained the age of thirty-five years, and been fourteen years a resident within the limits of the Confederate States, as they may exist at the time of his election.

(8) In case of the removal of the President from office, or of his death, resignation, or inability to discharge the powers and duties of the said office, the same shall devolve on the Vice-President; and the Congress may, by law, provide for the case of the removal, death, resignation, or inability both of the President and the Vice-President, declaring what officer shall then act as President, and such officer shall then act accordingly until the disability be removed or a President shall be elected.

(9) The President shall, at stated times, receive for his services a compensation, which shall neither be increased nor diminished during the period for which he shall have been elected; and he shall not receive within that period any other emolument from the Confederate States, or any of them.

(10) Before he enters on the execution [of the duties] of his office, he shall take the following oath or affirmation:

"I do solemnly swear (or affirm) that I will faithfully execute the office of President of the Confederate States, and will, to the best of my ability, preserve, protect, and defend the Constitution thereof."

SEC. 2. (1) The President shall be commander-in-chief of the army and navy of the Confederate States, and of the militia of the several States, when called into the actual service of the Confederate States; he may require the opinion, in writing, of the principal officer in each of the Executive Departments, upon any subject relating to the duties of their respective offices; and he shall have power to grant reprieves and pardons for offences against the Confederate States, except in cases of impeachment.

(2) He shall have power, by and with the advice and consent of the Senate, to make treaties, provided two-thirds of the Senators present concur; and he shall nominate, and, by and with the advice and consent of the Senate, shall appoint ambassadors, other public ministers, and consuls, Judges of the Supreme Court, and all other officers of the Confederate States, whose appointments are not herein otherwise provided for, and which shall be established by law; but the Congress may by law vest the appointment of such inferior officers, as they think proper, in the President alone, in the courts of law, or in the heads of departments.

(3) The principal officer in each of the Executive Departments, and all persons connected with the diplomatic service, may be removed from office at the pleasure of the President. All other civil officers of the Executive Departments may be removed at any time by the President, or other appointing power, when their services are unnecessary, or for dishonesty, incapacity, inefficiency, misconduct, or neglect of duty; and when so removed, the removal shall be reported to the Senate, together with the reasons therefor.

(4) The President shall have power to fill all vacancies that may happen during the recess of the Senate, by granting commissions which shall expire at the end of the next session; but no person rejected by the Senate shall be reappointed to the same office during their ensuing recess.

SEC. 3. (1) The President shall, from time to time, give to the Congress information of the state of the Confederacy, and recommend to their consideration such measures as he shall judge necessary and expedient; he may, on extraordinary occasions, convene both Houses, or either of them; and, in case of disagreement between them, with respect to the time of adjournment he may adjourn them to such time as he shall think proper; he shall receive ambassadors and other public ministers; he shall take care that the laws be faithfully executed, and shall commission all the officers of the Confederate States.

SEC. 4. (1) The President and Vice-President, and all Civil officers of the Confederate States, shall be removed from office on impeachment for, or conviction of, treason, bribery, or other high crimes and misdemeanors.

ART. III

SEC. 1. (1) The judicial power of the Confederate States shall be vested in one Supreme Court, and in such inferior courts as the Congress may from time to time ordain and establish. The judges, both of the Supreme and inferior courts, shall hold their offices during good behavior, and shall, at stated times, receive for their services a compensation, which shall not be diminished during their continuance in office. . . .

ART. IV

SEC. 1. (1) Full faith and credit shall be given in each State to the public acts, records, and judicial proceedings of every other State. And the Congress may, by general laws, prescribe the manner in which such acts, records, and proceedings shall be proved, and the effect thereof.

SEC. 2. (1) The citizens of each State shall be entitled to all the privileges and immunities of citizens of the several States, and shall have the right of transit and sojourn in any State of this Confederacy, with their slaves and other property; and the right of property in said slaves shall not be thereby impaired.

(2) A person charged in any State with treason, felony, or other crime against the laws of such State, who shall flee from justice, and be found in another State, shall, on demand of the executive authority of the State from which he fled, be delivered up to be removed to the State having jurisdiction of the crime.

(3) No slave or other person held to service or labor in any State or Territory of the Confederate States, under the laws thereof,

escaping or [un]lawfully carried into another, shall, in consequence of any law or regulation therein, be discharged from such service or labor; but shall be delivered up on claim of the party to whom such slave belongs, or to whom such service or labor may be due.

SEC. 3. (1) Other States may be admitted into this Confederacy by a vote of two-thirds of the whole House of Representatives, and two-thirds of the Senate, the Senate voting by States; but no new State shall be formed or erected within the jurisdiction of any other State; nor any State be formed by the junction of two or more States, or parts of States, without the consent of the Legislatures of the States concerned as well as of the Congress.

(2) The Congress shall have power to dispose of and make all needful rules and regulations concerning the property of the Confederate States, including the lands thereof.

(3) The Confederate States may acquire new territory; and Congress shall have power to legislate and provide governments for the inhabitants of all territory belonging to the Confederate States, lying without the limits of the several States, and may permit them, at such times, and in such manner as it may by law provide, to form States to be admitted into the Confederacy. In all such territory, the institution of negro slavery, as it now exists in the Confederate States, shall be recognized and protected by Congress and by the territorial government; and the inhabitants of the several Confederate States and Territories shall have the right to take to such territory any slaves lawfully held by them in any of the States or Territories of the Confederate States.

(4) The Confederate States shall guarantee to every State that now is or hereafter may become a member of this Confederacy, a Republican form of Government, and shall protect each of them against invasion; and on application of the Legislature, (or of the Executive when the Legislature is not in session,) against domestic violence.

ART. V

SEC. 1. (1) Upon the demand of any three States, legally assembled in their several Conventions, the Congress shall summon a Convention of all the States, to take into consideration such amendments to the Constitution as the said States shall concur in suggesting at the time when the said demand is made; and should any of the proposed amendments to the Constitution be agreed on by the said Convention—voting by States—and the same be ratified by the Legislatures of two-thirds thereof—as the one or the other mode of ratification may be proposed by the general convention—they shall thenceforward form a part of this Constitution. But no State shall, without its consent, be deprived of its equal representation in the Senate.

Art. VI

1.—The Government established by this Constitution is the successor of the Provisional Government of the Confederate States of America, and all the laws passed by the latter shall continue in force until the same shall be repealed or modified; and all the officers appointed by the same shall remain in office until their successors are appointed and qualified, or the offices abolished.

2. All debts contracted and engagements entered into before the adoption of this Constitution, shall be as valid against the Confederate States under this Constitution as under the Provisional Government.

3. This Constitution, and the laws of the Confederate States, made in pursuance thereof, and all treaties made, or which shall be made, under the authority of the Confederate States, shall be the supreme law of the land; and the judges in every State shall be bound thereby, any thing in the Constitution or laws of any State to the contrary notwithstanding.

4. The Senators and Representatives before mentioned, and the members of the several State Legislatures, and all executive and judicial officers, both of the Confederate States and of the several States, shall be bound, by oath or affirmation, to support this Constitution; but no religious test shall ever be required as a qualification to any office or public trust under the Confederate States.

5. The enumeration, in the Constitution, of certain rights, shall not be construed to deny or disparage others retained by the people of the several States.

6. The powers not delegated to the Confederate States by the Constitution, nor prohibited by it to the States, are reserved to the States, respectively, or to the people thereof.

Art. VII

1.—The ratification of the conventions of five States shall be sufficient for the establishment of this Constitution between the States so ratifying the same.

2. When five States shall have ratified this Constitution in the manner before specified, the Congress, under the provisional Constitution, shall prescribe the time for holding the election of President and Vice-President, and for the meeting of the electoral college, and for counting the votes and inaugurating the President. They shall also prescribe the time for holding the first election of members of Congress under this Constitution, and the time for assembling the same. Until the assembling of such Congress, the Congress under the provisional Constitution shall continue to exercise the legislative powers granted them; not extending beyond the time limited by the Constitution of the Provisional Government.

Adopted unanimously by the Congress of the Confederate States of South Carolina, Georgia, Florida, Alabama, Mississippi, Louisiana, and Texas, sitting in convention at the capitol, in the city of Montgomery, Alabama, on the Eleventh day of March, in the year Eighteen Hundred and Sixty-One.

HOWELL COBB
President of the Congress.

(Signatures)

Bibliography

The literature of the "Lost Cause" is indeed vast, and necessarily the materials mentioned here are but a sample. The sample is not random, however. This bibliography will emphasize by inclusion the "classic" works on the Confederate experience and attempt to summarize the best of recent scholarship. Because this is a survey, a third emphasis will be upon bibliographical guides to broader and deeper study.

Works specifically about the pre-Confederate South are not included here, although the footnotes to chapters 1 and 2 offer some introduction. Two other volumes in the New American Nation Series are more directly concerned with the Old South and the secession crisis—Clement Eaton, *The Growth of Southern Civilization, 1790–1860* (New York, 1960), and David M. Potter, *The Impending Crisis, 1848–1861* (New York, 1976)—and both of these books contain fine bibliographies. The materials cited here are intended to compose an introduction to the literature of the South as nation.

Guides and General Histories

For some years now, the most available general guides to the study of the Confederacy have been the relevant portions in the bibliography of James G. Randall and David Donald, *The Civil War and Reconstruction* (Boston, 1969), and Allan Nevins, James J. Robertson, Jr., and Bell I. Wiley (eds.), *Civil War Books: A Critical Bibliography* (Baton Rouge, La., 1967). Also helpful is David Donald's brief bibliography of the war years, *The Nation in Crisis 1861–1877* (New York, 1969), and appropriate chapters of Arthur S. Link and Rembert W. Patrick (eds.), *Writing Southern History: Essays in Historiography in Honor of Fletcher M. Green* (Baton Rouge, La., 1965). Reviews and articles in scholarly and some popular journals are the best sources of more recent scholarship. For Confederate history a few of the most significant national, regional, and period journals are: *American Historical Review, Journal of American History, Journal of Southern History, Civil War History, Civil War Times Illustrated,* and *Journal of Negro History.* State journals, especially those of Southern states, are also important, as are a number of regional and topical journals too numerous to cite here. Perhaps the best access to current periodical literature is the annual "Bibliography of Civil War Articles" published in *Civil War History* or similar annual guides published in the *Journal of Southern History* and the *Journal of American History.*

To locate unpublished research studies there are two basic guides: Warren F. Kuehl, *Dissertations in History* (Lexington, Ky., 1965), and the periodical *Dissertation Abstracts* (title varies) published by the University Microfilm Service, Ann Arbor, Mich. The number of cooperating institutions in the microfilm enterprise involved in the latter guide imposes some limits upon the scope of the material surveyed.

General histories of the Civil War period are often important for their content as well as for their use as bibliographical guides. Randall and Donald's *Civil War and Reconstruction* continues, despite numerous challenges, to be the most widely used general history, and its bibliography, although somewhat dated, remains basic to serious students. Perhaps the best one-volume history of the war is Raimondo Luraghi, *Storia della guerra civile americana* (Turin, Italy, 1966). Luraghi also has an intriguing study of *The Rise and Fall of the Plantation South* (New York, 1978). Among multivolume studies Allan Nevins' *Ordeal of the Union,* 2 vols. (New York, 1947), *The Emergence of Lincoln,* 2 vols. (New York, 1950), and *The War for the Union,* 4 vols. (New York, 1959–1971) have surpassed the older standard, James Ford Rhodes, *History of the United States from the Compromise of 1850 to . . . 1877,* 7 vols. (New York, 1893–1900). A more popular account is Bruce Catton's *Centennial History of the Civil War,* 3 vols. (Garden City, N.Y., 1961–1965). The major limitation of both Nevins' and Catton's projects is the tendency to hurry through the later war years in the last volumes. Shelby Foote's *The Civil War: A Narrative,* 3 vols. (New York, 1958–1975) is good, especially as military narrative.

Shorter studies of the period include Arthur C. Cole, *The Irrepressible Conflict, 1850–1865* (New York, 1934), and Thomas H. O'Connor, *The Disunited States* (New York, 1972), both of which emphasize the prewar years. Robert Cruden, *The War That Never Ended* (Englewood Cliffs, N.J., 1973), emphasizes the black experience. More balanced recent interpretations are William R. Brock, *Conflict and Transformation: The United States, 1844–1877* (Baltimore, 1973); Emory M. Thomas, *The American War and Peace, 1860–1877* (Englewood Cliffs, N.J., 1973); Robert H. Jones, *Disrupted*

Decades: The Civil War and Reconstruction Years (New York, 1973); Peter Parish, *The American Civil War* (New York, 1975); Roy F. Nichols, *The Stakes of Power, 1845–1877* (New York, 1961); and William L. Barney, *Flawed Victory: A New Prospective on the Civil War* (New York, 1975). Other brief, general works of note are Alan Barker, *The Civil War in America* (Garden City, N.Y., 1961); Harry Hansen, *The Civil War* (New York, 1962); and James A. Rawley, *Turning Points of the Civil War* (Lincoln, Neb., 1966).

Reference works and collections of documents relating to the Civil War era in general and to the Confederacy in particular include Mark Mayo Boatner III, *The Civil War Dictionary* (New York, 1959); David C. Roller and Robert W. Twyman (eds.), *The Encyclopedia of Southern History,* soon to be published by the Louisiana State University Press; E. B. Long, with Barbara Long, *The Civil War Day by Day: An Almanac, 1861–1865* (Garden City, N.Y., 1971); Henry Steele Commager (ed.), *The Blue and the Gray: The Story of the Civil War as told by Participants,* 2 vols. (Indianapolis, Ind., 1950); Otto Eisenschiml and Ralph G. Newman (eds.), *The American Iliad: The Epic Story of the Civil War as Narrated by Eyewitnesses and Contemporaries* (Indianapolis, Ind., 1947); Frank Moore (ed.), *The Rebellion Record: A Diary of American Events . . .,* 12 vols. (New York, 1861–1868); Albert Kirwan (ed.), *The Confederacy* (Cleveland, 1959); Richard B. Harwell (ed.), *The Confederate Reader* (New York, 1957); and *Historical Statistics of the United States: Colonial Times to 1957* (Washington, D.C., 1960).

Essays touching Confederate history abound. One of the best collections is David Donald (ed.), *Why the North Won the Civil War* (Baton Rouge, La., 1960), which might be more descriptively titled "Why the South Lost." David Potter, *The South and the Sectional Conflict* (Baton Rouge, La., 1968) contains some of the best efforts of its brilliant author, as does C. Vann Woodward's *Burden of Southern History,* revised edition (Baton Rouge, La., 1968) and *American Counterpoint* (Boston, 1971). Frank E. Vandiver (ed.), *The Idea of the South* (Chicago, 1964), is a collection of thoughtful pieces, as are Charles G. Sellers, Jr., *The Southerner as American* (Chapel Hill, N.C., 1960), and William R. Brock (ed.), *The Civil War* (New York, 1969). Vandiver makes some especially perceptive observations in his contribution to William F. Holmes and Harold M. Hollingsworth (eds.), *Essays on the American Civil War* (Austin, Tex., 1968). Two essays with essentially the same title written some years apart by different scholars are suggestive: Charles W. Ramsdell, "Some Problems Involved in Writing the History of the Confederacy," *Journal of Southern History,* II (1936), 133–147, and Frank E. Vandiver "Some Problems Involved in Writing Confederate History," *Journal of Southern History,* XXXVI (1970), 400–410. Finally, some reflections of a "master" are contained in Douglas S. Freeman, *The South to Posterity* (New York, 1939).

About the Confederacy *per se* a number of general histories exist. One of the most interesting is one of the oldest, Edward A. Pollard's *The Lost Cause: A New Southern History of the War* ... (New York, 1866). Pollard was a talented journalist who wrote from a pro-Southern, anti-Jefferson Davis bias. Somewhat more recently, the standard modern work has been Clement Eaton, *A History of the Southern Confederacy* (New York, 1954). E. Merton Coulter, *The Confederate States of America, 1861–1865* (Baton Rouge, La., 1950) is an encyclopedic work which presents more facts than interpretation. The best general reader's history is Frank E. Vandiver, *Their Tattered Flags: The Epic of the Confederacy* (New York, 1970). Other studies appealing to a general readership are Clifford Dowdey, *The Land They Fought For: The Story of the South as the Confederacy, 1832–1865* (Garden City, N.Y., 1955), and Robert S. Henry, *The Story of the Confederacy* (Indianapolis, Ind., 1931). The best short general history is still Charles P. Roland's *The Confederacy* (Chicago, 1960).

Among significant interpretive works on the Confederate experience, Nathaniel W. Stephenson's *The Day of the Confederacy* (New Haven, Conn., 1919) and Frank L. Owsley's *State Rights in the Confederacy* (Chicago, 1925) are older standards. Frank E. Vandiver's "The Confederacy and the American Tradition," *Journal of Southern History*, XXVIII (1962), 277–286 is seminal. Bell I. Wiley's *Road to Appomattox*, Atheneum edition (New York, 1968) focuses upon the negative aspects of Southern nationhood, while Emory M. Thomas' *Confederacy as a Revolutionary Experience* (Englewood Cliffs, N.J., 1971) emphasizes the positive.

There is a significant literature which attempts to determine the reason or reasons the "Lost Cause" lost. The best summary of this material is Henry Steele Commager (ed.), *The Defeat of the Confederacy* (Princeton, N.J., 1964). Further contributions include: Wiley's *Road to Appomattox;* Lawrence H. Gipson, "The Collapse of the Confederacy," *Mississippi Valley Historical Review*, IV (1918), 437–458; and Robert L. Kerby, "Why the Confederacy Lost," *Review of Politics*, XXXV (1973), 326–345.

Manuscript and Archival Materials

The rawest raw materials of Confederate history, manuscript, and archival materials, are fairly well scattered. Much official and personal material did not survive the Confederacy and more has perished since 1865 through fire, neglect, and like causes. Nevertheless, because the Confederacy and its war came very close to the Southern people, much abides, and still those interested in the study make "finds" among old trunks in attics.

Important to the location and use of this material are several guides. Henry Putney Beers, *Guide to the Archives of the Government of the Confederate*

States of America (Washington, D.C., 1968) is a veritable gold mine. Beers lists and locates records of the Confederate government, cites printed material, and notes secondary works which relate to the items listed. Moreover the guide offers the locations of manuscript collections of the papers of government and military officials. Since most archival material of the Confederacy is in the National Archives and most of it is contained in Record Group 109, the National Archives *Preliminary Inventory,* number 101, *War Department Collection of Confederate Records,* compiled by Elizabeth Bethel (Washington, D.C., 1957), is also useful.

For manuscript collections, the most important guide is U.S. Library of Congress, *National Union Catalog of Manuscript Collections,* which describes and locates the important collections of major repositories. Also useful are National Historical Publications Commission, *Guide to Archives and Manuscripts in the United States,* ed. by Philip M. Hamer (New Haven, Conn., 1961), which provides notes on the holdings of 1,300 repositories; and American Association for State and Local History, *Directory of Historical Societies and Agencies in the United States and Canada* (Nashville, Tenn., 1965).

Archives of the individual Confederate states as well as some city and county records are important. An introduction to British materials is Bernard R. Crick and Miriam Alman (eds.), *A Guide to Manuscripts Relating to America in Great Britain and Ireland* (London, 1961). The largest collection of district court records is in the Federal Records Center at East Point, Georgia. Most individual manuscript and archival repositories have a publication describing their holdings and facilities. These range in size and scope from pamphlets to Susan Sokol Blosser and Clyde Norman Wilson, Jr., *The Southern Historical Collection: A Guide to Manuscripts* (Chapel Hill, N.C., 1970).

Guides and lists are important. Too often, however, the researcher may in his or her haste overlook an even more significant resource: the people who work with the materials in a given repository. These professionals may often save many hours or locate items otherwise unknown. If nothing else they usually offer a sympathetic ear to a wandering scholar.

Printed Sources

In addition to the published material cited under "Biography and Personal Narratives," on page 331–349, there is a rich trove of eyewitness accounts in *The Southern Historical Society Papers, The Confederate Veteran,* and Clarence C. Buel and Robert U. Johnson (eds.), *Battles and Leaders of the Civil War,* 4 vols. (New York, 1887).

For contemporary statistical data and encyclopedic material see *The Eighth Census,* 1860, 4 vols. (Washington, D.C., 1864–1866); Frank Moore (ed.), *The Rebellion Record: A Diary of American Events* ... , 12 vols. (New York, 1861–1868); *The American Annual Cyclopedia* ... , 5 vols. (New York, 1862–1866); Rembert W. Patrick (ed.), *The Opinions of the Confederate Attorneys General, 1861–1865* (Buffalo, 1950); and the reports of the secretary of the treasury appended to Henry D. Capers, *The Life and Times of C. G. Memminger* (Richmond, Va., 1893). Confederate statutes are in James M. Matthews (ed.), *The Statutes at Large of the Provisional Government* ... (Richmond, Va., 1862–1864), covering all but the final session of Congress and some secret acts; and Charles W. Ramsdell (ed.), *Laws and Joint Resolutions of the Last Session of the Confederate Congress* ... *Together with the Secret Acts of Previous Congresses* (Durham, N.C., 1941).

State governments, too, printed legislative journals and statutes. These and other material published in the Confederacy are listed and located in Marjorie L. Crandall (comp.), *Confederate Imprints: A Check List Based Principally on the Collections of the Boston Athenaeum*, 2 vols. (Boston, 1955), and Richard B. Harwell (comp.), *More Confederate Imprints*, 2 vols. (Richmond, Va., 1957). The imprints cited in Crandall's and Harwell's volumes are available in microfilm edition compiled by the Lost Cause Press.

Basic to any military study and many civil topics as well is *War of the Rebellion: A Compilation of the Official Records of the Union and Confederate Armies*, 127 "serials" comprising 70 vols. (Washington, D.C., 1880–1901). Comparable materials on the navy and some diplomatic correspondence as well are in *Official Records of the Union and Confederate Navies in the War of the Rebellion*, 30 vols. (Washington, D.C., 1894–1922).

Periodicals

The standard study of magazines in the United States is Frank Luther Mott, *A History of American Magazines, 1741–1905*, 5 vols. (New York and Cambridge, Mass., 1930–1968). To locate periodicals the best guide is Winifred Gregory, *Union List of Serials in Libraries of the United States and Canada* (New York, 1943), *and Supplement* ... (New York, 1945); however microfilm has much reduced the need to travel in order to use periodicals.

Within the Confederacy the most significant magazines were:

The Countryman
De Bow's Review
Magnolia: A Southern Home Journal.
Record of News, History, and Literature
Richmond Age, A Southern Monthly Eclectic Magazine
Southern Cultivator
Southern Field and Fireside
Southern Illustrated News

Southern Literary Messenger
Southern Punch

Newspapers

For newspapers the best introductions are Dwight L. Dumond (ed.), *Southern Editorials on Secession* (New York, 1931), and especially J. Cutler Andrews, *The South Reports the Civil War* (Princeton, N.J., 1970). Frederick S. Daniel, *The Richmond Examiner during the War . . .* (New York, 1868), contains some of the best editorials to appear in that provocative paper. Also appropriate is the article by J. Cutler Andrews, "Writing History from Civil War Newspapers," *Western Pennsylvania Historical Magazine,* LIV (1971), 1–14. For the location of the files of specific papers, the standard guide is Winifred Gregory (ed.), *American Newspapers, 1821–1936, A Union List of Files Available in the United States and Canada* (New York, 1937). Perhaps even more helpful, though incomplete, is U.S. Library of Congress, *Newspapers on Microfilm,* 6th edition (Washington, D.C., 1967). Most recent information on newspapers on microfilm is available from the Micro Photo Division of the Bell and Howell Company.

A representative list of newspapers significant for the study of the Confederacy includes:

Athens *Southern Watchman*
Atlanta *Intelligencer*
Atlanta *Southern Confederacy*
Augusta *Chronicle and Sentinel*
Augusta *Constitutionalist*
Charleston *Courier*
Charleston *Mercury*
Chattanooga *Daily Rebel*
Columbia *South Carolinian*
Columbia *Southern Guardian*
Columbus *Enquirer*
Galveston *Tri-Weekly News*
Houston *Telegraph*
Jackson *Mississippian*
Knoxville *Register*
London *Index*
London *Times*
Lynchburg *Republican*
Lynchburg *Virginian*
Macon *Telegraph*
Memphis *Appeal*

Milledgeville *Confederate Union*
Mobile *Register and Advertiser*
Montgomery *Advertiser*
Montgomery *Daily Mail*
Nashville *Republican Banner*
Natchez *Courier*
New Orleans *Crescent*
New Orleans *Delta*
New Orleans *Picayune*
New York *Times*
New York *Tribune*
Norfolk *Day Book*
Raleigh *Confederate*
Raleigh *North Carolina Evening Standard*
Richmond *Dispatch*
Richmond *Enquirer*
Richmond *Examiner*
Richmond *Sentinel*
Richmond *Whig*
Savannah *Morning News*

Savannah *Republican*   Vicksburg *Whig*
Selma *Reporter*   Wilmington *Journal*

A special class of newspapers is described in Bell I. Wiley, "Camp Newspapers of the Confederacy," *North Carolina Historical Review* XX (1943) 327–335.

Physical and Graphic Sources

Confederate physical remains and reminders still exist in the South. Visits to cities such as Richmond or Charleston and automobile trips away from interstate highways in the Southern United States offer the opportunity to see houses and public buildings which date back to the Confederate era. Helpful for the traveler is Alice Hamilton Cromie, *A Tour Guide to the Civil War* (Chicago, 1965). The National Park Service does a generally outstanding job of administering sites at Chickamauga and Chattanooga, Stones River (Murfreesboro, Tennessee), Kennesaw Mountain, Shiloh, Fort Donelson, Vicksburg, Fort Pulaski, Antietam, Gettysburg, Manassas, Fredericksburg and Spotsylvania, Petersburg, Richmond, Fort Sumter, and Appomattox Court House. In addition state and municipal governments sponsor the preservation and administration of other places of historical interest. Organizations such as state historical societies and chambers of commerce also maintain sites and museums throughout the South.

The largest single collection of photographs dealing with the Confederacy and its war is that of Matthew Brady at the Library of Congress. Among published materials the most complete is Francis T. Miller (ed.), *The Photographic History of the Civil War*, 10 vols. (New York, 1912). A recent case study of photography during the period is William A. Frassanito, *Gettysburg: A Journey in Time* (New York, 1975).

The response of graphic art to the Confederacy and the war is usually represented in the works of Winslow Homer, for which see Julian Grossman, *Echo of a Distant Drum: Winslow Homer and the Civil War* (New York, 1974). However, other artists of varying abilities displayed their talents in a variety of media ranging from sheet music covers to illustrated letters. A fine collection of this material, originally published in *Battles and Leaders of the Civil War*, is Stephen W. Sears (ed.), *The American Heritage Century Collection of the Civil War Art* (New York 1974). For contemporary sketches, periodicals such as *Harper's Weekly, Frank Leslie's Illustrated Newspaper, The Illustrated London News*, and *The Southern Illustrated News* are quite good. Because the techniques of photography were still quite primitive, these sketches provide a counterpart of the modern action photograph. A good collection of drawings is *The Civil War: A Centennial Exhibition of Eyewitness Drawings*

(Washington, D.C., 1961.) Edited by Alfred H. Guernsey and Henry M. Alden, *Harper's Pictorial History of the Great Rebellion*, 2 vols. (New York, 1866–1868) is basic. Also good is the recent work on Alfred R. Waud, Frederic E. Ray's *Alfred R. Waud: Civil War Artist* (New York, 1974); and W. Stanley Hoole, *Vizetelly Covers the Confederacy* (Tuscaloosa, Ala., 1957). Collections of drawings, paintings, photographs, and the like include Richard M. Ketchum (ed.), *The American Heritage Picture History of the Civil War* (New York, 1960); David Donald (ed.), *Divided We Fought* (New York, 1952); Bell I. Wiley and Hirst D. Milhollen, *They Who Fought Here* (New York, 1959); and Bell I. Wiley, *Embattled Confederates* (New York, 1964). The current periodical *Civil War Times Illustrated*, too, contains excellent graphic work of the era. And on a more limited scale so do the magazines *Virginia Cavalcade* and *American History Illustrated.*

For maps the best collection is Calvin D. Cowles (comp.), *Atlas to Accompany the Official Records of the Union and Confederate Armies*, 2 vols. (Washington, D.C., 1891–1895). More readily available is Vincent J. Esposito (ed.), *The West Point Atlas of American Wars*, 2 vols. (New York, 1959).

Biography and Personal Narratives

Numerous reference works of collected biography offer introductions to the Confederate dramatis personae. Basic is Allen Johnson and Dumas Malone (eds.), *Dictionary of American Biography*, 22 vols., index (New York, 1928–1965). A forthcoming work to be published by Louisiana State Press, Davis C. Roller and Robert Twyman, *Encyclopedia of Southern History*, will doubtlessly be vital. In addition to Mark Boatner's *Civil War Dictionary* (cited on page 325, above) are Ezra J. Warner *Generals in Gray* (Baton Rouge, La., 1959); Ezra J. Warner and W. Buck Yearns, *Biographical Register of the Confederate Congress* (Baton Rouge, La., 1975); and Jon L. Wakelyn, *Biographical Dictionary of the Confederacy* (Westport, Conn., 1977). Besides these works, Thomas B. Alexander and Richard E. Beringer, *Anatomy of the Confederate Congress* (Nashville, Tenn., 1972), contains background data on individual members of the Congress. The standard guide to biographical literature is the *Biography Index* (New York, 1946–present), which provides an index of books and articles on American figures.

For personal narratives there are several excellent guides. See especially volume two of C. E. Dornbusch (comp.), *Regimental Publications and Personal Narratives of the Civil War: A Checklist*, 2 vols. (New York, 1961–1971). Travel literature is a valuable resource, and for materials see E. Merton Coulter, *Travels in the Confederate States: A Bibliography* (Norman, 1948); Frank Monaghan, *French Travellers in the United States, 1765–1932: A Bibliography* (New York, 1933 reprinted and supplemented by Samuel J. Marino, 1961); and

Allan Nevins, *America Through British Eyes* (New York, 1948), which contains thirty-one excerpts from travel accounts and an annotated bibliography. For diaries begun before 1861 (which often continue into the Confederate era) see William Matthews, *American Diaries: An Annotated Bibliography of American Diaries Written Prior to the Year 1861* (Berkeley, Calif. 1945), and the same author's volume on manuscript diaries, *American Diaries in Manuscript, 1580–1954: a descriptive Bibliography* (Athens, Ga., 1974). There is also a guide to autobiography, Louis Kaplan and others, *A Bibliography of American Autobiographies* (Madison, Wis., 1961).

The list which follows includes prominent Confederates (or authors of prominent narratives), their significant biographies and their own writings.

Warren Akin:
>Bell I. Wiley (ed.), *Letters of Warren Akin, Confederate Congressman* (Athens, Ga., 1959).

James Lusk Alcorn:
>Lillian A. Pereyra, *James Lusk Alcorn: Persistent Whig,* (Baton Rouge, La., 1966).

Edward P. Alexander:
>Maury Klein, *Edward Porter Alexander* (Athens, Ga., 1971). Edward P. Alexander, *Military Memoirs of a Confederate,* ed. by T. Harry Williams (Bloomington, Ind. 1962).

Henry W. Allen:
>Vincent H. Cassidy and Amos E. Simpson, *Henry Watkins Allen of Louisiana* (Baton Rouge, La. 1964).

James Patton Anderson:
>"Autobiography of General Patton Anderson," *Southern Historical Society Papers,* XXIV (1896), 57–72.

Joseph R. Anderson:
>Charles B. Dew, *Ironmaker to the Confederacy: Joseph R. Anderson and the Tredegar Iron Works* (New Haven, Conn., 1966).

Eliza Frances Andrews:
>Spencer Bidwell King, Jr. (ed.), *War-Time Journal of a Georgia Girl, 1864–1865* (Macon, 1960).

Turner Ashby:
>Frank Cunningham, *Knight of the Confederacy: Gen. Turner Ashby* (San Antonio, Tex., 1960).

Myrta L. Avary:
>Myrta L. Avary (ed.), *A Virginia Girl in the Civil War* (New York, 1903).

George William Bagby:
>George W. Bagby, *The Old Virginia Gentleman and Other Sketches,* 5th edition, Richmond, Va., 1948).

Pierce Gustave Toutant Beauregard:
  Hamilton Basso, *Beauregard: the Great Creole* (New York, 1933).
  T. Harry Williams, *P. G. T. Beauregard: Napoleon in Gray* (Baton Rouge, La., 1955).
  Alfred Roman, *The Military Operations of General Beauregard in the War Between the States, 1861 to 1865* . . . (New York, 1884).
Judah P. Benjamin:
  Pierce Butler, *Judah P. Benjamin* (Philadelphia, 1907).
  Robert D. Meade, *Judah P. Benjamin: Confederate Statesman* (New York, 1943).
  Rollin Osterweis, *Judah P. Benjamin: Statesman of the Lost Cause* (New York, 1933).
  Simon I, Neiman, *Judah Benjamin,* (Indianapolis, Ind., 1963).
Henry L. Benning:
  James C. Cobb, "The Making of a Secessionist: Henry L. Benning and the Coming of the Civil War," *Georgia Historical Quarterly,* LX (1976), 313–323.
Mary B. M. Blackford:
  L. Minor Blackford, *Mine Eyes Have Seen the Glory: The Story of a Virginia Lady, Mary Berkeley Minor Blackford* . . . (Cambridge, Mass., 1954).
William W. Blackford:
  War Years with Jeb Stuart (New York, 1945).
Albert T. Bledsoe:
  John B. Bennett, "Albert Taylor Bledsoe: Transitional Philosopher of the Old South," *Methodist History,* XI (1972), 3–14.
Heros von Borcke:
  Memoirs of the Confederate War for Independence, 2 vols. (New York, 1938).
Belle Boyd:
  Curtis Carroll Davis (ed.), *Belle Boyd in Camp and Prison,* (South Brunswick, N.J., 1968).
  Louis Adrien Sigaud, *Belle Boyd, Confederate Spy,* (Richmond, Va., 1945).
Braxton Bragg:
  Grady McWhiney, *Braxton Bragg and Confederate Defeat: Field Command* (New York, 1969).
  Don C. Seitz, *Braxton Bragg, General of the Confederacy,* (Columbia, S.C., 1924).
John C. Breckinridge:
  William C. Davis, *Breckinridge: Statesman, Soldier, Symbol* (Baton Rouge, La., 1974).
  Frank Hopkins Heck, *Proud Kentuckian, John C. Breckinridge, 1821–1875* (Lexington, Ky., 1976).

Albert G. Brown:
  James B. Ranck, *Albert Gallatin Brown, Radical Southern Nationalist*, (New York, 1937).
Joseph E. Brown:
  Louise B. Hill, *Joseph E. Brown and the Confederacy*, (Chapel Hill, N.C., 1939).
  Derrell C. Roberts, *Joseph E. Brown and the Politics of Reconstruction*, (Tuscaloosa, Ala., 1973).
  Joseph H. Parks, *Joseph E. Brown of Georgia* (Baton Rouge, La., 1977).
William M. Browne:
  E. Merton Coulter, *William Montague Browne: Versatile Anglo-Irish American, 1823–1883*, (Athens, Ga., 1968).
William G. Brownlow:
  William G. Brownlow, *Sketches of the Rise, Progress, and Decline of Secession*, (Philadelphia, 1862).
  E. Merton Coulter, *William G. Brownlow: Fighting Parson of the Southern Highlands* (Chapel Hill, N.C., 1937).
  Royal Forrest Conklin, *The Public Speaking Career of William Gannaway (Parson) Brownlow* (Athens, Ohio, 1967).
Franklin Buchanan:
  Charles Lee Lewis, *Admiral Franklin Buchanan, Fearless Man of Action*, (Baltimore, 1929).
Simon B. Buckner:
  Arndt M. Stickles, *Simon Bolivar Buckner: Borderland Knight* (Chapel Hill, N.C., 1940).
James D. Bulloch:
  James D. Bulloch, *The Secret Service of the Confederate States in Europe*, 2 vols. (New York, 1884).
  William P. Roberts, "James Dunwoody Bulloch and the Confederate Navy," *North Carolina Historical Review*, XXIV (1947), 315–366.
John A. Campbell:
  Henry G. Connor, *John Archibald Campbell, Associate Justice of the United States Supreme Court, 1853–1861.* (Boston and New York, 1920).
  Thad Holt Jr., "The Resignation of Mr. Justice Campbell," *Alabama Review*, XII (1959), 105–118.
  Paul J. Zingg, "John Archibald Campbell and the Hampton Roads Conference: Quixotic Diplomacy, 1865," *Alabama Historical Quarterly*, XXXVI (1974), 21–34.
Mary Boykin Chesnut:
  Isabella D. Martin and Myrta L. Avary, *A Diary from Dixie, as Written by Mary Boykin Chesnut . . .* (New York, 1905). New edition by Ben A. Williams, 1949.

Patrick R. Cleburne:
   Howell Purdue and Elizabeth Purdue, *Pat Cleburne, Confederate General:
   A Definitive Biography* (Hillsboro, Tex., 1973).
Howell Cobb:
   Robert P. Brooks (ed.), "Howell Cobb Papers," *Georgia Historical Quar-
   terly* V, VI (1921–1922).
   Zachary T. Johnson, *Political Policies of Howell Cobb*, (Nashville, Tenn.,
   1929).
   Horace Montgomery, *Howell Cobb's Confederate Career*, (Tuscaloosa,
   Ala., 1959).
   John Eddins Simpson, *Howell Cobb: The Politics of Ambition*, (Chicago,
   1973).
   Ulrich B. Phillips (ed.), "The Correspondence of Robert Toombs,
   Alexander H. Stephens, and Howell Cobb," *Annual Report of the Ameri-
   can Historical Association*, (Washington, D.C., 1911), II.
T. R. R. Cobb:
   "The Correspondence of Thomas Reade Rootes Cobb, 1860–1862,"
   Southern Historical Association Publications, XI (1907, 147–328 passim).
   Tom W. Brown, "The Military Career of Thomas R. R. Cobb," *Georgia
   Historical Quarterly*, XLV (1961), 345–362.
John Esten Cooke:
   John O. Beaty, *John Esten Cooke, Virginian* (New York, 1922).
   John Esten Cooke, *Wearing of the Gray*, (Bloomington, Ind., 1959).
   Richard B. Harwell, "John Esten Cooke, Civil War Correspondent,"
   Journal of Southern History, XIX (1953), 501–516.
   Jay B. Hubbell (ed.), "The War Diary of John Esten Cooke," *Journal of
   Southern History*, VII (1941), 526–539.
John J. Crittenden:
   Ann M. B. Coleman, *The Life of John J. Crittenden*, 2 vols. (Philadelphia,
   1871).
   Albert D. Kirwan, *John J. Crittenden: the Struggle for the Union* (Lexington,
   Ky., 1962).
Kate Cumming:
   Richard B. Harwell (ed.), *Kate: the Journal of a Confederate Nurse*, (Baton
   Rouge, La., 1959).
J. L. M. Curry:
   Edwin A. Alderman and Armistead Gordon, *J. L. M. Curry: A Biography*,
   (New York and London 1911).
   Jessie P. Rice, *J. L. M. Curry: Southerner, Statesman, and Educator*, (New
   York, 1949).
John M. Daniel:
   George W. Bagby, "John M. Daniel's Latchkey," in *The Old Virginia

Gentleman and Other Sketches, 5th edition (Richmond, Va., 1948).

Frederick S. Daniel, *The Richmond Examiner During the War* (New York, 1868).

Jefferson Davis:

Frank H. Alfriend, *Life of Jefferson Davis,* (Cincinnati and Philadelphia, 1868).

John J. Craven, *Prison Life of Jefferson Davis,* (New York, 1905).

Elisabeth Cutting, *Jefferson Davis, Political Soldier,* (New York, 1930).

Jefferson Davis, *The Rise and Fall of the Confederate Government,* 2 vols. (New York, 1958).

Varina Howell Davis, *Jefferson Davis, Ex-President of the Confederate States of America: A Memoir by his Wife,* 2 vols. (New York, 1890).

William E. Dodd, *Jefferson Davis,* (Philadelphia, 1907).

Hamilton J. Eckenrode, *Jefferson Davis, President of the South,* (New York, 1923).

Robert McElroy, *Jefferson Davis: The Unreal and the Real,* 2 vols., (New York, 1937).

Haskell Monroe, Jr., and James T. McIntosh (eds.), *The Papers of Jefferson Davis,* I, *1808–1840.* (Baton Rouge, La., 1971).

Edward A. Pollard, *Life of Jefferson Davis with a Secret History of the Southern Confederacy, Gathered "Behind the Scenes in Richmond."* (Philadelphia and Chicago 1869).

Dunbar Rowland (ed.), *Jefferson Davis, Constitutionalist: His Letters, Papers, and Speeches,* 10 vols. (Jackson, Miss., 1923).

Hudson Strode, *Jefferson Davis,* 3 vols. (New York, 1955–1964).

Hudson Strode (ed.), *Jefferson Davis: Private Letters, 1823–1889* (New York, 1966).

Allen Tate, *Jefferson Davis, His Rise and Fall,* (New York, 1929).

Robert W. Winston, *High Stakes and Hair Trigger: The Life of Jefferson Davis,* (New York, 1930).

James T. McIntosh (ed.), *The Papers of Jefferson Davis,* II, *June, 1841–July, 1846,* (Baton Rouge, La., 1974).

Frank Edgar Everett, Jr., *Brierfield, Plantation Home of Jefferson Davis* (Hattiesburg, Miss., 1971).

Varina Davis:

Ishbel Ross, *First Lady of the South: The Life of Mrs. Jefferson Davis* (New York, 1958).

Eron O. Rowland, *Varina Howell, Wife of Jefferson Davis,* 2 vols. (New York, 1927–1931).

Sarah M. Dawson:

James I. Robertson, Jr. (ed.), *A Confederate Girl's Diary* (Bloomington, Ind., 1960).

J. D. B. DeBow:
  Robert F. Durden, "J. D. B. DeBow: Convolutions of a Slavery Expansionist," *Journal of Southern History*, XVII (1951), 441–461.
  Otis C. Skipper, *J. D. B. DeBow: Magazinist of the Old South* (Athens, Ga., 1958).
  James Adelbert McMillen, *The Works of James D. B. DeBow*, (Hattiesburg, Miss., 1940).
Thomas Cooper DeLeon:
  Four Years in Rebel Capitals (Mobile, Ala., 1890)
  Belles, Beaux, and Brains of the 60's (New York, 1907).
Henry Kyd Douglas:
  Fletcher M. Green (ed.), *I Rode with Stonewall: the War Experiences of the Youngest Member of Jackson's Staff* (Chapel Hill, N.C., 1940).
Basil W. Duke:
  A History of Morgan's Cavalry, ed. by Cecil Fletcher Holland (Bloomington, Ind., 1960).
  Reminiscences . . . (Garden City, N.Y., 1911).
Jubal A. Early:
  Jubal A. Early, *Autobiographical Sketch and Narrative of the War between the States*, (Philadelphia, 1912). New edition titled *War Memoirs* . . . , with introduction by Frank E. Vandiver, (Bloomington, Ind., 1960).
  Millard Kessler Bushong, *Old Jube, A Biography of General Jubal A. Early*, (Boyee, Va., 1955).
  Frank Everson Vandiver, *Jubal's Raid: General Early's Famous Attack on Washington in 1864*, (New York, 1960).
George C. Eggleston:
  A Rebel's Recollections, new edition with introduction by David Donald, (Bloomington, Ind., 1959).
John W. Ellis:
  Noble J. Tolbert (ed.), *The Papers of John Willis Ellis*, 2 vols. (Raleigh, N.C., 1964).
Augusta Jane Evans:
  William Perry Fidler, *Augusta Evans Wilson, 1835–1909* (University, Ala., 1951).
  ———, "Augusta Evans Wilson as Confederate Propagandist," *Alabama Review*, II (1949), 32–44.
Richard S. Ewell:
  Percy G. Hamlin, *"Old Bald Head" (General R. S. Ewell): The Portrait of a Soldier*, (Strasburg, Va., 1940).
  Percy G. Hamlin, "Richard S. Ewell: His Humanity and Humor," *Virginia Cavalcade*, XXI (1971), 5–11.

George Fitzhugh:

Arnoud B. Leavelle and Thomas I. Cook, "George Fitzhugh and the Theory of American Conservatism," *Journal of Politics,* VII (1945), 145–168.

Harvey Wish, *George Fitzhugh, Propagandist of the Old South* (Baton Rouge, La., 1943).

Eugene D. Genovese, *The World the Slaveholders Made* (New York, 1971).

Henry S. Foote:

John E. Gonzales, "Henry Stuart Foote: Confederate Congressman and Exile," *Civil War History,* XI (1965), 384–395.

John E. Gonzales, "Henry Stuart Foote in Exile—1865," *Journal of Mississippi History,* XV (1953), 90–98.

Henry Stuart Foote, *Casket of Reminiscences,* (New York, 1968).

Rip Ford:

Stephen B. Oates (ed.), *Rip Ford's Texas* (Austin, Tex., 1963).

Nathan Bedford Forrest:

Robert S. Henry (ed.), *As They Saw Forrest* (Jackson, Tenn., 1956).

Robert S. Henry, *"First with the Most" Forrest* (Indianapolis, Ind., 1944).

Andrew N. Lytle, *Bedford Forrest and His Critter Company* (New York, 1931), new edition (New York, 1960).

Eric W. Sheppard, *Bedford Forrest, the Confederacy's Greatest Cavalryman* (New York, 1930).

John A. Wyeth, *Life of General Nathan Bedford Forrest* (New York, 1899), new edition titled *That Devil Forrest* (New York: 1959).

Arthur J. L. Fremantle:

Walter Lord (ed.), *The Fremantle Diary . . .* (Boston, 1954).

John B. Gordon:

John B. Gordon, *Reminiscences of the Civil War* (New York, 1903).

Allen P. Tankersley, *John B. Gordon: A Study in Gallantry* (Atlanta, Ga., 1955).

H. Dorgan, "A Case Study in Reconciliation: General John B. Gordon and the Last Days of the Confederacy," *Quarterly Journal of Speech,* LX (1974), 83–91.

Josiah Gorgas:

Frank E. Vandiver (ed.), *The Civil War Diary of General Josiah Gorgas* (University, Ala., 1947).

Frank E. Vandiver, *Ploughshares into Swords: Josiah Gorgas and Confederate Ordnance* (Austin, Tex., 1952).

Maxey Gregg:

Robert K. Krick, "Maxey Gregg: Political Extremist and Confederate General," *Civil War History,* XIX (1973), 293–313.

Wade Hampton:
  Manly Wade Wellman, *Giant in Gray: A Biography of Wade Hampton of South Carolina* (New York, 1949).
William J. Hardee:
  Nathaniel C. Hughes, Jr., *General William J. Hardee: Old Reliable* (Baton Rouge, La., 1965).
Constance Cary Harrison:
  Recollections Grave and Gay (New York, 1911).
Henry Heth:
  James L. Morrison Jr. (ed.), *Memoirs of Henry Heth* (Westport, Conn., 1974).
Ambrose Powell Hill:
  John Wheeler-Bennett, "A.P. Hill: A Study in Confederate Leadership," *Virginia Quarterly Review*, XXXVII (1961), 198–209.
Benjamin H. Hill:
  Haywood J. Pearce, Jr., *Benjamin H. Hill, Secession and Reconstruction* (Chicago, 1928).
Daniel H. Hill:
  Hal Bridges, *Lee's Maverick General: Daniel Harvey Hill* (New York, 1961).
W. W. Holden:
  William K. Boyd (ed.), *Memoirs of W. W. Holden* (Durham, N.C., 1911).
  Horace W. Raper, "William W. Holden and the Peace Movement in North Carolina," *North Carolina Historical Review*, XXXI (1954), 493–516.
John Bell Hood:
  John P. Dyer, *The Gallant Hood* (Indianapolis, Ind., 1950).
  John B. Hood, *Advance and Retreat*, new edition with intro. by Richard N. Current (Bloomington, Ind., 1959).
  Richard M. McMurry, "Disappointment in History: The Papers of John Bell Hood," *Prologue*, IV (1972), 161–164.
  Richard O'Connor, *Hood, Cavalier General*, (New York, 1949).
  Frank E. Vandiver, "General Hood as Logistician," *Military Affairs*, XVI (1952), 1–11.
Jedediah Hotchkiss:
  Archie P. McDonald, *Make Me a Map of the Valley: The Civil War Journal of Stonewall Jackson's Topographer* (Dallas, 1973).
Henry Hotze:
  Stephen B. Oates, "Henry Hotze: Confederate Agent Abroad," *Historian*, XXVII (1965), 131–154.
  Charles P. Cullop, *Confederate Propaganda in Europe, 1861–1865* (Coral Gables, Fla., 1969).

Samuel Houston:

Donald Day and H. H. Ullom (eds.), *The Autobiography of Sam Houston* (Norman, Okla., 1954).

Marquis James, *The Raven: A Biography of Sam Houston* (Indianapolis, Ind., 1929).

Amelia W. Williams and Eugene C. Barker, (eds.), *The Writings of Sam Houston 1813–1863,* 8 vols. (Austin, Tex., 1938–1943).

Llerena Friend, *Sam Houston: the Great Designer* (Austin, Tex., 1954).

Andrew Forest Muir, "Sam Houston and the Civil War," *Texana,* VI (1968), 282–287.

Edward R. Maher, Jr., "Sam Houston and Secession," *Southwestern Historical Quarterly,* LV (1952), 448–458.

R. M. T. Hunter:

Charles H. Ambler (ed.), *Correspondence of Robert M. T. Hunter, 1826–1876* (Washington, D.C., 1918).

Henry H. Simms, *Life of Robert M. T. Hunter: A Study in Sectionalism and Secession* (Richmond, Va., 1935).

W. S. Hitchcock, "Southern Moderates and Secession: Senator Robert M. T. Hunter's Call for Union," *Journal of American History,* LIX (1973), 871–884.

Thomas J. "Stonewall" Jackson:

Lenoir Chambers, *Stonewall Jackson,* 2 vols. (New York, 1959).

Burke Davis, *They Called Him Stonewall: A Life of Lt. General T. J. Jackson, C.S.A.* (New York, 1954).

G.F.R. Henderson, *Stonewall Jackson and the American Civil War,* 2 vols. (New York, 1898) new edition, 1936.

John Selby, *Stonewall Jackson as Military Commander* (Princeton, N.J. 1968).

Frank E. Vandiver, *Mighty Stonewall* (New York, 1957).

Robert G. Tanner, *Stonewall in the Valley: Thomas J. Stonewall Jackson's Shenandoah Valley Campaign Spring, 1862* (Garden City, N.Y., 1976).

Herschel V. Johnson:

Percy S. Flippin, *Herschel V. Johnson of Georgia, States Rights Unionist* (Richmond, Va., 1931).

Albert Sydney Johnston:

William P. Johnston, *The Life of Gen. Albert Sidney Johnston* (New York, 1878).

Charles P. Roland, "Albert Sidney Johnston and the Loss of Forts Henry and Donelson," *Journal of Southern History,* XXIII (1957), 45–69.

Charles P. Roland, "Albert Sidney Johnston and the Shiloh Campaign," *Civil War History,* IV (1958), 355–382.

Charles P. Roland, *Albert Sidney Johnston: Soldier of Three Republics* (Austin, Tex., 1964).

Joseph E. Johnston:
Gilbert E. Govan, and James W. Livingood, *A Different Valor: the Story of General Joseph E. Johnston, C.S.A.,* (Indianapolis, Ind., 1956).
Alfred P. James, "General Joseph Eggleston Johnson, Storm Center of the Confederate Army," *Mississippi Valley Historical Review,* XIV (1927), 342–359.
Joseph E. Johnston, *Narrative of Military Operations . . . during the Late War Between the States* (New York, 1874) new edition with introduction by Frank E. Vandiver, 1959.
Donald B. Sanger, "Some Problems Facing Joseph E. Johnston in the Spring of 1863," in Avery O. Craven (ed.), *Essays in Honor of William E. Dodd* (Chicago, 1935), pp. 257–290.

John Beauchamp Jones:
John Beauchamp Jones, *A Rebel War Clerk's Diary at the Confederate States' Capitol,* 2 vols. (Philadelphia, 1866) new edition, with introduction by Howard Swiggett (New York, 1935).

Robert G. H. Kean:
Edward Younger (ed.), *Inside the Confederate Government: The Diary of Robert Garlick Hill Kean,* (New York, 1957).

John McIntosh Kell:
Norman C. Delaney, *John McIntosh Kell of the Raider* Alabama (University, Ala., 1973).

Gazaway B. Lamar:
Edwin B. Coddington, "The Activities and Interests of a Confederate Businessman: Gazaway B. Lamar," *Journal of Southern History,* IX (1943), 3–36.
Thomas R. Hay, "Gazaway Bugg Lamar, Confederate Banker and Business Man," *Georgia Historical Quarterly,* XXXVII (1953), 89–128.

L. Q. C. Lamar:
Wirt A. Cate, *Lucious Q. C. Lamar* (Chapel Hill, N.C., 1935).
Edward Mayes, *Lucious Q. C. Lamar: His Life, Times, and Speeches, 1825–1893* (Nashville, Tenn., 1896).
James B. Murphy, *L. Q. C. Lamar: Pragmatic Patriot* (Baton Rouge, La., 1973).

Emma LeConte:
Earl S. Miers (ed.), *When the World Ended: the Diary of Emma LeConte* (New York, 1957).

Joseph LeConte:
Joseph LeConte, *'Ware Sherman: A Journal of Three Months Personal Experience in the Last Days of the Confederacy* (Berkeley, Calif. 1937).

T. D. Bozeman, "Joseph LeConte: Organic Science and a Sociology for the South," *Journal of Southern History*, XXXIX (1973), 565–582.

Robert E. Lee:

Gamaliel Bradford, *Lee the American*, (Boston, 1912).

Thomas L. Connelly, *The Marble Man: Robert E. Lee and His Image in American Society* (New York, 1977).

Avery Craven (ed.), *"To Markie:" the Letters of Robert E. Lee to Martha Custis Williams* (Cambridge, Mass., 1933).

Burke Davis, *Gray Fox: Robert E. Lee and the Civil War* (New York, 1956).

Peter Earle, *Robert E. Lee*, (New York, 1973).

Douglas S. Freeman, *R. E. Lee: A Biography*, 4 vols., (New York, 1934–1935).

Douglas S. Freeman (ed.) *Lee's Dispatches: Unpublished Letters of General Robert E. Lee . . . to Jefferson Davis . . .* (New York and London, 1915) new edition with additional dispatches and foreword by Grady McWhiney, 1957.

Stanley F. Horn (ed.), *The Robert E. Lee Reader* (Indianapolis, Ind., 1949).

J. William Jones, *Life and Letters of Robert E. Lee* (New York, 1906).

Robert E. Lee, [Jr.], *Recollections and Letters of General Robert E. Lee* (Garden City, N.Y., 1924).

Frederick Maurice, *Robert E. Lee, the Soldier* (New York, 1925).

Earl S. Miers, *Robert E. Lee: A Great Life in Brief* (New York, 1956).

Thomas N. Page, *Robert E. Lee: Man and Soldier* (New York, 1911).

Clifford Dowdey, *Lee* (Boston, 1965).

Clifford Dowdey and Louis H. Manarin (eds.), *The Wartime Papers of R. E. Lee*, (Boston, 1961).

Margaret Sanborn, *Robert E. Lee*, 2 vols. (Philadelphia, 1966–1967).

Stephen Dill Lee:

Herman Hattaway, *General Stephen D. Lee* (Jackson, Miss., 1976).

John Letcher:

F. N. Boney, *John Letcher of Virginia: The Story of Virginia's Civil War Governor* (University, Ala., 1966).

James Longstreet:

H. J. Eckenrode and Bryan Conrad, *James Longstreet: Lee's War Horse* (Chapel Hill, N.C., 1936).

James Longstreet, *From Manassas to Appomattox: Memoirs of the Civil War in America* (Philadelphia, 1896) revised edition, 1903; new edition with introduction by James I. Robertson, Jr., 1960.

Donald B. Sanger and Thomas R. Hay, *James Longstreet*, (Baton Rouge, La., 1952).

William W. Loring:

William L. Wessels, *Born to Be A Soldier: The Military Career of William Wing Loring of St. Augustine, Florida,* (Fort Worth, Tex., 1971).

Francis P. Lubbock:

C. W. Raines (ed.), *Six Decades in Texas or Memoirs of Francis Richard Lubbock, Governor of Texas in War Time, 1861–1863* . . . (Austin, Tex., 1900).

William Mahone:

Nelson M. Blake, *William Mahone of Virginia, Soldier and Political Insurgent* (Richmond, Va., 1935).

Stephen R. Mallory:

Joseph T. Durkin, *Stephen R. Mallory: Confederate Navy Chief* (Chapel Hill, N.C., 1954).

J. Franklin Jameson (ed.), "Letters of Stephen R. Mallory, 1861," *American Historical Review,* XII (1906), 103–108.

James M. Mason:

Virginia Mason, *The Public Life of . . . James M. Mason . . .* (Roanoke, Va., 1903).

Matthew F. Maury:

Charles L. Lewis, *Matthew Fontaine Maury, The Pathfinder of the Seas* (Annapolis, Md., 1927).

Frances L. Williams, *Matthew Fontaine Maury: Scientist of the Sea* (New Brunswick, N.J., 1963).

Samuel Bell Maxey:

Nancy Hobson, "Samuel Bell Maxey as Confederate Commander of Indian Territory," *Journal of the West,* XII (1973), 424–438.

Louise Horton, *Samuel Bell Maxey: A Biography* (Austin, Tex., 1974).

Christopher G. Memminger:

H. D. Capers, *The Life and Times of C. G. Memminger* (Richmond, Va., 1893).

John H. Morgan:

Cecil F. Holland, *Morgan and His Raiders: A Biography of the Confederate General* (New York, 1942).

Howard Swiggett, *The Rebel Raider: A Life of John Hunt Morgan* (Garden City, N.Y., 1937).

Edison H. Thomas, *John Hunt Morgan and His Raiders* (Lexington, Ky., 1975).

John S. Mosby:

Virgil C. Jones, *Ranger Mosby* (Chapel Hill, N.C., 1944).

John S. Mosby, *Mosby's War Reminiscences and Stuart's Cavalry Campaigns* (New York, 1958).

John W. Munson, *Reminiscences of a Mosby Guerrilla* (New York, 1906).
Charles W. Russell (ed.), *The Memoirs of Colonel John S. Mosby* (Boston, 1917) new edition with introduction by Virgil C. Jones (Bloomington, Ind., 1959).
Lucius B. Northrop:
Jeremy P. Felt, "Lucius B. Northrop and the Confederacy's Subsistence Department," *Virginia Magazine of History and Biography,* LXIX (1961), 181–193.
Thomas R. Hay, "Lucius B. Northrup: Commissary General of the Confederacy," *Civil War History,* IX (1963), 5–23.
Phoebe Yates Pember:
A Southern Woman's Story: Life in Confederate Richmond, ed. by Bell I. Wiley, (Jackson, Tenn., 1959).
John C. Pemberton:
John C. Pemberton, Jr., *Pemberton: Defender of Vicksburg,* (Chapel Hill, N.C., 1942).
Alexander "Sandie" Pendleton:
W. G. Bean, *Stonewall's Man: Sandie Pendleton,* (Chapel Hill, N.C., 1959).
Benjamin F. Perry:
Lillian A. Kibler, *Benjamin F. Perry, South Carolina Unionist* (Durham, N.C., 1946).
John J. Pettus:
Robert W. Dubay, *John Jones Pettus, Mississippi Fire-Eater: His Life and Times, 1813–1867* (Oxford, Miss., 1975).
George E. Pickett:
Arthur C. Inman (ed.), *Soldier of the South: General Pickett's War Letters to his Wife* (Boston and New York, 1928).
LaSalle C. Pickett, *The Heart of a Soldier as Revealed in the Intimate Letters of Genl. George E. Pickett, C.S.A.* (New York, 1913).
LaSalle Corbell Pickett, *Pickett and His Men* (Atlanta, Ga., 1900).
Albert Pike:
Robert L. Duncan, *Reluctant General: The Life and Times of Albert Pike* (New York, 1961).
Gideon J. Pillow:
Roy P. Stonesifer, Jr., "Gideon J. Pillow (1806–78); A Study in Egotism," *Tennessee Historical Quarterly* XXV (1966), 340–350.
Leonidas Polk:
Joseph H. Parks, *General Leonidas Polk, C.S.A.: The Fighting Bishop* (Baton Rouge, La., 1962).
Edward A. Pollard:
Jack P. Maddex, Jr., *Reconstruction of Edward A. Pollard: A Rebel's Conversion to Postbellum Unionism* (Chapel Hill, N.C., 1974).

Sterling Price:
Robert E. Shalhope, *Sterling Price: Portrait of a Southerner* (Columbia, S.C., 1971).
Albert Castel, *General Sterling Price and the Civil War in the West* (Baton Rouge, La., 1968).

Roger A. Pryor:
Robert S. Holzman, *"Adapt or Perish:" the Life of General Roger A. Pryor, C.S.A.* (Hamden, Conn., 1976).

Mrs. Roger A. Pryor:
Mrs. Roger A. Pryor, *Reminiscences of Peace and War* (New York, 1905).

Sallie Brock Putnam:
Richmond during the War: Four Years of Personal Observation (New York, 1867).

William Clarke Quantrill:
Albert Castel, *William Clarke Quantrill: His Life and Times,* (New York, 1962).

John A. Quitman:
J.F.H. Claiborne, *Life and Correspondence of John A. Quitman,* 2 vols. (New York, 1860).
James H. McLendon, "John A. Quitman, Fire-Eating Governor," *Journal of Mississippi History,* XV (1953), 73–89.

George Wythe Randolph:
Archer Jones, "Some Aspects of George W. Randolph's Service as Confederate Secretary of War," *Journal of Southern History* XXVI (1960), 299–314.

John H. Reagan:
Walter F. McCaleb (ed.), *Memoirs, with Special Reference to Secession and the Civil War,* by John H. Reagan, (New York, 1906).
Ben H. Procter, *Not Without Honor: the Life of John H. Reagan* (Austin, Tex., 1962).

Robert Barnwell Rhett:
Laura A. White, *Robert Barnwell Rhett, Father of Secession* (New York, 1931).

Fitzgerald Ross:
Cities and Camps of the Confederate States, ed. by Richard Barksdale Harwell (Urbana, Ill., 1958).

Edmund Ruffin:
Avery O. Craven, *Edmund Ruffin, Southerner: A Study in Secession* (New York, 1932).
William Koutman Scarborough (ed.), *The Diary of Edmund Ruffin,* I, *Toward Independence, October, 1856–April, 1861,* (Baton Rouge, La.,

1972), II, *The Years of Hope, April, 1861–June, 1863* (Baton Rouge, La., 1976).

William Howard Russell:

My Diary North and South (Boston, 1863).

Justus Scheibert:

Seven Months in the Rebel States during the North American War, 1863, trans. by Joseph C. Haynes, ed. by Wm. S. Hoole, (Tuscaloosa, Ala., 1958).

James A. Seddon:

Roy W. Curry, "James A. Seddon, a Southern Prototype," *Virginia Magazine of History and Biography,* LXIII (1955), 122–150.

Raphael Semmes:

Harpur A. Gosnell, *Rebel Raider: Being an Account of Raphael Semme's Cruise in the C.S.S. Sumter* (Chapel Hill, N.C., 1948).

Colyer Meriwether, *Raphael Semmes* (Philadelphia, 1913).

W. Adolphe Roberts, *Semmes of the Alabama* (Indianapolis, Ind., 1938).

Raphael Semmes, *Service Afloat, or The Remarkable Career of the Confederate Cruisers, Sumter and Alabama during the War between the States* (Baltimore, 1887).

Edward Carrington Boykin, *Ghost Ship of the Confederacy: The Story of the Alabama and Her Captain,* (New York, 1957).

Joseph Shelby:

Daniel O'Flaherty, *General Jo Shelby, Undefeated Rebel* (Chapel Hill, N.C., 1954).

R. Casellas, "Confederate Colonists in Mexico," *Americas,* XXVII (1975), 8–15.

William Gilmore Simms:

Mary C. Simms, Alfred T. Odell, and T.C. Duncan Eaves (eds.), *The Letters of William Gilmore Simms,* 5 vols., Columbia, S.C., 1952–1956).

William P. Trent, *William Gilmore Simms* (Boston, 1892).

Jon L. Wakelyn, *The Politics of A Literary Man: William Gilmore Simms* (Westport, Conn., 1973).

John Slidell:

Louis M. Sears, *John Slidell* (Durham, N.C., 1925).

Joseph G. Tregle, Jr., "The Political Apprenticeship of John Slidell," *Journal of Southern History,* XXVI (1960), 57–70.

Beckles, Willson, *John Slidell and the Confederates in Paris (1862–65)* (New York, 1932).

Edmund Kirby Smith:

Joseph H. Parks, *General Edmund Kirby Smith, C.S.A.* (Baton Rouge, La., 1954).

Robert L. Kerby, *Kirby Smith's Confederacy: the Trans-Mississippi South, 1863–1865,* (New York, 1972).

Mason Smith:
    Daniel E. H. Smith and others (eds.), *Mason Smith Family Letters, 1860–1868* (Columbia, N.C., 1950).
William Smith:
    Alvin A. Fahrner, "William 'Extra Billy' Smith, Governor of Virginia, 1864–1865: A Pillar of the Confederacy," *Virginia Magazine of History and Biography*, LXXIV (1966), 68–87.
G. Moxley Sorrel:
    G. Moxley Sorrel, *Recollections of a Confederate Staff Officer* (New York, 1905), new edition with introduction by Bell I. Wiley, 1958.
Alexander H. Stephens:
    Henry Cleveland, *Alexander H. Stephens, in Public and Private . . .* (Philadelphia, 1866).
    Richard M. Johnston and William H. Browne, *Life of Alexander H. Stephens,* (Philadelphia, 1878).
    Ulrich B. Phillips (ed.), "The Correspondence of Robert Toombs, Alexander H. Stephens, and Howell Cobb," *Annual Report of the American Historical Association* (Washington, D.C., 1911), II.
    E. Ramsay Richardson, *Little Aleck: A Life of Alexander H. Stephens, the Fighting Vice President of the Confederacy* (Indianapolis, Ind., 1932).
    Alexander H. Stephens, *A Constitutional View of the Late War Between the States . . .,* 2 vols. (Chicago, 1868–1870).
    Alexander H. Stephens, *Recollections of Alexander H. Stephens* (New York, 1910).
    Rudolph Von Able, *Alexander H. Stephens: A Biography* (New York, 1946).
Kate Stone:
    John Q. Anderson, *Brokenburn: the Journal of Kate Stone, 1861–1868* (Baton Rouge, La., 1955).
J. E. B. Stuart:
    Burke Davis, *Jeb Stuart: The Last Cavalier,* (New York, 1957).
    John W. Thomason, Jr., *Jeb Stuart* (New York, 1930).
Richard Taylor:
    Jackson B. Davis, "The Life of Richard Taylor," *Louisiana Historical Quarterly*, XXIV (1941), 49–126.
    Richard Taylor, *Destruction and Reconstruction: Personal Experiences of the Late War* (New York, 1879) new edition with introduction by Richard Harwell, 1955.
James H. Thornwell:
    Benjamin Morgan Palmer, *Life and Letters of James Henry Thornwell* (New York, 1969).
Robert Toombs:
    Ulrich B. Phillips (ed.), "The Correspondence of Robert Toombs,

Alexander H. Stephens, and Howell Cobb," *Annual Report of the American Historical Association* (Washington, D.C., 1911), II.

Ulrich B. Phillips, *The Life of Robert Toombs* (New York, 1913).

William Y. Thompson, *Robert Toombs of Georgia* (Baton Rouge, La., 1966).

George Trenholm:

Ethel Trenholm Seabrook Nepveux, *George Alfred Trenholm: The Company That Went to War, 1861–1865* (Charleston, S.C., 1973).

Zebulon Vance:

Richard S. Yates, *The Confederacy and Zeb Vance* (Tuscaloosa, Ala., 1958).

Frontis W. Johnson (ed.), *The Papers of Zebulon Baird Vance* (Raleigh, N.C., 1963).

Glenn Tucker, *Zeb Vance: Champion of Personal Freedom* (Indianapolis, Ind., 1966).

Earl Van Dorn:

Robert G. Hartje, *Van Dorn: The Life and Times of a Confederate General* (Nashville, Tenn., 1967).

Leroy Pope Walker:

William C. Harris, *Leroy Pope Walker: Confederate Secretary of War* (Tuscaloosa, Ala., 1952).

Sam R. Watkins:

"Co. Aytch," A Side Show of the Big Show, ed. by Bell I. Wiley (Jackson, Tenn., 1952).

Joseph Wheeler:

John P. Dyer, *"Fight'n Joe" Wheeler* (Baton Rouge, La., 1941).

Louis T. Wigfall:

Alvy L. King, *Louis T. Wigfall: Southern Fire-Eater* (Baton Rouge, La., 1970).

Henry A. Wise:

Clement Eaton, "Henry A. Wise, A Liberal of the Old South," *Journal of Southern History*, VII (1941), 482–494.

Clement Eaton, "Henry A. Wise and the Virginia Fire-Eaters of 1856," *Mississippi Valley Historical Review*, XXI (1935), 495–512.

Barton H. Wise, *The Life of Henry A. Wise of Virginia, 1806–1876* (New York, 1899).

William Lowndes Yancey:

Ralph B. Draughon, Jr., "The Young Manhood of William L. Yancey," *Alabama Review*, XIX (1966), 28–40.

John W. DuBose, *The Life and Times of William Lowndes Yancey* (Birmingham, Ala., 1892).

Alto L. Garner and Nathan Scott, "William Lowndes Yancey: Statesman of Secession," *Alabama Review*, XV (1962), 190–202.

Malcolm C. McMillan, "William L. Yancey and the Historians: One Hundred Years," *Alabama Review*, XX (1967), 163–186.

Austin L. Venable, "The Public Career of William Lowndes Yancey," *Alabama Review*, XVI (1963), 200–212.

Austin L. Venable, "William L. Yancey's Transition from Unionism to State Rights," *Journal of Southern History*, X (1944), 331–342.

Politics and Government

A good summary of the Montgomery Convention, which spawned the Confederacy, is Albert N. Fitts, "The Confederate Convention;" *Alabama Review* II (1949), 83–101, 189–210. The best eyewitness account is "The Correspondence of Thomas Reade Rootes Cobb, 1860–1862, "*Southern History Association Publications*, XI (1907), 147–185, 233–260, 312–328. On the chief work of the convention the best study is Charles R. Lee, Jr., *The Confederate Constitutions* (Chapel Hill, N.C., 1963). See also William M. Robinson, Jr., "A New Deal in Constitutions," *Journal of Southern History*, IV (1938), 449–461.

The convention evolved into the Confederate Congress, and for this body two works are crucial: Wilfred B. Yearns, *The Confederate Congress* (Athens, Ga., 1960) and Thomas B. Alexander and Richard E. Beringer, *The Anatomy of the Confederate Congress: A Study of the Influence of Member Characteristics on Legislative Voting Behavior, 1861–1865* (Nashville, Tenn., 1972). Two related articles which grew out of the quantitative research involved in the latter book are Beringer's "A Profile of the Members of the Confederate Congress," *Journal of Southern History* XXXIII (1967), 518–541 and "The Unconscious 'Spirit of Party' in the Confederate Congress," *Civil War History* XVIII (1972) 312–333. Members of the Congress were far less active than soldiers in leaving their memoirs for posterity. Henry Putney Beers in his *Guide to the Archives of the Government of the Confederate States of America* (Washington, D.C., 1968) lists the locations of papers of congressmen on pp. 33–35. Beyond manuscript collections the most significant material is J. L. M. Curry, *Civil History of the Government of the Confederate States, with Some Personal Reminiscences* (Richmond, Va., 1901) and Bell I. Wiley (ed.), *Letters of Warren Akin, Confederate Congressman* (Athens, Ga., 1959). Interpretative studies which attempt to assess the role or nature of the Congress include David M. Potter's essay, "Jefferson Davis and the Political Factors in Confederate Defeat," in David Donald (ed.), *Why the North Won the Civil War* (New York, 1962); Thomas B. Alexander, "Persistent Whiggery in the Confederate South, 1860–1877," *Journal Of Southern History* XXVII (1961), 305–329; and John Brawner Robbins, "Confederate Nationalism: Politics and

Government in the Confederate South 1861–65," Ph.D. dissertation (Rice University, 1964).

On the executive branch of the Southern government the best beginning is a study of the two men at the top, Davis and Stephens. Beside the books written by the men (Davis' *Rise and Fall of the Confederate Government* and Stephens' *A Constitutional View of the Late War between the States . . .*) and their biographies, there are two fine articles by James Z. Rabun which pretty well define the nationalism–state rights dilemma inherent in Confederate polity in terms of these two officials: "Alexander H. Stephens and Jefferson Davis," *American Historical Review,* LVIII (1953), 290–321; and "Alexander H. Stephens and the Confederacy," *Emory University Quarterly,* VI (1950), 129–146. The best summary work on the executive branch is Rembert W. Patrick, *Jefferson Davis and His Cabinet* (Baton Rouge, La., 1944). Also useful are Burton J. Hendrick, *Statesmen of the Lost Cause* (Boston, 1939); Robert D. Meade, "The Relations between Judah P. Benjamin and Jefferson Davis," *Journal of Southern History,* V (1939), 468–478; and Hudson Strode, "Judah P. Benjamin's Loyalty to Jefferson Davis," *Georgia Review,* XX (1966), 251–260.

Interpretations of the Southern government as a nationalist or state rights vehicle seem to fluctuate periodically. Frank L. Owsley in his *State Rights in the Confederacy* (Chicago, 1925) and his article "Local Defense and the Overthrow of the Confederacy," *Mississippi Valley Historical Review,* XI (1925), 490–525, argues that the Southern nation was doomed by its origins as a state rights confederation. Studies such as Frank E. Vandiver, "The Confederacy and the American Tradition," *Journal of Southern History,* XXVIII (1962) 277–286, Louise B. Hill, *State Socialism in the Confederate States of America* (Charlottesville, Va., 1936); Raimondo Luraghi, "The Civil War and the Modernization of American Society," *"Civil War History,* XVIII (1972), 230–250; Frank E. Vandiver, *Jefferson Davis and the Confederate State* (Oxford, Miss. 1964); May Spencer Ringold, *The Role of State Legislatures in the Confederacy* (Athens, Ga., 1966); and Curtis Arthur Amlund, *Federalism in the Southern Confederacy* (Washington, D.C., 1966) speak in some degree to an opposite emphasis. However a thoughtful work by Paul D. Escott on Davis and nationalism soon to be published by Louisiana State University Press reverts to the Owsley prospective.

The standard work on the Southern bureaucracy is Paul P. Van Riper and Harry N. Scheiber, "The Confederate Civil Service," *Journal of Southern History,* XXV (1959), 448–470. Related articles are Haskell Monroe, "Early Confederate Political Patronage," *Alabama Review,* XX (1967), 45–61; and Harrison A. Trexler, "Jefferson Davis and Confederate Patronage," *South Atlantic Quarterly* XXVIII (1929), 45–58.

The Confederate mail service is well studied in August Dietz, *The Postal*

Service of the Confederate States of America (Richmond, Va., 1929). Supplementary material is in Walter F. McCaleb, "The Organization of the Post-Office Department of the Confederacy," *American Historical Review,* XII (1906), 66–74; and Cedric O. Reynolds, "The Postal System of the Southern Confederacy," *West Virginia History,* XII (1951), 200–279.

In a class by itself as political-administrative history is Robert L. Kerby, *Kirby Smith's Confederacy: The Trans-Mississippi South, 1863–1865* (New York, 1972). Smith was a general who, in command of the Trans-Mississippi Department, assumed civil duties far beyond the norm and in essence exercised the Richmond government's prerogative west of the Mississippi. A case study in Smith's administration is James L. Nichols, "The Tax-in-Kind in the Department of the Trans-Mississippi," *Civil War History,* V (1959), 382–389.

The standard work on the Davis administration's fiscal policy is Richard C. Todd, *Confederate Finance* (Athens, Ga., 1954). Other material on the subject is contained in Ralph L. Andreano, "A Theory of Confederate Finance," *Civil War History,* II (1956), 21–28; John Munro Godfrey, "Monetary Expansion in the Confederacy," Ph.D. dissertation (University of Georgia, 1976); and three articles by Eugene M. Lerner: "Monetary and Fiscal Programs of the Confederate Government, 1861–1865," *Journal of Political Economy,* LXII (1954), 506–522; "Money, Prices, and Wages in the Confederacy," *Journal of Political Economy,* LXII (1955), 20–40; and "Inflation in the Confederacy 1861–1865," in Milton Friedman (ed.), *Studies in the Quantity Theory of Money* (Chicago, 1956), pp. 161–175.

On the interaction of the government and the economy, in addition to the Luraghi article and Hill book cited above, the best analysis is still Charles W. Ramsdell, *Behind the Lines in the Southern Confederacy* (Baton Rouge, La., 1944). Two of Ramsdell's articles are also important: "The Control of Manufacturing by the Confederate Government," *Mississippi Valley Historical Review,* VIII (1921), 231–249; and "The Confederate Government and the Railroads," *American Historical Review,* XXII (1917), 794–810. Also helpful is John C. Schwab, *The Confederate States of America, 1861–1865: A Financial and Industrial History of the South during the Civil War* (New Haven, Conn., 1901). On another aspect of political economy Ludwell H. Johnson's article, "Trading With the Union: The Evolution of Confederate Policy," *Virginia Magazine of History and Biography,* LXXVIII (1970), 308–325, is definitive. For materials relating more directly to the Southern economy, see the section on Confederate economy, pages 353–355.

About the judicial history of the Confederacy the standard work is William M. Robinson, Jr., *Justice in Gray* (Cambridge, Mass., 1941). Since the Confederacy had no supreme court, Rembert W. Patrick (ed.), *The Opinions of the Confederate Attorneys General, 1861–1865* (Buffalo, N.Y., 1950), and

J. G. deR. Hamilton, "The State Courts and the Confederate Constitution," *Journal of Southern History*, IV (1938), 425–448, are important. For case studies of the judicial process involving controversial legislation see Albert B. Moore, *Conscription and Conflict in the Confederacy* (New York, 1924); and John B. Robbins, "The Confederacy and the Writ of Habeas Corpus," *Georgia Historical Quarterly*, LV (1971), 83–101.

Disloyalty and disaffection in the Confederacy have received thorough study. The standard work is Georgia L. Tatum, *Disloyalty in the Confederacy* (Chapel Hill, N.C. 1934). Within a broader format Carl N. Degler in *The Other South: Southern Dissenters in the Nineteenth Century* (New York, 1974) discusses the phenomenon of Southern Unionism (pp. 99–187). Also important are Frank W. Klingberg, *The Southern Claims Commission* (Berkeley, Calif., 1955); Ella Lonn, *Desertion During the Civil War* (New York, 1928); Bessie Martin, *Desertion of Alabama Troops From the Confederate Army* (New York, 1932); Louise B. Hill, *Joseph E. Brown and the Confederacy* (Chapel Hill, N.C., 1939); and Richard E. Yates, *The Confederacy and Zeb Vance* (Tuscaloosa, Ala., 1958). Among a host of articles which deal with specific instances or locations of disloyalty and/or disaffection are: Horace W. Raper, "William W. Holden and the Peace Movement in North Carolina," *North Carolina Historical Review*, XXXI (1954), 493–516; Rosser H. Taylor (ed.), "Boyce-Hammond Correspondence," *Journal of Southern History*, III (1937), 348–354; Hugh C. Bailey "Disloyalty in Early Confederate Alabama," *Journal of Southern History*, XXIII (1957) 522–528; John K. Bettersworth (ed.), "Mississippi Unionism: The Case of Reverend James A. Lyon," *Journal of Mississippi History* I (1939), 37–52; Richard Bardolph, "Inconstant Rebels: Desertion of North Carolina Troops in the Civil War," *North Carolina Historical Review*, XLI (1964), 163–189; Hugh C. Bailey, "Disaffection in the Alabama Hill Country, 1861," *Civil War History*, IV (1958), 183–194; Meriwether Stuart, "Colonel Ulric Dahlgren and Richmond's Union Underground, April 1864," *Virginia Magazine of History and Biography*, LXXII (1964), 152–204; Angus J. Johnston II, "Disloyalty on Confederate Railroads in Virginia," *Virginia Magazine of History and Biography*, LXIII (1955), 410–426; Frank W. Klingberg, "The Case of the Minors: A Unionist Family within the Confederacy," *Journal of Southern History*, XIII (1947), 27–45; James Smallwood, "Disaffection in Confederate Texas: The Great Hanging at Gainesville," *Civil War History*, XXII (1976), 349–360. Barnes F. Lathrop, "Disaffection in Confederate Louisiana: The Case of William Hyman," *Journal of Southern History*, XXIV (1958), 308–318; Henry T. Shanks, "Disloyalty to the Confederacy in Southwestern Virginia, 1861–1865," *North Carolina Historical Review*, XXI (1944), 118–135; J. Reuben Sheeler, "The Development of Unionism in East Tennessee," *Journal of Negro History*, XXIX (1944), 166–203; Ethel Taylor, "Discontent in Confederate Louisiana," *Louisiana History,* II (1961), 410–428; Ted R. Worley, "The Arkansas Peace Society of 1861: A Study in Mountain Unionism," *Journal of Southern History,* XXIV (1958), 445–456; and Donald Bradford Dodd, "Unionism in Confederate Alabama," Ph.D. dissertation (University of Georgia, 1969). Against this powerful tide, Stephen E. Ambrose in his "Yeoman Discontent in the Confederacy," *Civil War History,* VIII (1962), 259–268, points out that the Southern plain folk were the backbone of the Southern nation; and Durwood Long in "Unanimity and Disloyalty in Secessionist Alabama," *Civil War History,* II (1965), 257–273, offers a balanced overview.

State studies include biographies of the governors, the Ringgold work on state legislatures, and the following: John E. Johns, *Florida During the Civil War* (Gainesville, Fla., 1963); E. Merton Coulter, *The Civil War and Readjustment in Kentucky* (Chapel Hill, N.C., 1926); John G. Barrett, *The Civil War in North Carolina.* (Chapel Hill, N.C., 1963); T. Conn Bryan, *Confederate Georgia* (Athens, Ga., 1953); Walter L. Fleming, *Civil War and Reconstruction in Alabama* (New York, 1905); Jefferson D. Bragg, *Louisiana in the Confederacy* (Baton Rouge, La., 1941); Roger W. Shugg, *Origins of Class Struggle in Louisiana* (University, La., 1939); John D. Winters, *The Civil War in Louisiana* (Baton Rouge, La., 1963); Arthur R. Kirkpatrick, "Missouri's Secessionist Government, 1861–1865," *Missouri Historical Review,* XLV (1951), 124–137; Michael B. Dougan, "Life in Confederate Arkansas," *Arkansas Historical Quarterly,* XXXI (1972), 15–35; Edwin C. Bearss, *Decision in Mississippi: Mississippi's Important Role in the War Between the States* (Jackson, Miss., 1962); John K. Bettersworth, *Confederate Mississippi: The People and Policies of a Cotton State in Wartime* (Baton Rouge, La., 1943); John K. Bettersworth and James W. Silver (eds.), *Mississippi in the Confederacy,* 2 vols. (Baton Rouge, La., 1961); Stephen B. Oates, "Texas under the Secessionists," *Southwestern Historical Quarterly,* LXVII (1963), 167–212; and William E. Parrish, *A History of Missouri,* III, *1860 to 1875* (Columbia, Miss., 1973).

Economy

Much of the recent work on the economic history of the Civil War era has focused upon the North. Thus despite the new methodology available to modern economic historians, the best overview of the Southern economy during wartime is still Charles W. Ramsdell's *Behind the Lines in the Southern Confederacy* (Baton Rouge, La., 1944). Raimondo Luraghi's article, "The Civil War and the Modernization of American Society," *Civil War History,* XVIII (1972), 230–250, offers the insight of a comparative analysis and points to a new direction for researchers to take when examining the Confederate South. Luraghi opens the intriguing possibility of perceiving the Confederacy as a case study in economic planning by a landed elite. Actually Louise B. Hill offered part of this insight in 1936 in her *State Socialism in the Confederate States of America* (Charlottesville, Va., 1936), though not with the sophistication of Luraghi's analysis. Until someone accepts the challenge of Hill's and Luraghi's ideas, however, the best work on the Confederate economy is among a number of older studies.

The section of this bibliography covering "Politics," pages 349–353, notes the articles of Ramsdell, Eugene M. Lerner, Ludwell K. Johnson, and Ralph L. Andreano and books by Richard C. Todd and John C. Schwab. In addition, see Lester J. Cappon, "Government and Private Industry in the Southern Confederacy," in *Humanistic Studies in Honor of John Calvin Metcalf* (New York, 1941), pp. 151–189; and Edwin B. Coddington, "A Social and Economic History of the Seaboard States of the Southern Confederacy," Ph.D. dissertation (Clark University, 1939). Paul W. Gates, *Agriculture and the Civil War* (New York, 1965), is the standard on farming in the nation as a whole. Charles P. Roland, *Louisiana Sugar Plantations during the American Civil War* (Leiden, Netherlands, 1957), offers an agricultural case study.

Mary Elizabeth Massey, *Ersatz in the Confederacy* (Columbia, S.C., 1952) explores the shortages and substitutes which characterized the Confederate consumer economy. Two works by Frank E. Vandiver offer good case studies of varied facets of the Southern economy: *Ploughshares into Swords: Josiah Gorgas and Confederate Ordinance* (Austin, Tex., 1952) details the activities of the most significant government war industry; and *Confederate Blockade Running through Bermuda, 1861–1865: Letters and Cargo Manifests* (Austin, Tex., 1947) reveals more about blockade running in general than the title suggests. Other good works on Southern industrial development include Vandiver's "The Shelby Iron Company in the Civil War," *Alabama Review*, I (1948), 12–26, 111–127, 203–217; Charles B. Dew, *Ironmaker to the Confederacy: Joseph P. Anderson and the Tredegar Iron Works* (New Haven, Conn., 1966); Kathleen Bruce, *Virginia Iron Manufacture in the Slave Era* (New York, 1931); George W. Rains, *History of the Confederate Powder Works* (Augusta, Ga., 1882); Robert C. Black III, *The Railroads of the Confederacy* (Chapel Hill, N.C., 1952); Angus J. Johnston II, *Virginia Railroads in the Civil War* (Chapel Hill, N.C., 1961); John D. Capron, "Virginia Iron Furnaces of the Confederacy," *Virginia Cavalcade*, XVII (1967), ii, 10–18; Ralph W. Donnelly, "The Bartow County Confederate Saltpetre Works," *Georgia Historical Quarterly*, LIV (1970) 305–319; Ralph W. Donnelly, "Confederate Copper," *Civil War History*, I (1955), 355–370; Richard J. Stockham, "Alabama Iron for the Confederacy: The Selma Works," *Alabama Review*, XXI (1968), 163–172; and W. Stanley Hoole, "John W. Mallet and the Confederate Ordnance Laboratories, 1862–1865," *Alabama Review*, XXVI (1973), 33–72.

Three articles by William F. Zornow describe efforts at relief and welfare: "State Aid for Indigent Soldiers and Their Families in Louisiana, 1861–

1865," *Louisiana Historical Quarterly,* XXXIX (1956), 375–380; "Aid for the Indigent Families of Soldiers in Virginia, 1861–1865," *Virginia Magazine of History and Biography,* LXVI (1958), 454–458; and "State Aid for Indigent Soldiers and Their Families in Florida," *Florida Historical Quarterly,* XXXIV (1956), 259–265. Related material is in Emory M. Thomas, "Welfare in Wartime Richmond, 1861–1865," *Virginia Cavalcade,* XXII (1972), i, 22–29.

Foreign trade is covered in the "Foreign Relations" section, on pages 361–364. Nevertheless the Ludwell Johnson article on contraband trade rates mention here, along with William Diamond, "Imports of the Confederate Government from Europe and Mexico," *Journal of Southern History,* VI (1940), 470–503; two articles on trade across the Rio Grande are: Ronnie C. Tyler, "Cotton on the Border, 1861–1865," *Southwestern Historical Quarterly,* LXXIII (1970), 456–477; and Marilyn McAdams Sibley, "Charles Stillman: A Case Study of Entrepreneurship on the Rio Grande, 1861–1865," *Southwestern Historical Quarterly,* LXXVII (1973), 227–240. See also Edwin B. Coddington, "The Activities and Attitudes of a Confederate Businessman: Gazaway B. Lamar," *Journal of Southern History,* IX (1943), 3–36.

In a class by itself is Ella Lonn's fine monograph, *Salt as a Factor in the Confederacy* (New York, 1933). Like so many other resources salt grew quickly scarce in the embattled South. Other shortages are detailed in such works as William N. Still, *Confederate Shipbuilding* (Athens, Ga., 1969) which points out the lack of facilities, skilled labor, and raw materials and Richard D. Goff, *Confederate Supply* (Durham, N.C., 1969), which notes among other failures the deficiencies in Southern transportation and production capabilities.

Social and Cultural Developments

There exists no comprehensive social or cultural history of the Confederacy. Some of the best material is in the letters and diaries of the period, many collections of which have been published. Edmund Wilson conducted a literary critique of some of the better-known writings in his *Patriotic Gore: Studies in the Literature of the American Civil War* (New York, 1962). Also good is Douglas S. Freeman, *The South to Posterity: An Introduction to the Writings of Confederate History* (New York, 1939). The diaries or journals of Kate Stone, John B. Jones, Mary Boykin Chesnut, Phoebe Yates Pember, Robert G. H. Kean, T. C. DeLeon, and Kate Cumming (all cited in the "Biography" section of this bibliography, pages 331–349) are well-known "classics." In addition, two works of family papers, arranged to form almost epistolary novels, deserve special mention. Robert Manson Myers (ed.), *The Children of Pride: A True Story of Georgia and the Civil War* (New Haven, Conn., 1972), chronicles the experiences of the Charles C. Jones family in Georgia; and

Betsy Fleet and John D. P. Fuller (eds.), *Green Mount: A Virginia Plantation Family during the Civil War* . . . (Lexington, Ky., 1962) displays wartime from the prospective of teen-aged Benjamin Robert Fleet and his family.

About cultural life in the Confederacy the best survey is Clement Eaton, *The Waning of the Old South Civilization* (Athens, Ga., 1968). There is an excellent guide to the literature of the era in Louis D. Rubin, Jr., *A Bibliographical Guide to the Study of Southern Literature* (Baton Rouge, La., 1969), and the check lists of Confederate imprints by Crandall and Harwell (cited in "Printed Sources, page 328) list works published in the South. Beside the works cited in Ruben's *Guide* and in Eaton's text and bibliography, Jon L. Wakelyn's *The Politics of a Literary Man: William Gilmore Simms* (Westport, Conn., 1973) is an important recent work on Southern *belles-lettres.* Richard B. Harwell has done three books of significance on aspects of wartime culture: *The Brief Candle: The Confederate Theatre* (Worcester, Mass., 1971); *Confederate Music* (Chapel Hill, N.C., 1950); and *Songs of the Confederacy* (New York, 1951). The best summary of the impact of the war upon schools and colleges is Wayne Flynt, "Southern Higher Education and the Civil War," *Civil War History,* XIV (1968), 211–225.

On the Confederate press the best work is J. Cutler Andrews, *The South Reports the Civil War* (Princeton, N.J., 1970). A number of articles are also significant: J. Cutler Andrews, "The Southern Telegraph Company, 1861–1865: A Chapter in the History of Wartime Communications," *Journal of Southern History,* XXX (1964), 319–344, and "The Confederate Press and Public Morale," *Journal of Southern History,* XXXII (1966), 445–465; C. Richard King, "Col. John Sidney Thrasher: Superintendent of the Confederate Press Association," *Texana,* VI (1968), 56–86; Peter Langley III, "Pessimism-Optimism of Civil War Military News: June 1863–March, 1865," *Journalism Quarterly,* XLIX (1972), 74–78; Richard Barksdale Harwell, "John Esten Cooke, Civil War Correspondent," *Journal of Southern History,* XIX (1953), 501–516; Harrison A. Trexler, "The Davis Administration and the Richmond Press 1861–1865," *Journal of Southern History,* XVI (1950), 177–195; Emory M. Thomas, "Rebel Nationalism: E. H. Cushing and the Confederate Experience," *Southwestern Historical Quarterly,* LXXIII (1970), 343–355; Robert Neil Mathis, "Freedom of the Press in the Confederacy: A Reality," *Historian,* XXXVII (1975), 633–648; Thomas H. Baker, "Refugee Newspaper: The Memphis *Daily Appeal,* 1862–1865," *Journal of Southern History,* XXIX (1963), 326–344; Lawrence Huff, "Joseph Addison Turner: Southern Editor during the Civil War," *Journal of Southern History,* XXIX (1963), 469–485; and Bell I. Wiley, "Camp Newspapers of the Confederacy," *North Carolina Historical Review,* XX (1943), 327–335.

There are a number of studies of religion in the Confederacy. Among older works perhaps the Reverend J. William Jones, *Christ in the Camp*

. . . (Richmond, Va., 1888) is the best summary. More recent material on religion in the army includes John Shepard, Jr., "Religion in the Army of Northern Virginia," *North Carolina Historical Review,* XXV (1948), 341–376; and Sidney J. Romero, "The Confederate Chaplain," *Civil War History* I (1955), 127–140. The best modern study of the topic is James W. Silver, *Confederate Morale and Church Propaganda* (Tuscaloosa, Ala., 1957). In addition to Silver's book a series of articles by W. Harrison Daniel are essential: "Southern Protestantism—1861 and After," *Civil War History,* V (1959), 276–282; "Protestantism and Patriotism in the Confederacy," *Mississippi Quarterly,* XXIV (1971), 117–134; "Southern Presbyterians in the Confederacy," *North Carolina Historical Review,* XLIV (1967), 231–255; "Virginia Baptists, 1861–1865," *Virginia Magazine of History and Biography,* LXXII (1964), 94–114; "Southern Protestantism and the Negro, 1860–1865," *North Carolina Historical Review,* XLI (1964), 338–359; "Southern Protestantism and Army Missions in the Confederacy," *Mississippi Quarterly,* XVII (1964), 179–191; "Protestant Clergy and Union Sentiment in the Confederacy," *Tennessee Historical Quarterly,* XXIII (1964), 284–290; "The Christian Association: A Religious Society in the Army of Northern Virginia," *Virginia Magazine of History and Biography* LXIX (1961), 93–100; and "Bible Publication and Procurement in the Confederacy," *Journal of Southern History,* XXIV (1958), 191–201. Other helpful studies include Bertram W. Korn, "The Jews of the Confederacy," *American Jewish Archives,* XIII (1961), 3–90; Samuel Horst, *Mennonites in the Confederacy: A Study in Civil War Pacifism* (Scottdale, Pa., 1967); J. Treadwell Davis, "The Presbyterians and the Sectional Conflict," *Southern Quarterly,* VIII (1970), 117–133; Ernest Trice Thompson, *Presbyterians in the South,* II, *1861–1890* (Richmond, Va., 1973); and Haskell Monroe, Jr., "The Presbyterian Church in the Confederate States of America," Ph.D. dissertation (Rice University, 1961).

About women in the Confederacy, besides the personal narratives cited above, there are three basic studies. Mary Elizabeth Massey, *Bonnet Brigades: American Women and the Civil War* (New York, 1966), is a somewhat traditional work based upon solid research. More interpretative is Anne Firor Scott, *The Southern Lady: From Pedestal to Politics, 1830–1930,* (Chicago, 1970). Also sound is Bell I. Wiley, *Confederate Woman* (Westport, Conn., 1975), which contains sketches of a few well-known Confederate women and a summary essay which justifies the title.

The art and science of medicine in the wartime South is the subject of Horace H. Cunningham, *Doctors in Gray: The Confederate Medical Service,* revised edition, (Baton Rouge, La., 1960). Cunningham's *Field Medical Services at the Battles of Manassas* (Athens, Ga., 1968) is also first rate. On medicines themselves, see Norman H. Franke, "Official and Industrial Aspects of Pharmacy in the Confederacy," *Georgia Historical Quarterly* XXXVII (1953),

175–187; and "Pharmacy and Pharmacists in the Confederacy," *Georgia Historical Quarterly,* XXXVIII (1954), 11–28.

The Confederate experience generated among many Southerners higher degrees of urban consciousness. Although no general study of Confederate urbanism exists, for the examples of individual cities see Emory M. Thomas, *The Confederate State of Richmond: A Biography of the Capital* (Austin, Tex., 1971); Louis H. Manarin (ed.), *Richmond at War: The Minutes of the City Council, 1861–1865* (Chapel Hill, N.C., 1966); Gerald M. Capers, *Occupied City: New Orleans under the Federals, 1862–1865* (Lexington, Ky., 1965); Kenneth Coleman, *Confederate Athens, 1861–1865* (Athens, Ga., 1968); and E. Milby Burton, *The Siege of Charleston, 1861–1865* (Columbia, S.C., 1970).

Although the Confederates wrote much of their own social history in personal narratives, two secondary works are important to the study: Bell I. Wiley, *The Plain People of the Confederacy* (Baton Rouge, La., 1943) and Mary Elizabeth Massey, *Refugee Life in the Confederacy* (Baton Rouge, La., 1964).

One other work of intellectual history deserves attention, although it defies classification. Michael Davis, *The Image of Lincoln in the South* (Knoxville, Tenn., 1971) is a fine bit of scholarship which delivers more than it promises.

Black Confederates

Ironically the most intriguing aspect of the black experience in slavery is one of the least studied: the experience of blacks within the Confederacy. The best commentary on this subject is Clarence L. Mohr, "Southern Blacks in the Civil War: A Century of Historiography," *Journal of Negro History,* LXIX (1974), 177–195. The standard bibliographical guide to black history, James M. McPherson, et. al., *Blacks in America* (Garden City, N.Y., 1971), reveals few works on this topic. The general study of slavery which best integrates the ante-bellum and bellum experience is Eugene D. Genovese, *Roll, Jordan, Roll: The World the Slaves Made* (New York, 1974). Mohr has begun rectification of the scholarly oversight in his "Georgia Blacks During Secession and Civil War, 1859–1865," Ph.D. dissertation (University of Georgia, 1974). Paul D. Escott has contributed, "The Context of Freedom: Georgia's Slaves During the Civil War," *Georgia Historical Quarterly,* LVIII (1974), 79–104. Otherwise the best work on black Confederates is still Bell I. Wiley, *Southern Negroes, 1861–1865* (New Haven, Conn., 1938). Other studies include Herbert Aptheker, *The Negro in the Civil War* (New York, 1938); Dudley T. Cornish, *The Sable Arm: Negro Troops in the Union Army, 1861–1865* (New York, 1956); James M. McPherson, *The Struggle for Equality: Abolitionists and the Negro in the Civil War and Reconstruction* (Princeton, N.J., 1964); James M. McPherson, *The Negro's Civil War: How American Negroes Felt and Acted during the War for Union* (New York, 1965); and W. E. B. DuBois, "The Negro and the Civil War," *Science and Society,* XXV (1961), 347–352—all of which emphasize the experience of black people who escaped the slave South during the war. James H. Brewer, *The Confederate Negro: Virginia's Craftsmen and Military Laborers, 1861–1865* (Durham, N.C., 1969) is good on impressed and industrial slaves. Yet beyond Mohr, Brewer, Wiley, and Genovese, the literature of Confederate slavery is pretty thin. See Herbert Aptheker, "Notes on Slave Conspiracies in Confederate Mississippi," *Journal of Negro History,* XXIX (1944), 75–79; Bernard H. Nelson, "Some Aspects of Negro Life in North Carolina during the Civil War," *North Carolina Historical Review,* XXV (1948), 143–166; Robert D. Reid, "The Negro in Alabama during the Civil War," *Journal of Negro History,* XXXV (1950), 265–288; Joe G. Taylor, "Slavery in Louisiana during the Civil War," *Louisiana History,* VIII (1967), 27–33; Edmund L. Drago, "How Sherman's March Through Georgia Affected the Slaves," *Georgia Historical Quarterly,* LVII (1973), 361–375; C. Peter Ripley, "The Black Family in Transition: Louisiana, 1860–1865," *Journal of Southern History,* XLI (1975), 369–380; and John W. Blassingame, *Black New Orleans, 1860–1880* (Chicago, 1973).

About the use of slaves as military laborers, see Ernest F. Dibble, "Slave Rentals to the Military: Pensacola and the Gulf Coast," *Civil War History,* XXIII (1977), 101–113; Tinsley L. Spraggins, "Mobilization of Negro Labor for the Department of Virginia and North Carolina 1861–1865," *North Carolina Historical Review,* XXIV (1947), 160–197; Bernard H. Nelson, "Confederate Slave Impressment Legislation, 1861–1865," *Journal of Negro History,* XXXI (1946), 392–410; and Harrison A. Trexler, "The Opposition of Planters to the Employment of Slaves as Laborers by the Confederacy," *Mississippi Valley Historical Review,* XXVII (1940), 211–224.

Fortunately there is an outstanding work on the Confederate scheme to employ black troops, Robert F. Durden, *The Gray and the Black: The Confederate Debate on Emancipation* (Baton Rouge, La., 1972). Durden's work, which emphasizes a documentary approach, supplants earlier studies: Thomas R. Hay, "The South and the Arming of the Slaves," *Mississippi Valley Historical Review,* VI (1919), 34–73; Nathaniel W. Stephenson, "The Question of Arming the Slaves," *American Historical Review,* XVIII (1913), 295–308; and Charles H. Wesley, "The Employment of Negroes in the Confederate Army," *Journal of Negro History* IV (1919), 239–253. Other material about white response to the black circumstance in the Confederacy includes Bell I. Wiley, "The Movement to Humanize the Institution of Slavery during the Confederacy," *Emory University Quarterly,* V (1949), 207–220; Bernard H. Nelson, "Legislative Control of the Southern Free Negro, 1861–1865,"

Catholic Historical Review, XXXII (1946), 28–46; and Bill G. Reid, "Confederate Opponents of Arming the Slaves, 1861–1865," *Journal of Mississippi History*, XXII (1960), 249–270.

Southern blacks who lived in or fled to areas controlled by federal troops encountered some form of governmental policy dealing with the transition from slavery to freedom. The literature of this experience is growing. The best beginning is Willie Lee Rose's book *Rehearsal for Reconstruction: The Port Royal Experiment* (New York, 1964). Two other important books on the subject are Peter Kolchin, *First Freedom: The Responses of Alabama's Blacks to Emancipation and Reconstruction* (Westport, Conn., 1972), and Louis S. Gerteis, *From Contraband to Freedman: Federal Policy Toward Southern Blacks, 1861–1865* (Westport, Conn., 1973). A number of articles relate case studies: Cam Walker, "Corinth: The Story of a Contraband Camp," *Civil War History*, XX (1974), 5–22; William F. Messner, "Black Education in Louisiana, 1863–1865," *Civil War History*, XXII (1976), 41–59; Martha M. Bigelow, "Freedmen of the Mississippi Valley, 1862–1865," *Civil War History*, VIII (1962), 38–47; Martha M. Bigelow, "Vicksburg: Experiment in Freedom," *Journal of Mississippi History*, XXVI (1964), 28–44; Robert D. Parmet, "Schools for the Freedmen," *Negro History Bulletin*, XXXIV (1971), 128–132; J. Thomas May, "Continuity and Change in the Labor Program of the Union Army and the Freedman's Bureau," *Civil War History*, XVII (1971), 245–254; Felix James, "The Establishment of Freedman's Village in Arlington, Virginia," *Negro History Bulletin*, XXXIII (1970), 90–93; and Sing-Nan Fen, "Notes on the Education of Negroes of Norfolk and Portsmouth, Virginia, During the Civil War," *Phylon*, XXVIII (1967), 197–207. Also useful is Henry Swint (ed.), *Dear Ones at Home: Letters from Contraband Camps* (Nashville, Tenn., 1966).

Cornish's *Sable Arm* is the basic work on blacks in the Union Army. Important, too, are John Hope Franklin (ed.), *The Diary of James T. Ayers, Civil War Recruiter* (Springfield, Ill., 1947); Thomas W. Higginson, *Army Life in a Black Regiment* (Boston, 1870); Benjamin F. Quarles, *Lincoln and the Negro* (New York, 1962); and V. Jacque Voegeli, *Free but Not Equal: The Midwest and the Negro during the Civil War* (Chicago, 1967). The following articles are useful: Lary C. Rampp, "Negro Troop Activity in Indian Territory, 1863–1865," *Chronicles of Oklahoma*, XLVII (1970), 531–559; James I. Robertson, Jr., "Negro Soldiers in the Civil War," *Civil War Times Illustrated*, VII, vi (1968), 21–32; Mary F. Berry, "Negro Troops in Blue and Gray: The Louisiana Native Guards, 1861–1863," *Louisiana History*, VIII (1967), 165–190; Brainard Dyer, "The Treatment of Colored Union Troops by the Confederates, 1861–1865," *Journal of Negro History*, XX (1935), 273–286; Roland C. McConnell (ed.), "Concerning the Procurement of Negro Troops in the South during the Civil War," *Journal of Negro History*, XXXV

(1950), 315–19; C. R. Gibbs, "Blacks in the Union Navy," *Negro History Bulletin,* XXXVI (1973), 137–139; Albert E. Cowdrey, "Slave into Soldier: The Enlistment by the North of Runaway Slaves," *History Today,* XX (1970), 704–715; and Richard H. Abbott, "Massachusetts and the Recruitment of Southern Negroes, 1863–1865," *Civil War History,* XIV (1968), 197–210.

The subject of white racist response to emancipation has a growing literature which lies outside the scope of this study. Two titles, however, are suggestive: Forrest G. Wood, *Black Scare: The Racist Response to Emancipation and Reconstruction* (Berkeley, Calif., 1968); and John S. Haller, "Civil War Anthropometry: The Making of a Racial Ideology," *Civil War History,* XVI (1970), 309–324.

Foreign Relations

An addition to the bibliographical guides cited above is Samuel Flagg Bemis and Grace G. Griffin, *Guide to the Diplomatic History of the United States, 1775–1921* (Washington, D.C., 1935). The best summary and interpretation of the diplomacy of the war era is D. P. Crook, *The North, the South, and the Powers, 1861–1865* (New York, 1974). On Confederate foreign relations the "classic" is Frank L. Owsley, *King Cotton Diplomacy: Foreign Relations of the Confederate States of America,* revised edition, (Chicago, 1959). Other general works on Confederate diplomacy include an older study, James M. Callahan, *Diplomatic History of the Southern Confederacy* (Baltimore, 1901); and a thoughtful article by Henry Blumenthal, "Confederate Diplomacy: Popular Notions and International Realities," *Journal of Southern History,* XXXII (1966), 151–171. Also of general interest are the essays in Harold Hyman (ed.), *Heard Round the World: The Impact Abroad of the Civil War* (New York, 1969).

The dated, but still useful, work on Great Britain is E. D. Adams, *Great Britain and the American Civil War,* 2 vols. (New York, 1925). More recent interpretations are in Max Beloff, "Great Britain and the American Civil War" *History,* XXXVII (1952), 40–48; Robert H. Jones, "Anglo-American Relations, 1861–1865, Reconsidered," *Mid-America,* XLV (1963) 36–49; and Kinley J. Brauer, "British Mediation and the American Civil War: A Reconsideration," *Journal of Southern History,* XXXVIII (1972), 49–64. Confederate efforts in England are the subject of Frank J. Merli, *Great Britain and the Confederate Navy, 1861–1865* (Bloomington, Ind., 1970), which provides an excellent overview of British policy as well as an appreciation of the work of James D. Bulloch. The latter spoke for himself in his *Secret Service of the Confederate States in Europe,* 2 vols. (New York, 1884). A companion work to Merli's is Richard I. Lester, *Confederate Finance and Purchasing in Great Britain* (Charlottesville, Va., 1975). A fine case study of Anglo-American diplomacy in action is Stuart L. Bernath, *Squall Across the Atlantic: American Civil War Prize Cases and Diplomacy* (Berkeley, Calif., 1970).

On the economics of British neutrality, see: Louis B. Schmidt, "The Influence of Wheat and Cotton on Anglo-American Relations during the Civil War," *Iowa Journal of History and Politics*, XVI (1918), 400–439; Eli Ginzberg, "The Economics of British Neutrality during the American Civil War," *Agricultural History*, X (1936), 147–156; Robert H. Jones, "Long Live the King?" *Agricultural History*, XXXVII (1963), 166–169; Amos Khasigian, "Economic Factors and British Neutrality, 1861–1865," *Historian*, XXV (1963), 451–465; and especially Eugene A. Brady, "A Reconsideration of the Lancashire 'Cotton Famine,' " *Agricultural History*, XXXVII (1963), 156–162.

There has been a continuing controversy in the literature concerning British public opinion regarding the American war. The issue is now perhaps at rest because of several fine studies: Mary Ellison, *Support for Secession: Lancashire and the American Civil War* (Chicago, 1972); Joseph M. Hernon, *Celts, Catholics and Copperheads: Ireland Views the American Civil War* (Columbus, Ohio, 1968); and Joseph M. Hernon, "British Sympathies in the American Civil War: A Reconsideration," *Journal of Southern History*, XXXIII (1967), 356–367.

About the *Trent* Affair, the older standard is Thomas L. Harris, *The Trent Affair* (Indianapolis, Ind., 1896), now supplanted by Norman B. Ferris, *The Trent Affair* (Knoxville, Tenn., 1975). Lynn Case in his part of Lynn M. Case and Warren F. Spencer, *The United States and France: Civil War Diplomacy* (Philadelphia, 1970), contends that the Confederates all but arranged their capture and argues the significance of the French influence on Washington. Articles of interest and/or importance to the incident include: F. C. Drake, "The Cuban Background of the *Trent* Affair," *Civil War History*, XIX (1973), 29–49; Charles Francis Adams, "The *Trent* Affair," *American Historical Review*, XVII (1912), 540–562; V. H. Cohen, "Charles Sumner and the *Trent* Affair," *Journal of Southern History*, XXII (1956), 205–219; Norman B. Ferris, "The Prince Consort, 'The Times,' and the 'Trent' Affair," *Civil War History*, VI (1960), 152–156; and Norman B. Ferris, "Abraham Lincoln and the *Trent* Affair," *Lincoln Herald*, LXIX (1967), 131–135.

Other studies of significance to Anglo-Confederate relations include: Martin P. Claussen, "Peace Factors in Anglo-American Relations, 1861–1865," *Mississippi Valley Historical Review*, XXVI (1940), 511–522; Milledge L. Bonham, *The British Consuls in the Confederacy* (New York, 1971); J. Franklin Jameson, "The London Expenditures of the Confederate Secret Service," *American Historical Review*, XXXV (1930), 811–824; Frank J. Merli and Theodore A. Wilson, "The British Cabinet and the Confederacy: Autumn, 1862," *Maryland Historical Magazine*, LXV (1970), 239–262; Robert L. Reid (ed.), "William E. Gladstone's 'Insincere Neutrality' during the Civil War," *Civil War History* XV (1969), 293–307; Frank Merli, "Crown versus Cruiser: The Curious Case of the *Alexandra*," *Civil War History*, IX (1963), 167–177; Wilbur D. Jones, "The British Conservatives and the American Civil War," *American Historical Review*, LVIII (1953), 527–543; David F. Krein, "Russell's Decision to Retain the Laird Rams," *Civil War History*, XXII (1976), 158–163; and Wilbur D. Jones, *The Confederate Rams at Birkenhead* (Tuscaloosa, Ala., 1961).

Relating directly to questions of neutral rights and the blockade are: James P. Baxter, "Some British Opinions as to Neutral Rights, 1861 to 1865," *American Journal of International Law*, XXIII (1929), 517–537; James P. Baxter III, "The British Government and Neutral Rights, 1861–1865," *American Historical Review*, XXXIV (1928), 9–29; Frank L. Owsley, "America and the Freedom of the Seas, 1861–1865," in Avery O. Craven (ed.), *Essays in Honor of William E. Dodd* (Chicago, 1935), pp. 194–256; and William M. Leary, Jr., "*Alabama* versus *Kearsarge:* A Diplomatic View," *American Neptune*, XXIX (1969), 167–173.

On Confederate relations with France the standard work is Case and Spencer, cited above. This study, however, is seriously marred by the omission of treatment of the French venture in Mexico. Fortunately there are a number of fine recent works which deal with that topic: Arnold Blumberg, *The Diplomacy of the Mexican Empire, 1863–1867* (Philadelphia, 1971); Alfred J. Hanna and Kathryn A. Hanna, *Napoleon III and Mexico: American Triumph over Monarchy* (Chapel Hill, N.C., 1971); and Nancy Nichols Barker, "France, Austria, and the Mexican Venture, 1861–1864," *French Historical Studies*, III (1963), 224–245. The Erlanger loan is well covered in Judith Fenner Gentry, "A Confederate Success in Europe: The Erlanger Loan," *Journal of Southern History*, XXXVI (1970), 157–188. Other material touching France and the American conflict includes: Henry Blumenthal, *A Reappraisal of Franco-American Relations, 1830–1871* (Chapel Hill, N.C., 1959); Daniel B. Carroll, *Henri Mercier and the American Civil War* (Princeton, N.J., 1971); and Serge Gavronsky, *The French Liberal Opposition and the American Civil War* (New York, 1968).

About Confederate diplomats and foreign agents the following studies are useful: C. S. Davis, *Colin J. McRae: Confederate Financial Agent* (Tuscaloosa, Ala., 1961); Charles P. Cullop, *Confederate Propaganda in Europe, 1861–1865* (Coral Gables, Fla., 1969); Charles P. Cullop, "Edwin de Leon, Jefferson Davis's Propagandist," *Civil War History*, VIII (1962), 386–400; Stephen B. Oates, "Henry Hotze: Confederate Agent Abroad," *Historian*, XXVII (1965), 131–154; W. Stanley Hoole (ed.), *Confederate Foreign Agent: The European Diary of Major Edward C. Anderson* (University, Ala., 1976); Virginia Mason, *The Public Life . . . of James M. Mason* (Roanoke, Va., 1903);

Louis M. Sears, *John Slidell* (Durham, N.C., 1925); Beckles Willson, *John Slidell and the Confederates in Paris (1862–65)* (New York, 1932).

Although Britain and France were the most emphasized targets of Confederate diplomacy, other foreign nations received attention or affected the Southern international position. The consequences of the rising in Poland is the subject of John Kutolowski, "The Effect of the Polish Insurrection of 1863 on American Civil War Diplomacy," *Historian*, XXVII (1965), 560–577. Concerning Canada see Robin Winks, *Canada and the United States: The Civil War Years* (Baltimore, 1960). About Southern activities in Northern Mexico, see Ronnie C. Tyler, *Santiago Vidaurri and the Southern Confederacy* (Austin, Tex., 1973). Three articles are important for the story of Confederate relations with the Indian nations: LeRoy H. Fischer, "The Civil War Era in Indian Territory," *Journal of the West*, XII (1973), 345–355; Kenny A. Franks, "The Implementation of the Confederate Treaties with the Five Civilized Tribes," *Chronicles of Oklahoma*, LI (1973), 21–33; and "The Confederate States and the Five Civilized Tribes: A Breakdown of Relations," *Journal of the West*, XII (1973), 439–454.

Finally the abortive attempts to achieve a negotiated peace with the United States deserve mention. For these see Edward C. Kirkland, *The Peacemakers of 1864* (New York, 1927); Ludwell H. Johnson, "Lincoln's Solution to the Problem of Peace Terms, 1864–1865," *Journal of Southern History*, XXXIV (1968), 576–586; and Paul J. Zingg, "John Archibald Campbell and the Hampton Roads Conference," *Alabama Historical Quarterly*, XXXVI (1974), 21–34.

Naval War

With the exception of the activities of the *Virginia* and the *Alabama*, the Confederate navy has assumed a distant second place to the army in the literature of the war. There is a bibliographical guide, Myron J. Smith, Jr., *American Civil War Navies: A Bibliography* (Metuchen, N.J., 1972); however the work is essentially an uncritical, alphabetized list of materials. There is a bibliography of the *Virginia*'s conflict with the *Monitor*, David R. Smith, *The Monitor and the Merrimac: A Bibliography* (Los Angeles, 1968). Also under the heading of guide is the Naval History Division of the Navy Department's *Civil War Naval Chronology 1861–1865* (Washington, D.C., 1971).

The best general history of the war on water is Virgil C. Jones, *The Civil War at Sea*, 3 vols. (New York, 1960–1962). Other general histories include: Bern Anderson, *By Sea and By River: The Naval History of the Civil War* (New York, 1962); and Howard P. Nash, Jr., *A Naval History of the Civil War* (New York, 1972). The fundamental collection of primary materials is *Official*

Records of the Union and Confederate Navies in the War of the Rebellion, 30 vols. (Washington, D.C., 1894–1922).

About the Confederate navy the best beginning is with J. T. Scharf, *History of the Confederate States Navy* (New York, 1887). Biographies of Mallory, Buchanan, Semmes, Maury, Bulloch, and Kell are important, as are works on purchasing activities in Great Britain (eg. Merli's *Great Britain and the Confederate Navy 1861–1865*). The best recent works on the Southern navy are those of William N. Still, Jr. Still has written two good books—*Confederate Shipbuilding* (Athens, Ga., 1969) and *Iron Afloat: The Story of the Confederate Armorclads* (Nashville, Tenn., 1971)—and a number of fine articles: "Confederate Naval Strategy: The Ironclad," *Journal of Southern History,* XXVII (1961), 330–343; "Facilities for the Construction of War Vessels in the Confederacy," *Journal of Southern History,* XXXI (1965), 285–304; "Confederate Naval Policy and the Ironclad, *Civil War History,* IX (1963), 145–156; "Selma and the Confederate States Navy," *Alabama Review,* XV (1962), 19–37; and "Confederate Shipbuilding in Mississippi," *Journal of Mississippi History,* XXX (1968), 291–303. Other studies of a general nature about the Confederate navy include: Tom H. Wells, *The Confederate Navy: A Study in Organization* (University, Ala., 1971); Milton F. Perry, *Infernal Machines: The Story of Confederate Submarine and Mine Warfare* (Baton Rouge, La., 1965); G. Melvin Herndon, "The Confederate States Naval Academy," *Virginia Magazine of History and Biography,* LXIX (1961), 300–323; and James M. Merrill, "Confederate Shipbuilding at New Orleans," *Journal of Southern History,* XXVIII (1962), 87–93.

On the *Virginia* the best account of the fight with the *Monitor* is William C. Davis, *Duel Between the First Ironclads* (Garden City, N.Y., 1975). Related studies of significance include: R. W. Daly, *How the Merrimac Won: The Strategic Story of the CSS Virginia* (New York, 1957); Harrison A. Trexler, *The Confederate Ironclad 'Virginia' ('Merrimac')* (Chicago, 1938); and T. Catesby Jones, "The Iron-Clad Virginia," *Virginia Magazine of History and Biography,* XLIX (1941), 297–303.

The best study of the *Alabama* is the memoir of its master, Raphael Semmes, *Service Afloat: Or, the Remarkable Career of the Confederate Cruisers, Sumter and Alabama, during the War between the States* (Baltimore, 1887). Other works include: W. Stanley Hoole (ed.), *The Logs of the CSS Alabama and the CSS Tuscaloosa, 1862–1863, Kept by Lieutenant (Later Captain) John Low, C.S.N.* (University, Ala., 1972); Edward Boykin, *Ghost Ship of the Confederacy* (New York, 1957); Edna Bradlow, *Here Comes the Alabama* (Cape Town, 1958); William M. Robinson, Jr., "The *Alabama-Kearsarge* Battle: A Study in Original Sources," *Essex Institute Historical Collections,* LX (1924), 97–120, 209–218; and the Kell biography (Kell was Semmes' first mate).

On the blockade and blockade running, see Robert Erwin Johnson, "Investment by Sea: The Civil War Blockade," *American Neptune,* XXXII (1972), 45–57; John B. Hefferman "The Blockade of the Southern Confederacy: 1861–1865," *Smithsonian Journal of History,* II (1967–1968), iv, 24–44; John Wilkinson, *The Narrative of a Blockade-Runner* (New York, 1877); Kathryn A. Hanna, "Incidents of the Confederate Blockade," *Journal of Southern History,* XI (1945), 214–229; Frank E. Vandiver, *Confederate Blockade Running Through Bermuda, 1861–1865* (Austin, 1947); plus the Owsley work cited under "Foreign Relations," on page 361, *King Cotton Diplomacy.*

The war on inland waters is the subject of: James M. Merrill, *Battle Flags South: The Story of the Civil War Navies on Western Waters* (Rutherford, N.J., 1970); John D. Milligan, *Gunboats down the Mississippi* (Annapolis, Md., 1965); H. Allen Gosnell, *Guns on the Western Waters: The Story of River Gunboats in the Civil War* (Baton Rouge, La., 1949); John F. Dillon, "The Role of Riverine Warfare in the Civil War," *Naval War College Review,* XXV (1973), iv, 58–78; Robert V. Bogle, "Defeat through Default: Confederate Naval Strategy for the Upper Mississippi River and Its Tributaries, 1861–1862," *Tennessee Historical Quarterly,* XXVII (1968), 62–71, Kenneth R. Johnson, "Confederate Defenses and Union Gunboats on the Tennessee River: A Federal Raid into Northwest Alabama," *Alabama Historical Quarterly,* XXX (1968), 39–60; Charles E. Frohman, *Rebels on Lake Erie: The Piracy, The Conspiracy, Prison Life* (Columbus, Ohio, 1965); and Allen M. Woolson, "Confederates on Lake Erie," *United States Naval Institute Proceedings,* XIC (1973), iv. 69–70.

The best material on privateers is in William M. Robinson, Jr., *The Confederate Privateers* (New Haven, Conn., 1928). Studies of individual ships include: Mary Elizabeth Thomas, "The CSS *Tallahassee*: A Factor in Anglo-American Relations, 1864–1866," *Civil War History,* XXI (1975), 148–159; Frank L. Owsley, Jr., *The CSS Florida: Her Building and Operations* (Philadelphia, 1965); Charles G. Summersell, *The Cruise of CSS Sumter* (Tuscaloosa, Ala., 1965); William Oliphant Rentz, "The Confederate States Ship *Georgia,*" *Georgia Historical Quarterly,* LVI (1972), 307–317; Lee Kennett, "The Strange Career of the [CSS] *Stonewall,*" *United States Naval Institute Proceedings,* XCIV (1968), ii, 74–85; Wallace Shugg, "Prophet of the Deep: The H. L. Hunley," *Civil War Times Illustrated,* XI (1973), x, 4–10, 44–47; Stanley F. Horn, *Gallant Rebel: the Fabulous Cruise of the C.S.S. Shenandoah* (New Brunswick, N.J., 1947); and W. Stanley Hoole, *Four Years in the Confederate Navy: The Career of Captain John Low . . .* (Athens, Ga., 1964).

Army

In the popular mind, Confederate history is the history of Southern armies and battles, and there is indeed a plethora of military studies. In

addition to the guides and general histories listed elsewhere, see Charles
E. Dornbusch, *Military Bibliography of the Civil War*, 3 vols. (New York, 1961–
1972). The *sine qua non* of any military work on the Confederate War is *War
of the Rebellion:* . . . *Official Records of the Union and Confederate Armies*, 128 vols.
(Washington, D.C., 1880–1901). A useful reference work is Clement A.
Evans (ed.), *Confederate Military History*, 12 vols. (Atlanta, Ga., 1899). At least
two general works are important for the Confederate military context:
Marcus Cunliffe, *Soldiers and Civilians: The Martial Spirit in America, 1775–
1865* (Boston, 1968); and Russell F. Weigley, *The American Way of War: A
History of United States Military Strategy and Policy* (New York, 1973). On
Confederate strategy there are a number of fine overviews, most of which
blame or defend Jefferson Davis for his conduct as commander-in-chief.
Archer Jones in *Confederate Strategy from Shiloh to Vicksburg* (Baton Rouge, La.,
1961); Grady McWhiney in "Jefferson Davis and the Art of War," *Civil War
History* XXI (1975), 101–112; and Thomas L. Connelly and Archer Jones
in *The Politics of Command: Factions and Ideas in Confederate Strategy* (Baton
Rouge, La., 1973) are critical of Davis (although the latter work presents
far more than a critique of Davis). The best defense of Davis as strategist
is Frank E. Vandiver, "Jefferson Davis and Confederate Strategy," in *The
American Tragedy: The Civil War in Retrospect*, ed. by Frank E. Vandiver and
Avery O. Craven (Hampden-Sydney, Va., 1959), in which the author soft-
ens some of his judgments made in an earlier, broader study, *Rebel Brass:
The Confederate Command System* (Baton Rouge, La., 1956). Also somewhat
supportive of Davis is William J. Cooper, Jr., "A Reassessment of Jefferson
Davis as War Leader: The Case from Atlanta to Nashville," *Journal of South-
ern History*, XXXVI (1970), 189–204. Robert E. Lee, too, has recently in-
spired controversy in regard to his strategic ability and vision. Thomas L.
Connelly is the primary critic and suggests some of Lee's shortcomings in
The Marble Man (cited under "Biography," page 342). A more pointed
debate is in an exchange of articles: Connelly's "Robert E. Lee and the
Western Confederacy: A Criticism of Lee's Strategic Ability," *Civil War
History*, XV (1969), 116–132; and Albert Castel, "The Historian and the
General: Thomas L. Connelly versus Robert E. Lee," *Civil War History*, XVI
(1970), 50–63. Important for its conclusions on Lee and generalship in
general is J. F. C. Fuller's *Grant and Lee* (Bloomington, Ind., 1957). Other
articles important to the study of Southern strategy include the essays by
Richard N. Current, T. Harry Williams, and David Donald in David Donald
(ed.), *Why the North Won the Civil War* (Baton Rouge, La., 1960); plus Ludwell H. Johnson, "Civil War Military History: A Few Revisions in Need of
Revising," *Civil War History*, XVII (1971), 115–130; Grady McWhiney "Who
Whipped Whom? Confederate Defeat Reexamined," *Civil War History*, XI
(1965), 5–26; and Archer Jones, "Jomini and the Strategy of the American

Civil War, a Reinterpretation," *Military Affairs,* XXXIV (1970), 127–131. Connelly and Jones, *The Politics of Command,* contains the best summary statement of the European context of Confederate military thought, and Jay Luvaas, *The Military Legacy of the Civil War: The European Inheritance* (Chicago, 1959), is best on the lessons Europeans did and did not learn from the American experience.

Concerning the military organization and supply, there are a number of solid works. In addition to books on and about the individuals associated with these functions (i.e. Davis, his Secretaries of War, Jones, Kean, Gorgas et al.), Vandiver's *Rebel Brass* and Connelly's and Jones' *Politics of Command* are the best summaries of command structure. Vandiver's biography of Josiah Gorgas, *Ploughshares into Swords: Josiah Gorgas and Confederate Ordnance* (Austin, Tex., 1952), is the best study of the Ordnance Bureau. About the individual weapons, see William A. Albaugh III and Edward N. Simmons, *Confederate Arms* (New York, 1957). Also useful is Vandiver's article, "Makeshifts of Confederate Ordnance," *Journal of Southern History,* XVII (1951) 180–193. Quartermaster and commissary operations are best covered in Richard D. Goff, *Confederate Supply* (Durham, N.C., 1969). See also Frank E. Vandiver, "The Food Supply of the Confederate Armies, 1865," *Tyler's Quarterly Historical and Genealogical Magazine,* XXVI (1944), 77–89; Frank E. Vandiver, "Texas and the Confederate Army's Meat Problem," *Southwestern Historical Quarterly,* XLVII (1944), 225–233; James J. Nichols, *The Confederate Quartermaster in the Trans-Mississippi* (Austin, Tex., 1964); Charles W. Ramsdell, "General Robert E. Lee's Horse Supply, 1862–1865," *American Historical Review,* XXXV (1930), 758–777; and William T. Windham, "The Problem of Supply in the Trans-Mississippi Confederacy," *Journal of Southern History,* XXVII (1961), 149–168. Works on bureaus and offices other than ordnance, quartermaster, and commissary include H.V. Canan, "Confederate Military Intelligence," *Maryland Historical Magazine,* LIX (1964), 34–51; Horace H. Cunningham, *Doctors in Gray: The Confederate Medical Service* (Baton Rouge, La., 1958); Robert W. Waitt, Jr., *Confederate Military Hospitals in Richmond* (Richmond, Va., 1964); James L. Nichols, *Confederate Engineers* (Tuscaloosa, Ala., 1957); William M. Robinson, Jr., "The Confederate Engineers," *Military Engineer,* XXII (1930), 297–305, 410–419, 512–517; Ralph W. Donnelly, "Scientists of the Confederate Nitre and Mining Bureau," *Civil War History,* II (1956), 69–92; Joseph H. Woodward II, "Alabama Iron Manufacturing, 1860–1865," *Alabama Review,* VII (1954), 199–207; Albert B. Moore, *Conscription and Conflict in the Confederacy* (New York, 1924); William B. Hesseltine, *Civil War Prisons; a Study in War Psychology* (Columbus, Ohio, 1930); and Ovid L. Futch, *History of Andersonville Prison* (Gainesville, Fla., 1968).

Individual armies and commands have their own literature. The ultimate work on the Army of Northern Virginia is Douglas S. Freeman, *Lee's Lieutenants: A Study in Command,* 3 vols. (New York, 1942–1944). On the Army of Tennessee see Thomas L. Connelly, *Army of the Heartland: The Army of Tennessee, 1861–1862* (Baton Rouge, La., 1967), and *Autumn of Glory: The Army of Tennessee* (Baton Rouge, La., 1971). Connelly's volumes have superseded Stanley F. Horn, *The Army of Tennessee: A Military History* (Indianapolis, Ind., 1941). The "model" unit history for the Confederacy is James I. Robertson, *The Stonewall Brigade* (Baton Rouge, La., 1963).

Works on soldier life are many—many more than can be cited under the "Personal Narrative" section beginning on p. 331. The best guides to this material are Dornbusch, *Regimental Publications and Personal Narratives of the Civil War,* II, and Nevins, Robertson, and Wiley, *Civil War Books,* II. Fortunately, Bell I. Wiley has compressed his intensive research on soldier life into *The Life of Johnny Reb: The Common Soldier of the Confederacy* (Indianapolis, Ind., 1943), a superb book. Related to this topic are two articles on morale: Pete Maslowski, "A Study of Morale in Civil War Soldiers," *Military Affairs,* XXXIV (1970), 122–126; Harry N. Scheiber, "The Pay of Confederate Troops and Problems of Demoralization: A Case of Administrative Failure," *Civil War History,* XV (1969), 226–236.

Campaigns and battles have an enormous literature. The magazine *Civil War Times Illustrated* alone has articles and sometimes entire issues about a large number of engagements and campaigns. A good, brief analysis is Vincent J. Esposito (ed.), *The West Point Atlas of American Wars,* 2 vols. (New York, 1959). An older work which is still quite useful for military analysis is Matthew F. Steele, *American Campaigns,* 2 vols. (Washington, D.C., 1909). The following list of campaign and battle studies is by no means exhaustive; it is meant to be representative and should be helpful, used with biographies of the commanders and broader works.

Fort Sumter: Samuel W. Crawford, *The History of the Fall of Fort Sumter* (New York, 1896); Roy Meredith, *Storm Over Sumter: The Opening Engagement of the Civil War* (New York, 1957); W. A. Swanberg, *First Blood: The Story of Fort Sumter* (New York, 1957); Richard N. Current, "The Confederates and the First Shot," *History,* VII (1961), 357–369; Ludwell H. Johnson, "Fort Sumter and Confederate Diplomacy," *Journal of Southern History,* XXVI (1960), 441–477; and Grady McWhiney, "The Confederacy's First Shot," *Civil War History,* XIV (1968), 5–14.

First Manassas: Robert M. Johnston, *Bull Run: Its Strategy and Tactics* (New York, 1913); William C. Davis, *Battle at Bull Run: A History of the First Major Campaign of the Civil War* (Garden City, N.Y., 1977).

New Mexico Campaign: Martin H. Hall, *Sibley's New Mexico Campaign*

(Austin, Tex., 1960); and David Westphall, "The Battle of Glorieta Pass: Its Importance in the Civil War," *New Mexico Historical Review,* XLIV (1969), 137–154.

Roanoke Island: Emory M. Thomas, "The Lost Confederate of Roanoke," *Civil War Times Illustrated,* XV (1976), ii, 10–17.

Forts Henry and Donelson: James J. Hamilton, *The Battle of Fort Donelson,* (New York, 1968).

Pea Ridge: Albert Castel, "A New View of the Battle of Pea Ridge," *Missouri Historical Review,* LXII (1968), 136–151; Homer L. Kerr, "The Battle of Elkhorn: The Gettysburg of the Trans-Mississippi West," in William F. Holmes and Harold M. Hollingsworth (eds.), *Essays on the American Civil War* (Austin, Tex., 1968), 31–44.

Shiloh: James Lee McDonough, *Shiloh—In Hell Before Night* (Knoxville, Tenn., 1976); Wiley Sword, *Shiloh: Bloody April* (New York, 1974); Charles P. Roland, "Albert Sydney Johnston and the Shiloh Campaign," *Civil War History,* IV (1958), 355–382.

Jackson's Valley Campaign: Robert G. Tanner, *Stonewall in the Valley* (Garden City, N.Y., 1976).

Seven Days Campaign: Clifford Dowdey, *Seven Days: the Emergence of Lee* (Boston, 1964).

Antietam: Edward J. Stackpole, *From Cedar Mountain to Antieteam* (Harrisburg, Pa., 1959).

Kentucky: Grady McWhiney, "Controversy in Kentucky: Braxton Bragg's Campaign of 1862," *Civil War History,* VI (1960), 5–42.

Chancellorsville: John Bigelow, *The Campaign of Chancellorsville: A Strategic and Tactical Study* (New Haven, Conn., 1910); Edward J. Stackpole, *Chancellorsville: Lee's Greatest Battle* (Harrisburg, Pa., 1958).

Vicksburg: Peter F. Walker, *Vicksburg: A People at War, 1860–1865* (Chapel Hill, N.C., 1960); Thomas L. Connelly, "Vicksburg: Strategic Point or Propaganda Device?", *Military Affairs,* XXXIV (1970), 49–53.

Brandy Station: Fairfax Downey, *Clash of Cavalry: The Battle of Brandy Station, June 9, 1863* (New York, 1959).

Gettysburg: Edwin B. Coddington, *The Gettysburg Campaign: A Study in Command* (New York, 1968); Warren W. Hassler, Jr., *Crisis at the Crossroads: The First Day at Gettysburg* (University, Ala., 1970); Archer Jones, "The Gettysburg Decision Reassessed," *Virginia Magazine of History and Biography,* LXXVI (1968), 64–66; Clifford Dowdey, *Death of a Nation: The Story of Lee and His Men at Gettysburg* (Harrisburg, Pa., 1958); George R. Stewart, *Picketts Charge: A Microhistory of the Final Attack at Gettysburg, July 3, 1863* (Boston, 1959); Glenn Tucker, *High Tide at Gettysburg: The Campaign in Pennsylvania* (Indianapolis, 1958); and William A. Frassanito, *Gettysburg: A Journey in Time* (New York, 1975).

Chattanooga: Fairfax Downey, *Storming the Gateway: Chattanooga, 1863* (New York, 1960).

Mine Run: Jay Luvaas and Wilbur S. Nye, "The Campaign that History Forgot: Mine Run," *Civil War Times Illustrated,* VIII (1969), vii, 11–36.

Red River: Ludwell H. Johnson, *Red River Campaign Politics and Cotton in the Civil War* (Baltimore, 1958).

Grant versus Lee: Edward Steere, *The Wilderness Campaign* (Harrisburg, Pa., 1960); Clifford Dowdey, *Lee's Last Campaign* (Boston, 1960); Earl Schenck Miers, *The Last Campaign: Grant Saves the Union* (Philadelphia, 1972); Frank E. Vandiver, *Jubal's Raid* (New York, 1960); Edward J. Stackpole, *Sheridan in the Shenandoah: Jubal Early's Nemesis* (Harrisburg, Pa., 1961); Rembert W. Patrick, *The Fall of Richmond* (Baton Rouge, La., 1960); William C. Davis, *The Battle of New Market* (Garden City, N.Y., 1975); Philip Van Doren Stern, *An End to Valor: The Last Days of the Civil War* (Boston, 1958); Burke Davis, *To Appomattox: Nine April Days, 1865* (New York, 1959).

Atlanta and After: Richard M. McMurry, "The Atlanta Campaign of 1864: A New Look," *Civil War History,* XXII (1976), 5–15; Samuel Carter III, *The Siege of Atlanta, 1864* (New York, 1973); Errol MacGregor Clauss, "The Atlanta Campaign 18 July–2 September, 1864," Ph.D. dissertation (Emory University, 1965); James F. Rhodes, "Sherman's March to the Sea," *American Historical Review,* VI (1901), 466–474; N. C. Hughes, Jr., "Hardee's Defense of Savannah," *Georgia Historical Quarterly,* XLVII (1963), 43–67; John G. Barrett, *Sherman's March Through the Carolinas* (Chapel Hill, N.C., 1956); Marion Brunson Lucas, *Sherman and the Burning of Columbia* (College Station, Tex., 1976).

Campaigns in the Far West: Wiley Britton, *The Civil War on the Border,* 2 vols. (New York, 1899; Ray C. Colton, *The Civil War in the Western Territories* (Norman, Okla., 1959); Stephen B. Oates, *Confederate Cavalry West of the River* (Austin, Tex., 1961); Jay Monaghan, *Civil War on the Western Border, 1854–1865* (Baton Rouge, La., 1955).

Hood in Tennessee: Thomas R. Hay, *Hood's Tennessee Campaign* (New York, 1929); Stanley F. Horn, *The Decisive Battle of Nashville* (Baton Rouge, La., 1956); Jacob D. Cox, *The Battle of Franklin, Tennessee, November 30, 1864,* (New York, 1897).

About the Confederates' Indian allies see: Frank Cunningham, *General Stand Watie's Confederate Indians* (San Antonio, Tex., 1959); George H. Shirk, "The Place of Indian Territory in the Command Structure of the Civil War," *Chronicles of Oklahoma,* XLV (1968), 464–471; and LeRoy H. Fischer and Jerry Gill, *Confederate Indian Forces Outside of Indian Territory* (Oklahoma City, Oka., 1969).

On cavalry raids some representative studies are: James Pickett Jones, *Yankee Blitzkrieg: Wilson's Raid Through Alabama and Georgia* (Athens, Ga.,

1976); Dee A. Brown, *The Bold Cavaliers: Morgan's 2nd Kentucky Cavalry Raiders* (Philadelphia, 1959); Dee A. Brown, *Grierson's Raid* (Urbana, Ill., 1954); and Basil W. Duke, *Morgan's Cavalry* (New York, 1906). See also William David Evans, "McCook's Raid," M.A. thesis (University of Georgia, 1976).

The best overview of guerrilla activities is Albert Castel's issue of *Civil War Times Illustrated*, "The Guerrilla War," XIII, vi (1974), 3–50. Biographies of Mosby and Quantrill present extremes of the spectrum on irregular combat. See also Michael R. Kirkby, "Partisan and Counter-Partisan Activity in Northern Virginia," M.A. thesis (University of Georgia, 1977).

On atrocities and alleged atrocities, see Liva Baker, "The Burning of Chambersburg," American Heritage XXIV, (1973), 36–39, 97; Hartwell T. Bynum, "Sherman's Expulsion of the Roswell Women in 1864," *Georgian Historical Quarterly*, LIV (1970), 162–182; Charles R. Mink, "General Orders, No. 11: The Forced Evacuation of Civilians during the Civil War," *Military Affairs*, XXXIV (1970), 132–136; William C. Davis, "The Massacre at Saltville," *Civil War Times Illustrated*, IX (1971), X, 4–11, 43–48; Ronald K. Huch, "Fort Pillow Massacre: The Aftermath of Paducah," *Illinois State Historical Society Journal*, LXVI (1973), 62–70; and John L. Jordan, "Was There a Massacre at Fort Pillow?," *Tennessee Historical Quarterly*, VI (1947), 99–133.

Finally, some miscellaneous studies merit mention: Warren Ripley, *Artillery and Ammunition of the Civil War* (New York, 1970); John Bakeless, *Spies of the Confederacy* (Philadelphia 1970); Francis A. Lord and Arthur Wise, *Uniforms of the Civil War* (South Brunswick, N.J., 1970); Archie P. McDonald (ed.), *Make Me a Map of the Valley: The Civil War Journal of Stonewall Jackson's Topographer* (Dallas, 1973); June I. Gow, "Chiefs of Staff in the Army of Tennessee Under Braxton Bragg," *Tennessee Historical Quarterly*, XXVII (1968), 341–360; and Jennings C. Wise, *The Long Arm of Lee: Or the History of the Artillery of the Army of Northern Virginia*, 2 vols. (Lynchburg, Va., 1915).

Index